CLEAR THINKING IN A BLURRY WORLD

Tim Kenyon
University of Waterloo

THOMSON

NELSON

Australia   Canada   Mexico   Singapore   Spain   United Kingdom   United States

THOMSON

NELSON

Clear Thinking in a Blurry World
by Tim Kenyon

Associate Vice President, Editorial Director:
Evelyn Veitch

Editor-in-Chief, Higher Education:
Anne Williams

Executive Editor:
Cara Yarzab

Acquisitions Editor:
Bram Sepers

Marketing Manager:
Shelley Collacutt Miller

Developmental Editor:
Heather Parker

Photo Researcher:
Mary Rose Maclachlan

Permissions Coordinator:
Nicola Winstanley

Content Production Manager:
Imoinda Romain

Production Service:
ICC Macmillan Inc.

Copy Editor:
Wendy Thomas

Proofreader:
ICC Macmillan Inc.

Indexer:
ICC Macmillan Inc.

Production Coordinator:
Ferial Suleman

Design Director:
Ken Phipps

Interior Design:
Greg Devitt

Cover Design:
Courtney Hellam

Cover Image:
Paul A. Souders/Corbis Canada

Compositor:
ICC Macmillan Inc.

Printer:
Thomson/West

Library and Archives Canada Cataloguing in Publication

Kenyon, Timothy, 1968-
Clear thinking in a blurry world / Tim Kenyon.

Includes index.
ISBN 978-0-17-625194-9

1. Critical thinking—Textbooks.
I. Title.

B809.2.K36 2007   160
C2007-903452-7

ISBN-13: 978-0-17-625194-9
ISBN-10: 0-17-625194-4

TABLE OF CONTENTS

PREFACE

In recent years no single theme has been more emphasized in education and professional training than critical thinking. The increased need for highly specialized education in many fields, and especially in scientific and technical disciplines, has left both educators and students sensitive to the need for general reasoning skills that apply to specialized and commonplace domains alike.

A nearly universal hope is that these general critical thinking skills can be taught as a secondary aim of courses in various other disciplines. One would be hard-pressed nowadays to discover a public school course curriculum at any level, in any academic area, that did not list critical thinking as one of the educational aims of the course. Even if this hope is reasonable, though, there remains an important role for the study of critical reasoning through books and courses dedicated to it. General reasoning issues cut across topics in ways that one cannot easily follow up when one is primarily focused on teaching or learning any one of those topics. When critical thinking itself is the subject of study, one is free to follow the issues across disciplines as necessary.

This book is intended to address the need for such a wide-ranging approach. This need may not seem very obvious, of course, given how many critical thinking books are already in print! Some of these books are excellent, but none, to my mind, takes the particular sort of multidisciplinary approach I describe in the Introduction: a synthesis of topics including arguments, fallacies, evidential reasoning, numeracy, probability, the psychology of biases, science, and media analysis. One simple reason for the novelty of this combination of topics is that almost all critical thinking books devote considerable resources to topics I do not raise: formal logic, categorical logic, and Venn diagrams in particular. These topics and techniques are popular because they are useful and worthwhile. Given the choice, however, I believe there is more to be gained for true critical thinking purposes—as opposed, say, to formal reasoning purposes—by emphasizing some higher-order or metacognitive aspects of critical thinking. In particular, I aim to emphasize reasoning about our own reasoning processes, and reasoning about the wider social and commercial factors that can affect the information we receive.

ACKNOWLEDGMENTS

I have benefited from the assistance and generosity of many people in writing this book and in teaching the course upon which it was based. Several authors kindly allowed me to reprint portions of their work; I deeply appreciate their permission. My colleague Chris Eliasmith has taught the same critical thinking course from a similar perspective and has shared many examples and much insight over the years. My colleagues Rolf George, Dave DeVidi, Jim van Evra, and Bill Abbott also contributed many interesting examples and did much to show me how to find critical and philosophical issues in every aspect of the workaday world. I received inspiration and very useful feedback on the idea of this book from Elena Lester. The whole project received a huge boost from Chris Viger's support at the early stages. I also got crucial feedback from the reviewers of the proposal and portions of the manuscript: my thanks to Leslie Burkholder, Don Dedrick, Wayne Henry, Catherine Hundleby, Murray Littlejohn, and Chris MacDonald for their thoughtful input. Thanks also to the fine people at Nelson Education Ltd.—Cara Yarzab, Katherine Goodes, Bram Sepers, and especially Heather Parker and Wendy Thomas—for their assistance and patience.

Jim van Evra, Roger Davidson, and Jeff Shallit proofed sections of the text helpfully, while Adam Jensen read over half of the text with a brilliantly keen eye. Most of all I owe my thanks to Colleen Kenyon, who read the whole thing and worked hard to make it better.

Introduction: Roadmap to This Book

CRITICAL THINKING BEGINS AT HOME

For many reasons, ranging from the aesthetic to the intensely practical, we prefer not to believe falsehoods. Believing truths, we typically feel, is a good thing—the kind of thing there really should be more of. Or, if truth is too rare a philosophical commodity, we would at least rather have our beliefs be reliable and justified than unreliable and unjustified. Unreliable beliefs lead us to act in misguided ways. An inability to distinguish good reasoning from bad reasoning leaves us open to various forces—people, businesses, political parties, what have you—whose primary concern can be quite literally to control (portions of) our minds, and thereby control things like our votes or our wallets. For reasons like these, everyone agrees that critical thinking is an important skill. When it comes to explaining how to get better at it, though, one can quickly be reduced to uttering clichés or platitudes: Think carefully. Be reasonable. Observe accurately. Yes, but how?

This book is really an attempt to answer that question in the least imperfect way possible. To begin motivating the approach I will take, let's consider two (deliberately simplified) representations of the goals and methods of critical thinking. One depicts critical thinking as a filter, acting to prevent bad arguments from getting inside our heads; the other portrays critical thinking most fundamentally as a set of **metacognitive skills**—that is, skills for thinking about the way we think and for monitoring our own thoughts.

A. *Critical thinking as a filter*

Me: Seeker of reasonable beliefs
The World: Repository of facts, some truth-tellers, some stupid people, and some liars
Critical Thinking: A set of skills that acts as a filter, letting truths in but keeping stupidity and lies out

B. *Critical thinking as metacognition*

Me: Sometimes seeker of reasonable beliefs, with tendencies to exaggerate, to mislead, to value ideology over accuracy, to be confused, and to be simultaneously overconfident and under-informed.

The World: Filled with other people much like me. (And a few stupid people and liars.)

Critical Thinking: The cognitive habit of paying attention to these tendencies in myself and others, and actively seeking to minimize them.

Again, these are caricatures of the views that actual people might hold. But what is realistic about the distinction is this: on the filter approach, critical thinking is primarily directed toward the trustworthiness and reliability of other people, other information sources. The point of critical thinking so conceived (especially, it seems to me, when it is assimilated to *sceptical* thinking) is to preserve the sanctity of one's own mind by letting the conclusions of good arguments in and keeping the conclusions of bad arguments out. The metacognitive approach, on the other hand, adopts the view that *critical thinking starts at home:* the person whose weak arguments and systematic biases I really have to monitor is *me*. An appropriate scepticism about other people is included in this approach, but it falls out of the more basic presumption that other people are no more reliable than I am, in the first instance. (And of course there are more of them. Their very complex interactions can make them either much less reliable or much more reliable than I might be, depending on the context.)

The second caricature is the better approach, I say, since it captures the breadth of the skills and the knowledge that effective critical thinking seems to involve, and it respects the active role that each person's own thoughts and actions play in their belief formation and belief revision. Feed people a diet of nothing but strict truths and they may still end up believing a vast array of falsehoods. How? By shading the interpretation of those truths, by overestimating how much they really know, by drawing unwarranted inferences from what they've been told, and by finding ways to reconcile the falsehoods they generate with the truths they have been given. The basic critical reasoning issue is not what *gets into* your head. The most basic issue is what *happens* in there.

Protecting your mind from the depredations of those seeking to exploit it in one way or another is a very important project—one that is a focus throughout this book. But restructuring your own ways of forming and revising beliefs is a more fundamental goal. Hence we will work throughout the book not only on understanding the differences between reliable and unreliable reasoning, but also on understanding why each sort occurs. This will help us predict and minimize reasoning errors, based on our sense of when and how they occur.

There is also a tendency for courses in critical thinking or informal reasoning to define the course goals in terms of formal logic. This can happen either by designing the critical thinking course as a precursor to a course in formal logic or simply by treating it as "Formal Logic Lite," intended for students who cannot quite handle the industrial-strength product. With some differences of attitude and focus, both approaches aim to ease students into the basic ideas of classical propositional calculus through natural language. Often the climax of the course is the introduction of the elementary logical formalism over the final few weeks. That is not what this book aims to do. Instead, it aims more directly at conveying a much broader set of knowledge, skills, and habits properly called critical reasoning faculties. While an ability to do formal logic is associated with many of these skills, it is not especially strongly linked with some others. My goal is broader: to help you improve your abilities to believe reasonable things in a wide range of contexts.

To that end, we will consider a range of topics, some of them standard fare for critical thinking texts and courses, and some of them less standard (for now). The approach taken here is based on a number of principles that can be made clear from the outset.

SOME PRINCIPLES OF CRITICAL THINKING

1. **Critical thinking can be effective only when it is a habit.**

The goal is not to acquire a self-contained skill that can be used deliberately when needed and set aside when not needed. Critical reasoning skills are neither generally nor specifically useful if they do not function automatically for the most part. There are at least two reasons for this.

First, if critical thinking is not a habit, it will be exercised too sporadically to be much use. It is rare that we consciously and deliberately tell ourselves, "Think critically!" Many of the situations in which we are not overtly on guard for unreliable reasoning are precisely the ones in which we ought to be concerned about making faulty judgments. But noticing errors or potential problems of a particular sort can become somewhat automatic, with hard work. An example that will be familiar to many people who have made the transition from student to teacher is that of noticing spelling or grammatical errors in writing. Some people have this gift (or curse) from the outset, but for many others, it comes as the result of grading and correcting many written assignments. This repetition ingrains the skill of detecting such errors, changing the way one reads documents automatically. Rather than having to laboriously scan text for errors, one finds that the errors seem almost to leap off the page, sometimes at a quick glance, sometimes from part of the page that one is not even aware of reading! Just as doing lots of writing yourself is less effective at instilling this ability than doing lots of grading, mere thinking is less effective at instilling critical thinking abilities than is practice at monitoring and evaluating thinking. By practising in this way, we can improve our ability to notice weak reasoning even when that's not what we're concentrating on. (Indeed, sometimes even when we'd rather not have noticed the weakness of some piece of reasoning. Consider yourself warned of this occasionally unpleasant side effect.)

Moreover, like many skills, critical thinking is simply too *hard* if not made into a reflexive habit. Anyone who has learned how to play a musical instrument, how to juggle, how to skate, or anything similar, will understand the enormous difficulty of trying to perform a complex task through the deliberate ordering of one's actions. As long as one is thinking about where to place each finger, playing the guitar is very hard work, and slow besides. It's only when the complex actions become second nature that they become easy. Since it is exhausting to do hard mental activity, critical reasoning skills that are not habitual will rarely be used effectively.

2. **Critical thinking is a matter of learning not to trust yourself.**

We all have ingrained biases, tendencies to find lousy reasoning of one sort or another quite plausible or compelling. Some of these biases or weaknesses are "factory-preset," like the nearly universal human tendency to be bad at intuitive reasoning about probability. Some are ingrained by custom, by education, by indoctrination, or by socialization. But it is relatively rare for people to set out deliberately to reason badly. For the most part, we do it because we do not notice when we're doing it—our biases make the unwarranted leaps in logic seem smooth and uncontroversial to us. Critically analyzing your own reasoning, then, means developing the habit of checking even the obvious and commonsense inferences against the list of known patterns of human cognitive weakness. In a nutshell, it means learning not to trust your first reactions and knee-jerk conclusions, in light of what you know about the kinds of mistakes that are likely in that kind of situation.

Hence understanding how our own reasoning and that of other people might be going wrong requires a knowledge of human cognition and its weaknesses. Recent and ongoing work in cognitive and social psychology has revealed a great deal about how our perception, recollection, and interpretation of evidence can be influenced by a surprising array of mechanisms both internal and external to our individual psychologies. Emotion, pre-existing beliefs, social pressures, time constraints, and many other factors are known to play powerful roles in shaping our beliefs beyond the point that our state of information might warrant. Learning how this happens is a crucial first step in recognizing specific occurrences in ourselves and others.

3. **Critical thinking requires the completely general use of some basic cognitive skills, and not the highly specialized use of expert cognitive skills.**

This is the good news, since it means that in some sense you already know most of what you need to know to improve your critical thinking faculties. It would be only slightly optimistic to assert that any graduate of a decent secondary school already has the particular skills necessary for critical thinking. What is needed over and above that fairly basic skill set is a sort of meta-skill: the ability to yoke those elementary abilities together at the right time, to deploy the correct ones, to recognize the informational or evidential patterns calling for their exercise. This meta-skill does not come naturally, nor does it come automatically with expertise in smaller groups of cognitive skills. An experimental scientist who is highly skilled at evaluating evidence in her specialized field might easily be duped by a con artist operating under uncontrolled conditions in a different context. This is because highly developed *domain-specific* abilities to recognize evidential connections can, and frequently do, fail to transfer to other domains, even in weaker forms. Critical thinking means *domain-general* reasoning about evidential connections. For our purposes, then, the breadth with which the skills are applied is more important than having real virtuosity in any one such skill. The bad news is that developing and maintaining this meta-ability is not just a matter of deciding to do it. Psychologists have discovered that learning itself tends to be highly domain-specific, so it is predictable that learning to apply skills domain-generally can be hard work. Practice and self-reflection are crucial to this process.

4. **Understanding, producing, and recognizing good reasoning require understanding the concepts and terminology that describe it.**

   This is straightforward. Like any intellectual issue, the topic of thinking well has its own jargon intended to help express complex ideas briefly. It is one thing to have a vague sense that a piece of reasoning has gone wrong somehow or other; but one's thoughts on the matter, and one's articulations of those thoughts, acquire a greater clarity when the precise category of the mistake can be picked out and the nature of the problem is explained with exactitude. Hence the first thing we will do is learn the terms used to characterize both good and bad reasoning: definitions of successful arguments, for example, and explanations of the major fallacies.

5. **There is no such thing as generally good critical reasoning skills without basic numeracy.**

   The level of numeracy required may be extremely low indeed—nothing more than arithmetic, really. But without the ability to add, subtract, divide, and multiply, and without the habitual exercise of this ability, one's reasoning skills are badly weakened. However, as noted above, very high levels of mathematical ability are not especially important from a critical thinking perspective. What matters is the habitual and domain-general deployment of relatively basic arithmetical ability.

   The basic calculating abilities required for domain-general critical thinking might not extend much beyond making ballpark estimates in order to check numerical statements for approximate truth. Yet related skills like the ability to interpret graphs and charts are also properly considered numerical. A great deal of information—advertising, news, persuasive claims, and arguments of many kinds—comes to us couched in numerical terms and visually packaged in the form of charts, diagrams, and graphs. If critical thinking is understood as a fundamentally linguistic activity, to the exclusion of numerical and "numero-graphical" expressions of fact and opinion, we will overlook vast swathes of communication and information that ought habitually to be subjected to critical analysis. When we are confused or intimidated by numerical statements and reasoning, the temptation is either to accept it unquestioningly or to reject it wholesale. Either way we lose. Good critical reasoning requires a willingness to work through at least simple calculations when confronted with numerical claims, and enough of a default familiarity with both arithmetic and the pitfalls of graphs and charts to spot red flags.

6. **Good reasoning about evidence involves some central concepts of probability and statistics.**

   I list this separately from the previous point about numeracy, both to emphasize its importance and because the sense in which one must be able to reason about probability is not entirely numerical. We are constantly receiving new information that we ought to recognize as raising or lowering the credibility of propositions we already believe or disbelieve. But this process is very rarely explicable by a precise arithmetical calculation or even a rough guess of the initial and revised probabilities of these propositions. Working out an equation of probability theory is sometimes very important, but more often, what matters is understanding the *rationale* behind such equations, to help us understand in more qualitative terms the significance and relevance of data we possess and of data we might try to acquire.

7. **Informed judgments about the evidence at our disposal require analysis of the processes by which we get the information.**

More bluntly: knowing whether evidence is good often amounts to knowing how it came to us. We acquire information—some of it reliable, much of it grossly unreliable—through a wide range of sources: interpersonal communication, entertainment media, news media, educational contexts, Internet sources, academic journals, and many others. One cannot properly interpret the significance of such evidence without reflecting on the way that each of these sources shapes the content and the emphasis of the information it delivers.

One enormously important set of avenues for the production and dissemination of information is known, collectively, as science. For generally good reasons, science is widely regarded as the most credible or reliable means of learning about the world, but like any human activity it can and does go wrong in many ways, to many degrees. Moreover, having acquired the trust of many people, the methods and trappings of science are naturally exploited by those whose claims are not supported by evidence in the way of good science. For these two reasons, if for no other, it is important to gain at least a basic understanding of how the sciences work—both in idealized theory and in frequently messy practice.

It is equally important to develop a sense of how the information media work more generally, including newspapers, news magazines, broadcast news, and documentary channels. Relevant factors here can include anything from the commercial aspects of information sources, to the interactions of information sources with the public, to the working conditions and social contexts of the people employed in producing and disseminating information. There are foreseeable connections between these factors and the kind of information one should expect to find in such sources, and expect *not* to find, irrespective of whether that information accurately reflects the facts.

8. **Critical thinking is work: when in doubt, do it yourself.**

A concept that will come up repeatedly throughout this book is that of a **red flag.** For our purposes it means a feeling (in particular a feeling that can be at least partially explained if one puts one's mind to it) that there is something uncertain, unreliable, strange, weird, or dodgy about a claim, statistic, graph, or argument. A red flag is a reason to worry that something's not quite right in a critical thinking context.

The idea is that when we encounter something that raises a red flag, we go back to basics. Going back to basics is a general notion itself, meant to include responses like checking some alleged bit of data against the original sources, performing some alleged calculation to confirm that it's correct, doing a slow and more painstaking examination of a chart or graph, or reconsidering some argument to confirm that it has the right structure or true premises.

Of course, another of the main themes of this book is that our immediate judgments, reactions, and intuitions themselves are often unreliable, being powerfully affected by our expectations, desires, or plain old misunderstandings. So the idea of a red flag has to walk a middle path. The suggestion cannot be that we *reject* some claim when it raises a red flag, since this would often have us discounting

INTRODUCTION: ROADMAP TO THIS BOOK

accurate information just because it defies our expectations or because it challenges beliefs to which we are emotionally attached. Instead, what we do when there is a red flag is *check it out*. We do not trust our instincts about reliability or accuracy to distinguish correct from incorrect information, but we take those instincts seriously by investigating, rechecking, and thinking carefully when a red flag is raised. With any luck, the process of tracking down raw data, finding original sources, and confirming calculations independently is one that eventually hones our instincts about reliability.

Overall, it is a mistake to suppose that critical thinking is a set of skills that exists inside your head, the exercise of which involves only thinking the right thing at the right time. What's inside your head is important for the first stage, that of habitually noticing red flags. After that, though, the materials relevant to critical thinking are more likely to be in a library than in your head. The activity of critical thinking will include actually doing the reading, chasing down the quotes, and checking the math.

9. Problems or failures in reasoning are multifaceted.

Diagnosing the errors in someone else's reasoning or minimizing errors in our own reasoning is most easily and most thoroughly accomplished when we understand how different levels of analysis can apply to these errors. In many cases, failed reasoning is multifaceted just because it is complex and more than one kind of error is committed; a single example may involve shoddy methods of collecting data as well as the misinterpretation of the data that are collected. An argument might involve several fallacies (I've encountered single statements that commit more fallacies than they have words). But there is also the fact that different *kinds* of analysis are relevant to many individual cases of poor reasoning.

That someone has committed the fallacy called Post Hoc Ergo Propter Hoc might be all we care about in some cases. But understanding the relation between this fallacy and the natural human bias for extracting patterns from random events can be a powerful means not just of understanding instances of the fallacy in a well-rounded way, but of being on guard for Post Hoc Ergo Propter Hoc in situations that predictably invite that bias. Similarly, even if all we care about is whether someone has made an error in arithmetical calculation, our sense of how this might occur, or under what circumstances an otherwise reliable person is likeliest to do this, may implicate information we possess about that person's expectations, convictions, prejudices, or preoccupations. For the purposes of analyzing arguments themselves, it is widely taken that we factor out or minimize considerations about the arguer and the context of presentation. There is something right about this thought, for a rarefied class of cases. But it cannot be a general approach to critical thinking, which frequently requires a broader conception of *how to get things right* and, conversely, *how things went wrong*. Many cases of public or private reasoning simultaneously implicate issues of argumentation, of competence in some discipline, and of susceptibility to biases of one sort or another. We don't fully see how to work toward getting things right more often, nor how things may have gone wrong in a case of poor reasoning, without considering such interrelated factors.

DETAILS MATTER

Boxes like this one will be used occasionally throughout the book to indicate when a multifaceted example is being considered. The box may direct you to other sections of the book in which the example is analyzed from other perspectives. These boxes also sometimes contain elaborations of important details, additional examples to those given in the main text, and the occasional plain old digression.

SUMMARY

These principles and themes motivate the general approach of the book and its structure: We first study how to recognize and categorize different sorts of arguments and problems with arguments; then we focus on reasoning from states of information (including via probabilistic concepts). We investigate the links between errors in reasoning and a wide range of biases that operate at the sub-personal, personal, and social levels; then we examine issues involving the media, science, and dubious popular beliefs to see how all the factors we've studied have broad and significant effects. The goal is to develop habits of monitoring our own thinking and the thinking of people around us in order to gradually improve our skills of distinguishing reliable from unreliable reasoning on the fly. This is a lifelong process for all of us, based on a willingness to entertain the idea that our reasoning is currently systematically flawed in various respects. The aim of this book is to stimulate and focus the long-term project of thinking critically.

The Parts of Public Thinking: Deductive Argument

Here is Shakespeare's Macbeth. After first being told by three witches that he will become both thane of Cawdor (a title equivalent to earl) and king of Scotland, Macbeth discovers that he has in fact been made thane of Cawdor. He muses to himself,

> This supernatural soliciting
> Cannot be ill; cannot be good: if ill
> Why hath it given me earnest of success
> Commencing in a truth? I am thane of Cawdor:
> If good, why do I yield to that suggestion
> Whose horrid image doth unfix my hair
> And make my seated heart knock at my ribs,
> Against the use of nature? (*Macbeth*, I, iii, 130–37)

Or, as one might say less elegantly but more accessibly:

> "Is this prediction by the witches good or evil? I can't decide. If it's evil,
> why has it foretold successes that have already started to appear, like my
> becoming thane of Cawdor? If it's good, why does it already have me
> thinking about murdering the king so I can take his place, even though
> the thought disturbs me deeply? I just don't know what to make of it all."

Macbeth in this passage is doing what we all do from time to time: taking a tangled collection of thoughts that weigh for and against some idea, and trying to lay them out in a coherent and easily surveyed form.

He's doing it by talking to himself, a practice unjustly frowned upon in some circles as a sign of being either slightly crazy or a professor. But every time you write something down for the purpose of making a problem clearer, in solving an arithmetic problem, for example, or sketching the outline of an essay, you are talking to yourself in more or less the same way. You are figuring out what it's reasonable to say, what it's reasonable to think, by putting your best reasons out where they can be seen and marshalling them into a form that clearly shows what follows from what.

Like many endeavours, this is much easier to do badly than well. For example, those of us lucky enough to be able to walk had to learn how to do it at some point, though we rarely remember the process. Walking is actually a difficult and fragile series of controlled falls from one foot to the other, and for a toddler just getting the hang of it, there's no shortage of ways it can all end in tears. But we manage to make a habit of it, eventually. We even adapt to difficult walking conditions—gravel, ice, cow pastures, stepping stones—by slowing down and moving more gingerly. When we're walking, we automatically recognize circumstances that call for greater care.

Reasoning too is easy to do badly and hard to do well. Unlike walking, we tend not to get much better at it when we are just left to our own devices. When it comes to skating or walking or aerial gymnastics, it's obvious if you're systematically doing it badly: if you wake up in the hospital, something has gone wrong. The same is not always true of critical thinking. There are many, many ways that errors in reasoning can be reinterpreted, overlooked, or rationalized away. So we tend not to be very effective at spontaneously minimizing our ways of reasoning poorly. It takes some special effort to gradually acquire the habit of pulling off those fragile manoeuvres called "good reasoning," or the closely related habit of automatically slowing down and being more careful when you encounter the rational equivalent of a cow pasture or slippery stones.

To acquire these habits is to become a more critical thinker. And a first step in this process is learning how to think clearly about thinking itself. That's where we are starting. This chapter introduces some basic concepts by which reasoning can be categorized and evaluated, and its various roles clarified. We'll begin by reflecting

FIGURE 1.1

Rational Slip-Ups Are Easy in Some Cognitive Terrain

Careful habits in thinking and reasoning are the cognitive equivalent of walking carefully when you know you are crossing a stream with tricky stepping stones. You need to pay attention to avoid the hazards and reach a successful conclusion.

Albert Normandin/Masterfile

on the *activity* of putting reasoning on public display, as Macbeth did, through the presentation of the fundamental unit of reasoning: the argument.

The rather specialized concepts relating to arguments that we will consider in this chapter involve some fairly powerful idealizations: for example, they treat some fuzzy matters as if they were sharp, in a way that will become clear as we move along. They are also some of the concepts most central to formal logic. Why are we starting this way, you might ask, when the point of this book is not to do formal logic, but to take the blurriness of the world seriously rather than idealizing it away?

There are three reasons. First, the idealized concepts are simpler and easier to get a handle on. We can complicate matters later. Second, lots of reasoning really is quite properly evaluated in accordance with the more idealized concepts. And third, starting off with a more idealized approach to arguments enables us to understand and evaluate non-ideal arguments (the sort much more likely to be encountered) by judging how closely they approximate the ideal. Once we have the basic concepts in place, we can work toward a more general approach to a sometimes clear but often blurry world: learning how to factor in and take seriously the subtleties and nuances of reasoning.

The main focus of this first chapter, then, will be on deductive arguments—the sort of arguments that are logically airtight (or are intended to be so, at least). With the relevant deductive concepts in place, we can then move on to discuss the more common, complex, and subtle arguments in the following chapters.

HAVING REASONS

An overarching goal we all share, presumably, is to hold reasonable beliefs. But what is it to believe something for a good reason? On the one hand, we sometimes say that an event happened for a reason and mean by this only that it had an identifiable cause, that it was not just random or inexplicable. On the other hand, there is a stricter use of the word, meaning that an action or a belief has a **justification** or **warrant**: in other words, it can be rationally defended on the basis of evidence. Not only are there reasons for our beliefs, in the sense that there are explanations for why we come to hold our beliefs, but we moreover *have reasons* for believing what we do. There are reasons why only one side of the moon faces Earth, but the moon does not have reasons for doing what it does. Unlike the moon, people are often in a position to offer a rationale for holding their beliefs or performing their actions.

In general we take ourselves to have reasons for our beliefs. For the most part we must be right, because so many of our beliefs are truisms like "The ground gets wet when it rains" or "Cars have four wheels." Our reasons for believing things like this are so obvious that we virtually never need to articulate them. Nor need we reflect on our justifications consciously. Having reasons for such beliefs is clearly not a matter of continually thinking about either the reasons or the beliefs themselves. It seems to be enough that we could, if necessary, call such reasons to mind. For many such beliefs, no such need will ever arise.

It is important that we could provide them if the need arose, though. From time to time, a belief that seems basic and straightforward to some people will turn out not to be shared by others. Sometimes this may not be worth bothering about. It just seems obvious to me that potatoes with gravy taste better than plain boiled turnips, but if you disagree, that's no problem. (In fact, you can have my turnips.) But under many circumstances, it will be important to find out whether one (or both) of the competing claims is a genuine mistake. The way to pursue an answer is for all sides to express their reasons for their beliefs. For the purposes of settling disputes, comparing explanations, and teaching new information, it becomes essential that we are able to make our reasoning *public*.

ASSERTIONS AND ARGUMENTS

The most basic kind of communication for each of these purposes is the practice of presenting statements as true. Typically the point of saying something we think is true is to have other people also accept that it's true. Or, even if they don't agree, at least it is useful and enlightening to have their disagreement explained, so we can see where they part ways with what's been said. To present some claim as if it were true is to **assert** it. Whether in a classroom, in the workplace, in social environments, or through the media, a great deal of our communicative exchanges consist of **assertions**, as we go about telling one another the facts as we see them. "It was a bad idea for Athens to invade Sicily during the Peloponnesian War." I think that's true, and I'd be fairly pleased for you to think so as well.

If issuing assertions were the full extent of such communication, though, there wouldn't be much point to it. If all we did in such contexts was to declare this or that to be true, then you'd say your piece, and I'd say mine. And if we disagreed? "No, no," you'd reply, "it was a perfectly good idea for Athens to invade Sicily." Then it would be my turn to repeat my assertion, and we'd both just keep repeating ourselves until we got bored or hungry.

Of course there is much more to it. To assert is, among other things, to undertake a kind of obligation: the obligation to *defend* or *retract* the assertion in the face of questioning or when confronted with evidence to the contrary. For this reason the fundamental units of rational exchange are not assertions, but **arguments**.

The word "argument" is often used to mean a disagreement or even a fight. "We had an argument," one might say, without meaning to suggest that anything particularly involving reasonableness or rationality took place. But there is also a common and natural sense of the word that means *the presentation of reasons*. That's the sense that we're refining for the purposes of explaining and analyzing critical thinking. An argument, we will say, is a set of statements that are presented as true and that have a very important internal relation: some of the statements are **premises**, which are intended to provide rational support for (and ideally to establish the truth of) a further statement, the **conclusion**. An argument is premises given in support of a conclusion.

The property of an argument that succeeds in supporting its conclusion is *soundness*. Strictly speaking, a sound argument proves that its conclusion is true. This property can be broken down into two sub-properties of the argument: first, that it is *valid*, and second, that it has all true premises. Like the term "argument" itself, "sound" and "valid" have ordinary uses that can vary widely. Below we will define them in more specialized ways that let us speak precisely about the virtues and failings of argument.

The overall picture, then, is that assertions rest on arguments that support them, usually implicitly, but that could be made explicit if necessary. It's somewhat analogous to a simple currency system, in which people exchange paper money instead of gold or goods because they're confident they can swap the paper for the goods when they need to. The idea of the gold or the goods, available if requested, underwrites the exchange of paper money and coins; the idea of reasoning and arguments, available if requested, underwrites the exchange of assertions. Speakers are not normally taken to be making wild guesses when they assert. The idea is that a speaker has an argument tucked in her pocket that can be pulled out if necessary; she could produce at least the bare bones of reasons that supported her assertion.

Moreover, just as we saw with Macbeth and his dilemma, it's important to understand that one of the people who might be informed and affected by some argument you produce in support of an assertion is *you*. One of the central themes of this book is that critical thinking begins at home, that its immediate application is in understanding how your own reasoning succeeds and fails. Quite apart from the effects of your argument on others, you may change your own mind in various ways by going through the process of mounting an argument. You might convince yourself of something altogether new, or you might strengthen or weaken some opinion you'd already held. You might even convince yourself that one of your beliefs should be rejected. The process of making reasons public is not just about persuading other people. It's also about evaluating one's own reasoning by putting it in the clearest and most explicit form possible. The image of the argument tucked in your pocket is doubly appropriate, given how hard it can be to precisely identify the jumbled contents of your own pockets: the best way of deciding what's really in there is to pull it all out into the open and get a clear look at it.

WHAT MAKES AN ARGUMENT (GOOD)?

There are at least two ways of approaching the study of arguments and arguing. Each approach carries with it a distinct conception of how arguments succeed and fail. We will make use of both notions of argument, which are closely related and normally travel together.

Definition 1: Argumentation is a rational practice.

This approach to arguments stresses the fact that arguing is a process, one that occurs in a communicative context. Argumentation is a practice by which we aim to show the reasonableness of an assertion, up to whatever standard of reasonableness is called for in that context. (Or, in failing to do so, to learn that the assertion was not as well founded as it had first appeared.) Presenting an argument is a way of making good on the obligation to support an assertion, and there are as many different practical aims of argument, in this sense, as there can be reasons for making an assertion. An argument can be a means of education or of explanation.

CHAPTER 1   *The Parts of Public Thinking: Deductive Argument*

It can be a way of rationalizing or ordering reasons, and it can be a way of explicitly weighing competing reasons against each other. In each of these roles, though, a good argument is the presentation of a collection of premises that jointly are rationally persuasive of a conclusion. Taken together, the premises make it reasonable to believe the conclusion.

Definition 2: Arguments are linguistic or logical objects.

It can also be very illuminating to think of an argument just as a set of sentences or propositions, factoring out considerations about the speaker, the audience, the context, and the broader goal of giving the argument. Are these sentences true, and do they jointly imply this conclusion? This way of asking whether the argument is a good one just sets aside worries like whether an audience will find the premises *reasonable*, worries that can be viewed as merely practical complications that arise when speakers use the argument. In other words, a good argument in this sense can be defined in terms of the truth of the premises and their logical relation to the conclusion, without any allusion to speakers or hearers or context. It is in this sense that a good argument is defined as sound. This means, first, that it is valid: its premises are relevant to its conclusion in such a fashion that if the premises are true, then the conclusion must be true. And, second, a sound argument has all true premises. More precisely (since an argument might contain some irrelevant premises) we should say that all its **essential premises**—the ones that would remain if all irrelevancies were removed—must be true.

Obviously the first definition is the less precise and less technical of the two. Indeed, the second definition is really a refinement of the first. The idea behind using this more technical definition is that the somewhat vague notion of reasonableness can be clarified in terms of the more exact and idealized notion of soundness. In particular, when some argument fails to show its conclusion to be reasonable, this can be diagnosed in terms of its unsoundness: either it has an invalid structure, or it has one or more premises that are not true. Still, it is important to understand how these two conceptions of argument can come apart.

For example, Definition 1 reflects the idea that a good argument is supposed to be an *effective* one. The reasonableness of an argument has to be measured, at least in part, by the effects the argument has, or would have, on a basically reasonable person. We need the qualification about basically reasonable people, because we don't want to end up saying that an audience can make a speaker's argument a bad one just by being sufficiently closed-minded or, for that matter, that an audience can make a lousy argument good just by being sufficiently gullible. As to how we precisely define a reasonable person, it's a hard question. The short and imperfect answer is, by extrapolating from how people reason in uncontroversial cases.

FURTHER REFLECTION

"I am bound to furnish my antagonists with arguments, but not with comprehension."
(Attributed to Benjamin Disraeli)

Definition 2, on the other hand, makes no mention of effectiveness. An argument's being sound does not mean that anyone believes, or even ought to believe, that it is sound. We all know that, in some contexts, something can be true even though the currently available evidence suggests otherwise. So suppose we had a sound argument containing such premises. Being sound, it would be a good argument in the sense of Definition 2, but it would not give anyone (in that context) a reason to believe its conclusion. It would fail by the standards of Definition 1, because, while all its premises were true, they would not themselves be reasonably acceptable as true.

Suppose, for example, that there were a species of lizard not yet discovered by anyone, hiding in the badlands of south-central Alberta. Suppose also that I was putting together a critical thinking lecture and made up a sample valid argument using the (entirely fictional, so far as I knew) premise that there is a new species of lizard hiding in the badlands of south-central Alberta. In my lecture I say, "Either there is a new species of lizard hiding in the badlands of south-central Alberta or five plus five equals eleven. But it's false that five plus five equals eleven. So there is a new species of lizard hiding in the badlands of south-central Alberta."

Now, that argument is valid (it's an instance of *Disjunctive Syllogism*, discussed below), and in the situation described, it would also be sound because both its premises are true. But in giving this sound argument by accident, without actually having reason to believe the first premise (in particular because I have no reason to believe the first half of the first premise), I don't *do* the kind of thing that arguments are useful for doing. That is, I don't give anyone—not even myself!—rational grounds to believe the conclusion. When engaged in the practical business of giving an argument, in other words, it is not enough to produce premises that happen to be true, independent of whether you possess or have presented reasons to think that they are true. It is important that your premises are mutually accepted between you and your audience if you aim not only to give a sound argument, but also to give one that will convince a reasonable person. These considerations frequently drop away when we are analyzing the argument merely as a set of statements in accordance with Definition 2. And they drop away entirely when we do formal logic, which is the fundamentally algebraic study of valid argument-forms.

In the context of communicating an argument, the issue of acceptable premises frequently leads to at least some degree of regress of justification: the need to give some new argument to support one of your original premises, when it turns out not to be acceptable to your audience. As arguments get spelled out in actual discussions, then, they tend to acquire complex structures (although sometimes they have complex structures as initially presented, too). An argument can have not just an overall conclusion, but various sub-conclusions as well—propositions that are supported by a sub-argument and that function as premises in the larger argument. In principle, this process of embedding one argument within another can go on indefinitely, since a sub-argument too might contain a premise that has to be defended. In practice, it can go on until everyone is bored *and* hungry. Certainly it isn't rare for the discussion of some initially tidy argument to expand in surprising and mentally taxing ways, as the premises of the arguer's supporting arguments at each level of regress are called into question.

Finally, the idealization represented in Definition 2 only captures the virtues of deductive arguments, a special class of arguments whose properties will be discussed below. Many other arguments fail to meet these standards, while still counting as reasonable by the lights of Definition 1. To evaluate these arguments we eventually need to refine further concepts besides validity and soundness, especially for arguments falling under the broad heading of **evidential reasoning**. To begin, however, we will think of arguments as aiming at soundness, while bearing in mind the more general idea of argumentation as a rational practice.

SOME BASIC VOCABULARY OF COMMUNICATION AND ARGUMENTATION

Assertion: The act of stating something as if it were true.

Proposition, statement, sentence, claim: What you say in order to make an assertion. I will use these terms interchangeably for the most part, though for some purposes there are important technical differences among them.

Premise: A statement intended to provide rational support for some other statement (a *conclusion*), often in conjunction with other premises.

Conclusion: A statement intended to be rationally supported by a set of premises.

Argument: A collection of premises that justify, or are supposed to justify, a conclusion.

Validity: A structural property of arguments. An argument is valid just in case there is no way for the conclusion to be false if all the premises are true.

Soundness: A two-fold property of arguments; an argument is sound if it (i) is valid and (ii) has all true premises. By definition, a sound argument proves its conclusion.

Inference: The act of reaching a conclusion on the basis of some premises.

$$\text{Premises} \begin{Bmatrix} \text{entail} \\ \text{logically imply} \\ \text{establish} \end{Bmatrix} \text{conclusions}$$

$$\text{Conclusions} \begin{Bmatrix} \text{are a logical consequence of} \\ \text{follow from} \end{Bmatrix} \text{premises}$$

$$\text{People} \begin{Bmatrix} \text{draw} \\ \text{infer} \end{Bmatrix} \text{conclusions}$$

IS GOOD ARGUMENTATION A MATTER OF BEING LOGICAL?

The term "logic" and its variant forms are often used in non-technical ways, and it may seem natural to think of the goal of critical thinking as *being logical*. On both the technical and non-technical understandings, this is probably a mistake.

First, the technical side, where "logic" has at least two distinct meanings. There is a broad sense in which it means something like the *study* of rules of correct inference, and there is a singular sense in which it means a particular system of

A common error is to confuse *infer* with *imply*. Implication is the abstract relation between the premises and conclusion of a valid argument. People infer conclusions; premises imply conclusions.

Sometimes *imply* is used to mean something like indirect or sly suggestion. Both senses of implication are distinct from *infer*. To keep the logical entailment sense of implication clearly separate from the suggestion or insinuation sense, it's useful to call the former *logical implication*.

Wrong: This evidence infers that we should support public libraries.

Right: I inferred from this evidence that we should support public libraries.

Right: This evidence implies that we should support public libraries.

inferential rules. In the latter sense we can speak of *a* logic or of *different* ones: logic is not a single universally received system of rules. In fact, there is considerable debate over what ought to count as logical laws, with each different set of proposed logical laws giving rise to a different system of logic. Inferences that are valid in one system may not be valid in another.

Historically, going back at least to Aristotle, it was thought that logic was **univocal**, meaning that the term had only a single meaning or interpretation. It was believed that true logic flowed from three basic axioms. Later, some philosophers even described these axioms as the "**Laws of Thought**":

The **Law of Identity** (For any proposition P: P if and only if P)
The **Law of Non-Contradiction** (Not both P and not-P)
The **Law of Excluded Middle** (P or not-P)

This collection of axioms gives us what's called **classical logic**. Today some logicians continue to see these axioms as definitive of genuine logic, but all logicians are aware that there are important challenges to the universal application of classical logic. I will explain a bit about these challenges, just as a means of acknowledging them and to provide the keywords for further investigation, should you be interested.

Intuitionistic logic, for example, is a well-developed formal system that does not include the Law of Excluded Middle as an axiom. This approach may tolerate vagueness and fuzzy boundaries better than classical logic, which tends to idealize and sharpen distinctions conveniently but (potentially) inaccurately. Intuitionism also sets the bar higher for certain kinds of proof, since, without Excluded Middle, you can't just take a disproof of not-P as a proof of P. You need a *direct* proof in intuitionistic logic.

Dialetheic logic, by contrast, keeps the Law of Excluded Middle, but gives up (or restricts) the Law of Non-Contradiction. The latter tells you that if a collection of propositions contains a contradiction, the collection is incoherent. But in some situations, dialetheists argue, this produces such unwelcome consequences that we should limit the application of Non-Contradiction. For instance, in a system of legal judgments, different precedents may deliver contradictory results for a single case without it being clear that one precedent has the priority. In that sort of case we can either look around for arbitrary grounds on which to claim priority for one precedent, or we can discard that subset of the legal system as incoherent, or we can accept that there is at least a small class of acceptable contradictions. Dialetheists take the third option to be the most reasonable, all things considered.

Other systems of logic are distinguished by their giving up other theorems besides the so-called Laws of Thought; examples are *Relevance logic* and *Quantum logic*, if you feel inclined to investigate this more yourself. The point is not really to explain any of these alternatives to classical logic, but just to flag the fact that what counts as logic is not a settled question. Still other logical systems are extensions of classical logic, with certain complications factored in. Such complications can include the formalization of more notions like *belief, knowledge, obligation, possibility*, and *temporality*, among others. These systems are called **modal logics**. Again, the overall lesson is just that logic is not monolithic. There is a great deal of variety and many live philosophical issues involving logic and logics. While you might still read or hear about the "Laws of Thought," it is probably safer to think of them as weaker and less absolute than that name suggests. Perhaps the "Municipal Bylaws of Thought" would be a better label, indicating that the sharp and convenient categories of classical reasoning apply within some city limits, but are not necessarily suited to the wider and wilder regions beyond. While neither the details of logical formalism nor the higher-order philosophical debates about logic are our focus here, they are important and conceptually rich topics of study.

On the non-technical side, there are uses of the word "logic" that are likely to cause or embody confusions if we run them together with the technical senses. In many cases the term is used casually as a loose synonym for "sensible" or "plausible" and is applied not just to inferences and statements but to people and their choices.

> "You'd rather have cold hands than wear gloves? That's just not logical."
> "If he's athletic, then it's logical to think that he's tried skiing at some point."
> "She's very logical, so she probably doesn't like art, poetry, and music."

Each of these looser uses of the word can be fine on its own terms, but none of them is what the study of logic is about. Science Officer Spock of *Star Trek*, for example, while forever expounding on what is logical and illogical, almost never uses the terms in any precise sense. In the strict sense, to call an inference logical is simply to say that it is valid, while a "logical truth" is not just (perhaps not even) a plausible statement, but one that must be true given the logical laws one is working with. Many of the non-technical claims that something or someone is logical or illogical are best understood merely as statements of agreement or disagreement, which invoke the term "logic" in an attempt to gain an aura of authority. Rather than using sloppy terms as code words for agreement and disagreement, our aim is to learn the most precise terminology for categorizing and diagnosing arguments. So we won't just call arguments logical or illogical, since that is a sloppy and unrevealing way of using the terms.

WHAT ISN'T AN ARGUMENT?

I once owned a wheeled office chair that had the unnerving habit of throwing me across the room if I leaned back in it. It had only three wheels, so it balanced poorly. Yet while it was not a particularly good chair, it still counted as a chair. In fact we might reason this way: *it was a lousy chair; hence it was a chair.* With one armrest removed, it would still have been a chair. But with both armrests, two wheels, the backrest, and part of the seat removed (and destroyed, if that affects your intuitions), the remaining bit might have been at most a *broken chair*, or maybe we would then have said that it was no longer a chair at all. So it is with most kinds of thing: the lines are blurry between good instances, bad instances, and non-instances.

We have made a start on explaining conceptions of a *good argument*. But as we will see below, some of the ways arguments can fail to be sound—by failing to be valid, for instance—are, when taken to extremes, ways that a set of statements can intuitively fail to be an argument altogether. It would be silly and awkward to say that only successful arguments count as arguments. On the other hand, it seems strange to suppose that any set of randomly chosen sentences counts as at least a bad argument, or a **fallacious argument**, as bad arguments are known. Fortunately not much hangs on this distinction in practice. For our purposes, we will treat something as an argument if the context in which it is presented indicates that it is *intended* as an argument. So whether something counts as a random outburst of unrelated statements or as a dreadful fallacy might depend, in context, on what we glean of the speaker's intentions.

Still, there are systematic forms of reasoning that are easily mistaken for arguments, even though they are better categorized in other ways. Insisting, repeating, declaiming, vowing, defining, and stipulating should not be confused with arguing (though of course such acts may be *part* of giving an argument). Nor should mere assertion itself. The common usage of the word "argue" might extend to saying that someone has argued when she has only given unsupported assertions. But in the sense of argument we are using—as the basic unit of rational exchange—mere assertions are not arguments.

EXPLANATION VERSUS ARGUMENT

More subtle is the distinction between arguments, in which evidence is given in the form of premises to defend a conclusion, and **explanations**, in which we appeal to some facts in order to rationalize, or make sense of, some other facts. Explanation is a form of reasoning that is broadly distinct from argument while often overlapping with it. A working definition of the difference is that arguments aim at showing some statement to be worth believing, while explanations aim to make better sense of something already believed. Take, for example, the following statement:

> "The ice is thicker at the far end of the rink because the ground slopes in that direction."

The context of utterance will determine whether a statement like this is functioning as an argument or as an explanation. If the speaker is proffering the slope of the ground as a reason to believe that the ice is thicker at the far end of the rink (especially if the latter is not yet known to be the case), then the utterance is intended as an argument. But if the audience is fully aware that the ice is thicker at the far end and simply wants to know *why* this is the case, then the utterance is better taken as an explanation. In other words, the speaker need not be trying to persuade us that the ice is thicker at the far end. That may well be known already, so the explanation is not, or need not be, an argument itself. Instead the aim may just be to make sense of some known fact by fitting it into a pattern of understanding: laws, regularities, and familiar experiences.

As we will see in the case of arguments, explanations can have implicit elements—parts that are supposed to be understood from the context. The explanation above is just such an example. The speaker presumably expects us to understand that ice can be made by flooding an area with large amounts of water, that water runs downhill, and that water doesn't freeze instantly, so that the water will have time to run downhill before freezing. There are different kinds of explanation, moreover. Sometimes an explanation is **causal**, describing (in part) the prior conditions that caused some event. The explanation for a bicycle chain's getting rusty might be that it got wet, for example. Other times an explanation aims to rationalize, to order reasons and definitions, or to sort priorities according to principles of reasoning. An explanation of why there are as many even numbers as there are even and odd numbers together makes no appeal to causes, for instance, but is no less an explanation.

The argument-explanation distinction cuts across other distinctions of reasoning. There can be causal arguments and causal explanations, moral arguments and moral explanations, mathematical arguments and mathematical explanations. But aside from general virtues like clarity, a specific key virtue of good arguments is shared with explanations: roughly speaking, both arguments and explanations are supposed to teach us something. Circular or question-begging arguments, as discussed in Chapter 4, fail this condition inherently; these are fallacious arguments of the form "P, therefore P." Explanations too are open to an analogous problem of **pseudo-explanation**, primarily a matter of providing a triviality or a mere label when an explanation is called for.

The French author and playwright Molière famously parodied the pseudo-explanations of the medical doctors of his era by having one of his characters explain the fact that opium causes drowsiness in terms of a "*virtus dormativa*" of the opium. That is, opiates have the power to cause sleep. To say that opiates cause

LINK

The interrelations of argument and explanation are a complex topic, the surface of which we will barely scratch. Chapter 2 discusses a form of reasoning called **abduction,** in which the fact that a hypothesis would *explain* known facts is cited as *justification* for believing that hypothesis.

CHAPTER 1   *The Parts of Public Thinking: Deductive Argument*

sleep because they have a *virtus dormativa*, however, is merely to label the thing requiring explanation, rather than explaining it. Explanations are not necessarily arguments, but explaining in a circle is as unhelpful as arguing in a circle.

UNDERSTANDING VALID ARGUMENT FORMS

So far we have a technical definition of a deductive argument, telling us that arguments aim to be sound, and that a sound argument is valid with all true premises. Why should this two-part definition of soundness be so heavily emphasized? There are plenty of good reasons that could be spelled out in terms of the noble goals of conceptual inquiry, but for now my answer is just this: because laziness is wonderful when you can get away with it.

The fact that there are two conditions that a sound argument must meet—being valid and having all its essential premises be true—means that there are broadly two ways an argument can fail to be sound: by having one or more false essential premises, or by having an invalid structure. In general it's harder to discover whether premises are true than to determine whether the argument is valid. To learn whether some alleged statement of fact is true, you might have to go out and actually *look at the world*. It can be a messy and time-consuming business. So it makes sense to evaluate an argument's structure before focusing on the truth of its premises. After all, an argument that would not support its conclusion even if its premises were true can be rejected without checking out the truth of its premises. If it's invalid, then it's unsound irrespective of whether the premises are true. This can be a very efficient way of evaluating an argument.

Let's clarify the ideas of validity and soundness by looking at a few examples. Some of these examples are deliberately strange, in order to make the truth or falsity of the premises and their relevance to the conclusion perfectly obvious.

First, here is an argument that is valid but unsound:

1. If Pierre Trudeau was the prime minister, then he was a professional dance instructor.
2. Pierre Trudeau was the prime minister.
Therefore,
3. Pierre Trudeau was a professional dance instructor.

Since Premise 1 is false, the argument is not just goofy but unsound. A sound argument has all true premises. Still, for all its silliness this argument has an important virtue: it is valid. Its premises relate to its conclusion in such a way that, *if* the premises were both true, then the conclusion would be true as well. The same can be said of the following argument, even though *both* its premises are false.

1. If John A. Macdonald, first prime minister of Canada, was a dentist, then he was a professional dance instructor.
2. John A. Macdonald, first prime minister of Canada, was a dentist.
Therefore,
3. John A. Macdonald, first prime minister of Canada, was a professional dance instructor.

The premises are not true, but if they *were* true, then the conclusion would be as well. That is, if you think of a far-fetched world in which these premises are true—one in which dentists all teach dance, and in which John A. Macdonald was a dentist—then you're thinking of a world in which John A. Macdonald taught dance. So this argument, however silly, satisfies one condition for soundness (it's valid) but fails the other condition (it has false premises). The argument is valid but unsound.

It should be clearer now what it means to say that validity is a *structural* property of arguments. We are not concerned with whether the particular premises are actually true when we evaluate the validity of some argument, but only with whether the conclusion would be true if the premises were true. This enables us to factor out the specific content of the premises. For instance, both of the arguments we just examined have the same structure:

1. If P then Q
2. P
Therefore,
3. Q

The arguments are valid because this is a valid *form* of argument; its technical name is **Modus Ponens**.

The letters P and Q in this argument form are just placeholders; they each stand for any declarative sentence that we might plug into that structure. So we can substitute any two (declarative) sentences for P and Q in this argument framework and produce actual arguments. To say that the structure is valid is to say that any choice of sentences for P and Q that makes both premises true also makes the conclusion true. Notice that having true *premises* does not necessarily mean having true Ps and Qs! If one premise in an argument is not-P (i.e., "It is not the case that P"), then only a *false* sentence P will make the premise not-P true. In the modus ponens case, as long as we pick P and Q in such a way that it's true both that P, and if P then Q, then Q will also be true. That's a structural property of the argument—a property that remains even if P and Q don't happen to make the premises true. Looking again at the first two sample arguments, then, we can see that even though they have false premises, they still possess at least the virtue of validity. If their premises were true, then their conclusions would be true as well.

Another basic and important valid argument form is called **Modus Tollens**:

1. If P then Q
2. Not Q
Therefore,
3. Not P

FURTHER REFLECTION

There are a few Latin terms that are almost unavoidable in critical thinking, since the study of reasoning goes back to antiquity and inherits many terms from that history. Where possible I will use English terms. In addition, for purposes of clarity I will capitalize the names of fallacies. In general, though, this is unnecessary.

Again, to say that this is a valid structure is just to say that any choices of P and Q that make both (1) and (2) come out true are guaranteed to make (3) come out true as well; there is no way for the conclusion to be false if the premises are true. For example, if P = "Canada is a republic" and Q = "Canada has no monarch," then both

1. If P then Q

and

2. Not Q

are true. (If Canada is a republic, then Canada has no monarch; and it is not the case that Canada has no monarch.) Since Modus Tollens is a valid argument form,

3. Not P

should be true as well . . . and so it is. Canada is not a republic.

So far we have seen two examples of arguments that are valid but unsound. Next we will see an argument having the opposite problem. This argument has all true premises—indeed, it has a true conclusion—but it is invalid, and hence unsound.

1. 42 is a number.
2. Continents drift.
3. Pigs grunt.
Therefore,
4. Socrates is Greek.

Here each of the premises is true, but. . . yuck. It's only because the parts of this argument are numbered, and connected with "therefore," that we'd even imagine it to be intended as an argument. The premises do not relate to the conclusion in any way; in particular, the premises could all be true even were Socrates from Lithuania. So this argument is invalid and hence is unsound. This is the case even though the argument has not just all true premises, but a true conclusion as well. It's unsound anyhow. A lousy argument with a true conclusion is a lousy argument: after all, the idea is not simply to have the alleged conclusion happen to turn out true. The idea is for the conclusion to be *supported* by the premises. (By the same token, a lousy argument for a conclusion does not mean that the conclusion is *false*, either. It just means that the argument gives us no reason to believe it.)

This argument, however, is sound:

1. Vixens are foxes.
2. All foxes are mammals.
Therefore,
3. Vixens are mammals.

As an aside, notice that for the sake of convenience the above argument is framed in what are called **categorical** terms: it's a matter of how the categories *Vixen*, *Fox*, and *Mammal* are related. This way of framing logical inferences was largely the extent of logic for many centuries and is still frequently taught as informal logic owing to its ease of use in natural language. Since the rise of modern logic in the late nineteenth and early twentieth centuries, a more rigorous and general treatment is given to inferences of this sort, fitting them into the form of

conditional reasoning (like "If P then Q"). In the above case, the same argument could be given using a **quantifier expression** (like "some" and "every") and a **variable** like *x* or *y*—a kind of placeholder for objects that could be plugged into the statement.

1. For every object *x*, if *x* is a vixen then *x* is a fox.
2. For every object *x*, if *x* is a fox then *x* is a mammal.
Therefore,
3. For every object *x*, if *x* is a vixen then *x* is a mammal.

I will not focus on the distinction between categorical and quantificational reasoning, nor on the axioms or deduction rules that characterize either approach to formal logic, beyond the cases useful for explaining validity and soundness. For example, we now have an argument with the valid form of **Hypothetical Syllogism**. The premises seem quite clearly true, given the definitions of "vixen," "fox," and "mammal." So the argument is sound; it proves its conclusion true.

Now let's consider an example of a sound argument that falls outside the conditional mould:

1. Either foxes are mammals or rabbits are birds.
2. Rabbits are not birds.
Therefore
3. Foxes are mammals.

This argument also has a valid form for which there is a name: **Disjunctive Syllogism**.

1. P or Q
2. Not Q
Therefore,
3. P

Again, the premises of the sample valid argument are clearly true, so the argument is sound. Finally, we can see how more complex arguments can chain together such basic argument forms, proving intermediate conclusions along the way. This argument makes use of both Disjunctive Syllogism and Modus Ponens.

1. Either foxes are mammals or rabbits are birds.
2. If foxes are mammals, then vixens lactate.
3. Rabbits are not birds.
Therefore
4. Foxes are mammals.
Therefore,
5. Vixens lactate.

Lines 1 and 3 imply line 4 by Disjunctive Syllogism, then 2 and 4 imply 5 by Modus Ponens.

While people rarely present their reasoning in such a regimented format, this is the refined conception of what arguments are. Even when they don't come packaged in this way, arguments *can* be packaged in this way for the purposes of clarifying and assessing them. When we assess them—when we are interested in their

CHAPTER 1   *The Parts of Public Thinking: Deductive Argument*

soundness, or at least in their approximation to soundness—it is useful to put them in the format of numbered premises and conclusions. Throughout the book we will see examples of how to do this.

CHECKING AN ARGUMENT'S VALIDITY: THE METHOD OF COUNTER-EXAMPLE

Now we are in a better position to appreciate the utility and convenience of testing an argument's soundness by first testing its validity. What is needed, then, is a method for discovering whether an argument is invalid. There are several such methods, but a particularly quick and useful way of testing for invalidity is called the **Method of Counter-example**.

Our definition of validity tells us that there is no way for the conclusion of a valid argument to be false if all the premises are true. This means we can tell that an argument is invalid if we can think of ways for the premises all to be true while the conclusion is false. That's the Method of Counter-example in a nutshell: think of a situation in which the premises would be true but the conclusion would be false. If you can think of such a situation (or "construct a model," as some say), then the argument is invalid. The truth of its premises doesn't guarantee the truth of its conclusion, because you've thought of at least one situation in which the premises would be true but the conclusion false.

To take a simple example: every natural number has an immediate successor (i.e., the number you get by adding 1 to it); therefore, every natural number is the successor of some other natural number. A quick and easy way to see that this is an invalid argument is to look for a counter-example: some number that is consistent with the premise but inconsistent with the conclusion. Since 0 is clearly such a number, it shows the invalidity of the argument. Consider too this slightly more complex example:

1. The club president appoints the treasurer.
2. The chair of the club's board of governors appoints the vice-president.
Therefore,
3. The treasurer and the vice-president are appointed by different people.

Here again we can test for invalidity by thinking of scenarios that are consistent with (1) and (2), but inconsistent with (3). What about the scenario in which a single person serves both as president and as chair of the board of governors? Nothing in the premises rules this out, yet the conclusion would be false in that situation. So the argument is invalid; its premises would be true and its conclusion false if the president was also the chair.

Again, if all we're concerned with is whether a deductive argument provides grounds to accept its conclusion, it makes a great deal of sense to first consider its validity. Assessing the truth of premises can be hard work; we circumvent that problem altogether if we can see that *even were the premises true* they would not support the conclusion.

Here is an argument that a reader could reject without even knowing what the key terms *mean*, still less whether the premises are true:

1. If something is a dioxin then it's a polycyclic compound.
2. Some polycyclic compounds are carcinogens.

Therefore,

3. If something is a dioxin, then it's a carcinogen.

Because validity concerns an argument's form alone, a valid argument should remain valid (though not necessarily sound!) if we uniformly substitute one predicate or name for another throughout the argument. We can test the above argument for validity by substituting some more familiar terms for the potentially unfamiliar ones and seeing whether we can thereby make the premises true and the conclusion false.

1. If something is a fox, then it's a mammal.
2. Some mammals are herbivores.
Therefore,
3. If something is a fox, then it's a herbivore.

Clearly this argument is invalid—both premises are true and yet its conclusion is false. But structurally it's the same as the argument above it. Using the same argument structure (i.e., just uniformly substituting "fox" for "dioxin," "mammal" for "polycyclic compound," and "herbivore" for "carcinogen" everywhere those terms occur) we've found an interpretation that makes the premises true and the conclusion false. Hence the original argument—*whatever* its key terms mean—is invalid. That's not to say its conclusion is false; it's just to say that that argument doesn't give us reason to *believe* the conclusion. So the argument fails.

Now you might think, "But what if I'd chosen 'carnivore' instead of 'herbivore'? Then the premises and conclusion would all have been true." That's correct, but it's irrelevant. An invalid argument can happen to have true premises and a true conclusion; even in that case it still fails the condition that the premises are what *establish* the truth of the conclusion. The existence of even one counter-example—either a scenario in which the actual premises are true and the conclusion false, or a scenario on which a structurally identical argument has true premises and a false conclusion—shows that an argument is invalid. So when we test for invalidity, we have to actively search for counter-examples.

Overall, then, testing for validity is a very useful first tool in the evaluation of arguments. It can cut short a potentially long and difficult investigation into the argument's soundness. Of course, one might nevertheless want to investigate the truth of the argument's premises—just in the interests of learning and thoroughness. A complete evaluation of an argument will still consider both validity and the truth of the premises.

VALID ARGUMENT FORMS

Here is a selection of further argument forms recognized as (classically) valid.

Simplification

P and Q
Therefore,
P

"Eric and Ellen are both doctors. Therefore, Ellen is a doctor."

It might seem that such a simple and obvious inference rule could never need to be invoked in everyday communication. But this sort of inference can be usefully invoked in setting aside irrelevancies, as in "If she's a convicted criminal but truthful, then she's truthful, and her word can be trusted." It may also apply to complex claims of predication, sometimes flagged with the Latin term **a fortiori**, meaning "with stronger reason."

> A: "The rules say that prisoners aren't allowed to vote."
> B: "Well, that probably doesn't apply to *repentant* prisoners."
> A: "A fortiori, a repentant prisoner is a prisoner. So the rule applies to them too."

A's reply here implicitly invokes a simplification rule, moving from "repentant and prisoner" to "prisoner." (Not all predications will fit this logical mould, however. For example, a *young head of state* might simply be young *for* a head of state, rather than both young—period—and a head of state.) We've already seen another example of a fortiori reasoning, in the case of my office chair: it was a lousy chair; a fortiori, it was a chair.

Conjunction

1. P
2. Q
Therefore,
3. P and Q

> "Eric is a doctor. Ellen is a doctor. Therefore, Eric and Ellen are both doctors."

Notice that putting the conclusion in this way, rather than just writing "and" between the two premises, requires that the term "doctor" is being used univocally—that is, with one meaning, non-metaphorically in both cases.

Addition

1. P
Therefore,
2. P or Q

> "Foxes are mammals. Therefore, either foxes are mammals or cows are mammals."
> "Foxes are mammals. Therefore, either foxes are mammals or lizards are mammals."

Here it does not matter whether the statement added using "or" is true or false. For reasons discussed below, the resulting statement is true as long as *at least* one of the sub-statements is true. If we already know that P is true, this guarantees that "P or Q" is true—no matter what Q is.

This shows how truth conditions can come apart from the conditions for a cooperative or useful assertion. We might be guaranteed to say something *true* with "Foxes are mammals or lizards are mammals," if we know that foxes are mammals. But normally it would be uncooperative or misleading to assert such a truth if we know that lizards are not mammals, or even if we have no idea either way.

Hypothetical Syllogism

1. If P then Q
2. If Q then R
Therefore,
3. If P then R

> "If the dollar is devalued, exports will rise. If exports rise, then unemployment will fall. Therefore, if the dollar is devalued, unemployment will fall."

Constructive Dilemma

1. P or Q
2. If P then R
3. If Q then S
Therefore,
4. R or S

> "Either it will snow tomorrow or there will be a quiz in class. If it snows tomorrow, classes will be cancelled. If there's a quiz in class tomorrow, I'll fail it. So either classes will be cancelled tomorrow or I'll fail a quiz tomorrow."

Destructive Dilemma

1. If P then R
2. If Q then S
3. Not R or not S
Therefore,
4. Not P or not Q

> "If Zainab called her mother, the answering machine took a message. And if her brother called her mother, the line was busy. But the machine didn't take a message, or the line wasn't busy. So Zainab didn't call her mother, or her brother didn't."

You should be able to see how some of these valid forms are constituted out of simpler forms. Of course, one can have fabulously long and complicated argument forms; here I list just some simpler ones to aid in the recognition of valid arguments when you encounter them in natural language.

OTHER STRUCTURAL PROPERTIES OF ARGUMENTS

Besides being valid or invalid, an argument can be organized in a range of ways important to assessing the support it gives to its conclusion. Most of the arguments we have examined so far can be classified as **linked arguments**: their premises essentially tie together to support a single overall conclusion. Modus Ponens is a clear and simple example of this: by themselves, neither P nor *If P then Q* are grounds to conclude Q. But together they link up to imply the conclusion. Linked arguments are really the most fundamental sort of argument. But arguments can be structured in more complex ways that build on linked arguments.

One example is a **convergent argument**, in which a range of independent grounds for a conclusion are assembled together as premises. No premise in a convergent argument requires the other premises in order to support the conclusion; rather, each premise directly supports the conclusion. Suppose, for example, that I said, "Cars are bad for the environment. They burn petroleum, which pollutes the atmosphere, and the methods of their construction involve mining and industrial practices that pollute the soil and water as well." Here a collection of reasons are given for thinking that cars are bad for the environment, none of which rests on any of the others. In the case of deductively valid arguments, this kind of argument can amount to overkill, since just one sound argument for a conclusion is sufficient to establish its truth. But it's one thing to present an argument as sound, and another thing for one's audience to accept it as sound. Often it makes sense to provide convergent reasoning in the hopes that an audience who denies the truth of one premise or the validity of one of the premise-conclusion inferences will still find another of the converging lines of argument persuasive. That is, maybe someone is unconvinced that automobile exhaust is particularly bad for the environment, but accepts that mining and industrial practices are. Even if both lines of argument are sound, in this case casting the net more widely ensures that the argument is effective.

In the case of evidential reasoning, discussed in Chapter 2, convergent arguments are especially important. A collection of convergent premises, each independently supporting the conclusion *to a degree*, can add up to a stronger argument than any of the premises on its own. We can think of convergent arguments as collections of distinct simpler arguments. This is important for the purposes of analyzing arguments, because finding a false premise in a convergent set of reasons doesn't entail that the overall argument isn't sound. The other lines of reasoning in the convergent argument might nevertheless be sufficient to entail the conclusion.

Another way of putting together basic arguments into complex forms is through **sequential arguments**. These are cases in which premises establish intermediate conclusions, which then serve as premises for some further conclusion.

1. Literacy is an important life skill.
2. Anyone who gets accepted to a major university is literate.
3. Jill got accepted to a major university.
Therefore,
4. Jill is literate.

Therefore,

5.   At least one person is literate.

Therefore,

6.   At least one person has an important life skill.

In this argument, lines (4) and (5) are both intermediate conclusions that follow from earlier premises and premises from which subsequent conclusions follow. Many arguments are sequential in this fashion, proving intermediate conclusions for the purpose of making the move to the main conclusion especially clear and self-evident.

Finally, arguments can incorporate elements of all three structures, with complex hierarchical orderings. Someone (in particular my mother-in-law) might say:

> "Oat bran is healthy, and it's tasty. Besides, it's affordable and can be
> added to many different dishes. This makes it good value for the money.
> So it's a good ingredient to have in the pantry."

This reasoning really consists of four convergent lines of argument for an intermediate conclusion, with a main conclusion that follows sequentially. But the convergent arguments aren't entirely independent of one another; plausibly, it's the fact that oat bran is healthy that makes its (alleged) tastiness and affordability relevant. After all, automotive antifreeze might be tasty and affordable, but it's poisonous—so these properties on their own wouldn't really count in its favour as a food choice. The argument is partly convergent, then, but with some implicit linkage or interdependence between some of the convergent lines of reasoning.

Constructing an effective argument is partly a matter of understanding these sorts of dependence relations among the premises and being able to make them clear, just as analyzing an argument effectively requires perceiving these relations. In the case just given, for example, it would be a serious mistake to think that the other convergent lines of argument remained in force if it turned out that oat bran was in fact unhealthy.

TRUTH CONDITIONS

The first element of soundness is validity; now let's consider the second element. What does it mean to say that a premise is true? When we evaluate the truth of a premise, we are in effect checking to see whether there is an appropriate fit between the state of the world and the how the claim represents the world as being. We use the term **truth conditions** to mean how things would have to be in order for the statement to be true.

In many cases it may seem that explaining the truth conditions of a sentence is as simple as removing the quotation marks from it. The sentence "Felix the cat is on the mat" has truth conditions that are simply explained as a matter of Felix the cat's being on the mat. But this is not much of an explanation in a wide class of cases. Even this apparently simple case is complicated by there being more than one cat named Felix in the world, so particular *uses* of the sentence will have different truth conditions. My utterance of that sentence in a room with a salient cat named "Felix" that is on a mat will normally be judged true, even if there are thousands of cats named Felix around the world that are not on mats at that moment. But even in that sort of immediate context, it still might be clear to everyone involved that I am actually making a claim about some other cat named Felix, perhaps far away (in an attempt to display my psychic abilities, say). Under *these* conditions, the presence of the local Felix on the local mat would not suffice to make my statement true. When we are considering what makes some statement true, a range of such interpretive issues can arise. Some of these are discussed below; others are examined in detail in Chapter 3.

TRUTH AND REASONABLENESS

It is arguments, and not single statements, that are valid or invalid, sound or unsound. On the other hand, it is statements and not arguments that are true or false. The term "reasonable" is broad enough to apply at various levels, but we will use it, like truth, to apply to individual statements rather than arguments. A reasonable statement on our definition is one with sufficient evidence, all things considered, to render it acceptable in a given state of information.

We often call statements true even though we are rarely, if ever, in a position to know that they are perfectly accurate, immune to falsification by any subsequent discovery of evidence. This is a significant difference between truth and reasonableness, though. If our assertion later turns out to have been mistaken, we say that it was false, but this is consistent with continuing to hold the assertion was reasonable at the time it was made. While we *aim* at the truth in making and defending our assertions, the means by which we aim, and typically the only virtue we can be certain our assertions have, is their reasonableness according to our information at any given time.

Truth is often formally understood to be a discrete concept: either a statement is true or it is false, with no intermediate cases. Another way of putting this is to say that statements have one of only two **truth values**. Strictly speaking, statements are not "sort of true" or "pretty much true." On this view, the word that means "approximately true" is "false."

An important philosophical question is how to characterize truth in general. For example, we may wish to admit the possibility of statements that are neither true nor false. But admitting this possibility is still consistent with the idea that statements are either true or not true, with no middling cases; it's just that there could be more ways of being not-true than of simply being false. However, even if we accept truth as **bivalent** (having only two possible truth values), this does not mean that we talk nonsense if we say that some statement is only approximately true. We might just interpret such talk as not quite literal. Such claims could be understood as meaning that there is some *other* statement, quite similar to the one in question, that really is true. When we say, "It's approximately true that Ted lied," we could be understood to mean "It's true that Ted did something approximately like lying." In other words, we need not suppose that an approximately true statement has some property of *semi-truth*; certainly it's simpler to suppose that such a statement is strictly false, but has a similar meaning to a (genuinely, fully) true statement.

There are philosophically deep waters here. Whatever we end up saying about truth, though, *reasonableness* clearly comes in degrees. The evidence available in support of some statement can range anywhere between overwhelming, considerable, marginal, and none. Understanding how we can reliably measure the degree of evidence for a statement is a major aspect of critical thinking. In general it is a mistake to suppose that we can call a valid argument unsound only if one or more premises are absolutely known to be false. An argument still fails by the lights of Definition 1 in the event that there's no positive reason to accept the premises; we don't actually need positive reasons to *reject* the premises in order to say that the argument fails. For in the case where there's simply no reason to accept the premise(s), there is correspondingly no reason to accept the conclusion. But that's what an argument was supposed to give us.

On the other hand, just as a matter of the meaning of the word *true*, the following seems correct: enough reason to accept some claim is enough reason to accept it as *true*—however provisionally. To the extent that we regard a statement as worth asserting, and to the extent that we are even interested in the *possible* truth of some statements, sound arguments will be crucial for revealing what entails and what is entailed by those statements. So even though the definition of soundness implicates truth rather than degrees of reasonableness, the standards of deductive reasoning remain relevant to our assessment of the consequences of sets of beliefs or claims, virtually without regard to what we say specifically about the standards for regarding claims as true—that is, without regard to how much evidence makes it reasonable to assert a claim.

NECESSARY TRUTHS AND DEFINITIONAL TRUTHS

An important class of true statements is those that *must* be true, either because they are truths of logic and mathematics, or because they are true by definition in a broader sense. Many philosophers of logic and language would say, for example, that when you realize the following sentence is true—It is not the case both that all bears hibernate and that not all bears hibernate—you are realizing something not about bears, but about logic. That sentence is an instance of a logical law, the Law of Non-Contradiction: not both P and not-P. Because it holds for all declarative sentences, irrespective of their subject matter, the truth of any instance of the law is really a matter of logic and not about the workings of the world. Even if an utterance of the sentence "Felix is on the mat" is true in some situations, this is merely a **contingent truth**; things might have turned out differently. But to the extent that Non-Contradiction is a logical law, the sentence above and any other instance of the law are **necessary truths**: they would be true no matter how things might have turned out (even if there were no bears at all).

Propositions of mathematics are standard examples of necessary truths, since they too, if true, could not have been false. Their truth follows from the definitions of the basic objects and operations of mathematics. Necessarily, then, 15 is greater than 6; this is simply a matter of the definitions of "15," "greater than," and "6." But other definitions abound in the way we communicate, including in argumentation, without their status always being so obvious. Someone learning about football might hear it said that the ground can't cause a fumble if the quarterback slides feet-first. This might sound like an assertion about the proper way to avoid having the ground cause a fumble—i.e., by sliding with the proper technique. In fact it's true by definition; someone who said this would not be making a claim about the causal powers of the ground, but rather laying down part of the definition of a fumble in football. According to the rules, if the quarterback slides feet-first and the ground knocks the ball loose, it doesn't count as a fumble.

Because necessary or definitional truths are often said to really be about logic or language, many people find it tempting to say that they are only *trivially* true, or that they convey no genuine information. There is little point to taking such a view, from our perspective. What matters is recognizing what sort of truth we are dealing with. Naturally if a premise in an argument is recognized to be true by definition, this removes any concern about confirming its truth by investigating facts or demanding further proof. But it's also important to be sensitive to at least two possibilities when dealing with such premises. First, there is the prospect that a claim equivocates between definitional and contingent status—that it gets used in both ways within the same argument. This is the problem with the No True Scot fallacy, for instance, discussed in detail in Chapter 4. And there is also the serious question about the power of definitions and who recognizes them. The fact that one side in a discussion thinks that a premise is true by definition does not settle the question; there are many, many examples of definitions that properly change over time to accommodate new discoveries or new perspectives.

When nineteenth-century scientist John Dalton re-introduced the ancient Greek notion of the *atom* to physics and chemistry, he defined atoms as indivisible (which is even what the word "atom" means, in Greek). But clearly it would not have made sense, upon the later discovery that atoms could be split, to say, "No, this discovery must be mistaken; after all, it's true by definition that atoms are indivisible!" Similarly, there was a time in most nations and cultures, including Canada, at which the legal definition of "voter" excluded women. The fact that this was true by definition, in some sense, was not a good argument against extending the right to vote to women, since the very question at issue was whether this was a *good* definition of voter. Premises can be treated as true by definition only if the acceptability of the definition itself is not contested.

Finally, questions of definition give rise to the important distinction between **necessary and sufficient conditions**. Objects or types of object are often defined in terms of a set of conditions that they satisfy. For example, the definition of a mammal typically includes such properties as being warm-blooded, having body hair, and nursing offspring by lactation. When we reason about how such properties or concepts fit together, we need to see the logical relations that such a definition imposes.

We can say that being warm-blooded is a necessary condition for being a mammal; if it's not warm-blooded, it's not a mammal. But the opposite is not true. Being a mammal is not a necessary condition for being warm-blooded. (Birds are warm-blooded too, so something can be warm-blooded without being a mammal.) Rather, being a mammal is a sufficient condition for being warm-blooded; if it's a mammal, it's guaranteed to be warm-blooded. Nor is being warm-blooded sufficient for being a mammal, since the other conditions must also be satisfied.

It is often important to note these distinctions. "Terry must be a good teacher," someone might assert. "After all, she's very enthusiastic about her subject area." Here we can reply that enthusiasm is at most a necessary condition for being a good teacher, but not a sufficient condition. Other things besides enthusiasm are needed. For the same reason, the inference from "Terry is not a good teacher" to "Terry is not enthusiastic about her subject area" also does not follow. Terry might fail to be a good teacher by failing to satisfy other necessary conditions instead. As a final example that we have already explained, notice that an argument's validity is a necessary condition for its soundness, while its soundness is a sufficient condition for its validity.

Of course some relations between conditions are neither necessary nor sufficient. Having excellent diction might be *correlated* with being a good teacher, in the sense that speaking clearly makes it *likelier* that one is a good teacher, without being necessary for it.

TRUTH CONDITIONS OF COMPOUND SENTENCES

Premises and conclusions are rarely all simple statements. Usually the claims made in an argument are complex in some respect—for instance, involving two or more sentences joined together. For this reason the assessment of an argument requires that we pay attention to the truth conditions of such complex sentences, since the way they are joined makes all the difference to what they entail and what entails them.

Simple (or atomic) statement: A sentence that does not contain another sentence as one of its parts. For example, "My dog has fleas" and "Continents drift."

Conjunctive statement, or conjunction: A compound statement containing two or more sub-statements (called **conjuncts**), usually joined with the words "and" or "but." A conjunction is true if and only if both of its conjuncts are true. To put it slightly more technically, a statement of the form "P and Q" is true just in case P is true and Q is true. Near-synonyms like "as well as" might be used instead. A term like "but" indicates a different speaker's attitude than "and" but also creates a conjunction. (This point is explored in the section on *rhetoric* in Chapter 3.)

Disjunctive statement, or disjunction: A statement of the form "P or Q" is true just in case at least one of P and Q is true.

A compound statement containing two sub-statements (called **disjuncts**), joined with the word "or" or near-equivalents like "alternatively." A disjunction is true if and only if one of its disjuncts is true.

Famously the word "or" can be understood *inclusively* or *exclusively*. To say that a disjunctive statement uses the inclusive "or" is to say that *at least* one of the listed disjuncts is true; in other words, the disjunction is also true if *both* its disjuncts are true. The exclusive "or," by contrast, applies when one and only one of the disjuncts is true. "Fish or cut bait!" is an idiom meaning "Do one thing or the other, but not both"—that is, it exhibits the exclusive "or." But for most purposes, it is best to treat "or" inclusively, as far as the meaning of the word itself, and to regard the exclusive "or" as an artifact of **implicature** in some contexts: that is, a further interpretation that goes beyond the strict and literal meaning of the words. (Implicature is discussed in more detail in Chapter 3.)

The intuitive difference between disjunctive and conjunctive statements, for the purposes of logic and evidential analysis, is that it's particularly easy for a disjunctive statement to be true. A disjunctive statement is true provided *any* of its disjuncts are true, while a conjunctive statement is true just in case *all* of its conjuncts are true.

Conditional statements: A statement of the form "If P then Q" is true unless P is true but Q is false.

Conditionals are sentences with an if-then form. In the above example, we would call P the **antecedent** (the "if" part), and Q the **consequent** (the "then" part).

The question of the truth-conditions of conditional statements is surprisingly complicated, so the definition given above should be taken as quite tentative. This is the definition of the if-then symbol employed in classical formal logic, so it has considerable currency, but it does have some unhappy consequences. For example, by this definition the sentence "If continents drift, then grass is green" is true, as is "If continents don't drift, then grass is purple." (You can check these examples against the above definition to confirm that they count as true.) Why should we adopt such a definition?

The short answer is this: because it captures many of our intuitions when understood properly. Often when we *use* a conditional statement, we intend to convey some sort of explanatory relation between the antecedent and the consequent—for instance, that P is what *made it the case* that Q. But that too can often be explained as something like an implicature. What matters for the sake of argument analysis, in any event, is whether an argument containing conditional statements *requires* them to be interpreted in the explanatory sense or not. As long as we're clear on what the argument requires, the task is just to determine whether it succeeds on that interpretation.

It can be an easier matter to identify a conditional statement in English than to recognize which *direction* the if-then relation runs, since the antecedent need not come before the consequent on various constructions. For example, each of the following makes the same conditional claim:

Abigail swims if Bill bikes.
If Bill bikes, Abigail swims.
Bill bikes only if Abigail swims.
Only if Abigail swims does Bill bike.

The latter two of these sentences may seem surprising at first. Why should two such strong-sounding claims have the same truth-conditions as the first two? The answer emerges quickly upon reflection. If it really is true that *if Bill bikes, then Abigail swims*, then there is no case in which Bill bikes but Abigail doesn't swim. But that's just to say that Bill bikes only if Abigail swims. The sentence need not be telling you anything about the explanation for Bill's biking or Abigail's swimming; it need not be proposing a causal connection between the two events. It just specifies a correlation between the truth-values of the two sub-sentences: that whenever "Bill bikes" is true, then so is "Abigail swims." In general, then, the following two formulations are logically equivalent.

CHAPTER 1   *The Parts of Public Thinking: Deductive Argument*

If P then Q
Q only if P

On the other hand, their different word orders and different emphases can mean that the two logically equivalent formulations are suited to convey different messages in practice. This, again, we can treat as a matter of **rhetoric** and implicature, discussed in Chapter 3.

There is a genuine distinction between two kinds of conditional statement in natural language, however. They are **indicative conditionals** and **subjunctive conditionals**.

Basic indicative conditional: If P then Q.

Subjunctive conditionals: If it were to be the case that P, then it would be the case that Q. There are some important differences in how to analyze reasoning that employs these two kinds of sentence. However plausible the definition of truth conditions for conditionals given above (a refined definition that's usually called the **material conditional**), it cannot be correct for conditionals in the subjunctive mood. For example, the argument form Hypothetical Syllogism is valid for indicative conditionals, interpreted as material conditionals, but fails for subjunctive conditionals since there are counter-examples to it. The following argument looks like Hypothetical Syllogism, yet even though each premise seems plausible, and the conclusion formally appears to follow from them, the conclusion is intuitively false.

1. If baseball player Nolan Ryan had thrown a cricket ball, he would have been a cheater.
2. If baseball player Nolan Ryan had played cricket, he would have thrown a cricket ball.
Therefore,
3. If baseball player Nolan Ryan had played cricket, he would have been a cheater.

With true premises and a false conclusion in this example, Hypothetical Syllogism is clearly not a valid form for subjunctive conditionals.

Now, you might notice that in this argument I've switched the order of the premises, in comparison to the Hypothetical Syllogism argument form defined earlier. The order of premises normally should not affect the validity of an argument. Why do you think I made this switch, then?

The reason is that the order of premises does affect the interpretation here. Subjunctive conditionals are often used to express **counterfactuals**, or statements about the way things might have been but are not. This idea is sometimes expressed in terms of various **possible worlds**, a convenient shorthand for talking about how things might have been. The reason the above argument goes wrong is that both premises are counterfactual conditionals, but they are about *different* possible worlds—different ways that things might have been. The possible world in which Nolan Ryan is a baseball player but uses a cricket ball anyhow is different from the one in which he uses a cricket ball because he is a cricket player. If you look at the above argument and take its premises in reverse order, chances are that your interpretation of which possibilities are under consideration would have been initially set by your interpretation of Premise 2. That is, if Premise 1 followed Premise 2, it would ring false—reading them in that order, you would begin by thinking of the situation in which Premise 2 is true, and *in that possible world* Premise 1 is false. To make the counter-example more effective, then, I reversed the order of the premises. As written, the argument makes it easier to interpret each premise as true, relative to different possible worlds. But the rules of inference we've sketched so far don't allow for that particular subtlety.

Formally spelling out valid inferences for counterfactual conditionals requires the resources of modal logic, mentioned earlier as a family of different logics that allow for talk of possibility and necessity (among many other things). We won't delve into this topic, but informally we can draw an important lesson: whenever we are confronted with complex reasoning about possibilities, including assertions about what would have happened under different circumstances, we have to bear in mind how the different possibilities fit together. For similar reasons, the conjunction rule also fails in modal contexts: from "Possibly P" and "Possibly Q," we can't conclude "Possibly P and Q." Consider the case in which Q is *not-P*, for example. It's possible the Canucks will win the Cup in the year 2020, and it's possible the Canucks will not win the Cup in 2020, but it's not possible that the Canucks will both win and not win the Cup in 2020. The details of the possibilities in question are often essential to making reasonable arguments about would have been the case, what might occur, or what must have happened.

Negation: A statement of the form "Not-P" (that is, "It is not the case that P") is true if and only if P is false.

It is only three letters in English, but the word "not" is tricky. Like a range of related terms and prefixes like "no," "non-," "anti-," and "false," it performs the logical role of negation. In one sense, negation is simple: we use it to say what isn't the case. But there are many different ways of doing so, while the meaning of "not" itself is less precise and less univocal than it may seem. From logic to linguistics to computer science, finding a complete and correct account of negation is a much-sought goal.

If we were going to do formal logic, we would have to elaborate considerably on the *meaning* of negation, especially by taking a stand on whether not-not-P is equivalent to P. (An inference rule known as **Double-Negation Elimination**, its plausibility as an axiom essentially reduces to that of the Law of Excluded Middle.) While this enormously simplifies a logical formalism, it doesn't always square with our use of negation in natural language. For instance, when asked a question like "Is Ted pleasant?" one might answer, "Well, he's not unpleasant." For predications that can be of this neither-nor sort, Double-Negation Elimination seems to force sharp distinctions where none can be found. Bearing in mind that it can be an over-simplification, though, for the most part we can use the simplest and most obvious story: not-P is true when P is false. For our purposes, then, the more important subtleties involve the interpretation of ambiguities that arise from the negation of compound and complex statements. When we encounter an utterance like "Seabiscuit was not the fastest, prettiest, gutsiest racehorse," it's important to recognize that we don't know exactly to what the negation applies, at any level more precise than the whole predication: it could be any subset of *fastest, prettiest, gutsiest, racing,* and *horse* that is being denied.

> This is a kind of **scope ambiguity,** discussed in more detail in Chapter 4.

This is an especially common ambiguity when negations are uttered as "prosentences"—words that stand for sentences the way that pronouns stand for nouns. If someone says "Continents drift" and I reply "Yes" or "True," I am using a prosentence to endorse their utterance, as a handy way of agreeing without uttering the sentence myself. Essentially I too am saying, "Continents drift." But if someone says, "Three members of Grant Devine's provincial cabinet were criminally prosecuted," and I reply, "No" or "False," it is far from clear what I'm saying *except* that I deny the whole utterance exactly as worded. Is it because I deny that it was Devine's cabinet members that were prosecuted? Or do I deny that those prosecuted were cabinet members? Or that they were criminally prosecuted, as opposed to civilly sued or not prosecuted at all? Do I deny that there were as many as three, or might I be taking exception to some understatement, on the grounds, say, that there were in fact *more* than three or that they were not simply prosecuted but convicted and sent to prison? Since the mere negation of a complex statement does not reveal such distinctions, the assessment of a negated premise or conclusion must be based on the least specific interpretation available, unless the surrounding context really does make clear what is intended. And by the same token, when we are constructing arguments ourselves, we should place our *not*s carefully to communicate our views as clearly as possible.

COMPLEX STATEMENTS

A crucial aspect of analyzing reasoning is understanding how much information a quite short statement can express—how many distinct claims are encoded by a grammatically complex sentence.

> Ted was cranky and annoying despite getting his way, as usual.

The truth-conditions of this sentence include all of the following:

1. Ted was cranky.
2. Ted was annoying.
3. Ted got his way.
4. Either Ted is usually cranky and annoying, or Ted usually gets his way, or both. (This is disjunctive because it's unclear what the phrase "as usual" modifies in the initial sentence.)

Hence if any of 1 to 4 is false, so too is the original sentence. A compound and complex sentence like this can end up embodying many distinct factual claims, each of which must be evaluated if the statement is offered as a premise or a conclusion.

Overall the lesson is that being really precise in one's claims requires great care in how one frames them. On the flip side, someone else's claims may require very careful evaluation to separate what's reasonable and clear in them from what is vague and unreasonable. An imprecise or ambiguous statement can seem plausible and significant on a quick reading, even when one interpretation of it is plausible but trivial, while another interpretation is exciting but implausible. Sensitivity to the precise effects of particular word choices and to the effects of context is a crucial ingredient in assessing claims that we encounter and in making reasonable statements ourselves. This is harder work than one might expect, given that we've used language most of our lives. But little of our everyday use of language provides us with the skills to write or speak with the great clarity that some situations require.

FACTUAL AND NON-FACTUAL STATEMENTS

Many thinkers in various fields have thought it plausible that certain kinds of statements do not really have truth conditions at all, or have very different truth conditions than they seem to have. The most-discussed class of statements for which these views have been widely held are value-theoretic statements: that is, statements involving moral concepts like right and wrong, good and evil, and statements involving aesthetic notions like beauty and ugliness.

Both within and without professional philosophy, many people have thought that moral statements either have no real truth conditions—they are neither true nor false—or they have truth conditions involving something other than what the statement seems to be about. Some people have thought that a statement like "Killing innocent people is morally wrong" is really just an expression of emotion, on a par with "*Booooo* to killing innocent people!" or "Killing innocent people? Yuck!" Since utterances of the latter two sorts arguably are neither true nor false, the same can be said of moral statements in general on this view. Others have taken ethical statements to contain an implicit reference to some behavioural code, so that our example would be more clearly rendered as "By the standards of my culture, killing innocent people is unacceptable." On this view our sample moral statement does have truth conditions, but they implicate facts about our culture more than any facts about killing *per se*. And on the aesthetic front, it has reached the status of folk wisdom that "beauty is in the eye of the beholder" or, as an older saying had it, *De gustibus non est disputandum*: on matters of taste there can be no argument.

None of these views is entirely accepted by philosophers today. Partly this is because it's difficult to spell out just what kinds of talk are and are not beyond the categories of truth and falsity. If we think of a statement's truth as consisting in some arrangement of physical things, for instance, on the model of the cat's being on the mat, then certainly it's difficult to think of some straightforward truth condition for the statement that something immoral has occurred. But it is equally hard to visualize just what arrangement of physical things would suffice to make true various other kinds of statement that may seem less contentious than the moral or aesthetic cases. What are the truth conditions for the claim that monetary inflation has occurred, for example? That there are now more ways than ever of proving some theorem? That celebrity is a fetish within the mainstream media? In each case we might answer the question by appeal to other concepts inherent to the relevant field—economics, logic, sociology—but so too in the moral case might we appeal to justice, fairness, rights, and so forth. Tracing the important differences between

The Dog Walking Ordinance[1]

The following reputed transcript of a borough council meeting in England illustrates the potential difficulty of finding precise and unambiguous language to express something that seems like a simple idea.

Councilor Trafford took exception to the proposed notice at the entrance of South Park: "No dogs must be brought to this Park except on a lead." He pointed out that this order would not prevent an owner from releasing his pets, or pet, from a lead when once safely inside the Park.

The Chairman (Colonel Vine): What alternative wording would you propose, Councilor?

Councilor Trafford: "Dogs are not allowed in this Park without leads."

Councilor Hogg: Mr. Chairman, I object. The order should be addressed to the owners, not to the dogs.

Councilor Trafford: That is a nice point. Very well then: "Owners of dogs are not allowed in this Park unless they keep them on leads."

Councilor Hogg: Mr. Chairman, I object. Strictly speaking, this would prevent me as a dog-owner from leaving my dog in the back-garden at home and walking with Mrs. Hogg across the Park.

Councilor Trafford: Mr. Chairman, I suggest that our legalistic friend be asked to redraft the notice himself.

Councilor Hogg: Mr. Chairman, since Councilor Trafford finds it so difficult to improve on my original wording, I accept. "Nobody without his dog on a lead is allowed in this Park."

Councilor Trafford: Mr. Chairman, I object. Strictly speaking, this notice would prevent me, as a citizen, who owns no dog, from walking in the Park without first acquiring one.

Councilor Hogg (with some warmth): Very simply, then: "Dogs must be led in this Park."

Councilor Trafford: Mr. Chairman, I object: this reads as if it were a general injunction to the Borough to lead their dogs into the Park.

Councilor Hogg interposed a remark for which he was called to order; upon his withdrawing it, it was directed to be expunged from the Minutes.

The Chairman: Councilor Trafford, Councilor Hogg has had three tries; you have had only two...

Councilor Trafford: "All dogs must be kept on leads in this Park."

The Chairman: I see Councilor Hogg rising quite rightly to raise another objection. May I anticipate him with another amendment: "All dogs in this Park must be kept on the lead."

This draft was put to the vote and carried unanimously, with two abstentions.

value-theoretic discourse like aesthetics or morality and other discourses is a subtle matter; in the absence of such subtlety it is unwarranted to dismiss moral and ethical claims as meaningless, or as lacking truth values.

For our purposes it is safest to treat moral discourse as differing from other discourses, not in being non-factual where they are factual, but in being less apt to general agreement on fundamental assumptions. Statements about morality, humour, etiquette, aesthetics, and other matters with some significant degree of subjectivity can be perfectly acceptable as premises in an argument, provided the interlocutors share the relevant assumptions. If at first they do not, then discussion may bring them around to agreement; otherwise, however, it may be difficult for them to have a meaningful exchange. But then, this much is true whenever fundamental assumptions are not shared, no matter what their topic.

This is not to say there are no lasting philosophical issues regarding the alleged contrast between **subjective** and **objective** statements or disciplines. I am, however, counselling that we treat the distinction (whatever it amounts to) as irrelevant, focusing instead on the more general communicative problem of settling on premises acceptable to those involved in a discussion. Labels like "objective" and "subjective" can easily do more harm than good, leading us to polarize the categories under discussion, so that we take the terms deemed objective to be immune to conceptual criticism while lumping the subjective issues in with matters of whim or fleeting conventions. While many writers over the past few decades have claimed that objectivity isn't all it's cracked up to be, an equally important observation is that strictly subjective ways of speaking—ones that implicate human responses or judgments in their truth-conditions—are also much more robust than a simplistic conception would have it. Judgments about colour, for example, are in some sense subjective. But if "Hurting the innocent is wrong" were no worse off truth-wise than "The sky is blue," there would be no obvious general reason to worry about arguments involving allegedly subjective moral statements!

People considering the following argument, for example, might agree on the first (non-moral) premise but disagree over the second (morally loaded) premise.

Mixed moral and non-moral premises in argument:

1. If we allow inflation to rise, then the shoe manufacturers will lose their jobs.
2. It would be unjust for the shoe manufacturers to lose their jobs.
Therefore,
3. If we allow inflation to rise, then something unjust will occur.

But then, they might just as easily disagree over the truth of the first premise while all accepting the second. Either way, the argument appears valid, and it seems entirely reasonable for someone defending the argument to offer reasoning in support of *either* disputed premise. So we end up treating value-theoretic statements much the same way we treat statements more generally: as open to disagreement, but effective in argument provided they are acceptable to all discussants. Reasoning about values is discussed in more detail in Chapter 3.

CONCLUSION

For the most part we want to believe reasonable things and to communicate our beliefs in a way that makes their reasonableness clear. Arguments are the basic units of these processes. The clearest and most idealized conception of argumentation is that of deductive argument, according to which a good argument is a sound one—an argument that is valid and has all true essential premises. An argument is valid just in case there is no way for its premises to be true and its conclusion false; the idea is that if the premises are true, they prove the conclusion. To say that the premises are true is to say that they describe the world accurately, or that they are laid down as commonly accepted definitions. Premises can be treated as true for argumentative purposes when they are jointly acceptable to both the speaker and audience. If they are not accepted by the audience then, whether or not the premises are true, further argument in support of them may be required as a practical measure for the argument to be rationally persuasive. The truth values of compound premises and conclusions are determined by the truth values of their subsentences and vary according to the way those subsentences are connected. Validity and soundness are technically all-or-nothing threshold concepts, though we will see how this idealization is usually only approximated to some degree in actual argumentation.

REVIEW QUESTIONS

1. For every valid argument form listed in this chapter, construct your own example.
2. Explain the concepts of linked, convergent, and sequential arguments. Which is the most fundamental kind, and why?
3. Read through recent national or local newspapers to find examples of ambiguous negation. For each example, explain the different possible interpretations of what is being denied.

NOTES

1. From R. Graves and A. Hodge, *The Reader Over Your Shoulder* (New York: Macmillan, 1943). Reprinted in E. Nagel, "Symbolic Notation, Haddocks' Eyes and the Dog-walking Ordinance," in *The World of Mathematics*, Vol. III, ed. J. Newman, 1890–91 (New York: Simon and Schuster, 1956).

Evidence Adds Up

Consider the plight of Lois. She wants to know the secret real-life identity of her favourite superhero, but she's finding it hard to get good evidence. She has her colleague Clark to help her in her quest, but the information he can offer is limited by the fact that he always seems to disappear in the crisis situations where super-heroic acts are being performed. She concludes that he's easily frightened. Then one day Lois happens to catch a glimpse of Clark without his glasses. She pictures him wearing a skin-tight outfit (this is probably a violation of workplace ethics on her part, but never mind) and—*presto!*—suddenly it all makes sense. Clark *is* the superhero.

There are a few interesting things about this story, for our purposes. One is that Lois doesn't really seem to *infer* that Clark is the superhero on the basis of an argument. It's a creative conjecture on her part, one that might leap to mind for any number of reasons and then be recognized as having various explanatory virtues. Another is that Lois doesn't have to give up any of her previous evidence, any of the premises in her earlier reasoning about Clark, in order to reach this new judgment. The new piece of evidence changes how she interprets her previous stock of information, but it doesn't force her to reject anything except the conclusion she was drawing from it. Clark's disappearances during crises seemed to be good evidence for the conclusion that he was avoiding danger. In the context of the new evidence and new hypothesis, though, that very same information supports the very opposite conclusion—that in fact Clark was *seeking out* dangerous situations.

How can we make sense of reasonable arguments that are weakened or over-turned by the addition of new evidence, even though the old evidence remains in force? What conception of argument allows for degrees of strength in the support that evidence can lend to a conclusion? And where in our scheme of reasoning does Lois's sort of "Aha!" moment of insight fit?

To answer these and similar questions, we need to consider the differences between deductive and ampliative reasoning.

In describing validity and soundness, we have so far been defining deductive arguments. A deductive argument is in some respects the gold standard of reasoning, because deductive validity amounts to a *guarantee* of a true conclusion given true premises. Deductive reasoning provides this guarantee because, in some sense, all the information contained in its conclusion is also expressed in its premises. In various domains of reasoning this is exactly the right general approach: in mathematics, for example, or in formal logic itself. In these disciplines it appears that the standards for a sound argument are the ones that most clearly matter, both because strict validity is what's wanted (a mathematical proof is supposed to be a way of being *sure*, not just *confident*), and because we are frequently in a position to treat premises as known with certainty. And if you can get such a guarantee, naturally it's a good thing to have. But this conception of argument can amount to a powerful idealization, especially in situations where our reasoning aims to express how our imperfect knowledge supports some conclusion only to a degree.

This presupposes that we have some background notion of *support* for a conclusion that is independent of valid entailment by true premises, since validity does not strictly come in degrees. We can use the term "**cogency**" for this broader notion of support. An argument is **cogent** just in case it makes its conclusion rationally credible—that is, rationally believable. We can then qualify this notion to reflect the degrees of rational believability that a set of premises can confer on a conclusion. A strongly cogent argument provides a high degree of justification for its conclusion, while a weakly cogent argument might provide only a tentative or easily overturned justification for its conclusion. A deductively sound argument is fully cogent by these definitions: with true premises and valid structure, it demonstrates the truth of its conclusion. But the broader notion of cogency leaves open the prospect of arguments that are cogent, perhaps even strongly cogent, despite being unsound. Such arguments might provide a high degree of support for their conclusions, despite not being deductively valid.

VALID, INVALID, AND AMPLIATIVE ARGUMENTS

In a wide class of cases, of course, arguments that are invalid simply don't work; they are **logical fallacies**. These are arguments presented as valid, the success of which would require their validity, but which have invalid forms. These are discussed in depth in Chapter 4. In many other cases, arguments are technically invalid in the sense that they have premises that are left unstated, which the audience is supposed to understand from the context. Such arguments are called **enthymemes** and are discussed in more detail in Chapter 3. A deductive argument too can be an enthymeme if some of the premises required for it to be valid are left implicit. But the goal of this chapter is to define and examine the large class of arguments that are deductively invalid in a more interesting sense than enthymemes and fallacies. These are **ampliative arguments**: arguments in which the conclusion amplifies on the premises, expressing information that cannot be validly inferred from them. While strictly unsound, ampliative arguments can nevertheless be cogent to varying degrees.

We can think of a valid deductive argument as one in which the conclusion expresses no more information than the premises jointly express. This allusion to "amounts" of information is hard to make precise, but the intuitive idea is that the conclusion of a deductive argument takes some of the content of the premises and presents it in a different form, but without adding anything new. Consider this argument:

1. Ted is a human.
2. All humans are mammals.
Therefore,
3. Ted is a mammal.

The conclusion that Ted is a mammal is already *there*, in some sense, within the two premises that Ted is a human and that all humans are mammals.

The conclusion to a deductive argument can still be surprising, of course; we can be astonished to discover just what was packed into some set of premises, especially if there are lots of premises and they are complicated.

1. If either Agnes got the job or Bill went on vacation, then if either Candice bought a pet or Darren found a dance partner, then Ellen is jealous.
2. Candace bought a pet.
3. Ellen is not jealous.
Therefore,
4. Agnes did not get the job and Bill did not go on vacation.

For most people, it is far from immediately obvious that the three premises of this deductively valid argument contain the information expressed in the conclusion; we genuinely learn something from such arguments. And they can be much more complicated than this example! Anyone familiar with the long (and ultimately successful) mathematical quest to prove Fermat's Theorem can regard that proof as a fabulously complex unpacking of information somehow implicit in a few basic axioms about whole numbers. Even though it may not be immediately obvious, there is some sense in which all the information in the conclusion is already in the premises—perhaps distributed over several premises—if the argument is deductively valid.

An ampliative argument is one for which this is not the case. In an ampliative argument the conclusion expresses information that is not explicitly or implicitly expressed by the premises. Consider an example:

> "Eric's always carrying on about the RCMP spying on private citizens without proper warrants. I think he's got something to hide."

We use and encounter this sort of reasoning every day. Clearly nobody would take such an utterance as an attempt to give a deductively sound argument, though—not even an enthymematic one. The idea (an over-optimistic idea, in this case, since it's obviously a weak argument) is just that the premise supplies enough evidence to make the assertion of the conclusion reasonable, or at least more reasonable than other alternatives, and not that the truth of the premise guarantees the truth of the conclusion.

Guarantees aside, however, some ampliative conclusions *can* be regarded as extremely likely in light of their premises, as with the following argument.

1. Ted was found standing over the body when the police broke down the locked door.
2. Ted was holding a smoking gun.
3. The gun Ted was holding was matched by experts to the bullet that killed the victim.
4. There were no windows or other doors to the room.
5. Only Ted's fingerprints were found on the gun.
6. Ted had a powerful motive to kill the victim.
Therefore,
7. Ted killed the victim.

Why does it matter that such arguments are ampliative? The surprising thing we have already noted is that, by our initial definitions of validity and soundness, this argument *isn't valid*. Simply put, if the conclusion expresses some information not included in the premises, then there is a way for the premises to be true and the conclusion false. That's invalidity. The sample argument immediately above would be regarded as a *great* argument in a courtroom context, yet there are lots of ways that the premises could all be true and the conclusion false. Homicidal aliens who shoot the victim and then toss Ted the gun before teleporting away just as the police break down the door—this would be consistent with each of the premises, but inconsistent with the conclusion. So whatever we say about the rational virtue of this argument, we can't say that it amounts to the truth of its premises *requiring* the truth of the conclusion. It seems more accurate to say that we recognize the strength of this argument when we recognize that any other explanation for premises (1) to (6) is, in the absence of further information, vastly less probable than (7), the conclusion.

The analysis of arguments therefore begins in much the same way whether we're considering deductive or ampliative reasoning. In both cases, the question of whether the premises would support the conclusion (were they true) can be approached by looking for scenarios on which those premises, or others that are genuinely structurally the same, could be true without the conclusion being true. In the deductive case, finding such a scenario shows that the argument is invalid. The only remaining question is whether the invalidity could be eliminated by adding an extra premise that is itself defensible or acceptable. In the ampliative case, we are guaranteed to find such scenarios (because the argument is strictly invalid), with the subsequent question being whether those alternatives that are inconsistent with the offered conclusion are (singly or in aggregate) more likely than the conclusion itself. In both cases we want to explore the prospect of scenarios on which the premises are true and the conclusion false. For a deductive argument, the existence of the possibility alone is enough to scuttle the argument's validity (at least, as written), while for an ampliative argument we are concerned not merely with the *possibility* that the conclusion is false, but with the *probability* that it's false.

In the normal run of events we just don't worry about ruling out such exotic possibilities as homicidal teleporting extraterrestrials, nor is it clear how we could insert a premise that would rule out such possibilities in any case. Reasoning based on the preponderance of evidence rather than strict validity (**evidential reasoning**, as we might also call it) is absolutely everywhere in our talk and our understanding of the world; it's fair to say that human reasoning is largely ampliative. So whatever else we say about such arguments, we can't simply say, "They're invalid; so they're unsound; so junk 'em." For one thing, there is no coherent way of junking them since they underwrite the bulk of what we know. Science largely works by formulating and testing general theories on the basis of specific observed events, and then predicting and explaining specific unobserved events on the basis of those theories. Scientific reasoning, everyday reasoning about causes and effects, even our reliance on memory—in short, the statements and arguments called **empirical,** or *based on experience,* are virtually all justified in ampliative terms. So it's simply not an option to consider giving up this kind of reasoning on the grounds that it's invalid.

In any case, such a radical measure would ignore the powerful resources at our disposal for distinguishing between better and worse ampliative arguments. We can make much more fine-grained judgments than merely noting that all such arguments are deductively invalid. We can carefully and rigorously qualify our acceptance of their conclusions in accordance with the degree of support they provide, through the application of probabilistic and statistical methods. This is why we will look at probability and statistics in some detail in Chapter 6.

In sum, if we think of the premises as the stock of evidence at our disposal, ampliative reasoning is characterized by drawing a conclusion *based on* the evidence, yet *going beyond* the evidence. There are a few different ways this can happen.

VARIETIES OF AMPLIATIVITY

INDUCTIVE REASONING

The most important and widespread form of ampliative reasoning is **inductive argument,** in which one draws conclusions about unobserved cases from premises about observed cases. Roughly speaking, the inductive judgment is that the still-unobserved cases are (in some relevant sense) *more of the same.* Of course this makes it possible for the premises (the evidence about observed cases) to be true while the conclusion (a claim about unobserved cases) is false, as will happen whenever the evidence in our possession does not accurately represent the reality beyond our current experience. Hence inductive arguments are not intended to be deductively valid. Still they can be cogent, even strongly cogent, according to our definition of cogency.

Equally importantly, they can be mediocre arguments, or weak but not entirely failed arguments. Again, the success of evidential arguments can vary by degrees instead of being an all-or-nothing affair, as is the case with deductive arguments. Consider again arguments like the one just seen above:

> Eric's always carrying on about the RCMP spying on private citizens without proper warrants. I think he's got something to hide."

Or similarly:

> "My team lost the last three games of the season. We're going to be eliminated from the playoffs pretty quickly."

Obviously in neither case does the truth of the premise guarantee the truth of the conclusion. In both examples the sole premise provides only a degree of justification for its conclusion—a degree that the speaker might take to be sufficient, but which we might take to be very weak as it stands.

Of course, adding more information might make both arguments better, without making either of them valid. The first speaker might add, "Also, Eric says he gets cold sweats at the thought of the police examining his bank records between 1994 and 1997." The second speaker might say, "We won our fourth-to-last game of the season, but lost ten straight before that, too." Both of those utterances would add a substantial degree of support to the respective conclusions of the two arguments, though both arguments would still be deductively invalid. Additional information might also make both arguments *worse* instead: the first speaker might instead have added, "To be fair, Eric has a long history of supporting positions based solely on principle rather than self-interest. Still . . ." And the second speaker might instead have noted, "Of course, for those last three games we were missing our best player, who'll be back with us for the playoffs." *These* new premises would cast the original premises in quite a different light, weakening the support they lend to their conclusions. But as soon as we start talking in such terms—degrees of justification, sensitivity to added information, and so forth—it's clear that we're no longer talking about validity or soundness as the virtues of such reasoning. Those are all-or-nothing properties that don't strictly admit of degrees or approximation.

A simple form of induction is an **enumerative argument**: an argument based on counting off specific observed cases, then drawing an inference about one or more unobserved cases. For example:

1. Rose 1 is red.
2. Rose 2 is red.
3. Rose 3 is red.
   . . .
100. Rose 100 is red.
Therefore,
101. All roses are red.

The argument proceeds by enumerating instances that have a property and concluding that an unobserved instance will also have that property. Clearly the conclusion goes beyond the aggregate information of the premises.

This would be so even if it happened that there were only 100 roses in existence, since that information is not given in the premises. Indeed, if we added that information as an additional premise, then the argument would be deductively valid. Any ampliative argument can be rendered deductively valid simply by adding one or more carefully chosen premises—e.g., "Unobserved cases resemble observed cases." But this just papers over the ampliativity, since such a premise must then itself be justified. If there is a good reason that the argument was ampliative in the first place, only an ampliative argument will be available to justify the added premise. As long as we are drawing an inference from observed cases about unobserved cases, the argument is inductive. It takes a stock of evidence in our possession—sometimes called the **inductive base**—as a sort of guideline for deciding what is the case in areas (or times) we haven't directly examined. In general, the larger and more representative the inductive base, the stronger the argument for the conclusion.

Inductive arguments are not just those that go from specific statements to general statements, however.

1.   Every currently observed rose is red.
Therefore,
2.   The next rose observed will be red.

This argument is inductive, even though its premise is of the universal form *Every x is F* and its conclusion is a specific claim. It nevertheless moves from a class of observed cases to an unobserved case.

With sufficient evidence presented in appropriately related premises, inductive arguments can satisfy the most general conception of a good argument; they can be rationally persuasive of their conclusions. To denote this kind of success, we've introduced the term *cogency*: an argument is cogent when it provides sufficient grounds for the rational belief of its conclusion. Deductively sound arguments are of course cogent, but so too are sufficiently strong evidential arguments, despite being strictly unsound. With cogency being a property they can share, it is important also to note the key differences between deductive and inductive arguments.

A. *Deductive arguments*

*   satisfy, or aim to satisfy, the definition of validity.
*   do not strictly become more valid or more sound by degrees.
*   if sound, remain sound no matter what other premises might be added.

B. *Inductive arguments*

*   are strictly deductively invalid, being ampliative.
*   lend only a degree of support to their conclusion; the degree can vary.
*   are sensitive to subsequent information that may be added.

We can see the distinctions between inductive and deductive arguments more clearly by considering some examples.

1.   If something is a fox, then it is a mammal.
2.   Renard is a fox.
Therefore,
3.   Renard is a mammal.

This argument, obviously, is deductively valid, and let's say it has all true premises, so it is sound. Suppose, however, that we add some true premises to the argument so it ends up looking like this:

1.   If something is a fox, then it is a mammal.
2.   Renard is a fox.

CHAPTER 2   *Evidence Adds Up*

Notice what this example shows about the notions of an *essential premise* and of soundness, introduced in Chapter 1. Premises 2.1 to 2.3 could all be false without affecting the argument's soundness. So while stating that a sound argument has *all* true premises provides a guarantee that a valid argument will be sound, this is not a *requirement* for soundness without further restricting what counts as an argument. To make having all true premises a requirement we would need to stipulate that the argument is also maximally elegant: meaning, in other words, that it contains no unnecessary premises.

2.1. Continents drift.
2.2. Pigs grunt.
2.3. Acrophobes tremble.
Therefore,
3.   Renard is a mammal.

Now we have an inelegant and somewhat confusing argument, but it is as sound as ever. The extra premises are distracting, but they neither disrupt the truth of the original premises, nor undo the valid connection between those premises and the conclusion. By contrast, suppose we have this argument:

1.   Between Monday and Wednesday we examined 200 roses at random, and each was red.
Therefore,
2.   It's reasonable to expect that the first rose we examine on Sunday will be red.

Assuming that the premise is true, this inductive argument provides some degree of support for its conclusion—never mind how great a degree for now. All that matters is that this degree of support would be lowered by the addition of further true premises like this one:

1.5 Between Wednesday and Saturday we examined 300 more roses at random, and 200 were yellow.

The resulting argument might still constitute *some* support for the original conclusion, but clearly much less support than it did at first. As new information comes in, ampliative arguments can be weakened or overturned altogether—not (or not necessarily) by overturning the initial premises, but by changing their significance for the conclusion. Ampliative reasoning is **defeasible**, in other words: no matter how confident we may be in the cogency of an inductive argument, in principle it remains possible that some new information will weaken or overturn it. This concept is discussed in more detail later in this chapter.

DEDUCTION AND INDUCTION WORK TOGETHER

I explained earlier that human reasoning is largely ampliative. This is, however, consistent with its also being largely deductive. Deductive and evidential reasoning very often intertwine. Consider as an example the following letter published in the

Toronto Star, regarding the official inquiry into the killing of Dudley George by Ontario Provincial Police in 1995. George was one of a group of native protestors occupying Ipperwash Provincial Park, part of a tract of land expropriated from the Stony Point Reserve by the federal government to create a military training camp in 1942, and never returned when World War II ended. Mike Harris, the newly elected premier of Ontario, held a meeting with police representatives and various cabinet ministers shortly before the shooting. Among those present was Harris's attorney general, Charles Harnick, who later testified to the inquiry that Harris had shouted profanely that he wanted the protestors out of the park. In his testimony at the inquiry, Harris denied both the shouting and the profanity. The letter writer clearly uses both deductive and evidential thinking in presenting his view of Harris's testimony.

> [C]ommon sense tells us that Charles Harnick and Harris both can't be telling the truth. So, who is lying? Common sense also tells us that Harnick has essentially nothing to gain by lying. In fact, he could have quite easily not recalled the alleged Harris statements and avoided much controversy and unpleasantness in his personal life. Therefore, it appears he was honest in spite of the negative consequences for himself. Harris, on the other hand, has some very important reasons to be disingenuous in his accounts. It sure does not look flattering, to say the least.[1]

The basic structure of the deductive argument is that of disjunctive syllogism: P or Q; not-P; therefore Q. The second premise, however, is not presented as true, but only as more likely than the available alternative. The author is arguing from indirect evidence: since one of the two men must be "lying" (the writer errs in not mentioning the possibility of mistaken memory), we should consider which of them has incentive or disincentive to lie or misremember. This reasoning is based essentially on implicit inductive evidence to the effect that people are unlikely to tell a lie that will foreseeably do them no good or even harm them, but are more likely to lie if they believe they will benefit from it. Since Harnick is allegedly made worse off by telling his version while Harris stands to benefit from telling his version, it's likelier, the author argues, that Harnick is telling the truth. This is a common sort of interrelation of deductive and evidential argument: a valid argument form provides the general outlines of the argument, while evidential reasoning (of whatever quality) is invoked to defend the premises.

Not only do induction and deduction work together in most arguments, but the initial approach to evaluating both kinds of reasoning can be very similar. Even if an argument is evidential rather than deductive, the Method of Counter-example, for instance, is a useful analytical tool. That's really what we saw with this sample argument, introduced earlier.

1. Ted was found standing over the body when the police broke down the locked door.
2. Ted was holding a smoking gun.
3. The gun Ted was holding was matched by experts to the bullet that killed the victim.
4. There were no windows or other doors to the room.

5. Only Ted's fingerprints were found on the gun.
6. Ted had a powerful motive to kill the victim.
Therefore,
7. Ted killed the victim.

In this case, the question is not whether the argument is strictly valid (of course, it isn't valid). The question is whether any of the possible alternative scenarios on which the premises are true and the conclusion false have anything like the plausibility of (7) itself, given the premises. We can understand plausibility here not merely as meaning the appeal some proposition has for a person, but in terms of its fit with our available evidence and our best theories more generally. Ted's guilt and the existence of teleporting aliens are both scenarios that are *consistent* with premises (1) through (6), but our best wider evidence about the world fits well with the former and very poorly with the latter. The greater the plausibility of the alternative scenarios, though, the less confidence an evidential argument confers on its conclusion.

This sort of application of the method of counter-example is an important tool for determining the cogency of an evidential argument.

In the context of scientific evidential arguments, and especially arguments based on experiments or studies, such counter-example scenarios are called **confounds** (emphasis on the first syllable), a noun coined from the verb form "to confound" (emphasis on the second syllable), meaning to confuse or defeat. An experimental confound is an alternative explanation for why a particular result was observed, distinct from the conclusion offered by the experimenter. Just as a good scientific experiment is one that eliminates or minimizes confounds, a good evidential argument more generally eliminates or minimizes plausible alternative scenarios on which the premises are true and the conclusion false. The coherence of any counter-example establishes the invalidity of an argument, while the number and plausibility of counter-examples can establish a lack of cogency.

ABDUCTIVE REASONING

When Lois is contemplating the identity of her favourite superhero, she is faced with a range of facts. Some of these seem obviously related to the problem and some seem unrelated or only distantly related. But when she contemplates the thought that Clark is secretly her superhero, she has a sort of "Aha!" moment. She realizes, in particular, that Clark's being a superhero would *explain* most or all of a set of facts that were previously unexplained and even seemed unrelated. It's a hypothesis that makes sense of otherwise scattered data, better sense than any other hypothesis that occurs to her, and in particular better than the default assumption that those facts really *are* unrelated. The explanatory role that her new hypothesis plays, in relation to those data, amounts to an ampliative argument for its correctness.

In effect, the previously known facts, plus the higher-order fact that the new hypothesis would explain them, are premises in an argument whose conclusion is the hypothesis that Clark is a superhero. This style of reasoning is sometimes known as **Inference to the Best Explanation**. It is an instance of what many scientists and philosophers call **abductive reasoning**, a term modelled on "inductive" by the philosopher Charles Sanders Peirce and used to mean a leap to a conclusion that unifies, explains, or rationalizes a set of facts. Unlike inductive argument, abduction doesn't (or needn't) involve anything like a "more of the same" judgment about unobserved cases. Like inductive argument, though, it is clearly ampliative. For all that a hypothesis seems suddenly plausible in light of its explanatory force, it may be wrong nevertheless. The set of data it unifies will certainly not deductively entail it. Like ampliative reasoning more generally, too, abduction is both common and ineliminable; it is a crucial element of scientific reasoning and drives our ordinary thinking about many problems.

For example, my brother-in-law is an auto mechanic. Every day he accepts cars into his shop to be repaired. Both his time and the replacement parts for the vehicle are expensive, so he and his customers both want the problem to be diagnosed correctly the first time rather than fixing one potential problem after another until the root cause is discovered. So there is a diagnostic problem to be solved for many vehicles. Sometimes this is easily done, when the malfunction is immediately visible—a pipe dragging on the ground, say. But in many cases, when the problem occurs only intermittently or is something subtle and internal (like an annoying noise that is heard only after driving for an hour), he is faced with a problem calling for an abductive solution. He asks the owner for all the information that might be relevant to the problem—information about when and how the symptoms occur—then he employs a wide range of other evidence-gathering techniques, of varying degrees of directness. These include reading data off the car's computer system, listening to the sounds it makes while running, and looking at or even smelling the engine or other vehicle systems.

This process produces a large body of facts, some of which are relevant to the underlying problem, with any luck, and most of which are not. How does the difference emerge? As with deduction and induction, there is of course an interplay of various styles of reasoning here. His past experiences with vehicles exhibiting certain behaviours may well provide a partial inductive justification for the conclusion that this particular vehicle has the same problem as those earlier vehicles turned out to have. But abduction is also typically required: with this large set of data in hand, he will consider and reject hypotheses until he hits on one that makes particularly good sense of (some key subset of) the data. That will be his best guess for what to try fixing first. And if the customer wants to know *why* he's trying that solution first, the *justification* will come in the form of an abductive argument: this hypothesis (about underlying causes) is the best available explanation for these particularly significant facts, so, given those facts, this hypothesis is reasonable to believe—or to act upon, at least.

The line between abductive reasoning and other forms of "Aha!" moments can be blurry, partly due to variation in definitions and partly due to the slight differences in cases. There is a famous story about the ancient Greek mathematician and inventor Archimedes, who had been given the task of determining whether the King of Syracuse's goldsmith had cheated the king. The king's worry was that the goldsmith might have substituted an equal weight of silver for some of the gold he'd been given to create a crown, keeping the extra gold for himself. Archimedes is said to have pondered the problem of how to discover, without harming the crown itself, whether this had been done. When he settled into a tub of water at the baths he noticed the water level rising as he immersed himself, and the answer came to him in a flash. According to the Roman historian Vitruvius, Archimedes leaped out of the bath and ran home naked through the streets of Syracuse, shouting *"Eureka!"*— a Greek term meaning either "I've found it!" or "Somebody hand me a towel!"

What Archimedes was supposed to have suddenly grasped was the prospect of solving the problem by determining whether the crown displaced more water than an equivalent weight of gold would. Silver being lighter than gold, a partially silver crown would take up more volume, hence raising the water level higher when submerged, than a crown of pure gold with the same mass. (It's a great story but almost certainly didn't help Archimedes with his task, since a Greco-Roman crown is too small and the density of silver and gold too similar for the debasement of a crown's metal to have been measured with any confidence by differences in water displacement alone, unless the debasement was so extreme as to be identifiable by other means). Archimedes' cry of discovery has become a byword for the unexpected insights that pepper scientific history and which are familiar to most of us from our own experience as well.

We often draw conclusions about some matter or see solutions to a problem not as the direct product of a conscious and laborious calculation of evidence, either inductive or deductive, but as a kind of mental leap from a puzzling set of data to a hypothesis that would, if true, explain the data. For that matter, sometimes explanations or solutions to problems pop into awareness when we are not even consciously thinking about the problem—in the middle of a meal, during a conversation about an entirely different topic, while drifting off to sleep, and so forth. Some writers reserve the term "abduction" for the first sort of phenomenon alone; others use it to include more concrete problem-solving discoveries like that of Archimedes, or even for "Aha!" moments in general. In any case, how should we characterize these flashes of insight from a critical thinking perspective?

CONTEXT OF DISCOVERY AND CONTEXT OF JUSTIFICATION

It is important not to think of flashes of insight or hypothesis-formation as being especially reliable forms of thought, over and above serving as a source of *potential* solutions and explanations. For one thing, while the stories about flashes of insight that turn out to be correct tend to be told and retold, there is no very good reason to tell and retell the stories (even our own stories, within our own personal memories) of those "Eureka!" moments that turn out to be instantly mistaken. On occasions of group problem-solving, it may happen several times that someone begins to say animatedly, "Hey, I know!" only to stop abruptly and conclude, "No, never mind," without even bothering to explain the idea. These false starts are easily forgotten after someone really does hit upon a workable solution "out of the blue." Given the ways in which anecdotes spread or fail to spread, discussed in more detail in Chapter 8, popular discussions of our own reasoning and of the history of science are likely to over-represent the successes and minimize the failings of such intuitive leaps of judgment, giving us a mistaken idea of their reliability.

In any case, when abductive judgments do turn out to be correct, their correctness is *recognized*, not necessarily through "Aha!" processes themselves, but through the more systematic, conscious, and explicit forms of reasoning we've already introduced. Philosophers of science have emphasized this point by distinguishing between the **context of discovery**, which might include any number of arational, accidental, and sheer-dumb-luck explanations for someone's having that "Aha!" judgment, and the **context of justification**, in which we adduce the evidence that makes it reasonable to regard the abductive judgment as one of the successes. You might have a dream through which you discover that there are infinitely many "twin primes"—pairs of prime numbers of the form p, $p+2$—but merely reciting your dream to mathematicians will quite properly not convince them of your discovery. The context of justification is more demanding, from the perspective of the argument required, since the feeling of having a sudden insight is not amenable to rational exchange. Abductive discoveries in the more restricted sense mentioned above can be converted into ampliative arguments, via appeal to inference to the best explanation. But hypothesis formation in the broader sense can include all manner of factors that have no good role in the context of justification. Hence two kinds of related mistake in reasoning associated with this distinction are to undervalue and to overvalue a claim on the basis of its context of discovery, overlooking the role of the justification provided for the claim. If a hypothesis arose from entirely arational processes but, once generated, turned out to be highly explanatory and predictive of further evidence, its arational origins do not justify dismissing it. And if a hypothesis arose from the most careful, explicit, and deliberate attempt to abductively explain a set of data, this still would not justify believing it, if it did not turn out to be usefully explanatory or if it made nothing but false predictions. Both of these mistakes are instances of the **Genetic Fallacy**, discussed in Chapter 4.

ANALOGICAL ARGUMENTS

Yet another important kind of ampliative argument is the argument from analogy. This sort of reasoning works by examining a familiar or uncontroversial case, noting some feature of it, and then arguing that some other case is **relevantly similar**—so the feature must also be found in the other case.

We may think of analogical arguments as cross-classifying other ampliative arguments. Sometimes an analogical argument will have the "more of the same" character of an inductive argument. More often, though, the strength of the analogy won't reduce to the number of analogical cases (i.e., the size of the inductive base); these cases might be viewed as having an abductive component, so that the hypothesis of relevant similarity to the familiar case is what explains or makes coherent the features of the unfamiliar case. For example, a Canadian broadcasters' association recently ran a commercial spot in which a boy is caught shoplifting candy and is brought home by the police. His father lectures him on the evils of stealing, to which

L I N K

Most commercials aim to modify your purchasing behaviour by completely non-rational means, rather than by giving something intended as even a bad argument. They work at a level more appropriately analyzed by the concepts in Chapters 7 and 8.

the boy replies, "But you steal cable!" This commercial, unlike most, seems to contain at least an implicit argument.

The implicit argument in this commercial, moreover, is clearly analogical.

1. Shoplifting is unacceptable.
2. Receiving cable (or arranging to receive cable) reception without paying for it is *relevantly similar* to shoplifting.

Therefore,

3. Receiving cable (or arranging to receive cable) reception without paying for it is unacceptable.

I say "arranging to receive cable" because we might think there's a significant ethical distinction between, say, moving into an apartment and just discovering that you happen to get cable reception there without paying for it, and taking actions specifically intended to "turn on" the cable reception to your apartment without paying for it. In the former case you're receiving cable without paying; in the latter case you are *arranging* to receive it without paying. The analogy with shoplifting is probably closer to the latter than it is to the former. (Maybe a better analogy for such a situation would be if something fell into your shopping bag accidentally, and you knew it had. Would you consider it stealing to leave the store without paying?)

Arguments from analogy are very common. They are even harder to make rigorous than most evidential arguments, though. Statistical reasoning that might refine and clarify some kinds of inductive arguments will rarely apply to a case like the shoplifting example. Ultimately what ends up bearing the weight of such an argument is the claim of relevant similarity between the case presumed to be clear and the contested case. But this is a tricky business. Similarity itself is a vague notion, and under some interpretations is simply too weak a relation to bear out any conclusions: everything is similar to everything else in some way or other. And judgments of relevance can be quite subjective as well. It is easy for an analogy to appeal only to those already convinced of the conclusion in question.

So the appropriateness of an analogical argument has to be assessed not merely by enumerating relevant similarities, but also by looking for **disanalogies**—that is, relevant *differences* between the two things or situations compared. There is no formula for calculating when these disanalogies render an argument defective, though. The stronger the analogy the better the argument; conversely, analogical arguments resemble evidential arguments more generally in that they can fail by degrees. For example, consider this use of analogical reasoning:

> Some people seem to think that it's morally optional to donate money to alleviate starvation in far-off countries. But would you consider it merely optional to give money or food to someone literally starving to death on the street, if you could afford a few cents for a meal? A starving person is a starving person. If it would be monstrous to watch someone die of starvation in front of your house while you had lots of spare food, it's hard to see how the distance from which you watch it happen could make a morally relevant difference. Donating money to worldwide famine relief is therefore morally *required;* it is basic decency.

The argument here draws an analogy between failing to donate money to famine relief and failing to help someone starving before your very eyes. The attitude we take toward the latter inaction is the one we ought to adopt toward the former inaction as well, according to this argument. Indeed, the passage even anticipates the need for analogical arguments to be based on a genuinely relevant similarity, as the arguer aims to forestall the objection that the distance between you and the famine victims amounts to a disanalogy.

What can we say about this argument? First, there is an issue having little direct connection to analogy, namely, the difference between the moral evaluation of events or outcomes and the moral evaluation of actions, motives, and people's characters. The argument makes its conclusion a matter of whether a certain kind of *action* (or inaction) would be "monstrous" rather than specifically a matter of how bad some *outcome* would be. One might agree that (other things being equal) one person's death is an outcome as bad as any other person's death, irrespective of where those deaths occur, without thinking that any two actions causing those deaths, or any people's reactions to those deaths, are therefore morally equivalent. In this case the arguer seems to be talking about the moral qualities of one's character or one's reaction to an event, rather than the moral qualities of the event itself.

With that noted, we can see that there is at least one potentially important disanalogy in the reasoning—the very one that the arguer tries to defuse. When we evaluate someone's motives or moral character, at least, we do seem to distinguish between a person who isn't deeply and viscerally disturbed by the thought that somebody is suffering somewhere, and someone who isn't disturbed by the immediate presence of someone in obvious suffering. The tendency to be emotionally moved by witnessing a specific person's plight is typically considered a moral virtue. People who have this ability we don't generally convict of inconsistency, even if the theoretical knowledge that someone or other is always in such a plight doesn't lead them to be consumed with sympathy all the time. It might be monstrous to not care that one's own sibling has just died, but most people who die are *someone's* sibling, and yet it doesn't seem monstrous not to spend all one's time distressed about the sheer number of people dying from all causes at every instant. The existence of direct personal connections seems to matter to the question of what's a morally reasonable response to an event or situation.

So at first blush it seems that our moral evaluation of people's attitudes toward the suffering of others allows that at least basic moral decency might demand more of people in personal interactions (including face-to-face physical presence) than in the case of more general or theoretical knowledge of far-off events. If that's right, then it's not obvious that we can move from judgments about what's morally required in cases of personal interaction to judgments about what's morally required in other cases. Yet that's how this analogical argument works.

On the other hand, it's not a terrible analogy either. Granting that we frequently don't hold our behaviour regarding far-off events to the same standards we employ for immediate or personally charged events, there is a question of whether we *ought* to do so. We might regard this analogical argument as an attempt to put a burden of proof on the dissenter—forcing someone who rejects the conclusion to say exactly *why* mere distance or the existence of some personal connection should be morally relevant factors.

An analogy may fail because of a large number of individually minor disanalogies or because of one particularly gross disanalogy. Here are excerpts from an episode of the public affairs show *Fresh Air*, broadcast in the United States on National Public Radio. Host Terry Gross interviews Grover Norquist, head of Americans for Tax Reform and a Republican Party campaign strategist. They are discussing the elimination of the "estate tax," a tax on large inheritances. Norquist, opposed to the tax, presents an argument by analogy.

Gross: The estate tax is only paid by somebody who gets over $2 million in inheritance . . . . That's a line people don't cross a lot.

Norquist: . . . The argument that some who played at the politics of hate and envy and class division will say, "Yes, well, that's only 2 percent [of the population]," or as people get richer 5 percent in the near future of Americans are likely to have to pay that tax. I mean, that's the morality of the Holocaust. "Well, it's only a small percentage," you know. "I mean, it's not you, it's somebody else." . . .

Gross: Excuse me. Excuse me one second. Did you just . . .

Norquist: Yeah?

Gross: . . . compare the estate tax with the Holocaust?

Norquist: No, the morality that says it's okay to do something to a group because they're a small percentage of the population is the morality that says that the Holocaust is okay because they didn't target everybody, just a small percentage. What are you worried about? It's not you. It's not you. It's them. And arguing that it's okay to loot some group because it's them, or kill some group because it's them and because it's a small number, that has no place in a democratic society that treats people equally. The government's going to do something to or for us, it should treat us all equally. . . .

Gross: So you see taxes as being the way they are now terribly discriminating against the wealthy comparable to the kind of discrimination of, say, the Holocaust?

Norquist: Well, what you pick—you can use different rhetoric or different points for different purposes, and I would argue that those who say, "Don't let this bother you; I'm only doing it"— I, the government. The government is only doing it to a small percentage of the population. That is very wrong. And it's immoral. They should treat everybody the same. They shouldn't be shooting anyone, and they shouldn't be taking half of anybody's income or wealth when they die.

Source: "Fresh Air with Terry Gross," produced in Philadelphia by WHYY and distributed by NPR.

So does this analogical argument succeed or fail? Like very many broadly evidential arguments, the answer is somewhere between "Neither" and "It depends." Unlike many evidential or inductive arguments, however, there is little we can do to make the extent of its success clearer; we can't, for instance, say that the argument gives us reason to regard its conclusion as at least 40 percent likely to be true.

None of this means that arguments from analogy are no good. They have an important role in argument generally. Often they are used for the purpose of **Reductio Ad Absurdum**—a proof technique that consists in showing that a statement or argument leads to an absurd conclusion and must therefore be false.

Analogical arguments frequently have that sort of upshot: if *this* argument worked, then *that* relevantly similar argument would work too; but that relevantly similar argument leads to a conclusion we know to be false; so this initial argument can't work, either. (It's a version of Modus Tollens.) Arguments by analogy are also very useful for encouraging new ways of thinking by drawing potentially relevant, even surprising, connections between situations or issues that might otherwise seem unrelated. The key cautionary note is that such arguments deserve careful scrutiny with respect to both relevant similarities and relevant dissimilarities.

CAUSAL REASONING

We have used the term "empirical" to denote statements and arguments based on or justified through experience, as opposed to axiomatic or purely definition-based reasoning. Naturally this turns out to be an enormous category, including everything from ordinary statements about the events of one's day to abstract theoretical reasoning in the sciences. It is not an extra kind of ampliativity but, like other concepts we've examined, the empirical cross-classifies and interacts with inductive, deductive, abductive, and analogical reasoning.

Perhaps the most important sort of empirical reasoning is that relating to causes and effects. Many of our inductive inferences aim at identifying a cause for oft-observed events; many of our abductive inferences identify some hypothetical cause as the best explanation for previously unexplained events. It is worth acquainting ourselves with the varieties of causal reasoning and explanations that occur in these contexts.

The philosopher John Stuart Mill proposed a thorough set of guidelines to reasoning about cause and effect relations. **Mill's Methods**, as they are known, are useful for identifying causes in complex circumstances. They don't tell us much about the concept of causation, and they have limitations that are discussed below. But they are useful for beginning to distinguish between intuitive causes and mere **correlations**, or patterns of co-occurrence among various factors.

There are five basic methods, the first of which is called the *Method of Agreement*. It hinges on the idea of factors common to a range of circumstances. Suppose some effect E is produced in two situations, S1 and S2. If there is only one factor F common to S1 and S2, then F is (or is integral to) the cause of E. So, for example, if public health officials are investigating an outbreak of some illness, they will look at information regarding the patients' jobs, travel history, diet, and so forth, to see if there is some one factor they all share. If all the victims in an outbreak of hepatitis turn out to have eaten at the same restaurant within the same week, this is powerful evidence that the restaurant is causally implicated in their illness (perhaps via an infected cook, or a contaminated food supplier).

The second method is the *Method of Difference*. If S1 and S2 share every factor except that S1 contains F and S2 does not, then if E occurs in S1, F is (or is integral to) the cause of E. This is essentially the rationale behind having a **control group** in experimental studies, a practice discussed in detail in Chapter 9. By creating two groups that are carefully controlled to have all identical or highly similar properties except for one, we can greatly increase our confidence that any eventual differences between the groups are causally explained by that sole distinguishing factor.

Of course, in practice any two circumstances are likely to have both a substantial overlap and substantial differences in their properties. So neither method in isolation may narrow down the causal relations very precisely. The third method, the *Joint Method of Agreement and Difference,* addresses this problem by combining the first two. When comparing a range of complex circumstances, we look for a pattern that has some factor common to all the circumstances in which the effect occurred and absent from all the circumstances in which the effect didn't occur.

Mill's fourth method is intended to apply when fate or our research budget doesn't permit us to find or construct distinct circumstances in which properties or effects are entirely absent. The *Method of Concomitant Variations* basically tells us to look for **co-variation,** or coordinated changes, in the degree to which some factor is present and the degree to which an effect is present in various circumstances. Maybe we can't entirely eliminate our subjects' exposure to cigarette smoke over the course of many years, in an observational study of their health. But if we see that the more our subjects are exposed to cigarette smoke, the more they suffer health problems, we can infer that cigarette smoke plays a causal role in health problems.

Finally, Mill proposed the *Method of Residues*. If we know that a particular range of factors causes a particular range of effects, and we notice that all those factors minus F cause all those effects minus E, then F is (or is integral to) the cause of E.

What do Mill's Methods tell us? They codify intuitions about cause and effect that are, or ought to be, obvious in principle but are surprisingly easy to forget in practice. Simple adherence to the Joint Method eliminates some of the most alluring fallacies of causal argument or explanation and is a corrective for various biases in reasoning about causes. For at least this reason it is useful to think first in terms of Mill's Methods when formulating or evaluating causal explanations. Equally important, though, is what the methods don't tell us. They don't tell us how to *individuate*— roughly, how to carve up—situations, nor do they tell us which factors in a situation are potentially causally relevant. Since situations or circumstances or contexts will have vast numbers of properties if we are permissive about what counts as a property, Mill's Methods are seriously incomplete. But they are a useful first pass at explaining how we can identify causes when situations and causally relevant factors are at least loosely understood.

In fact it's hard to say exactly what a causal relation amounts to. Someone once said that cause and effect is ultimately a matter of *bumping*. Certainly our stereotype of what it is for one event to cause another might include things knocking into one another in the world of "medium-sized slow-moving objects" like fish, pickles, baseballs, and people. But it's hard to see how this stereotype might extend to relations between more abstract things, and it's hard to see how cause, understood in this way, might be inferred on the basis of correlations. Explaining the (or a) notion of cause is an extremely difficult problem in the philosophy of science for these and related reasons. Straightforward explanations of the concept, like "A causes B when A makes B happen," or " . . . when A brings it about that B" don't seem very explanatory after all. Often writers discussing statistics and correlations treat causation simply as if it were intuitively understood. They focus instead on what it *isn't*. It is often asserted that causation must be distinguished from (mere) statistical correlation; the problem, on this approach, is then how to think of correlation.

There are, moreover, various sorts of causes that we might appeal to in an empirical argument or explanation, and different purposes behind seeking a causal explanation. Sometimes it is important to distinguish immediate or **proximate causes** from ultimate or **remote causes,** for example. If we imagine a chain of causes over time leading up to event E, the first items in the chain are the remote causes of E, while the events just prior to E are proximate causes. We usually can give principled grounds for regarding some event as the first in a chain, without actually going back to the beginning of the universe. Depending on our explanatory purposes we might regard the beginning of Canada as occurring with the first settlement of humans on what is now Canadian soil, or with the imposition of a nation-state politics on the area, or with the formal event of Confederation— among other candidates.

Another distinction between causes to which an explanation might allude is that between **efficient causes** and **structuring causes**. The former are normally just what we mean by "cause," the direct event leading to some outcome. The latter constitute the framework of factors that enables a chain of efficient events to occur at all. These two kinds of distinction can both apply to a situation. When one curling stone knocks another out of the rings, the proximate efficient cause of the second rock's moving is the collision with the thrown stone; a remote efficient cause is the action of the player who threw the stone; a proximate structuring cause is the work of the sweepers; and a remote structuring cause is the presence of the plumbing that enabled the ice to be installed.

Any one of these things, or all of them, might be what we're asking for when we inquire about the cause of some event. Causal explanations can be given (or attempted) in such fine-grained detail, or tracing so far back in time, or with such enormous breadth of structuring factors, that we always have to use the context to decide what sort of causal explanation would be appropriate to ask for, or to provide if someone else asks for it. The question "What (or who) caused E?" can also be a way of asking what the easiest way of *preventing* E would have been or will be in future similar circumstances. It can be a way of seeking to assign blame or praise to someone, for that matter. In these contexts, the distinctions between structuring, efficient, remote, and proximate causes can be crucial.

In each case, the evidence for a causal claim will be empirical, whether directly observational or based on a theory that is itself concerned with describing or predicting empirical outcomes. This evidence will most fundamentally be a matter of correlations between events of particular kinds and may also crucially involve appeals to mechanisms, possibly highly theoretical, that are taken to relate the events. With a sufficiently large stock of good evidence and powerful theoretical resources, we can have great confidence in causal claims; inference to the existence of a cause can be strongly cogent. Like ampliative reasoning more generally, though, such claims and conclusions are always open to being strengthened, weakened, or overturned altogether as new evidence comes in.

STATES OF INFORMATION

A key idea for understanding ampliativity, and especially for inductive reasoning, is that of a **state of information**: the total evidence at our disposal when we consider the proposition or some course of action. If we aim to reason reliably in any given case of incomplete knowledge, the fundamental problem is to come up with an accurate assessment of our state of information relative to the issue at hand. It is easy to overlook relevant information, on one hand, and easier still to over-estimate the amount and relevance of information that we do possess, on the other hand.

Taking seriously the idea of a state of information requires us to set aside some widespread attitudes about how we know things, and even our intellectual pride. It is quite common for people to talk and think as if the rational believability (the **credibility**) of some proposition is an all-or-nothing matter: if there's too little reason to believe it, then you're irrational to believe it; but if you get enough evidence you cross the credibility line, at which point someone blows a whistle and you now count as being justified in your belief. Of course there is no such line, or at least not a sharp one. States of information lend support to claims by degrees. So as our state of information improves gradually, the rational credibility of some belief can increase gradually—and the same goes for decreasing credibility, too.

Thinking of credibility as a sharp line can easily be a way for us to hang onto unjustified beliefs, by regarding increases or decreases in evidential support for some belief as falling on the wrong side of the line to really make a difference. ("Oh, sure, the evidence is mounting for your view, but it's not enough to tip the scales" or "Oh, sure, that's *some* evidence against my view, but not enough to make it unjustified.") Notice that this does not mean that we don't sometimes have to just pick one of several imperfectly justified beliefs and *act* on it; for the purposes of that specific action, our commitment to that belief crosses a threshold of sorts. But this ought not lead us to suppose that our warrant for that belief is all-or-nothing, nor that our reliance on it must extend beyond the context in which we act on it.

A crucial fact about our empirical or inductively justified beliefs is that new information can rationally require that we revise them. Our states of information change, and it is not always easy for us to keep our beliefs fitted to them appropriately. When our actions are based on nothing more than best guesses, for example, it is important that we bear the guesswork in mind subsequently. Sometimes we just need a best-available belief to guide our actions in a situation, but it can be tempting to hang onto that belief afterwards. It is easy to regard a belief that was arrived at quickly and under pressure as justified, not just by the state of information under which it was formed, but by subsequent states of information as well—even when subsequent information reveals those decisions to have been mistaken or subop-timal. Understanding the idea of defeasible states of information is an important step in giving up the idea that the justification for our beliefs is all-or-nothing and always-and-forever.

"When the facts change, I change my mind—what do you do, sir?"

Economist John Maynard Keynes

DEFEASIBILITY

To see the importance of defeasibility, consider the following bit of reasoning. Obviously, believing that some proposition P is true means believing that not-P is false. If you believe that "Weebles wobble" is true, then you must believe that "Weebles don't wobble" is false. This in turn requires that if some other statement *entails* that not-P, then it too is false. For example, since "Nothing wobbles" logically implies "Weebles don't wobble," you have to reject it too. It follows that if you believe that P, then you must reject as false any proposition entailing that P is incorrect. But that sounds like a way of saying that if potentially new information is brought to your attention, and it contradicts one of your current beliefs, then rationally you must reject that new information. Apparently it is irrational to reject any currently held belief on the basis of new evidence, because your current belief should require you to reject that new evidence instead!

Clearly something has gone wrong with this line of thought. Changing your mind in light of new evidence is often the *only* reasonable thing to do. What is missed by the reasoning sketched above is the fact that our beliefs can be held on the basis of a current state of information without greatly constraining what it would be rational to believe under some *other* (more complete) state of information. Believing that some proposition is true, in the sense in which the term is ordinarily employed, is consistent with open-mindedness about the possibility that it will be overturned.

To recognize the defeasibility of a belief is not necessarily to lack confidence in its truth. One can be highly justified in some belief while acknowledging its defeasibility. For example, I am very confident indeed that there exist no backward-flying winged horses who solve calculus puzzles while delivering pizza to the president of Ecuador. By the ordinary, non-technical, use of the term "certain," I'd even say I'm *certain* there are no such things. But *in principle* I recognize that this belief is defeasible. It might take a great deal of evidence over a long term to convince me otherwise, but it could happen. That kind of recognition is what keeps our belief-revision processes sensitive to changes in our state of information.

Defeasibility is a key feature of empirical beliefs. In logic or mathematics the idea is that once a proposition is proved, it stays proved; proofs do not become defunct. This is not to say that we can't make mistakes in logic or math, of course. It's just that when we do make mistakes, what we are mistaken about is whether we really had a proof at all. Because we are less than perfect reasoners, we can erroneously think that a non-proof is a proof—because of its complexity and length, for example. In the empirical case, though, a belief that was first justified by the available evidence can later be overturned without this meaning that the apparent evidence wasn't really evidence in the first place. It might just mean that as more evidence accumulated, it came to point in a different direction.

NEUTRALITY: IGNORANCE AND EVENLY BALANCED EVIDENCE

Another key element of evidential reasoning is the ability to recognize when we are in a **neutral state of information**, and to condition our judgments appropriately. This ability does not seem to come very naturally to most of us. We might just have an inherent tendency to imagine better evidence than we really possess, or there may be in part a cultural norm according to which admitting one's ignorance is seen as being wishy-washy or just plain stupid. Whatever the explanation, there is no question that even when we attempt to explicitly flag some state of information as neutral, we sometimes read information into the situation whether it's there or not.

Consider UFOs, for example. What reasonable person believes in UFOs?

I do.

This may seem a surprising admission, but then, I have three small children at my house. I see unidentified flying objects every single day, usually out of the corners of my eyes. Was it food? A sock? The cat? Sometimes I just can't tell; all I know is that it was flying. Hence there are unidentified flying objects—lots of them, presumably, the world over.

Now, it could quite rightly be objected that I'm committing the Fallacy of Equivocation, discussed in Chapter 4, in which one illicitly uses a single term in two different ways. After all, most people nowadays use the term "UFO" to mean something like "alien spaceship." But that is precisely the point: an acronym explicitly abbreviating the word "unidentified" easily comes to be a label for something purportedly identified, at least as a general kind. Similar effects are found in the widespread use of phrases like "the unknown" or "the unexplained" in popular pseudo-documentaries or television series about alleged supernatural events. In such contexts, these phrases are often just used to *mean* "the psychic" or "the supernatural." On a similar note, one researcher describes how various media outlets began reporting exaggerated estimates of the number of murders by serial killers in the 1980s, calculated by going through national statistics for homicides and interpreting all the murders categorized as having unknown perpetrators as meaning that serial killers were responsible.[2] We do not appear to find it very natural to admit that we just have no idea what is going on with some phenomenon. Even our attempts to do so tend to become labels that are used to suggest that we really *do* have quite a good idea.

Sometimes a state of information is neutral with respect to some proposition, not because we have no information, but because the information we have seems to divide roughly equally between supporting and undermining the proposition. These are tricky judgments to make about a state of information, since they involve the evaluation and weighing of various bits of evidence. But this is a process that we can easily rig in favour of whatever side of the issue we are predisposed to favour. A danger from the perspective of monitoring your own reasoning for bad habits is that it is easy to over- or under-interpret evidence bearing on a claim to which one is emotionally attached in some way. This can even be a matter of concluding that some question is entirely open, rather than recognizing that the preponderance of the evidence is on one side.

Think back to the quote from Shakespeare's *Macbeth* at the beginning of Chapter 1. Macbeth lays out the evidence for and against the thought that the

FIGURE 2.1

Not a UFO

By definition, a UFO is "an *unidentified* flying object," not a "flying saucer." However, this label denoting a neutral state of information is now widely understood as the equivalent of "alien spaceship."

Digital Art/Corbis Canada

witches' prediction is a good thing and concludes that it's really a tie (the prediction "cannot be ill, cannot be good"). It can't be a bad thing, because Macbeth has been appointed thane of Cawdor. And it can't be good, because the prediction has Macbeth considering the murder of the current king. But surely it's an indication of Macbeth's ambition (and inclination to amorality) that he considers this a tie! One might reasonably respond: "The upside here might be good *for you*, but that hardly shows that the witches' plan isn't evil anyhow. And the evil side is *really* evil. Seriously, you're already contemplating murdering the king? That's not a tie or a toss-up. This whole business stinks."

The upshot is that thinking critically from imperfect evidence requires monitoring our tendencies to misread our own states of information—that is, it requires reflecting not just on what evidence we possess, but on how to weigh that evidence.

A first step here is to recognize and employ forms of speech that express (or are at least consistent with) the modest limits of what we may know in a situation. Compare the following examples.

1. I believe that there are exactly five apples at the corner store.
2. I believe that there are not exactly five apples at the corner store.
3. I do not believe that there are exactly five apples at the corner store.

Notice that (3) is a weaker claim than (2), in terms of the rational commitments of the speaker. In the normal run of events, my state of information is much likelier to be (3) than (1) or (2), since I will rarely know the exact number of apples in a store. Merely holding (3) is consistent with neither believing that there are five nor believing that there are not five. I just might not know either way; hence I don't believe that there are five. Nor, similarly, do I believe that the number of apples at the corner store is not five, though I might think this more probable than that there are five, just because there are far more ways for there not to be five apples than for there to be five apples. This is also a general point about the interaction of the term "believes" with negation; we can't automatically move from "A does not believe that P" to "A believes that not-P," since the former but not the latter is consistent with a neutral state of information regarding P.

All in all, when the evidence with respect to some statement P is impoverished or (upon careful reflection) seems equally balanced, and when no action that assumes either P or not-P is absolutely necessary, the reasonable thing to do is to *suspend judgment:* that is, to recognize the neutral state of information and to neither accept P nor accept not-P, pending further discovery. What remains is to think about how we can get a precise and reliable sense of the quality of our state of information, relative to some proposition. That is largely what probability and statistics are about, the main concepts of which are explored in Chapter 6.

PROVING A NEGATIVE

It is often said that it is impossible to prove a negative statement; that is, impossible to prove that something is not the case, or that something does not exist. There is a kernel of truth to this, but also a lot of confusion stemming from the difference between deductive and inductive or empirical standards of proof.

First, the notion of *proof* is not univocal (it does not have just one meaning in all contexts). We have already seen that we need to clearly distinguish deductive proof from inductive proof. Some people don't like applying the word "proof" to the empirical case, but this is a standard usage of the term; in ordinary parlance, the police *proved* that Enron executives committed fraud—though of course proof in this sense is defeasible.

As long as you stick to one conception of proof or the other, there is no principled reason to say that one cannot prove a negative claim. Consider first the deductive case. Here non-existence proofs abound. There exist no round squares. There exist no spherical cubes. There exists no even prime greater than 2. In this sense, clearly, one can prove negatives quite easily. So what about empirical cases? Suppose I say, "There is no elephant in this room." Can I prove that negative statement? By empirical standards, again the answer is yes. I can look all around, including behind the couch cushions and fail to find an elephant.

"But," one might reply, "what if your eyes are deceiving you? What if you're hallucinating? What if a cunning paint job has put the elephant in special living room camouflage? What about exceedingly tiny elephants?"

Let's allow that these are all possibilities. All this means is that broadly ampliative standards of proof are in principle defeasible, as we already discussed. But this has little specifically to do with proving a *negative* claim. For the positive case is much the same. Suppose I say, "There *is* an elephant in this room," and then go on to empirically establish this by looking around and finding an African elephant (balancing atop the television, say). Notice that the same or similar questions apply in this case: What if your eyes are deceiving you? What if you're hallucinating? What if a cunning paint job only makes it look for all the world like there's an elephant there? The *general* possibility of being mistaken is just another aspect of the fact that empirical standards of proof do not amount to logico-mathematical certainty. But this point applies equally to positive and negative existence claims. *Within* the standards for inductive proof, one can often prove negatives with the similar confidence that one can prove positives; most defeating conditions for evidence in the negative case are defeating conditions in the positive case as well.

What is fair to say is that empirically proving a negative *in a large domain*, especially in an indefinitely large domain, can be anywhere from practically difficult to physically impossible. The real argumentative issues usually turn out not to be whether one can always or ever prove a negative, but what we should conclude in the absence of the evidence, and who has the burden of proof when a negative claim is offered in an argument. The saying "You can't prove a negative" is a misleading slogan that papers over the real distinctions between negative existence claims that are highly probable, given what we know of how the world works (like "There exist absolutely no flying winged horses") and those that seem uncertain or hard to assess (like "Absolutely nobody in history has ever spontaneously recovered from simultaneous malignant tumours in five major organs"). The specifics of such claims, their relations to our particular and theoretical knowledge, and the context of communication in which they are uttered are all relevant to whether we can or even need to judge them as sufficiently probable to accept.

CONCLUSION

An ampliative or evidential argument is one in which the conclusion expresses more information than the premises express in total. These arguments can be better and worse by degrees and are cogent when their premises are sufficiently plausible and sufficiently supportive to warrant believing their conclusions. Inductive, abductive, and analogical reasoning are all ampliative in nature. Causal reasoning too is broadly evidential and can involve a range of related yet distinct concepts of cause, as well as an element of interest-relativity.

Critical thinking about evidence requires understanding how one's state of information can lend degrees of support to some proposition, including a neutral degree of support. We seem naturally to resist recognizing neutral or nearly neutral evidential situations, in which we know too little about something to form a very solid opinion. Moreover these degrees of support can (and ought to) change as more evidence comes in, because the character of the new evidence may be different or because it may undermine evidence we previously had.

REVIEW QUESTIONS

1. Summarize three main distinctions between deductive and ampliative arguments.
2. Think of a proposition for which you think you have (for all practical purposes) a neutral state of information. Explain your choice.
3. Consult local or recent media to find two examples of analogical arguments: one you believe clearly illustrates a successful analogy, and one clearly showing how analogical arguments can fail.

NOTES

1. *The Toronto Star*, February 18, 2006, p. H07.
2. J. Best, *Damned Lies and Statistics* (Berkeley, Calif.: University of California Press, 2001), 74–76.

Language, Non-Language, and Argument

Suppose I am working as a bank teller, and you enter the bank and find my boss. "Kenyon is not a thief!" you tell the bank manager. "He has not been under investigation by the RCMP for fraud. Nothing for you to worry about—he's really not a thief. And no fraud investigations. Not that guy. No way. Goodbye!"

Should I feel in this case that you haven't called my honesty or background into question? It seems quite obvious that you've communicated doubts about me, simply by choosing to single me out for attention. The fact that you're raising the question of my honesty and reputation for no apparent reason will communicate more than the fact that you're strictly and literally saying that I'm not a thief. So in the absence of genuine reasons to doubt my honesty, your behaviour certainly is not justified by either the truth of your utterances or their positive *literal* meaning. It may be a good thing to not be under investigation, but by choosing to *say* that I'm not, in this singular way, you clearly convey that there are (or ought to be) worries about me. The lesson is that it is perfectly possible to mislead and misinform while sticking to statements that are strictly true. To understand how premises and conclusions are conveyed, we have to take seriously the distinction between the actual words a speaker chooses and the propositions that are communicated by the use of those words in the context at hand.

SENTENCES, UTTERANCES, AND COMMUNICATIVE DEVICES

This example shows that what is *asserted* often goes well beyond the content of the sentences uttered. (Writing is a kind of utterance, as we'll use the term.) Typically a reasonable audience will consider not merely what was said, but *the point of saying it*. This distinction is involved in a great deal of communication. As the makers, recipients, and evaluators of reasoning, we must therefore be highly sensitive to it. Why would someone point out that one employee isn't a thief, unless that employee was already known to be a suspect or as an indirect way of making the charge? If I was neither a thief nor (reasonably) suspected of being one, and you were to defend your action with the claim that what you'd said about me was in fact true of all the bank's employees, there would still be the obvious question of why you had chosen to focus on me in particular.

In general, good critical reasoning requires some reflection on the range of linguistic and extra-linguistic devices implicated in the communication of arguments and, occasionally, in the commission of reasoning errors. These are the focus of this chapter.

SAYING ONE THING AND (THEREBY) DOING ANOTHER

Language is used for many different purposes, ranging from ordering pizza to swearing when the pizza's late. Many of these purposes are **performative**—that is, they result in the accomplishment of some act rather than just describing it. Saying "I love you" does not bring it about that the speaker loves the audience; it's just a purported description of the speaker's state of mind. But saying "I promise you," uttered under the appropriate circumstances, brings it about that the speaker promises something to the audience. It's not just a description of what the speaker has in mind; the utterance is itself the promise. Similarly, saying "I thee wed" or "I do" suffices to get you married under the right circumstances. (So be careful.) Our uses of language extend to include issuing commands, asking questions, and making assertions.

Commanding, questioning, and asserting are different kinds of **speech-act**. In the clearest cases, performing these linguistic acts is a matter of employing the appropriate kind of sentence, since sentences have various grammatical moods that typically correspond to different kinds of speech-act. Imperative sentences are used to give orders, interrogative sentences are used to ask questions, and indicative or declarative sentences are used to assert.

> Imperative mood: Take out the trash.
> Interrogative mood: Did you take out the trash?
> Indicative mood: You took out the trash.

Constructing and analyzing arguments is largely a matter of making and identifying the assertions that function as premises and conclusions in the reasoning. Because there is such an obvious fit between grammatical mood and the kind of speech-act one performs by uttering a sentence, one might think that premises and conclusions in an argument can be identified more or less grammatically, by just looking for declarative sentences. That's too hasty, though. There are at least two reasons that we need to read or listen more carefully to what someone says in order to make sense of their argument.

First, assertions can be made without employing indicative sentences. The most common example is that of **rhetorical questions**. (Could *anything* be more obvious?) It is quite common to encounter a rhetorical question in an argument where it is plainly intended to function as a premise. In such a case it is best to think of the rhetorical question as an assertion with the same content. So, for example, someone who says, "How could anything be more important than keeping our streets crime-free?" might best be understood as simply saying, "Nothing could be more important than keeping our streets crime-free." Thinking of a rhetorical question in this way often reveals that it was framed rhetorically for a reason: the effect of putting the premise in the form of a question is to oblige the audience to look for evidence against the claim, rather than the speaker providing evidence in its favour. This tactic of shifting the **burden of proof**, discussed in more detail later in this chapter, often indicates that there is little or no good evidence to be given in support of the premise. And second, premises and even conclusions can be **implicit**—that is, not written out in any form at all, but intended to be obvious from the context.

Rhetorical questions and the like are part of a general way of indirectly setting out a premise or a conclusion, known as **conversational implicature**. This is the practice of using an utterance to convey a meaning beyond its literal meaning. Sarcasm most obviously employs this effect to communicate the opposite of a literal meaning, but the general use of intended inference, over and above literal meaning, is pervasive. Someone who looked at local scenery in the morning and then went for a drive in the afternoon could claim not to utter a literal falsehood in saying, "I went for a drive and saw some scenery." After all, the uttered sentence does not strictly say that the events occurred in the order they are presented in the sentence. That's a further inference, although one that is normally intended by such an utterance.

A careful reconstruction of an argument containing apparent uses of implicature should explicitly note them, and either choose the most plausible interpretation given the context (that is, either strictly and literally or factoring in implicatures), or analyze the argument twice—once with each interpretation. Consider this example of implicature in an argument:

> "The theft occurred at the party at midnight. But I said good night at 11:30 p.m. So I couldn't have witnessed the crime."

In a case like this one, charity obviously dictates interpreting the speaker as saying not merely that she "said good night" at 11:30, but that she also left the party (or at least went to bed, if the party was at her house) at that time. That is a normal or typical intended inference for that way of speaking. But if we have reason to think that the speaker might be trying to shade the truth, to mislead without directly lying, we might at least make a note of the possibility that the premises are strictly true (she *said* "goodnight" at 11:30) while the conclusion is false (she didn't leave until after the theft and hence could have witnessed the crime).

A related phenomenon is **presupposition**: a proposition that may not be explicit in some statement, but which must be granted if the statement is to be meaningful or felicitous. The statement "Jerry's middle child won an award" doesn't explicitly say that Jerry has more than one child, nor that Jerry has an odd number of children. But both of these propositions must be true for Jerry to have just one middle child, so we can say that the statement presupposes them. Presuppositions of this sort enable fast and elegant communication that would be laborious to express

Among other things, we have in these phenomena an explanation of the distinction between the **truth conditions** of a statement and the conditions for its felicitous or intelligible use. For example, looking at the Addition rule from Chapter 1, it should be easy to see that if P is true, then the disjunction (P or Q) is true. The latter requires only that at least one of its two sub-sentences be true, so if we already know that P is true, we can use "or" to add any other statement we like, and still produce a sentence that is literally true. But in any case where we take a statement P that's known to be true, and add a statement Q *not* known to be true (and worst of all if Q is known to be false!), to then simply assert the disjunction (P or Q) would be horribly misleading. It would wrongly communicate that for all the speaker knows each sub-sentence might be true. *Saying* something true is very often far too limited a requirement, if the aim is to have one's audience come to *believe* something true (and nothing false) on the basis of one's utterance.

explicitly. In Chapter 4 I discuss the fallacies and rhetorical tricks that can arise from incautious or sneaky uses of presupposition.

RHETORICAL EFFECTS

The concept of *rhetoric* is sometimes defined broadly as the study and use of effective communication, including cogent argumentation. Often, though, rhetoric is distinguished from strict considerations of truth, accuracy, validity, and soundness. We will use this more specific definition, under which rhetoric consists of ways of speaking or writing intended to *persuade* independently of the strength of the speaker's argument.

There are many different kinds of rhetorical devices in this sense, ranging from the inclusion of subtle value judgments in assertions to the use of implicatures and aspects of *prosody,* or the actual manner of speaking one employs. Most of these devices are invisible from the perspective of truth conditions as represented by formal logic or formal semantics. For example, we have already noted that the word "but" is a form of conjunction similar to "and." From the perspective of formal logic, these terms are not merely similar—they are indistinguishable. Yet they have very different rhetorical effects. The difference between the first pair of sentences is, if not entirely negligible, at least much less than the difference between the second pair of sentences.

Louis Riel showed brilliance and Gabriel Dumont was thoroughly competent.
Gabriel Dumont was thoroughly competent and Louis Riel showed brilliance.

Louis Riel showed brilliance, but Gabriel Dumont was thoroughly competent.
Gabriel Dumont was thoroughly competent, but Louis Riel showed brilliance.

In the second pair of sentences, the use of "but" suggests, in the first sentence, that competence is more important than brilliance, and in the second sentence, that brilliance is the more important. The order in which we place statements joined with "but" conveys an emphasis and a value judgment on the part of the speaker: the statement *after* the "but" is normally taken to be emphasized or particularly relevant. This is a subtle rhetorical device, a way of saying something without saying it in as many words. In this way a speaker can convey an attitude, even have other people adopt that attitude, without even being recognized as having made the attempt.

Rhetoric can be a matter of choosing between words that would loosely be regarded as synonyms. Depending on the context, talking about Ellen's *mother* can convey slightly different attitudes about the woman in question than talking about Ellen's *mom* would, the former being perhaps more formal or less warm than the latter. A rhetorical effect may also be achieved by the insertion of a word not strictly necessary from a truth-conditional perspective, but that imposes an attitude or presupposition nonetheless. In the least subtle cases, these *interjections* or *expletive* terms are profanities or insults (which is often just what "expletive" is used to mean). There is no real difference in the truth conditions of the following pair of sentences, but a clear difference in rhetorical effect.

> The Blue Jays will win the Pennant this year.
> The damned Blue Jays will win the Pennant this year.

The latter, obviously, communicates a negative attitude (not necessarily dislike; it could also be something like frustration) in a way that the former does not. Other interjections have a subtler effect. Compare:

> Ted intends to sue, and we should support him.
> Ted intends to sue, and surely we should support him.

The use of the term "surely" in the second sentence suggests that supporting Ted is not just the speaker's recommendation but is the *obvious* course of action. Anyone disagreeing will automatically be depicted as unreasonable.

Verbal communication offers particularly rich opportunities to employ rhetorical devices. Besides the rhetorical devices we've already seen, spoken language also enables rhetorical effects that are difficult or impossible to achieve in writing: tones of voice, facial expressions and gestures that powerfully influence the message conveyed by the utterance of the sentence itself. Still, the hesitations in speech that can convey an emphasis are at least partially communicable in writing through the use of commas and ellipses (...). And the use of italics in writing can help one approximate the range of tonal emphases conveyable in speech.

> You should *give* Zainab the calculator.
> You should give *Zainab* the calculator.
> You should give Zainab the *calculator*.

In the first sentence, the vocal emphasis on "give" suggests a contrast with some other means of Zainab's getting the calculator—say, your selling it to her. The second sentence insinuates that it's who receives the calculator that is under consideration. And the third conveys the presupposition that Zainab's to be given something or other in any case, with the speaker recommending that the gift be the calculator. Other **prosodic** features of speech (roughly, those dependent on how something is said, rather than what is said) are rarely made explicit in writing: for example, the manner in which someone else's speech is reported.

In an extreme case, we might make the phenomenon explicit.

> According to Eric, Mary left at midnight after saying, "This was a great party!"
> According to Eric, Mary left at midnight after saying, "Thish wash a greeaaat party!"

The way in which Eric reports Mary's utterance communicates as much as or more than the sentence he reports her as uttering—in this case, perhaps, that she was drunk. We might go out of our way to make the character of his report explicit, as the second sentence does by using phonetic spelling, but the manner a speaker imposes on a report can come in all degrees, few of which can neatly be made explicit. Had Eric chosen instead to use just a very slightly dopey voice in quoting Mary, he might have been quite effective in influencing his audience's perception of Mary without their being aware that he was colouring their views in this way. Indeed, Eric himself might not be aware of doing this.

One of the aims of critically analyzing arguments or assertions is to detect and defuse rhetorical flourishes. Rhetorical effects can be perfectly legitimate in an argumentative context, to be sure. They can be elegant and stylish ways of communicating one's judgments or of making assertions by way of presupposition. But we are obliged to ensure that these judgments and assertions are not sneaking in via the back door when we encounter arguments, and that they are not covertly doing all the work in our own arguments. To the greatest extent that's practical, the analysis of an argument should make its rhetorical devices explicit, so they can be evaluated like any other premise.

Qualifiers, Quantifiers, and Weasel Words

Suppose you are thinking about buying a small refrigerator from a friend, sight unseen. "How small is it?" you want to know. "Pretty small," your friend replies.

If you show up to collect the refrigerator and discover that it will not fit in your car, you might legitimately feel misled. But in this case it is much more difficult to say exactly what the truth conditions of your friend's utterance really amounted to. Adding the qualifier "pretty" makes the resulting claim loose and imprecise, over and above the fact that "small," like many adjectives, is a *context-sensitive* word. (That is, your friend might defend the description by noting that the fridge is small *for a full-sized refrigerator,* which was what your friend thought you were talking about in that context.) Determining whether a similarly qualified premise is false, or determining what would count as justifying such a conclusion, can be a tricky business. There may simply be no fact of the matter, in which case the most illuminating thing to say is that the claim is not really communicating very much.

Similar remarks apply to unspecific quantifying expressions, like *most, some, plenty, lots,* and *many.* There are few definite rules associated with the use of such terms, or, at least, the rules that apply to them do not have very precise implications. Take "most," for instance. How many people out of 100 have to vote for me, in order for me to honestly state that most people did? The answer is not straightforward. If I got 51 votes, then it's uncontroversial that I got *the most* votes of any candidate. But it would still seem to stretch the truth to say that *most of the voters* chose me; this phrasing connotes more decisive support than just the slenderest majority. The subtleties are greater if there are more than two choices as well. If there were four candidates, and I win the election with 26 votes, the accuracy of my description of things becomes particularly sensitive to wording: I can still correctly say that I received the most votes—the most of any candidate, in other words—but now it's clearly a mistake to claim that I received most of the votes.

The term "many" is less precise still. Again, out of 100 people, how many have to like carrots before it is reasonable to say "Many of these people like carrots"? A majority is not required for "many"; my intuition is that 20-ish would make the claim defensible, but intuitions may vary. Three is clearly too few while 50 is clearly enough, but besides setting such upper and lower bounds we may not be able to give any definite answer.

Words of this sort are extremely useful and are often perfectly legitimate, especially when the context of use serves to partially refine their intended meaning. We don't always have precise figures conveniently to hand, and sometimes precise figures aren't available at all; but general trends may be evident anyhow, and so we need words pitched at a level to capture the generalities without conveying a false precision. Once we have these words, though, they can be used as "weasel words"— terms chosen specifically to let the arguer weasel out of any refutation.

Here is an example of weasel words in action:

> A: "This policy will benefit a lot of Canadians."
> B: "What do you mean? It will only benefit a hundredth of one percent of Canadians."
> A: "Well, that's around three thousand people. That's a lot of Canadians. Try fitting them all in a phone booth!"

In this way a qualified or imprecisely quantified statement can come to seem empty, if its speaker goes on to defend a weaselly interpretation of it. Analyzing an argument containing such terms sometimes results in the conclusion that the relevant claim is either false, if the terms are taken to say something substantive, or trivial, if the terms are used as weasel words.

Vagueness

When vagueness is understood as mere imprecision, the critical thinking issues it raises are essentially those raised by weasel words. There is a more specific sense, however, in which calling a predicate or a concept vague can be a way of making a technical observation about the puzzling logic that characterizes statements employing the vague term. In this sense, vague terms are those subject to **Sorites reasoning**, a label that comes from an ancient Greek paradox.

A classic example is the concept of a heap. To say that this notion is vague is to point out a certain puzzle associated with it: one grain of sand is not a heap. And if something is not a heap, then adding one grain of sand to it will not make it a heap. But then no amount of sand is a heap, since one could get from one grain to any number of grains just by adding one more grain to a non-heap. Of course the conclusion is absurd—that's what makes it a puzzle—but it's hard to say how to block the reasoning. In particular, it's hard to see how we could non-arbitrarily choose some number of grains of sand to be the cutoff point at which we suddenly have a heap but below which we do not. There are two broad kinds of critical reasoning issues associated with vague predicates. It is possible to reason poorly by disregarding vagueness, but also by over-interpreting it.

The former kind of mistake comes when we fail to allow for blurred boundaries and partial results, treating situations as if they must be definitely one way or definitely the opposite way. In the wake of the 2004 presidential election in the United States, for example, there was a good deal of joking in the media and in cyberspace about the so-called Blue States seceding from the United States, with the aim of joining Canada. But what are these Blue States? American socio-political discourse, including Canadian discussion of American politics, involves widespread allusions to Red States, that is, states that have elected a Republican representative, and Blue States, or those electing a Democratic representative. There is a tendency for commentators to spin out long discussions on the different values, religions, pastimes, and politics of the Red and Blue states' residents—apparently forgetting that many of these states count as red or blue merely as a result of elections in which candidates won by a tiny fraction of the popular vote. To carry the metaphor over, most states are in fact close to the same shade of purple: the socio-political *attitudes* of a region usually are much less definite than the all-or-nothing outcome of an election. However wistfully some "Blue State" advocates may have told the jokes about splitting away from other states and joining Canada, the fact is that overall there is both a split of voters within most states and an enormous overlap of interests and attitudes across most states—far more, plausibly, than between any "Blue State" and Canada. It is too easy to move from noticing a small difference to inferring a deep difference, overlooking the tendency for many distinctions to come in degrees.

On the other hand, it is also important not to draw the inference that because there is grey, there is no black or white. An important aspect of understanding vague language is distinguishing between being unable to say where a difference lies and there being no difference at all. We can't say when a heap becomes a non-heap, and it may well be there is no precise point at which that happens, but this does not in itself mean that there are no heaps (nor that everything is a heap).

To choose a weightier example, think of the concepts like *maturity* and *responsibility*. Even if there is no principled line distinguishing an immature and irresponsible person from a mature and responsible person, there can still be a genuine difference between mature and immature people. This is relevant to the justification for choosing what we might call a *locally arbitrary but globally principled* cutoff point for access to things like driver's licences and the ability to purchase alcohol legally. The idea is that choosing a person's nineteenth birthday as the point at which they can legally buy alcohol seems entirely arbitrary in comparison to choosing the day before their nineteenth birthday or the day after. But that doesn't mean it's arbitrary relative to choosing their fifth birthday or their fiftieth birthday as the legal age. There may be no single day—certainly no single minute or second—between the ages of five and nineteen distinguishing responsible and irresponsible people, but that doesn't mean there is no difference between the responsibility of five-year-olds and nineteen-year-olds. Similarly, even though it might be difficult or impossible to determine precise truth-conditions for a statement involving vague terms, the statement may still be reasonable on broader grounds.

Ambiguity

Calling a statement or description ambiguous might mean only that it is imprecise or indeterminate. Vagueness and ambiguity are often run together in our normal way of speaking. But there are some more precise conceptions of ambiguity relevant to argument and interpretation.

The first is **syntactic ambiguity**. This occurs when a sentence has a *structure* that can be read in more than one way. "She kicked me in an unpleasant place" is a syntactically ambiguous sentence, having one reading in which what was unpleasant was the spot on my body where the kick landed, and another reading in which the whole event occurred in a location that was unpleasant. Cases of negation like those examined in Chapter 1, in which a negation statement like "That's not true" or the prosentence "No" is applied to a complex sentence (e.g., "Ted angrily shouted"), are also syntactically ambiguous, since the negation itself doesn't specify which aspect of the complex sentence is being denied.

The correct understanding of an argument requires care in imposing both the *proper* interpretation and a *single* interpretation on a syntactically ambiguous statement. We want to understand the argument as it was intended, and we want to avoid flipping between interpretations of terms in different premises or conclusions of a single argument—a fallacy known as **equivocation**, discussed in Chapter 4. Naturally this also means that we should enhance the clarity of our own communication by avoiding the use of syntactically ambiguous statements as much as possible.

A greater worry from a critical reasoning perspective is probably **lexical ambiguity**: multiple meanings for a single expression. (I say "expression" rather than "word" because it is common to distinguish words by their meanings; on this understanding of "word" the idea of a single word with different meanings would not make sense.) The basic idea is quite simple. For example, the expression "bug" can mean an insect, a secret listening device, or the act of bothering someone. One expression, three meanings/words—that's lexical ambiguity. Lexically ambiguous statements are particularly susceptible to the fallacy of equivocation, especially when the ambiguity is of a subtle or mild sort known as **polysemy**. This is a term indicating an ambiguity between related meanings of an expression, as opposed to **homonymy**, the existence of two or more unrelated meanings for a single expression. So, for example, the word "bank," meaning a financial institution, is polysemous with "bank," the act of doing business with a financial institution, but both of these are merely homonymous with the unrelated word "bank," meaning the shore of a river. As we will see in Chapter 4, closely related meanings for a single expression make it easy to read the expression one way in a premise, but a slightly different way in a conclusion. An argument so constructed may appear sound, yet the shifting interpretations render it invalid (or, if the interpretations are made explicitly distinct, one of the two statements may more clearly emerge as false).

A problem in many cases of argument, or communication more generally, is controversy over the definitions of particular words. Chapter 1 and Chapter 4 both discuss the uses of definitions in argumentation.

THE USE AND ABUSE OF QUOTATION

Quotation is a slippery instrument. Great care must be exercised both in using quotation and in interpreting someone else's use of it. **Direct quotation**, using actual quotation marks, is a particularly powerful rhetorical tool since it purports to let the quoted person speak for herself. **Indirect quotation**, in which the gist or effect of someone's utterance is presented, is useful because it can be made sensitive to the context of utterance. But it has a still greater potential to incorporate the quoter's agenda, too.

Direct quotation: Larry said, "Mike's a good guy."

Indirect quotation: Larry said that Mike is a good guy.

Indirect quotation (uttered to Mike's sister): Larry said that your brother is a good guy.

Indirect quotation (from someone who dislikes Mike): Larry said that the biggest idiot in town is a good guy.

In different contexts, each of these can be a perfectly straightforward way of communicating. But they each must be predicated on an accurate understanding of what Larry actually said. An audience who knows enough about the speaker's state of mind will understand that the final example does not imply that Larry uttered anything like the sentence "The biggest idiot in town is a good guy." The speaker's editorial contribution will be recognized by an audience who understands the speaker's attitude toward Mike or who perceives this attitude on the basis of the mismatch between Larry's alleged positive attitude toward Mike and the derogatory character of the phrase "the biggest idiot in town." But careless reading or unscrupulous writing can make such distinctions unclear in many cases.

If I say, "My friend John says he's tired of working for his boss, who's a complete doofus," my utterance is ambiguous. Is John calling his boss a doofus, or am I? Linguist and media critic Noam Chomsky notes an example from the *Boston Globe* newspaper, in which the president of Nicaragua is indirectly quoted as announcing measures in response to attacks by the Contras. These were U.S.-armed military forces who opposed the Sandinista government and who launched attacks on Nicaraguan territory from bases in Honduras.

> President Daniel Ortega of Nicaragua said yesterday his government suspended civil liberties last week to "guarantee" his army's defeat of US-backed resistance forces. . . . [H]e said, however, that defeat of the resistance forces could create an even more "dangerous situation." . . .[1]

Reading this passage, one might get the impression that Ortega himself had twice referred to the attackers as "the resistance forces." But this phrase carries rhetorical connotations of a morally just cause, even heroism, from its association with movements like the French Resistance during World War II. Ortega considered the military Contra forces to be terrorist in nature and would never have characterized them as "the resistance." The effect may seem subtle, but consider the difference in the news report had the journalist chosen a word like "terrorist" or "raider" in place of "resistance."

The most obviously misrepresentative form of direct quotation is the **misquote**. This just amounts to attributing words in quotation marks to someone who did not actually use those words—or at least a direct translation of them. It doesn't matter what someone thought or what their views imply; what matters for the sake of direct quotation is what they said. For example, by normal standards of honesty, it is not a misquote to cite René Descartes as having written, "I think, therefore I am," even though Descartes of course did not write in English. But it would be a misquote to cite Descartes as having written, "Our minds cannot influence our behaviours." Some people have thought that Descartes' stated views actually *entail* this result, but he did not actually write that sentence nor any reasonable translation of it.

Some misquotes are complete fabrications, some a matter of a changed word or phrase in something that was actually said. Of course, even a single word changed in a sentence can radically change the character of the utterance. (Leaving out the word "not," for example, can have a major effect.) But misquotes can also have quite subtle effects—and can be widely recited because of those effects.

Misquotation can result from deception or an honest mistake, but the repetition of the misquote very often is linked to its potential to cast a negative light on one side in a personally, politically, or religiously charged issue. In 2004, U.S. presidential candidate John Kerry said at a union rally, "There isn't one of us here who doesn't like NASCAR and who isn't a fan," as an introduction to some remarks about lost jobs in the automotive industry. *New York Times* columnist Maureen Dowd, however, who was not present at the rally, wrote an article in which she misquoted Kerry as having said, "Who among us does not like NASCAR?" Dowd poked fun at Kerry for his bumptiousness in using such a formal construction to claim an interest in such a low-brow sport as stock car racing. Over the ensuing days, this misquote was repeated in the *Times* (eventually becoming "Who among us does not love NASCAR?" in one *Times* article) and widely in other media venues. The misquote, small from some perspectives, made for a good news story because its grammar conveys a sense of self-important seriousness, which, in contrast with its subject matter, makes it seem phony and contrived. Kerry was widely ridiculed as a result of the misquote.[2]

Misattribution is another form of misquoting; it occurs when one speaker's words are attributed to another. For example, amateur religious critic Joseph Wheless, whose still-cited *Forgery in Christianity* appeared in 1930, took issue with the writings of Augustine of Hippo. Now, Augustine wrote two short treatises on the topic of lies and lying—both very worthy treatments of language and communication even today. Augustine's general perspective on lying was rather strongly negative, moreover. Except in the rarest of cases, he said, it is entirely the wrong thing to do. Wheless, however, was unimpressed:

> The great Bishop did not, however, it seems, read his own code when it came to preaching unto edification, for in one of his own sermons he thus relates a very notable experience: "I was already Bishop of Hippo, when I went into Ethiopia with some servants of Christ there to preach the Gospel. In this country we saw many men and women without heads, who had two great eyes in their breasts; and in countries still more southly, we saw people who had but one eye in their foreheads" (Augustine, Sermon 37).[3]

These obvious falsehoods seem to convict Augustine not just of lying, but of hypocrisy besides.

Yet Augustine never said that. The quote is actually from an old work called *Sermons to the Brother in Africa,* attributed to someone known to historians only as Pseudo-Augustine. It purports to be written by Augustine, but clearly dates from around the twelfth century CE (that is, roughly 800 years too late to have been written by Augustine). Pseudo-Augustine fabricated these quotes at great length, and through poor scholarship Wheless misattributed them to Augustine himself. That misattribution continues to circulate today, mainly on the Internet.

To choose a more recent example, feminist writer Catherine MacKinnon is widely said to have written that "all heterosexual sex is rape" or words to a similar effect. MacKinnon rose to some public prominence in Canada when she played a role in the formulation of more stringent laws governing pornography. There is, however, no evidence that she ever uttered the quote so widely reproduced and repeated on web pages or talk radio. In 1999, American syndicated columnist Cal Thomas mused:

> Those Sixties bra-burners got pretty exercised about rape. Catherine MacKinnon wrote in *Professing Feminism*: "In a patriarchal society all heterosexual intercourse is rape because women, as a group, are not strong enough to give meaningful consent."[4]

Again, there no evidence that MacKinnon wrote any such thing, but if she did, it could not have been in the book *Professing Feminism*—which was in fact written by Daphne Patai and Noretta Koertge. Misattributions stacked one atop the other! Yet Thomas's misquote is itself widely requoted on the Internet as if it were authoritative and is often used as evidence of the ridiculous extremism of feminists.

Yet another pitfall in the argumentative use of quotations is the out-of-context quote, or **quote-mining**. This is strictly distinguished from misquoting, in that a mined quote need not get the speaker's words wrong. A mined quote is a correctly

How often are suspiciously juicy quotes actually misquotes or mined quotes? No rigorous work exists on the subject, partly because the notion of a suspiciously juicy quote is hard to define. My experience, for what it's worth, is this: even after years of having my faith in human nature shrivelled to a sad husk, I'm still surprised at how often juicy quotes in wide circulation have been trimmed or massaged or just plain made up. Your results may differ—I hope they do, in fact—but only the willingness to track down original sources will enable you to gradually develop your own "sniff test" for poor quotation. Be prepared for this process to be difficult, moreover. Sometimes original quotes are very difficult to track down, Internet or not. But this fact itself should be seen as useful evidence. The harder you find it to directly confirm a quotation from some obscure source, the less likely that those repeating the quotation have checked it themselves—making it reasonable to reject the popularity of the quote as evidence of its accuracy.

quoted sentence or phrase that is reported without the surrounding context that changes or qualifies its meaning and is therefore falsely presented as characteristic of the speaker's views. For example, a writer might begin a paragraph with the sentence "Here is the view I will argue against." To leave out that sentence while quoting the rest of the paragraph, even if the quote were correct, would be to misrepresent the writer's views by making it seem as if the writer were asserting the very view being rejected. In the case of shorter phrasal quotes, quote-mining involves mixed quotation—partially direct and partially indirect.

A stitched-together sort of mixed quotation is a red flag, since this can amount to quote-mining combined with unquoted *interpretations* of the speaker's alleged views. For example, one website that campaigns against "speech codes" on university campuses presents a list of outrageous limitations placed on free speech by various universities and colleges. Virtually every example in the list, however, is constructed of mixed quotes like this:

> Brown University banned "verbal behavior" that produces "feelings of impotence, anger, or disenfranchisement," whether "intentional or unintentional."[5]

Even if Brown University has adopted policies containing those short phrases, we have no idea whether the policies have the overall effect ascribed by the website, nor even whether these are from a single document. In fact, we have at least a basic reason to doubt that Brown University has such a policy: the fact that no *straightforward* quote can be provided showing it. This is initial reason to doubt such claims, placing the burden on the website authors to provide enough context to make the claims stick. From a reader's perspective, these examples suggest quote-mining and the creative assembly of disparate phrases.

In general, quotes that seem too radical to be believed are red flags and should be directly confirmed. And "directly" means *directly*: misquotes and mined quotes may circulate so widely that a casual Internet search will turn up lots of instances of people repeating the quote even (perhaps especially) if it is bogus. So finding the same quote reproduced elsewhere is quite weak evidence for its accuracy and representativeness. As critical reasoners we ought neither to internalize nor to perpetuate dubious quotations, however much they may appeal to our preconceptions (or our senses of humour). Go back to the data, hunt down citations and page numbers, and find the original words in the original context.

RECOGNIZING ARGUMENTS ON THE HOOF

So far, in Chapters 1 and 2, we have mainly looked at some deliberately exaggerated examples of arguments, in order to get a feeling for what validity and soundness amount to. Of course, in most contexts people offer arguments for less strange conclusions than that Ted is made of peanut butter. That's not to say that arguments are just for formal purposes, though. Among the things we provide reasons for in the course of a normal day are such claims as these:

- The boss's new strategic business plan is basically the same as the old one
- The Canucks will be better this year
- Tracy's new friend, that guy, the one we met, is a complete jerk
- No way is *Harry Potter* better than *Lord of the Rings*

and all manner of other more and less mundane statements. The reasoning we offer for these kinds of claims, and even the arguments spoken and written in much more formal contexts, almost never come prepackaged into labelled premises and conclusions like those of our examples, though. For example, if the boss's old strategic business plan made reference to "licensed learners" and the new makes reference to "empowered information-users," an actual workplace conversation might go like this.

> **Angela:** Do you think the new plan is really different from the old one?

> **Beatrice:** Empowered information-users? Licensed learners.

And in context this reply might clearly communicate the argument that "empowered information-users" is really just another way of saying "licensed learners," which in turn is a reason to think that the new plan is merely a trivial variation on the old one. But Beatrice need not *say*, "The new plan is just a trivial variation on the old one." Indeed, that might well be a very strange thing for Beatrice to utter in that context, even if it's the most precise way of summarizing what she means by what she does utter.

Even in academic writing it is exceedingly rare for arguments to be strictly valid as written, with every single necessary assumption made explicit. Usually written arguments are communicated in paragraphs or even single sentences, by people who aim to exploit shared assumptions where possible. The order in which the claims are made need not follow the model of premises first, conclusion last; sometimes premises, and even the conclusion, can be entirely unstated; and overall the information given explicitly tends to be fragmentary and disorderly to some degree.

As mentioned in Chapter 2, an argument having implicit premises is called an **enthymeme**. It turns out that virtually every actual argument is an enthymeme, though, so the word is best reserved for cases in which the implicit premises of an argument are particularly significant (because they are implausible, for example, or because the argument is ostentatiously invalid). Almost every argument will leave at least *some* basic assumptions unstated, because making them all explicit would be at least inelegant and maybe even impossible. Consider:

"Ted was caught in a heavy rain with no shelter; hence he got wet."

Strictly speaking, this apparently simple argument makes all manner of assumptions not entered as premises, like that Ted is male and that rain makes you wet. So, strictly speaking, it's invalid. But these assumptions are uncontroversial; naturally we ought to think of them as "being there." It's when an argument has an implicit premise that someone might wish to *deny*, or when an implicit argument might be overlooked, that we ought to make a special note of the fact by calling it an enthymeme.

This point extends to arguments having implicit conclusions. These too should be treated as if the conclusion was really there—provided the content of the intended conclusion is obvious. If it isn't obvious, then we may still entertain various choices for what the intended conclusion might be, but we have then to be more guarded in our attributions. We might have to say simply that it's unclear what conclusion the speaker is getting at. Often, though, it is perfectly straightforward. For example,

"Only the wind or the neighbour's kids could have knocked over my garbage can yesterday. And there's been no wind for three days."

This is plainly an argument, and the conclusion is equally plain. (One might have doubts about how the first premise could itself be justified, though.) If we were rewriting the argument to make it clear, we would represent it as explicitly having the conclusion that the neighbour's kids knocked over the speaker's garbage can.

Moreover, it is very rare for arguments outside of a few academic disciplines to have their premises and conclusions flagged *as* premises and conclusions. Even when all the (major) premises and the conclusion are explicitly written out, it may take time and careful thought to distinguish premises from conclusions, and, if the argument is sequential, to distinguish intermediate conclusions from the overall conclusion. The most obvious signs of such distinctions are what we might call **Terms of Entailment**: words that indicate the speaker's intent to draw an inference or reach a conclusion. The following words and similar ones are associated with the presentation of conclusions:

thus
therefore
hence
so
because
consequently
as a result

Any of these expressions is a powerful cue enabling us to understand the argumentative structure of a passage or utterance. Still, there is no algorithm or precise recipe for determining the best interpretation of an argument. It's really a matter of reading the passage, getting an overall sense of the reasoning, and then reconstructing it as precisely as possible, in a way that best represents both the speaker's broad intent and specific wording.

This makes it more than a little tricky coming up with an interpretation of the argument that is intelligible and as plausible as possible, given what was actually said. A key principle in this interpretive process is **charity**. The idea is that one should always engage, not necessarily the argument exactly as spoken or written, but the best version of the argument that is roughly consistent with the speaker's words and recognizable intent. Sometimes people misspeak, sometimes they make simple and obviously correctable mistakes in otherwise interesting arguments. The principle of charity cautions against trying to score cheap points when this happens. Interpret arguments generously instead: fix these mistakes on behalf of your interlocutor, and engage the improved version of the argument.

One reason to do this is not to be a jerk. But another reason is to make your contribution meaningful. If you give a criticism that can be easily avoided just by modifying the original argument in some way that charity would have suggested anyhow, then you've wasted your time. The criticism will be short-lived and pointless. But if you can present a genuine criticism of the best version of the argument that you can construct on your interlocutor's behalf, you're likelier to have made a point that will stick—one worth taking seriously because it cannot be vitiated by a simple rewording.

The principle of charity itself does not always dictate one particular kind of response to an argument. When interpreting or reconstructing someone's argument, we are sometimes in the position of being able to trade obvious invalidity for obviously false premises; in this case it's difficult to say what charity requires. Suppose someone says, "There's no way Jill's read any great literature; I mean, she drinks generic beer!" As uttered, this reasoning is glaringly invalid. But which is more charitable: to depict the speaker as believing that this obviously invalid argument is valid, or to insert on the speaker's behalf a dopey implicit premise along the lines of *People who drink generic beer never read great literature*? (In fact, the most charitable assumption might be that the speaker was joking. Sadly, there are many such cases in which the speaker is clearly serious.) What really matters is that the argument is unsound either way.

SPECIAL STYLES OF REASONING AND ARGUMENTATION

The most straightforward cases of argumentation are those we started with: explicit premises, clearly identified conclusions, couched in language that is as literal as possible. So far in this chapter we have seen a variety of complications common to arguments as they are actually formulated and communicated: implicature, rhetorical effects, premises and conclusions containing vague and ambiguous terms, and others. Some styles of argumentation have more characteristic properties, though, due to their particular content or to the methods by which they work.

Moral Arguments

In most ways moral reasoning is like reasoning more generally. I explained in Chapter 1 that for most purposes the premises in an argument about morality or ethics can be treated similarly to those in other kinds of arguments. Moreover, when we consider not just the truth of the premises but also the kinds of inferences characteristic of moral or ethical discourse, it's fair to say there are few or no canons of good reasoning that apply only to the moral domain. The general requirements of argumentation apply, but any further standards in the form of moral principles tend to be culture-specific guidelines or moral theories of varying degrees of generality and plausibility. Many common fallacies in moral discourse, too, are not unique to moral discourse. For example, the assessment of praise and blame is frequently subject to fallacies of **false dichotomy**, discussed in detail in Chapter 4. In brief, it is a mistake in reasoning to assume that there are only two options where other options may also be open. But this line of thought seems particularly tempting when moral responsibility is under consideration. Consider how often reasoning like the following surfaces: "It's stupid to blame violent behaviour among children on the manufacturers of violent video games and movies. Parents are responsible for what their kids watch and play." This reasoning clearly assumes that it's not an option to hold both parents *and* the entertainment industry partially responsible for (certain cases of) such violence. Blame is very often treated as an all-or-nothing thing, but this pattern of poor reasoning extends widely beyond the moral domain.

Some patterns and pitfalls in argumentation are unique to or highly characteristic of moral discourse in particular, though. One example is the **Tu Quoque Fallacy,** a fallacy of distraction or relevance (these categories are discussed in Chapter 4). One commits Tu Quoque—Latin for "You too!" roughly—when one responds to a moral criticism by pointing out that someone else (especially the person issuing the criticism) is also open to a moral criticism.

Molly from France: "Canadians haven't always been the good guys, you know. Didn't Canadian soldiers torture and murder someone in Somalia?"
Eric the Canadian: "Aren't you forgetting that French agents bombed a Greenpeace boat, murdering a photographer in the process?"

In this example, Eric commits the Tu Quoque Fallacy, since the French military has no bearing on the truth of Molly's claims and the cogency of her reasoning (which is strong, mostly because her conclusion is so easily satisfied; nobody is *always* the "good guys," after all). On the other hand, there are contexts in which that response might be relevant; in that case, it would not be a fallacy.

Molly from France: "France is a better international citizen than Canada. Didn't Canadian soldiers torture and murder someone in Somalia?"
Eric the Canadian: "Aren't you forgetting that French agents bombed a Greenpeace boat, murdering a photographer in the process?"

Here we should say that while Molly and Eric are both offering extremely weak single pieces of evidence, relative to Molly's broad general claim, Eric's response is at least not a Tu Quoque fallacy. In this case he raises a point relevant to Molly's *comparative* claim.

Another issue in reasoning characteristic of moral discourse stems from a major problem in the history of moral philosophy, the **Is-Ought problem**. The eighteenth-century philosopher David Hume was the first person to really make the problem explicit: namely, that no collection of premises stated in purely non-moral vocabulary seems deductively sufficient to prove a moral conclusion. You can't get an Ought from an Is, as the saying goes (nor from a bunch of Is's, for that matter). The saying is somewhat inaccurate, on the other hand, since in one sense nothing stops us from invoking a premise like "Murder *is* wrong." The idea behind the Is-Ought problem is better communicated as a problem of inferring conclusions containing moral terms from premises not containing moral terms. So in this respect the issue is again quite general, applying to arguments of all kinds: you can't validly introduce predicates in the conclusion that you didn't have in the premises.

Another long-standing question within moral philosophy is whether the inability to prove moral statements from non-moral statements somehow reflects badly on moral claims—whether it means that moral statements aren't factual or meaningful, for instance. But for our purposes, the concern is simply that people often do seem to infer moral conclusions from non-moral premises. Since no successful such argument is known, how can we understand these arguments? The two broad explanations are that such arguments have implicit premises or that they are simply fallacious.

Sometimes arguments that appear to extract an Ought from an Is just have implicit premises expressing moral concepts. These can be perfectly good moral arguments. I might argue:

> "Ted tricked senior citizens into giving him their savings. Therefore he should be legally prosecuted."

Clearly this argument is invalid at it stands, since from the fact that Ted tricked senior citizens it does not logically follow that he should be legally prosecuted. But a charitable audience would understand me to be assuming some sort of moral principle as an implicit premise; something like "Anyone who tricks senior citizens out of their savings should be prosecuted." Then the argument is valid:

1. Ted tricked senior citizens into giving him their savings.
2. Anyone who tricks senior citizens out of their savings should be prosecuted.
Therefore,
3. Ted should be legally prosecuted.

If my audience accepts the truth of the premises, this will make the conclusion rationally compelling. If they don't accept one or more premises, of course, I'll have to defend those premises with further argument—again, without merely offering non-moral considerations as premises, if my argument is to be valid. As discussed in Chapter 1, this process can lead to an indefinite regress, in principle. But this fact alone does not distinguish moral reasoning from argument more generally, which can often involve regresses of justification for premises. So there's no special reason to reject moral arguments on this score, only reason to look for shared moral principles upon which to base discussions.

In other cases, however, arguers might genuinely attempt to extract a moral conclusion from alleged facts about the world. This is called the **Naturalistic Fallacy**. Here is an illustrative passage from Thomas Aquinas:

> [W]hatever is in accord with nature is best, for in all things nature does what is best. Now every natural governance is governance by one. In the multitude of bodily members there is one which is the principal mover, namely, the heart; and among the powers of the soul one power presides as chief, namely, the reason. Among bees there is one king bee, and in the whole universe there is One God, Maker and Ruler of all things. And there is a reason for this. Every multitude is derived from unity. Wherefore, if artificial things are an imitation of natural things and a work of art is better according as it attains a closer likeness to what is in nature, it follows that it is best for a human multitude to be ruled by one person.[6]

This is a stark example of the Naturalistic Fallacy. Aquinas gives some examples of nature intended to establish that rule by a single power *is* the norm in nature, and therefore *ought* to be the arrangement for humans as well. While Aquinas's examples largely amount to false or dubious premises (for instance, it is far from clear what it would mean for any single organ of the body to be "the principal mover," and Aquinas seems to think that beehives are organized around a king rather than a queen), the bigger problem is that the argument is invalid. Even if Aquinas had written about queen bees rather the king bees, there would be the same gap in his argument: the inference from how things *are* to how they *ought* to be.

There are a few red flags suggesting that the Naturalistic Fallacy is being committed: an arguer's explicit references to alleged facts about nature when a moral question is under discussion; claims about what is natural or unnatural, especially when these terms are used in a way that indicates an implicit moral judgment; or just analogies linking human moral questions with natural phenomena. Not all such invocations of nature in moral discussions are fallacious, of course. If two people agree that providing food for hungry people is morally important in a situation, then it is clearly no fallacy for one of them to argue that it's morally best to plant a particular strain of wheat, since that strain grows best in the relevant conditions and will produce the most food. This brings facts about nature into a moral argument, but non-fallaciously, since no one is arguing that the moral principle itself *follows from* what's natural. In the above example, by contrast, Aquinas attempts to infer what is morally or politically right for humans from some alleged examples of what is natural, making it an instance of the fallacy.

It is especially common for the Naturalistic Fallacy to occur in negated form, moving from premises about what is unnatural to defend the claim that some human action is wrong. Here too the inference fails, on virtually any interpretation of what "unnatural" means.

It is substantive but morally irrelevant to say that something is unnatural, if this means only that it is not characteristic of nature—for instance, if it's relatively rare. In this sense, phenomena like comets passing within 10,000 kilometres of Earth and very rare physical elements would count as unnatural or aberrant. Since there's little sense to the idea that lanthanum, terbium, and other rare elements are wrong or evil, there's no reason to accept a moral inference from *unnatural* to *wrong* in this sense of the term. At the other extreme, calling something unnatural might just be another way of calling it evil or wrong. One might say that "unnatural" means "wrong" just as a matter of stipulative definition. This would get the intended connection between appeals to nature and morality, but would make any claim of the form "X is wrong because X is unnatural" completely trivial.

Are there interpretations that fall somewhere in between these extremes? Some candidates suggest themselves. Sometimes what people seem to mean by calling something unnatural is just that they find it *distasteful*. "Unnatural" may be an acceptable word for indicating disgust in some contexts, but again this interpretation supports no moral conclusion. I find raw oysters rather disgusting, but this is insufficient grounds to conclude that people who eat them are morally defective. Another intermediate use of the term is roughly to distinguish objects or events caused by humans from those not caused by humans, so that "unnatural" means something like "artificial." Something like this notion of artificiality, combined with the earlier conception of naturalness as typicality, seems to be involved when, for example, we discuss whether someone died of *natural causes*. This is meant to exclude not just homicide and suicide, but also accidents—in the sense of *atypical deaths*—of most sorts. We normally would not say that someone who was killed in a cougar attack died of natural causes, even though cougars are perfectly natural creatures, and attacking humans is a perfectly natural thing for them to do. Again there is no moral "payload" to this notion of naturalness. The whole of medicine is a human intervention, so unless curing childhood diseases is wrong, there can be no general inference from artificiality to immorality. And of course the very distinction between human and nature is far from clear. It may be no less natural for humans to kill each other than for ants to do so; in this sense, homicides are as natural as heart attacks.

A final conception of what's unnatural involves the more basic notion of a "proper function": what a system in nature is *for*. This idea can seem very intuitive, especially in biological contexts. What is the body's immune system for? To fight off disease. What is a chameleon's camouflage for? To make it less visible to predators and prey. And so forth. Here we do get at least some notion of right and wrong out of the concept of the natural, since it's quite reasonable to say that there's something *wrong* with an immune system that stops fighting germs or with a chameleon that can't change colour. But this is not a moral notion of wrongness; it's a functional notion of wrongness. In this sense, we can talk about even a robbery going wrong, when the police catch the robbers. Clearly this does not mean that the robbery became *morally* wrong only when the police intervened. So this way of connecting what's unnatural with what's immoral also does not succeed. This is especially obvious when we consider the move from non-human to human examples.

Counter-examples abound. Lions (that is, males of the species) are known to kill any lion cub they encounter except for their own, a system that seems every bit as functional a natural arrangement as the examples just listed. What is a lion's cub-killing behaviour *for*? Maximizing its own genetic representation in the pride, apparently. (Killing another lion's cubs leaves the mothers prepared to mate again, giving the infanticidal lion a chance to impregnate them.) This system may function well, all things considered, but there's no temptation to say that the lions are doing a morally good thing in killing cubs. Nor, especially, is there any temptation to say that a man should behave similarly, on pain of being unnatural! All sorts of things occur among other animals that would (and do) horrify us if committed among humans. But it's completely unprincipled to argue from what's natural when we like the conclusions, while disowning parallel arguments when the conclusions are grotesque. Arguments from what's unnatural to what's wrong frequently are just such rationally unprincipled ways of selectively invoking aspects of nature in a moralistic argument.

Looking at things from the other direction, moreover, we find that some of what we consider highly moral behaviour is uncommon in the rest of the animal world—unnatural, if you will. Long-term dedicated projects devoted to altruistic ends, such as sending food or financial aid for years on end to people one has never met, have no very clear analogue in the rest of nature. Moreover, there is a vast range of human pleasures and satisfactions that depend on non functional uses of biologically functional systems. It's hard to defend the idea that our taste buds are particularly *for* enjoying a large banana split or a fudge brownie, yet presumably we'd resist the conclusion that it is unnatural, hence immoral, to enjoy such pleasures. Naturalistic fallacies have just such a way of proving far too much to be ultimately plausible.

For example, a pastor complaining about the homosexual rights movements provocatively writes:

> One does not need a Ph.D. to realize that homosexuality is anatomically aberrant; that is, there is a created biological order intended in our sexuality. As an editorialist at Harvard's *Peninsula* journal writes: "How can (homosexual) people be happy when they're persistently deceiving themselves, believing that it is just as natural for sperm to swim into feces as it is to swim into eggs?"[7]

This reasoning from what's natural and unnatural may seem superficially convincing to people whose prejudices it indulges. But on closer inspection, the overwhelming majority of Canadians turn out to fall on the wrong side of the line it tries to draw. After all, if we take the natural purpose of sperm to be "to swim into eggs," as the cited quote tells us, then it is equally unnatural for sperm to swim into non-ovulating or otherwise infertile uteruses, into condoms, tissue, saliva, or into thin air. But if we aren't willing to reject *these* "unnatural" practices as morally or socially defective, then there's no principled argument on offer here. The writer's main error is not a factual one about what the biological order really is—not even if he's wrong about that. Different answers might be defended on that question, depending on what our explanatory interest is. The real whopper is the attempt to extract a conclusion about what is right or wrong, worthwhile or pointless, happy or unhappy, based solely on a claim about the natural order.

Included in moral argument is reasoning that attempts to assess responsibility for actions, especially for the purposes of assigning praise and blame. Much argument of this sort incorporates non-moral reasoning; for example, causal reasoning

CHAPTER 3 *Language, Non-Language, and Argument*

about whether some outcome would have occurred had someone not acted as she did. Assigning blame for some event often crucially involves deciding who played the most direct, or the most avoidable, causal role in bringing it about.

But other factors come into play as well, including especially the *intention* with which an act was performed. An important consideration is whether someone *means* specifically to produce the outcome regarded as harmful or beneficial, immoral or moral. (We normally don't think that someone has to want to act immorally in order for their action to be immoral.) Whether some outcome was intended or accidental is normally a relevant factor for moral argument. If the latter, this is often taken to reduce the moral weightiness of the action, good or bad. I might accidentally foil a robbery by causing a traffic accident that delays the robber, but all other things being equal, in this situation I would not merit praise for my action. Similarly, when accidental occurrences lead to harm, there may not be anyone who actually deserves criminal blame. This is not to say that intention makes all the difference, however. Especially when it comes to applying borderline moral-legal categories like *accountability*, as opposed to moral blameworthiness, the actual action I performed, or its effects, may prove far weightier than what I meant to do when it comes to assessing blame. Judging someone's actions irresponsible or negligent is often a matter of emphasizing the actual consequences of their actions over the intention with which they were performed.

Comparative and Individual Reasoning

One important contrast between styles of reasoning or contexts that require particular approaches to a problem can be seen in situations that call for the singular evaluation of a single thing or case and those calling for a comparison between two things. We might call these **individual reasoning** and **comparative reasoning**. Some contexts of reasoning are properly comparative and some are not, once we factor in the nature of the problem and our interest in it. To confuse either sort of context with the other is a recipe for error.

Clear examples of comparative reasoning arise when we look at the frequent necessity of choosing between the options available in a situation. As a voter in an election, I may have four or five choices: to vote for one of Candidates A, B, C, or D, or not to vote at all. As I reflect on the positive and negative consequences of each possible choice, I may well wistfully think, "If only the Rhinoceros Party of Canada still existed! I'd like to vote for them." But this preference is irrelevant to the choice before me. My individual preference for the Rhino Party doesn't play a role in the comparative reasoning at hand, because the Rhino Party is not one of the available choices. By the same token, individual reasoning about the options that *are* at hand is also insufficient. I might decide, on the basis of individual reasoning about each of them, that each of A, B, and C are not good candidates and conclude that voting for candidate D therefore makes sense, or that not voting at all makes sense. But however reasonable my judgments about A, B, and C are, taken individually, it remains open that D is the worst choice of all. (Not voting at all might also amount to the worst choice, since not voting effectively helps whoever actually wins; the only difference your voting could have made is a negative one, from the winner's perspective.)

This is one situation in which comparative reasoning must be explicitly employed, then. It is a mistake to reason that, because each of A, B, and C has some negative property, D is therefore the best choice. The question isn't whether each candidate is good or bad. The question is which is the best among the available options, and, moreover, whether voting for any is better than, say, deliberately spoiling one's ballot by way of protesting an unappealing slate of candidates. (It is because so many contexts of action are comparative that critical thinking often implicates the field known as **decision theory**: the formal study of how to weigh competing choices in the most rational way.)

The opposite error can also arise. Many questions and problems call for answers framed in terms of standards or criteria, and not merely a comparison between individuals or options. If traffic law explicitly requires that you come to a complete stop at an intersection, there is no point in arguing in court that you at least slowed down more than other people who were ticketed for not stopping. In some cases, however, it's unclear which style of reasoning is appropriate to the circumstances. For example, teachers, professors, and students are frequently exercised by the question of whether the grades in a course will be "belled" or standardized— that is, whether they will be mathematically bumped up or down in varying complex ways, in order to get a particular average grade or distribution for the class as a whole. This is essentially the question of whether to set the individual grades according to each student's performance (measured against independent standards) or to set them by comparison to other grades. Working from criteria or rubrics that list the properties that the work should have in order to get each level of grade, one might accept that it's at least possible for every student in a class to get an A, or to get an F for that matter, depending only on how each piece of work measures up to those standards. Working from the assumption that grading is really a comparison of each student with the other students, one might decide instead that a particular grade—say, a C+—conventionally designates an average performance and then adjust the grades of a group so that the average is C+. In practice, aspects of both approaches are likely to figure in a teacher's approach to grading, at least implicitly, with differences between teachers amounting to a *degree* of preference for comparative or individual evaluations.

Visual Argument: Communicating with Pictures

Language has been around for a long, long time, and so have been the basic tools for analyzing linguistic argumentation. So while language is both ubiquitous and deeply influential on our thinking abilities and thought contents, there are also well-developed ways of understanding how some of its strengths, like its emotive force, its connotations, and its context-sensitivity, can facilitate poor reasoning (in the form of rhetoric, slanting language, and equivocation, for example—discussed at greater length in Chapter 4).

By contrast, the communicative and argumentative roles of visual imagery have gone from marginal to central in little more than a century, beginning with the rise of mass media capable of printing photographs and illustrations. Most of this shift has occurred within the past fifty years, as broadcast and other electronic media have become widespread. This represents an explosive increase in the influence of photography and video upon our thinking, an increase the scope of which has not been matched by analytical and educational measures aimed at encouraging critical thinking about communicative imagery.

It might be a cause or an effect of this lack of development that categorizing the methods of visual communication is particularly difficult. For our purposes it's almost enough to emphasize the fact that photographs and video clips *can* function as premises, conclusions, or even as implicit arguments themselves. Being aware of these functions is the crucial first step in recognizing and analyzing the information, deliberately formulated or not, that a particular piece of imagery conveys.

Obviously the message communicated or the effect achieved by a visual image is a matter of the objects or events depicted in the image. The message can be more or less precise depending on such factors as the number, kind, arrangement, and presentation of the objects. A photograph of a starving child may communicate any number of things through a kind of implicature, centring on the presumably shared view that childhood starvation is a horrible thing. A photograph of a starving African child standing back-to-back with a plump middle-aged Canadian white man plausibly conveys a more specific message about the injustice, or maybe hypocrisy, or both, implicit in the different standards of living of rich and poor.

A basic means of communicating a point through imagery is by this technique of picturing two things together, known as juxtaposition. But there are many more approaches to communicating or persuading via pictures. As we saw in the case of implicature, what is not said in an utterance can be its most communicatively significant aspect. Similarly, what's left out of a picture is as important as what's in it.

One of the most powerful aspects of a photograph is the way that it captures and isolates an instant, turning a fraction of a second of some event into a permanent object of attention. But this is also one of the main red flags of photographs when used as evidence or to shape opinions: they entirely erase the *temporal* context. What happened a moment earlier or a moment later? What happened an hour earlier, an hour later? A photograph rarely contains enough information to answer such questions, yet it tempts us to regard it as an authoritative record. Parallel considerations apply to video imagery, which of course depicts an interval of time, but still has a start and a finish.

In fact, any photograph or video would raise this red flag, but the fact that imagers (to invent a term covering photographers and videographers) and image publishers are involved makes the issue more important. Photographers rarely shoot pictures randomly, and publishers (be they based in newspapers, television, magazines, or the Internet) *never* publish them randomly. Photographs and video make their way into the public record because the imager tried to capture something interesting, and because the images that were judged interesting, significant, or persuasive were subsequently selected. This means that a range of interests other than—and possibly inimical to—the goal of accurate representation of events is almost always part of the process by which photographic or videographic information reaches us.

One of the most historically significant Canadian examples of the missing context of images relates to the 1974 federal election, in which Progressive Conservative party leader Robert Stanfield's public image was damaged by a photograph of

FIGURE 3.1

Robert Stanfield Drops the Ball

This 1974 photograph of Robert Stanfield dropping a football is a historic example of how one picture may not reveal the full context of an event. A picture may be worth a thousand words—but one image may not tell the whole story.

CP Photo/Doug Ball

him awkwardly dropping a football. During a refuelling stopover in North Bay, Ontario, Stanfield spent time throwing the football with an aide; though the photographer took many pictures of him catching passes, the one picture of Stanfield dropping the ball was printed on the front page of many newspapers across Canada (Figure 3.1).[8] A single awkward moment, with no hint of the surrounding context, was taken by some to symbolize Stanfield's bid to be prime minister. (He lost.)

Similar worries attach to the *spatial* cropping of images. Every image is implicitly framed by its edges, and the possibility always exists that something just outside the frame would change our interpretation of what's in the image, were we aware of it. For example, a famous set of photographs and video footage shot during the multinational invasion of Iraq in April 2003 seemed to show a large crowd of Baghdad citizens celebrating the destruction by American soldiers of a statue of defeated dictator Saddam Hussein. By framing the scene tightly around the Iraqi civilians present for the event, both kinds of image gave the impression of a large, thronging crowd. Images of this sort were widely published and rebroadcast in the news media for days, even weeks after the event. Yet later analysis of wider-angle images indicated that the crowd was relatively small; virtually everyone present was squeezed into the most widely circulated photographs and video. Whatever the reasons for the more popular tight cropping—it may have been merely aesthetic—one effect of it was seemingly to bolster a prediction made before the invasion by some of its advocates: that foreign troops would be enthusiastically welcomed as liberators by Iraqi citizens. Viewed in wide angle, the images did not convey that sense.

Similarly, a photograph that saw considerable newspaper distribution in Canada was a 2002 image of Prime Minister Jean Chrétien onstage listening to Finance Minister Paul Martin give a speech. Stories of a rift between the two had been common in the news, and when a picture became available of Chrétien

FIGURE 3.2

Jean Chrétien: Piqued or Parched?

Is Jean Chrétien angry at Paul Martin's speech or does he have a mouthful of water? Viewers who saw the photo without the water bottle, or who saw the photo with a caption describing Chrétien as annoyed, probably thought the former. The parts of a photograph that are left in or out, as well as contextual information we are given about it, can affect our perceptions of what the photograph conveys.

CP Photo/Tom Hanson

blowing his cheeks out in petulance or frustration at Martin's speech, it was widely published (Figure 3.2).

Yet far down at the bottom of the picture, nearly cropped out altogether and lost in the visual clutter, another explanation sits. Chrétien in fact is replacing the lid on a bottle of water: he is not making a face; he is taking a drink. An observant reader might notice this, but with only a little more cropping the true explanation of the photograph would have become completely invisible.

When we deal with video imagery, cropping can come to take on the character of visual "quote-mining," with bits and pieces stitched together to create a misleading impression. One of the more prominent examples of this phenomenon with video imagery came in the case of American coma patient Terri Schiavo, who existed for over a decade in a "persistent vegetative state" after entering a coma in 1990. In 2005 she died after her feeding tube was removed at her husband's request. But many legal, political, and public opinion battles were fought over the case, as Schiavo's parents and many other people contended that she retained some basic personality and cognitive functions.

The most influential factor in motivating public and political support for this conclusion was a collection of video evidence, several minutes long, which seemed to show Schiavo interacting with her family and reacting mindfully to questions and other stimuli. These video clips of a few seconds in length were repeatedly played on television news or were circulated on the Internet. Some of these, showing a smiling woman who makes eye contact with her mother, for example, powerfully suggested the presence of a mind. An opinion columnist in one magazine wrote of the case:

> [A] picture is worth 1,000 words. Videotapes of Terri clearly show her responding to requests. For example, a closed-eyed Terri is asked to open her eyes by a doctor. Her eyes flutter and she does as he requests. She is asked in another video to follow a balloon with her eyes, and she does. In a heartbreaking video, Terri's mother kisses her on the cheek and Terri smiles and responds, clearly happy that her mom is with her.[9]

Striking though these images were, they turned out to have been culled from hours of footage; seen in that context, the few publicized clips seem to show random rather than reasoned behaviour. In context, for example, Schiavo's apparently looking into her mother's eyes and smiling is revealed to be a fixed gaze and fixed expression, with her mother moving into the eye-line. Without context, the clip appeals powerfully to our tendency to read intention into human face-to-face interaction.

These video clips clearly played a role in the deep public polarization over the case, with many of those who opposed the withdrawal of life support accusing the courts of condoning the murder of someone who *obviously* retained cognitive functions. Yet the autopsy performed on Schiavo confirmed that she was not merely in an untreatable vegetative state, but was altogether blind. She simply could not have been watching balloons, still less seeking and maintaining eye contact with people.[10] Powerful as the edited clips were, they misled their viewers by presenting stitched-together randomness and reflex in a way that created the appearance of intention and interest.

INTERPRETING AND ANALYZING ARGUMENTS: DETAILED EXAMPLES

We almost always give arguments in ways that require substantial interpretation and reconstruction by anyone who wants to analyze the argument carefully. Part of presenting an argument well is minimizing the amount of reconstruction your audience has to perform on it. But even writers and speakers who are uncommonly good at presenting ideas will often have us thinking hard to understand *exactly* how their reasoning is supposed to work. I will work through an interpretation and analysis of one such passage, as a means of showing what is involved in these processes.

The example I will use is a passage from John Stuart Mill's famous 1863 essay "Utilitarianism." Mill is defending the idea that there is a fundamental moral requirement to maximize utility, that is, to increase happiness.

Mill's argument:

> No reason can be given why the general happiness is desirable, except that each person, so far as he believes it to be attainable, desires his own happiness. This, however, being a fact, we have not only all the proof which the case admits of, but all which it is possible to require, that happiness is a good: that each person's happiness is a good to that person, the general happiness, therefore, a good to the aggregate of all persons.

Clearly there is at least one argument on display here. But saying just what it is can be difficult. One plausible way of interpreting the argument is as two inferences one after the other.

Mill's argument clarified:

1. Each individual person desires his or her own happiness.

Therefore,

2. Happiness is a good to each person.

Therefore,

3. The general happiness is a good to everybody.

Let's focus on this particular argument to get a sense of how argument analysis works.

For one thing, you can see that the reconstruction does not quite follow the order of the points in the quoted passage. That's because the quote starts off with a claim that does not really get represented in my reconstruction, namely, that "the general happiness is desirable." Why not? When I read the passage, I see Mill basically doing two things: moving from what is desired to what is good, and moving from the individual case to the general case. The argument I've given puts these moves in just that order, so the generalizing move comes after the move from what's desired to what's good. That's the order in which Mill summarizes his reasoning in the last sentence, after all. But in the first sentence he seems to put things in the opposite order. Since this doesn't seem to make much difference, I've chosen what seems the more elegant way of presenting the argument.

The question, then, is whether (3) really follows from (1) via (2). And does (3) mean what Mill needs it to mean?

First, the inference from (1) to (2) is invalid if "good" in (2) is understood as "morally good" rather than just "good, from that agent's perspective." In other words, that a person happens to desire x does not entail that she *ought* to desire x. There seem to be two notions of goodness in play, with too little effort to keep them distinct. Of course, anyone who desires something may, to that extent, regard the object of desire as a good. But there seems to be a difference between "good for me" (call this good-1, for convenience) and "morally good" (good-2), and Mill's argument does not respect this difference, since (1) is about good-1, but utilitarianism presumably aims at having individual people maximize the happiness of other people as well, so it must involve good-2. Mill can't be arguing that *in fact* everyone desires the general good; surely his argument is that they *should*, whether they do or not.

Suppose, though, that we interpret the argument as involving good-1 all the way through. That way, we at least get the inference from (1) to (2). Still, in order to get the inference to (3) we are forced to equivocate on the notion of the aggregate of all persons, or "everybody," as I have put it. (To equivocate means to use a single word in two different ways, as is discussed in the next chapter.) If we understand this to mean, literally, the collection of all individuals, then there is a sense in which (3) follows from (2). However, it is a rather strange sense, since *collections* do not seem the right sort of things to have happiness, nor to seek the moral good, for that matter. It is *persons* who have and do these things.

In any case, since utilitarianism is a moral theory, Mill's argument is supposed to establish that the general happiness is a good for *each* person. Otherwise utilitarianism would not tell us, as individual agents, to maximize the general utility, but only our own particular happiness. So the term "everybody" must refer to each person individually if it is to support Mill's position. On that reading, though, (3) follows from (2) only if "happiness," in (2), means the *general* happiness—while we have already seen that it means the *personal* happiness of each individual. This is like arguing, about a group of twenty people.

1. Each person donated five cents.
Therefore,
2. Everybody donated one dollar.
Therefore,
3. Each person donated one dollar.

There is a sense in which we can move from (1) to (2), and a sense in which we can move from (2) to (3), but these are obviously not the *same* sense. Hence the argument from (1) to (3) commits the fallacy of equivocation. Mill's seems to require just this sort of move, too.

The fact that each person's goal is her own happiness does not entail that the goal of each person actually is to maximize the amount of all happiness. Nor does it mean that each person *ought* to have that, or any, goal. The argument expressed in the passage quoted above thus appears invalid on at least two counts.

If that seems a great deal of argument analysis for a passage consisting of two sentences, it's worth noting that we could easily go into much *more* detail here. For instance, I have not "anticipated objections"—that is, I haven't considered just how Mill (or a defender of Mill) might reply to my analysis at each stage, nor have I explored how I might in turn reply to his counter-objections. This is an important element of effective argument and critique, which I am shortchanging in this case for the sake of brevity. There is a general lesson lurking here: that offering an idea can be quick and easy, while carefully making sense of the idea can be slow and difficult. And this is all true of the passage from Mill, which is actually quite clear and helpful by normal standards of argumentation. Much of our discourse consists of arguments on which it is much harder to impose any degree of rigour.

Compare, for example, an utterance like the following:

> We've tried listening to experts, and look at the state of the world. Who could come up with something better, the government? Yeah, right! Democracy is about you and me getting our say. Shouldn't we try that instead?

This, I submit, is the sort of thing that is offered as an argument quite frequently in ordinary conversation. How might we go about taking it seriously? We might upon reflection read this utterance as containing anything from zero to several different arguments. I think there are two roughly distinct lines of reasoning "in there," but neither can be made both sound and interesting.

CHAPTER 3 *Language, Non-Language, and Argument*

First argument:

1. Our society (perhaps the whole world?) has made an effort to formulate laws and (or?) policies on the basis of what experts (of some sort) say.
2. This effort has led to unspecified bad consequences.
3. It is implausible that the government could do any better than the intellectuals already mentioned, at whatever task had been entrusted to them.
4. You and I (the majority?) have not yet had our say in formulating laws/policies.
5. There is some reason to believe that you and I would do no worse at formulating laws/policies than does the current arrangement.

Therefore,

6. You and I (the majority?) should formulate laws/policies.

Second argument:

1. According to the principles of democratic government, you and I should have our say in formulating laws/polices.
2. The principles of democratic government are correct.

Therefore,

3. You and I (the majority?) should have our say in formulating laws/policies.

Even supposing we could build in enough principles to make the first argument valid, it clearly suffers from a serious lack of precision in its premises. And where precise enough to evaluate, as with (1) and (4), the premises are very dubious and probably outright false. The second argument, extracted from the last two sentences of the passage, is at least valid. Its premises also have a pretty good claim to truth; as far as it goes, this looks like a sound argument. But it's hard to see what this is offered as an argument *against*. The interest or relevance of the second argument depends upon the truth of premises from the first argument—specifically premises like (1) and (4), which we have already noted as dubious. Uttering that (fictional) quote is the work of a few seconds in the course of a conversation, while working through it to determine whether it offers good reason to believe any significant conclusion is an awkward and difficult business. In this way a great deal of sloppy reasoning or pseudo-reasoning can seem to make a point with at least some sort of force, without it ever being revealed that it supports no relevant conclusion.

CONCLUSION

Arguments are communicated directly through the explicit content of language, and indirectly through gesture, tone, imagery, and rhetorical devices. By paying careful attention to these mechanisms of communication, we can recognize arguments and parts of arguments that may not be obvious, and we can detect more direct attempts to shape a discussion or influence opinions. Various styles of argument have potential red flags worth guarding against. Argument via quotation is susceptible to varieties of misquoting, for example, while moral argument is susceptible to the Naturalistic Fallacy and Tu Quoque Fallacy. Communication and persuasion through imagery can be powerful and vivid sources of information, but are also a style of argument open to misrepresentation through various means.

Now we have in place the vocabulary to discuss the components, kinds, and virtues of arguments. We have also got a feel for how to recover or interpret arguments from the things people write and say. In order to extend and refine the ability to understand arguments and to diagnose the problems they may have, our next step is to focus further on argument fallacies: how we make common mistakes in reasoning, and how useful debates are derailed.

REVIEW QUESTIONS

1. French author Anatole France wrote, "The law, in its majestic equality, forbids the rich as well as the poor to sleep under bridges, to beg in the streets, and to steal bread." Using concepts and categories discussed in this chapter, discuss the style(s) of reasoning and communication employed here.
2. Explain the key differences between vagueness and ambiguity.
3. Find and present a recent example from the Canadian media of either a quote or a photograph that is a red flag. Clearly explain just what you think red-flags the example you chose.

NOTES

1. Associated Press story, *Boston Globe*, October 21, 1985. Cited in Noam Chomsky, *Turning the Tide*, 2nd ed. Montreal: Black Rose Books, p. 121.
2. M. Pesca, "Fumble on the Kerry: The Truth about John Kerry's Sports Flubs," *Slate*. http://www.slate.com/id/2107251/ Posted Tuesday, Sept. 28, 2004. Accessed December 29, 2005.
3. J. Wheless, *Forgery in Christianity* (Moscow, Idaho: Psychiana), p. 16.
4. C. Thomas, "Silence of the Feminist Lambs" © 1999, Los Angeles Times Syndicate. http://www.capitolhillblue.com/Feb1999/022699/silence022699.htm. Posted February 26, 1999. Accessed December 15, 2005.
5. Freedom for Individual Rights in Education (FIRE), "About Speech Codes." http://www.thefire.org/index.php/article/5822.html. Accessed December 30, 2005.
6. T. Aquinas, *On Kingship,* Chapter 2, reprinted in *The Political Ideas of St Thomas Aquinas* (New York: Hafner Press, 1953), p. 180.
7. J. P. Gudel, *Christian Research Journal* (Winter 1993), p. 8. Citing R. Wasinger, "If You're Gonna Call Me Names . . ." *Peninsula* 3:2 (October/November 1991), p. 25.
8. CTV News, December 20, 2005. "Photographers Share Secrets Behind Enduring Photos." Published at http://www.ctv.ca/servlet/ArticleNews/print/CTVNews/20051220/lifeonapresspass_051220/20051220/?hub=CanadaAM&subhub=PrintStory. Accessed July 11, 2006.
9. W. J. Smith, "Schiavo's Date with Death: A Florida Woman Needs Non-dehydration Intervention." *National Review.* Published at http://www.nationalreview.com/comment/comment-smith090503.asp. September 5, 2003. Accessed July 3, 2006.
10. Associated Press report, "Schiavo Autopsy Shows Irreversible Brain Damage." Published at http://www.msnbc.msn.com/id/8225637/. June 15, 2005. Accessed June 10, 2006.

CHAPTER 4

Fallacies: When Arguments Turn Bad

We have seen that reasoning and argument are like most things—there are many more ways of doing them badly than there are of doing them well. Some errors or wrong turns in reasoning seem particularly enticing to us, though. Mistakes in argument tend to cluster into some recognizable patterns called **fallacies**. (Calling them mistakes is not necessarily to say that they are *accidental* mistakes, mind you; some forms of unreliable reasoning are deliberate attempts to mislead.) We can identify these forms of unreliable reasoning or misleading argument because they occur again and again. By labelling them and working out just what the recognizable patterns have in common, we can provide brief and useful diagnoses of the problem when we encounter it.

This chapter will lay out some broad distinctions among fallacies and explain the idea behind each kind by using a few examples. The three categories we will employ are Logical Fallacies, Evidential Fallacies, and Procedural or Pragmatic Fallacies. It's fair to say that the notion of a fallacy applies in a broader way in each successive category; the most general definition might be *a way of arguing that is unreliable*. Often the word is defined more specifically to mean something like an unsound argument or an argument that seems sound but isn't. But for better or worse (better, I think), the standard recognized literature on fallacies contains many entries that are best understood, not as specific ways for an argument to be unsound, but as ways for the process of discussion and argumentation itself to be undermined or sidetracked. The broader definition includes these examples.

This chapter by no means presents an exhaustive catalogue of known fallacies. Not even close. These are just enough common or otherwise important fallacies to give a sense of how different kinds of fallacies work. Some examples have already been discussed in earlier chapters; further examples will be added throughout the book as we consider different issues and as we look at explanations of *why* we are so susceptible to fallacious reasoning.

LOGICAL FALLACIES

One important class of fallacies, the logical fallacies, can be given formal or quasi-formal definitions with regard to argument structure. In one pretty obvious sense, any structurally invalid argument is logically fallacious; its premises do not suffice to logically determine the truth of its conclusion. In this sense logical invalidities are the largest class of fallacies, since both deductive and ampliative arguments that fail to bear out their conclusions will count as invalid. But not even all invalid arguments offered as deductive are logical fallacies of an interesting sort—that is, having some re-identifiable property worth recognizing on various occasions. And while non-cogent evidential arguments are (like cogent evidential arguments) also invalid, they too are categorized as fallacies for evidential, and not logical, reasons. With these provisos added, the class of logical fallacies becomes relatively small. If I say, "Pumpkins are orange; therefore, professional athletes are overpaid," clearly this is logically invalid (besides being ridiculous). But there's no very interesting fallacy committed there. The most precise logical diagnosis of the failure of that inference would just be that it's a **non sequitur**—a Latin term loosely translated as *it doesn't follow*. Another catch-all Latin term for such an argument is **ignoratio elenchi**: an argument with an irrelevant conclusion. Yet neither label says much more than that the argument is invalid. Sometimes, though, a much more precise category can be used to classify and explain an invalid argument. This section will review some illustrative examples of logical fallacies.

CONDITIONAL FALLACIES

Two well-known logical fallacies involving conditional arguments are **Denying the Antecedent** and **Affirming the Consequent**. Recall that the "if" part of a conditional statement is the antecedent, while the "then" part is the consequent. You can see that the names of these fallacies are based on what happens in the second premise of the argument-schemas below.

Affirming the Consequent:

1. If P then Q
2. Q
Therefore,
3. P

Denying the Antecedent:

1. If P then Q
2. It is not the case that P
Therefore,
3. It is not the case that Q

These are fallacies that are explicable in terms of their logical structures; in other words, arguments having these forms are invalid. The sentences we substitute for P and Q have no bearing on this fact. What makes these more interesting, fallacy-wise, than my example about pumpkins and athletes is their having re-identifiable structures, and the fact that people quite commonly confuse them for valid arguments. You could note that Affirming the Consequent half resembles Modus Ponens, while Denying the Antecedent is easily confused with Modus Tollens.

In fact it might not be obvious that these *are* fallacies the first time you glance at them. We can test their validity by the Method of Counter-example: interpretations that make the premises come out true, but the conclusion false. Again, if we can find such a counter-example, the argument-structure is not valid.

Affirming the Consequent:

1. If three plus three equals four, then three plus three equals an even number.
2. Three plus three equals an even number.
Therefore,
3. Three plus three equals four.

Clearly something's gone wrong here. Let's consider the other conditional fallacy before remarking on what it might be.

Denying the Antecedent:

1. If Kim Campbell's party won an election under her leadership, then Kim Campbell became prime minister.
2. Kim Campbell's party did not win an election under her leadership.
Therefore,
3. Kim Campbell did not become prime minister.

What's going wrong? The same thing in both cases, really. A conditional premise tells us that the truth of its antecedent is sufficient for the truth of its consequent. But that doesn't mean that the truth of the antecedent is necessary for the truth of the consequent. All sorts of different things may also be sufficient for the truth of the consequent, such as that six is an even number, in the first example, or that one can also become prime minister just by winning the leadership of the current majority party, in the second example—as Kim Campbell did in 1993. The point is quite general, moreover. If something is a fox, then it's a mammal, but there are lots of ways for something to be a mammal without being a fox, too.

In other words, both of these fallacies ignore the possibility that the consequent of a conditional is true even when its antecedent is false. Because this is a possibility with a conditional statement, we can't conclude from the truth of the consequent that the antecedent is true, nor from the falsity of the antecedent that the consequent is false. Suppose that if it's raining then it's cloudy; still we can't conclude from its being cloudy that it's raining, nor from its not raining that it's not cloudy. But that, respectively, is what Affirming the Consequent and Denying the Antecedent try to do.

SCOPE FALLACIES

Everyone shops for clothing at a store in town. Can we conclude that that store gets everyone's business? The question presupposes something contentious: that everyone shops at the *same* store. The sentence "Everyone shops for clothes at a store in town" displays an ambiguity of logical form, consistent with both (1) and (2).

1. Every person shops for clothing at one store (or another) in town.
2. There is one (particular) store in town at which every person shops for clothing.

Notice that (2) implies (1), but not vice versa; these are not the same claims. An argument that infers a specific statement like (2) from its unspecific version like (1) commits a **Quantifier Scope Fallacy**. This name for the fallacy indicates that it consists in a misordering of a **universal quantifier** (*all*, *every*, *each*) and an **existential quantifier** (*some, a, the, one*), resulting in an invalid inference. When an existential quantifier falls within the scope of a universal quantifier, as in (1) above, we cannot validly rewrite this with the universal quantifier falling within the scope of the existential quantifier, as in (2). Putting it in more concrete terms, from the statement that every patient saw a doctor, it's a fallacy to conclude that some one doctor was seen by every patient.

We already saw some formal problems with scope in Chapter 1, when we discussed negation in complex sentences. Those cases share with the quantifier cases the general problem of determining how logical operators or adjectives interact with other elements in a sentence. A Scope Fallacy is committed straightforwardly in the move from (1) to (2). It is committed indirectly if we take an ambiguous sentence like "Everyone shops for clothes at a store in town" and use a shifting interpretation of it—alternating between *treating it* as (1) and as (2). This shifting interpretation makes such an instance of the Quantifier Scope Fallacy into a complex sort of equivocation.

EQUIVOCATION

Consider the following argument, loosely based on an actual passage from a political lobby group:

> We spend a great deal of time and energy trying to get children to do what we expect of them. It's a real parenting success when your children make an effort to live up to your expectation that they be polite, honest, decent people. So we have to be very careful of the messages we send about what we expect. That's why it's a bad idea to teach condom use in schools. Some people say that if teens are likely to be sexually active, then they should be taught both the importance of abstinence and the proper way to use condoms. But as soon as adults teach young people about condom use, we clearly give them the message that we are expecting them to have sex. Why else would we be teaching about condoms? Of course our displaying this expectation will simply encourage more teens to become sexually active.

Here is one way of regimenting this argument:
1. Teens, like people in general, often make an effort to do what is expected of them.
2. Teaching condom use to teens shows that adults expect sexual activity among them.

Therefore,
3. Teaching condom use to teens will encourage them to become sexually active (or to try, at least).

There might be several things wrong with the argument given in this passage. A major problem, though, is that the argument commits the Fallacy of Equivocation: it disguises an invalid inference by using a single expression in two different ways. We saw this in the argument from John Stuart Mill in the previous chapter, in his use of the expressions "good" and "all persons." In this case the word is "expect."

In Premise 1 the word is used to mean *set a standard*. On this understanding, to tell someone you expect them be punctual is to indicate that punctuality is desired or obligatory. To indicate your expectations in this sense is indeed to encourage someone to meet them. But teaching condom use (especially in conjunction with emphasizing sexual abstinence) hardly imposes any sort of *request* or *obligation* to have sex, so this can't be how the term is being used in Premise 2. In the second premise, "expect" must be understood to mean the more minimal and neutral notion of "predict," since it is at least plausible that teaching condom use communicates that one is *predicting* that some people will have sex. The two interpretations are very different. It would be confusing but could be logically coherent to say, "I expect you to be punctual but I don't expect you to be punctual"—meaning "I'm holding you to the standard of punctuality, but I predict that you won't meet this standard."

But if the two premises are not really using the same word, or the same interpretation of a word, then Premise 2 is not appropriately related to Premise 1 and the conclusion. It's only the orthographic accident that "expect" (encourage) looks like "expect" (predict) that makes the argument seem valid. To argue by switching between meanings in this way is to *equivocate*. We could represent this fallacy as one of general soundness, on the grounds that, if the problematic expression is interpreted *univocally* (as having one meaning) then at least one of the premises containing it must be untrue, or at least implausible. But it can also be represented as a strictly logical fallacy by making the equivocal interpretation explicit—we could just replace "what is expected of them" with "what they are encouraged to do" in Premise 1 and "expect" with "predict" in Premise 2. Then the logical invalidity of the argument is obvious.

Now the sense in which these are logical fallacies should be clear: the arguments are presented as deductively valid, but they fail. And as we saw in comparing deductive arguments with ampliative arguments, in the deductive case there are no degrees of failed validity, at least not once we factor in implicit premises and conclusions. Either the argument is valid or the argument fails. But we've already seen that even though inductive or otherwise ampliative arguments are strictly deductively invalid, we cannot think of them as inherently fallacious. Just as the success conditions for arguments that deal in degrees of evidence are not a matter of deductive validity, the interesting ways in which such arguments can fail are not a matter of failures of validity. To examine the common patterns of mistaken reasoning in evidential arguments, we need to distinguish evidential fallacies from logical ones.

EVIDENTIAL FALLACIES

A good evidential argument shows its conclusion to be reasonably likely—with all the vagueness and context-dependence that "reasonably likely" suggests. Evidential fallacies are defined in terms of the failure to meet this aim. Of course, a fallacious evidential argument must also be logically unsound, but the diagnosis of its failure typically provides more information than this fact alone. Recall that any inductive argument is logically invalid, even a *strong* inductive argument—that is, one that provides reasonable grounds for its conclusion—so just pointing out that an inductive argument is unsound doesn't explain why it isn't even a good evidential argument. For that we need to think about the relationship between a state of information and some conclusion.

Consider, for example, the evidential fallacy known as Argument from Ignorance.

ARGUMENT FROM IGNORANCE

1. We have no evidence that P.
Therefore,
2. It is not the case that P.

This is considered a fallacy, for reasons that can be made quite intuitive. We all know of occasions on which we could have asserted a version of (1) about some claim, even though it later turned out that we found evidence, perhaps overwhelming evidence, for the relevant claim. In short, the mere fact that we're ignorant as to whether something is true doesn't mean that we're licensed to assert that it's false.

Putting the problem in terms of what we're entitled to assert is very different from diagnosing the fallacy in terms of its logical invalidity. Of course the Argument from Ignorance is invalid, but we wouldn't really capture what's interesting about the fallacy if that were all we noted about it. Indeed, it's not rare for the Argument from Ignorance to be (badly) explained in something like the following way: *From the mere fact that we don't have evidence that P, it doesn't follow that P is false.* This is correct, as far as it goes. But if that were what the fallacy amounted to, then one would commit precisely the same fallacy in arguing as follows:

Not the Argument from Ignorance:

1. We have excellent evidence that P.
Therefore,
2. P.

Notice that this argument too is logically invalid; the truth of a claim does not *validly* follow from the fact that we have excellent evidence in its favour. But it is clearly a better argument than the Argument from Ignorance. In fact, it seems obvious that this argument entirely succeeds by a standard that the Argument from Ignorance does not meet—that is, by the standards for evidential reasoning: showing the conclusion to be reasonable in light of the information available.

We need some way of characterizing the fallacy, then, so that it applies to the first argument but not to the second. All of which means that, even though the Argument from Ignorance is logically invalid, this fact is not what we're interested in when we point out that it's a fallacy. While evidentially fallacious reasoning is deductively invalid, it ought also to count as fallacious relative to *good* evidential reasoning, which is also deductively invalid. What distinguishes evidential fallacies from logical fallacies is their failure to provide good evidence for their conclusions. Evidential fallacies are patterns of reasoning that are frequently appealing, despite having weak or absent evidential connections between premises and conclusion. Fallacies of this sort are frankly more subtle, more numerous in kind, and much more frequently committed than logical fallacies; much of what follows will touch on evidential fallacies in one way or another.

What, then, of the Argument from Ignorance? Actually, it can be understood as the fallacious version of some broader reasoning we might call the **Argument from Missing Evidence**, a kind of reasoning that also has **non-fallacious instances**: arguments that share defining features with the fallacy but are cogent nonetheless. The real problem with arguing from ignorance is that there's no reason to think our mere lack of evidence shows much of anything, unless we can be confident that we are relatively well informed. In other words, we have to say more about how hard we've looked for evidence and how good we think our best methods are, relative to what evidence might be there for the finding, before we can reasonably take our lack of evidence for some claim as evidence against its truth.

Suppose I'm considering whether rhinoceroses exist, and what I do by way of evidence-gathering is this: I stand in my closet, take a hard look around it, and fail to discover any rhinoceroses. So there we have it: there are no such things as rhinos; another deep question settled. But obviously a lack of evidence after such a limited search of the world says nothing about the existence of rhinos in general. Just as evidential claims succeed by degrees of support, so do non-existence claims; strange as it may seem, my rhino-free closet would provide a degree of evidence, however uselessly weak, against the general existence of rhinos. If I had started from complete zoological ignorance, I could gradually increase that degree of evidence by surveying the Earth one rhino-free closet-sized area at a time, until, if I got unlucky, I had surveyed a really substantial portion of the planet without finding one and would then be in possession of non-trivial evidence that there were no rhinoceroses. (Eventually, of course, my sampling would take me to a zoo or to Africa, and I would learn firsthand both the inherent defeasibility of inductive reasoning and the inherent danger of being in closet-sized proximity to a rhino.)

If all we can say about P is that we have no evidence for it, then it is a fallacy to regard this as evidence that P is false. But if we can say that we have no evidence for P *after a thorough search using appropriate methods,* then this is itself a kind of positive evidence against P. Of course, we *might* always be just one closet-area away from the rhino, and this must always be borne in mind, but the more we look without finding one, the more confident we can be that we are not. In particular we ought to look in ways that seem well-suited to the search for that kind of thing; in this respect the rhinoceros example is a serious oversimplification. After all, we wouldn't just encounter the word "rhinoceros" and set off in search of one. That's probably an incoherent thought, in fact. We would have at least some sort of *definition* of a rhino, and this would give us theoretical grounds to restrict our search in helpful ways. For example, we might at least be able to rule out arid deserts and places with long cold winters in advance. In general, our searches for relevant information are powerfully informed by our best theoretical guesses about how to find it.

OVERGENERALIZATIONS

The broadest kind of evidential fallacy (really it's a family of fallacies) is that of drawing a general inference too strong for the specific evidence in hand. Framed in such imprecise terms, this makes for plenty of uncertain cases, examples that are only borderline fallacies. But some examples are clear enough to be diagnosed uncontroversially as **Hasty Generalizations** or **Sweeping Generalizations**. If I hear Ted say something stupid on two occasions, it is a Hasty Generalization for me to assert, "Ted is always saying something stupid." This is too strong a conclusion even if those are the only two occasions on which I have met Ted. Similarly, if I see several consecutive news reports about very corrupt Third World governments, I generalize sweepingly if I conclude that all, or even most, Third World governments are very corrupt. I've seen only a small sample of a fairly large domain, and there is of course reason to think that the sample was not random; chances are, those specific governments made the news precisely because they in particular were corrupt. As with the Argument from Ignorance, it can be important in diagnosing a Hasty Generalization to have some sense of the size and potential variations in the whole set of things about which one is generalizing.

CONSPIRACY THEORIES

A conspiracy is just a planned cooperative effort, usually to do something illegal and usually with the aim of keeping it quiet. Understood in these terms, conspiracies happen all the time. Yet to call something a conspiracy theory, or to call some person a conspiracy theorist, is usually not a compliment. It suggests a general nuttiness, with overtones of paranoia. Why?

When we talk about Conspiracy Theories as fallacies, we mean to identify a particular style of reasoning: a theory that says the conspiracy in question is so powerful, so widespread, that *all* evidence for its existence is carefully shielded or erased. Indeed, the conspiracy may even be thought capable of planting evidence that positively indicates its non-existence. The problem with this sort of theory is that, if it were true, an absence of evidence for its truth is exactly what we should expect to find. But since *this* outcome is what would normally lead us to reject the theory, in such a case the very conditions normally leading us to reject a theory are invoked as the best grounds for supposing the theory is true. On the face of it, the Argument from Conspiracy is a strange twist on the Argument from Ignorance.

1. There is no evidence that P.
2. No evidence is exactly what we should expect, if P is true.
Therefore,
3. P.

Naturally this is a recipe for all sorts of nonsense—the more a belief looks false, the better its conspiracy-theoretic claim to truth!

On the other hand, merely asserting the existence of a conspiracy is not intellectually disreputable or fallacious. There can be good evidence, direct or indirect, for the existence of a conspiracy—even a powerful conspiracy that makes some successful efforts to suppress evidence of its existence and operation. This is a point that can easily be lost when the term "conspiracy theory" takes on inherently negative connotations. For example, the United States Department of State posted a set of guidelines for journalists on its website, encouraging the journalists to "identify misinformation" by a set of criteria. The first criterion was whether a story "fits the pattern of a conspiracy theory." But the guidelines went on to run together conspiracy theories in the obviously fallacious sense with conspiracy theories in the more general sense:

> Does the story claim that vast, powerful, evil forces are secretly manipulating events? If so, this fits the profile of a conspiracy theory. Conspiracy theories are rarely true, even though they have great appeal and are often widely believed. In reality, events usually have much less exciting explanations.[1]

Of course, "evil" is a pretty subjective classification of purported conspiracies, but large and powerful forces quite commonly attempt to manipulate events in secret ways. To say that conspiracy theories *in this sense* "are rarely true" is a claim requiring detailed argument and might even be depicted as an attempt to *Poison the Well*—a fallacy discussed below. The main rational constraint on such theories is just that the evidence for the conspiracy can't itself be a lack of evidence for the conspiracy.

The more complex the story explaining why evidence for the conspiracy is hard to come by, the less plausible the theory itself is. The suddenly popular idea that the moon landings were faked, for instance, has to be evaluated against reflections on just how many people would have to have been involved in the fakery without piping up about it—and not just secret agents or intelligence officials, but camera operators, television network officials, food caterers, the astronauts themselves, and dozens or hundreds of scientists. What would be involved, given what we know of human nature, in keeping so large and diverse a group completely quiet about the trick for any length of time, still less for decades afterwards?

But when evidence for the existence of a conspiracy is available, dismissing the evidence on the grounds that the speaker is just giving a conspiracy theory is evasion—a rhetorical distracter. Real conspiracies can thrive and succeed either by being confined to small groups—either a single small group, or "cells" of people none of whom know about the other groups, like French and Polish resistance groups during World War II—or by remaining just secret enough, for just long enough, in order for the aim to be accomplished. In 1964, American Secretary of Defense Robert McNamara told the United States Congress that undeniable evidence showed that North Vietnamese forces had repeatedly attacked American naval forces (the "Gulf of Tonkin incident"). Doubts about the truth of this claim circulated at a low level almost from the outset and were publicly confirmed by memoirs and declassified papers over the next twenty-five years, showing that at least two consecutive governments kept secret the information that no attack of the sort McNamara described had occurred. Though the conspiracy gradually came to light, it was successful in at least one key sense: in the short term the story resulted in a 416–0 vote in the United States Congress supporting the open use of armed force in Vietnam. Political experience makes it foreseeable that a decision of such gravity is not normally reversed even if it turns out that the justification was fabricated or based on obviously flawed intelligence; a war supplies its own justifications very quickly, and the original reasons for the conflict can come to seem irrelevant. Depending on the circumstances, then, conspiracies may not need to remain secret for very long in order to succeed.

VICARIOUS AUTHORITY

Much of our information about the world is based on testimony from sources we take to be reliable. These can range from people we meet in the flesh, to the media workers whose claims we encounter in print or by broadcast, to the expert authors of books and other educational materials. In light of this, it cannot generally be a mistake to justify some claim by quoting the opinions of experts. But there are many ways of getting such a justification wrong—ways of giving fallacious appeals to vicarious authority.

If a famous authority is cited in defence of some claim, an important preliminary step is to distinguish the *evidential* force of their authority from the *rhetorical* force of their fame. The effectiveness of celebrity endorsements in advertising, from entertainment or sports figures unlikely to have a neutral opinion (since they're getting paid for it!) or real expertise, suggests that we tend to over-value the authority of the famous. So we may be too easily impressed by a quotation from Albert Einstein owing merely to his being famous, instead of asking whether he is the proper sort of authority for the claim in question. If the argument really reduces only to the fact that Einstein said so-and-so, we have the fallacy of **Argument from Authority**, a species of a broader class of errors called the **Genetic Fallacy**: evaluating a claim on the basis of irrelevant facts about its origins, rather than on the basis of the evidence for it. But if the claim is justified by appeal to a proper authority, the justification may be evidentially cogent.

What does the proper authority amount to? It is important to note that no single person—and virtually no institution—counts as an entirely general authority. People and groups are authorities only *relative to a field*. In order to count as an authority for the purposes of some specific claim, the person cited ought to have recognized expertise on that particular topic. This expertise will normally be a matter of having an appropriate educational background, preferably the highest qualification available, as well as a record of research on the topic. But in some contexts it might include having the right sort of experience—work experience, upbringing, or lived experience. The difference will usually be clear given the context. For a claim about the spread of viruses, the opinion of an expert virologist is properly authoritative, while the opinion of someone who has merely had a viral infection is not. For a claim about how a viral infection feels, both a virologist and a victim might count as some sort of authority—the former may have much testimonial and observational experience of people suffering from viruses, while the latter has direct, if limited, experience with it. Either way, if the person cited as an authority has an appropriate expertise then the appeal to authority establishes at least a default reason to regard the claim as correct.

Dr. Jonathan Wells is prominent within the community of people who reject evolutionary explanations of biological speciation. The author of two books attacking evolutionary theory (and evolutionary theorists), Wells is often cited by non-experts who oppose evolutionary theory as an expert authority who rejects the theory. Wells is regarded as an expert because he holds a doctorate in biochemistry from the University of California at Berkeley—a relatively high-profile university. This qualification strikes some people as giving his claims strong evidential support.

Apart from the general point that Argument from Authority is particularly weak when the cited authority's opinion differs sharply from the consensus opinion among experts, the Wells example shows something interesting about how we regard the proper role of expert testimony. Wells, a member of the Unification Church, is on record as having decided to "devote [his] life to destroying Darwinism" *before*

seeking an education in biochemistry—an education program for which he claims to have been selected by the head of his church, the Reverend Sun Myung Moon. This discovery removes what little force remained to the already weak argument from Wells's single or rare idiosyncratic authority, and it shows something about what we actually want from a reasonable appeal to expertise. We want not just someone with qualifications speaking on the topic central to those qualifications; we moreover want their opinion to have been *shaped* in some fundamental way by the expertise they acquired in gaining those qualifications. That is, we value the testimony of experts, when we value it, because we think their testimony somehow *depends* upon their expert knowledge. If their taking a position is essentially unrelated to their apparent expertise, the appeal to their authority is not merely weak but a testimonial misfire of sorts.

Naturally, this sort of evidence is defeasible, and especially if only one authority is cited, however relevantly qualified. People are a mixed bunch, after all, and all the qualifications in the world are no guarantee of holding uniformly reasonable views, even within one's area of expertise. Every discipline has its mavericks, its loners, and its out-and-out wingnuts. Sometimes these people are sources of valuable new insights, but as a rule the balance of evidence within a field is represented by the balance of opinion among its qualified experts. A successful appeal to authority is one that implicates the received view among those best qualified to judge the matter—the citation of a widely used university text, for example. This goes some distance toward factoring out the unusual opinions that any one expert might have. If we discover that a cited expert holds a view on the claim in question that is marginal relative to other experts in that field, this is sufficient to greatly weaken, and perhaps nullify altogether, the degree of justification that expert authority confers on a claim.

Another way of looking at this is to note that there are two main ways for Argument from Authority to turn into a fallacy. The problem just mentioned is that of citing an expert with unorthodox views relative to most other experts. The other main problem is that of having a mismatch between the claim to be supported and the expertise of the person cited. I have no idea whether Stephen Hawking believes that divorce law in Italy needs to be revised, but if he did, the mere fact that he is a *savant* in astrophysics would give us no reason to take his opinions about Italian law any more seriously than we would take anybody else's opinions.

The sort of fallacious Argument from Authority that conflates areas of expertise is often couched merely in reference to the authority's intelligence. If one were to say, "Galileo and Kepler both believed in astrology; do you think you're smarter than they were?" the intended inference is that only someone "smarter" than these authorities is qualified to reject any belief they held. But this example is mistaken in more than one respect. First, it assumes that intelligence is an entirely general ability, when accomplishments in one cognitive domain are no guarantee of reliability in others. As the writer Frederic Raphael pointed out, Einstein was great and Einstein was a violinist, but Einstein was not a great violinist.[2] The astrology claim moreover commits a variety of the error already considered: Galileo and Kepler are still rightly *famous*, and they still command respect for their contributions, but they no longer count as *authorities*—not even in the fields to which they made their greatest contributions. The fields have moved on in the meantime, after all. The example can appeal to them only as famously smart people, then, but this sort of appeal is essentially empty.

The relevance of training and experience to a particular question can also be hard to judge simply because the relations between topic and expertise can be very fine-grained. It may seem obvious that police and other law-enforcement officers have expertise on questions relating to laws—that is, both what the laws are and what they ought to be. So, for example, the official statements of groups representing police officers and polls of opinions among police officers are frequently cited as expert views on the question of whether to legalize various drugs that are currently illegal. Upon reflection, though, there are few grounds to regard such opinions as expert in the relevant sense: police are highly trained in techniques for law *enforcement*, in conflict resolution, and in a range of other skills, but they are not trained to measure or predict broad socio-political effects of changes in laws or policies.

Also clouding the issue of relevant expertise is the fact that experts themselves may have an overdeveloped sense of the breadth of their insight. Famous computer scientists have theories about economics; famous biologists have theories about theology; famous physicists have theories about consciousness. (As an expert on arguments in general, of course, I'm licensed to poke my nose into everyone else's business.) Such theories can be better or worse, depending on the quality of the arguments offered for them. But the expertise of their other-disciplinary champions simply ought not be a factor in how we evaluate them—mismatched expertise does not even provide weak default justification. There is no good reason to think that an expert in field X will have any special insight into field Y.

APPEAL TO POPULAR OPINION

What do you call a falsehood that lots of people believe? Whether rumour, legend, myth, anecdote, history, or theory—whatever else it might be, it remains a falsehood. So reasoning along the following lines is obviously invalid.

1. It is widely believed that P.
Therefore,
2. P.

If the fallacy of Appeal to Popular Opinion amounted to nothing more than this strictly logical fallacy, though, it would be hard to see anyone's ever falling victim to it. In fact the fallacy is evidential.

Appeal to Popular Opinion might come in the form of a rhetorical question addressed to someone who denies the popular view, along the lines of "Do you really think that all these people could be wrong?" or "If there is such an obvious problem with P, how come so many people believe it?" Lurking in the background here may be an implicit fallacy of False Dichotomy: either the popular belief is correct, or the people who hold it are stupid. Of course it's conceivable that they are all stupid, but that's an unhappy explanation. It ends up seeming more reasonable, not to mention more polite, to suppose that most people are correct in holding the contested belief.

There are various middle paths that such reasoning does not consider, however. Whenever contemplating the evidential significance of the fact that one or many people hold some belief, it is important to bear in mind that generally reasonable people can hold unreasonable beliefs. It is no blanket slur on the reasoning abilities of a set of people to point out that they share a false belief, nor even that they share an unreasonable belief.

The occasional tendency for people to regard popularity as a measure of reasonableness may just be an artifact of not having studied or reflected on this fact.

Another point to bear in mind is that often when someone invokes the Appeal to Popular Opinion, by saying something like "But how could everyone be wrong?" the more careful question they ought to be asking is "But how could everyone *I associate with* be wrong?" Beliefs can be widespread within a population or subculture while being only minority opinions in the bigger picture. What's more, one's sense of how many other people share one's beliefs can be badly skewed.

On the other hand, a version of the argument from popularity can be evidentially forceful when we are considering a sub-population that has expertise on the topic in question. That's essentially what we have in a proper argument from authority, which is why there can be a strong default justification for accepting the consensus opinion among genuine experts in a field. Without this constraint of expertise in the population, however, the Appeal to Popular Opinion is really just an aggregate of the worst possible arguments from authority: "P is true because my dad said so; and my aunt said so; and my neighbour said so. . . ." Whether the aggregated testimony of non-experts provides *any* reason to believe a claim depends on the nature of the claim, among other things. But whatever evidence it does provide is tentative; in the presence of more immediate evidence suggesting that not-P, the fact that many people *irrespective of competence* believe that P is not compelling.

LINK

Chapters 7 and 8 explore the many nuanced ways in which false beliefs can come to be widespread.

FALLACIES OF CAUSAL REASONING

Anthropologists and social psychologists sometimes use the expression "**magical thinking**" as a blanket term for biases toward seeing a causal connection where none exists. The simplest kind of magical thinking is the fallacy of **Post Hoc Ergo Propter Hoc**: in effect meaning *after, therefore because.*

1. A black cat crossed my path, and then I got hit by a bus.
Therefore,
2. I got hit by a bus because a black cat crossed my path.

Here only the relation of temporal succession serves as the basis for inferring a causal connection. A happened before B happened, the magical thinker reasons, therefore A caused B. Obviously this way of thinking leads to massive over-attribution of causal connections! But at least this much can be said for it: temporal succession is a feature of most, perhaps all, genuine cases of cause and effect. Other kinds of magical thinking lack even this dubious virtue—for example, the so-called **Law of Similarity**. This is a label for the tendency of people—sometimes one sees "primitive" or "pre-technological" people listed as the main culprits—to conclude that factors *similar* to some effect must have the power to *cause* the effect. Some traditional medicine recommends rhinoceros horn as a cure for erectile dysfunction, for example. Why? A range of fallacies and biases discussed in this and subsequent chapters may sustain and consolidate such a belief once it exists, but the basic explanation is the Law of Similarity. In this case, the similarity is visual: if the rhino had a horn drooping pessimistically downward, it might have had fewer hunters. (Though not a great deal fewer, since much of the medicinal use of rhinoceros horn seems to have been for conditions other than impotence.)

The problem with such reasoning is two-fold. First, similarity is cheap; there are innumerable ways for one thing to strike us as similar to another thing. And second, there is no good reason to think that what strikes us as similar to an effect is in any way disposed to be a cause for that effect. Moreover, while it's true that magical thinking especially characterized pretechnological societies, in every culture there are at least some traditional socio-cultural practices and habits of thought that continue to embody it. People wear good luck charms, hang symbols from the rear-view mirrors in their cars, and subscribe to various "alternative therapies" that are based on the Law of Similarity even in the most technologically advanced cultures. Scientific thinking merely joins magical thinking in much allegedly sophisticated society, rather than replacing it.

MULTIPLE ENDPOINTS

The last evidential fallacy we will consider (for now) is arguably the most significant threat to the proper use of statistical reasoning and the methods of good science. One of the most common and important uses of evidential reasoning is to detect and characterize correlations—between objects, trends, or more abstract phenomena. But it is not a simple matter to conclude that two things are in fact correlated in some interesting way. Correlations that look for all the world as if they are important, surprising, and significant can be virtually meaningless if they are established or reported in an unprincipled manner. The most common way of misdiagnosing correlations is known as the fallacy of **Multiple Endpoints**. It is not as simple a fallacy as some we have considered, though.

The short version is this: most objects and events have enough traits that *as a matter of chance alone* there will be unusual relations between objects in a collection. We can make it look like there are interesting connections between things, provided we don't specify in advance what will count as interesting connections. How does this work? At the risk of stating the obvious, objects or events have many different properties. A ball is round, but can be brown, wooden, and hand-crafted in Auckland; or blue, plastic, and mass-produced in Guangzhou. A vehicle accident can be fatal or non-fatal, involve cars or trucks or motorcycles, occur in Toronto or Sherbrooke or Regina. Each such property—colour, mass, name, gender, velocity, distance from Winnipeg, or whatever—is a dimension along which we can compare the elements in a sample.

Think of the old *Sesame Street* television show's game "One of These Things Is Not Like the Others." Three items would be shown to children, the idea being that they should pick out the item that was different—or, equivalently, identify the two items that were most similar. In trying to teach concepts of classification to children, the show always presented two naturally similar articles and one deliberately dissimilar article. For example, there might be a dog, a cat, and a hammer; naturally the two animals are most obviously similar by the standards of virtually everyone, and certainly by the classification schemes of small children. But suppose we wanted to be contrarians about the game. How technical or picky could you be in playing it? What properties of objects or events could you appeal to, in order to correlate two objects? Take objects A, B, and C, for instance.

A ▨   B ◯   C ✕

A and C, but not B, have straight lines. A and B, but not C, are shapes with enclosed areas. B and C, but not A, lack right angles . . . and so forth. If we don't specify in advance which sort of properties we're interested in, then it is usually easy, even trivial, to find properties that some things have in common, which is another way of saying that we can find correlations among them with respect to some properties or other.

So if we just take some collection of objects or events or other data points and look for unusual connections between the elements of the collection without deciding in advance what properties we're interested in, we will often be able to find an *apparently* low-probability confluence of properties in a sample. Still, it is a relatively high probability that by randomness alone a sample will show commonalities along *some* dimension of comparison or other. The Multiple Endpoints fallacy is committed when we first gather data and then look for significance, instead of first deciding on a hypothesis and then testing it.

An analogy commonly used to explain this idea is that of a set of bullet holes in a piece of paper: we can draw conclusions about a shooter's accuracy if we first set up a target, ask her to aim at the centre, and see how her shots are grouped. It wouldn't show anything if we first looked to see where some shots were clustered, and *then* decided to paint the target with that cluster at the centre. After all, we weren't antecedently interested in that spot, and we know that just by chance it's likely that the shots will land more densely in some areas than in others. If we choose one of the denser areas and decide *after* the fact to regard it as the centre of the target, we commit the Multiple Endpoints fallacy in concluding that the shooter is skilled. Hence the Multiple Endpoints fallacy is sometimes called the **Sharpshooter Fallacy**.

In June 2001, the British newspaper the *Telegraph* reported on the strange case of a "message balloon" (a random pen-pal request sent via a helium-filled balloon) that had found its way to a ten-year-old girl named Laura Buxton, in Milton Lilbourne, England. The balloon was sent from Stoke-on-Trent, Staffordshire, over 150 kilometres away. The facts of the case were first summarized in a small local newspaper, but were quickly picked up worldwide as an interest piece. The focus of the story was the string of amazing coincidences relating the person who sent the balloon and the person who ended up with it. In particular, the balloon had been sent by another young girl, who was also ten years old. Her name, remarkably, was also Laura Buxton! Both girls were fair-haired, and both had a black Labrador dog, a guinea pig, and a rabbit. The story was presented as an unfathomable string of coincidences. But was it really that amazing or inexplicable?

For current purposes the issue is the method by which the coincidences, even the genuine ones, were collected and reported. For like most other objects, these two girls each have an astronomical number of identifiable properties. This means that there are an astronomical number of ways for them to have *something or other* in common.

MULTIFACETED EXAMPLE

In Chapter 8 we examine the key point that much of the media coverage on the Two Lauras carefully omitted a crucial detail: the balloon was actually found by someone else, not by the second Laura Buxton. That aspect of the example is not strictly a fallacy of any sort; it is actually a case of what is called *levelling*—the transmission of testimony in a way that minimizes details that provide context and explanation for the main point of a story.

Just to get the flavour of the situation, consider a very, very few of the dimensions along which the girls could be identical:

Shoe size* Body mass* Eye colour* Middle name* Mother's name* Father's name* Grandfathers' names* Grandmothers' names* Teachers' names* Best friends' names* Number of siblings* Genders of siblings* Siblings' names* Name of school* Religion* Hobbies* Athletic achievement* Academic achievement* Volunteer work* Artistic ability* Telephone number* Street address* Favourite shop* Favourite music* Favourite food* Favourite actor* Favourite colour* Favourite film* Favourite book* Favourite stuffed toy* Favourite television show* Favourite computer/video game* Favourite restaurant* Favourite drink* Part-time job* Past vacation destinations* Brand of bicycle* Medical history (Both had tonsils out? Wow!)* Birthday* Place of birth* Time of birth* Day of week of birth* Mother's birthday* Father's birthday* Grandfathers' birthdays* Grandmothers' birthdays* Siblings' birthdays* Best friends' birthdays . . .

Does it seem a bit extreme to suppose that anyone would resort to comparing such remote relational properties, in order to manufacture correlations between the girls? Consider the closing paragraph of the article in the local newspaper that first reported the story:

By an even greater coincidence the grandparents of Laura, from Stoke on Trent, Terry and Margaret Buxton, are currently travelling the Kennet and Avon Canal and were moored at Wootton Rivers.[4]

For those less than intimate with English geography, the reporter is remarking on the coincidence that the grandparents of one Laura were vacationing in roughly the same part of England where the other Laura lives. So add "General geographical region occupied for some duration by girl or some member of her extended family" to the list! Taking this list and its obvious extensions into account, we can distinguish two questions:

1. Selecting one of these properties in particular—say, grandmother's name—what are the odds that two randomly chosen people will be the same with respect to that particular property? (I.e., what are the odds that two randomly chosen people will have a grandmother with the same name?)
2. What are the odds that two randomly chosen people will be the same with respect to *one of these properties or another*?

The answer we give to Question 1 obviously depends on which property we've asked about. Some properties are relatively likely to be shared between two randomly chosen people (like having two nostrils), and some are relatively unlikely to be shared (like being over seven feet tall). The key point is that the probability of two people sharing at least some *individually* unlikely property is relatively high; it is likely that any two people share some property or other that would seem surprising if we had set out to ask whether they shared that particular property. So if we don't specify what dimensions of comparison will count as interesting before we look for similarities, we can pick and choose from all the similarities that exist in order to get some that look surprising. Each of these possible similarities is like a ticket in the lottery; deciding what we're interested in *after* we see the results is like waiting until the winning lottery number has been drawn before deciding which ticket to buy. Each number in the lottery might be individually unlikely to be chosen, but *some* such unlikely number will be the winner. I might end up richer, if a lottery was foolish enough to let me pick my number after I knew the outcome of the draw, but I would still be wrong to claim that my ending up with the winning ticket was a surprising or low-probability event requiring further explanation. It is a similar mistake to think that some observed correlation requires explanation (beyond appealing to chance alone, that is) if it was chosen after the fact, from among many other correlations, for the specific purpose of looking surprising or significant.

So whether we should regard the case of the Laura Buxtons as baffling comes down to whether the reporters were analyzing the event along the lines of Question 1 or of Question 2—that is, whether the newspapers were independently interested in hair colour and guinea pigs, or were just looking for any shared properties that would round out the story. The answer is quite clear. Suppose that the two girls had not had the same colour hair. Is it plausible that the news reports would have made that *difference* part of the story? Of course not. As the old saying goes, DOG BITES MAN is a lousy newspaper headline while MAN BITES DOG is a great one. There is no way that a story with the headline LOCAL MAN FINDS BALLOON; NO REAL SURPRISES would have been written, and no question of its being picked up by the international media even if it had been written.

The lesson is that we do not get truly significant correlations by trawling through masses of insignificant correlations until we find a few that *would* have been significant had they been what we were investigating from the outset. Such discoveries can be weak evidential grounds to undertake a more systematic investigation, but are not themselves significant results of an investigation.

PROCEDURAL AND PRAGMATIC FALLACIES

Procedural and pragmatic fallacies are argumentative or conversational moves that undermine good reasoning by distracting the discussants from the real issues or otherwise damaging the procedure for exchanging ideas and evidence.

DISTRACTORS

Some fallacies are ways of communicating that shift attention from the argument at hand, rather than poor arguments in themselves, though they may be understood as **fallacies of relevance**—those introducing irrelevant factors to the real issue under discussion. These may be deployed deliberately as rhetorical devices.

Red Herring

When careful argument is required, staying on the precise topic of discussion is one of the hardest things to do. The issues that get raised in the process of giving an argument tend to draw us into assertions and objections that are *related* to the topic, but not precisely *relevant* to the argument. Statements or objections that lead the discussion away from the key point are called **Red Herrings**, especially when there is some suggestion that this is done deliberately.

The term seems to date back to the practice of dragging a herring through the woods in order to teach hunting dogs how to track a scent; a red herring invites the audience to follow a false trail. For example:

> Jill: "In Canada it's illegal to even question whether the Holocaust happened. That's ridiculous."
> Ted: "Is that true? I thought it was only speech likely to incite hatred that was illegal. What law are you talking about?"
> Jill: "Well, it's like they're trying to legislate morality. Can you really make people perfect by passing laws about what they should think?"

Here Jill has introduced a Red Herring in her reply, raising a substantially different question that would take the discussion in another direction, rather than addressing Ted's query about her initial claim. It should be clear that various kinds of distractor fallacies, including many that also have more precise descriptions, will broadly count as Red Herrings.

Straw Man Fallacy

This term refers to the fallacy of misrepresenting an argument or a view in order to refute a dumbed-down version of it. (The idea behind the name is that you build a dummy opponent out of straw instead of confronting the actual opponent.) This fallacy typically results from ignoring the importance of charity in reconstructing or interpreting the arguments of one's fellow discussants.

> "Jill, you argue that since the federal government reneged on its contractual promises to various Aboriginal groups, it owes them reparations. Well, since you think that everyone who ever broke a promise should have to give up all their belongings, maybe you should give up all of yours! Or haven't you ever broken a promise? Only a nut could believe such a crazy view."

The speaker here is very uncharitable, since (if the first sentence is correct) Jill did not argue that "everyone who ever broke a promise should have to give up all their belongings." Nor does that follow from what she did argue. This is a Straw Man reply, since it sets up a much less defensible argument than the one actually presented and attacks it instead. If done deliberately for rhetorical effect, this sort of thing is a pointless exercise in bad faith. More often, though, it's a mostly unintentional result of thinking the worst of one's opponent. If you think your opponent is stupid, it will seem natural to ascribe a stupid view to him or her. The idea behind charity in argumentation is to come up with the best argument you can reasonably make out of your opponents' words.

Many different phenomena count as instances of the Straw Man fallacy, ranging from deliberate deception to poor scholarship. The discussion of quotation in Chapter 3 can be subsumed under this heading in its entirety, for example, since direct and indirect quotations are the most obvious ways of attributing views to other people. Misquotation and quote-mining are inherently misrepresentative.

Ad Hominem

Literally "argument against the man," Ad Hominem is another species of Genetic Fallacy. Ad Hominem involves dismissing an argument on the basis of personal facts about the arguer. This can be a matter of saying something insulting or nasty about someone, but it need not be. Moreover, a speaker's saying something nasty or insulting about the arguer does not necessarily mean that the speaker has committed the Ad Hominem fallacy. Some insults are not really intended to change the topic, only to deliver an insult in the course of arguing. And some negative remarks that *are* intended to derail a discussion don't even pretend to impugn the argument on the basis of the allegedly negative properties of the arguer, but only to make a fuss. Such insults are more like sticking one's tongue out or issuing a loud yell during the discussion: rude, off-putting, and distracting, but not really Ad Hominem in themselves. Consider some examples.

> "Jill, you argue that since the federal government reneged on its contractual promises to various Aboriginal groups, it owes them reparations. But you're a dolt, so of course your argument doesn't work."

The speaker in this case is clearly committing the Ad Hominem fallacy, attributing the failure of Jill's argument to her alleged stupidity. Notice that the failure of the argument is not a matter of the falsity of the allegation, though it may well be false. The problem is that even if Jill *is* a dolt, her argument still might be correct in this case. What's required is to engage the argument, not the personal properties of the arguer. And this is true whether those personal properties are alleged to be negative or positive, as we see in this case:

> "Jill, you argue that since the federal government reneged on its contractual promises to various Aboriginal groups, it owes them reparations. But this is a matter of the evil and cynical world, Jill, while you're so personally innocent, spiritually beautiful, and morally upstanding that of course your argument doesn't work."

Again, clearly an Ad Hominem. Even though the speaker is attributing positive properties to Jill rather than the negative properties more usually associated with the fallacy, the reasoning is the same non sequitur from her (alleged) personal traits to the failure of her (alleged) argument.

The related sorts of cases mentioned above can also be seen by example.

> "Jill, you argue that since the federal government reneged on its contractual promises to various Aboriginal groups, it owes them reparations. But you're a dolt, which probably explains why you never bothered to figure out that contractual promises are not binding between a government and an informal tribe, which is why your argument doesn't work."

Here the speaker really does offer a counter-argument and seems to be rejecting Jill's argument on the basis of genuine reasoning. (Of what calibre, we will not remark.) So this is not a very clear case of Ad Hominem, nor a stark example of any fallacy.

Really, it's just the speaker being an ass. On the other hand, a *mere* insult looks like more of a rhetorical distractor or derailment strategy.

> "Jill, you're a dolt."

In this case there is neither an independent counter-argument nor even an attempt to link the alleged personal properties to Jill's argument. Here too the speaker is being an ass, but this appears even less argumentatively cooperative than the previous example; it is more akin to putting one's fingers in one's ears.

Finally, it is important to note that not every case of Ad Hominem is fallacious. A personal fact about the arguer, such as that she is a known liar, would be irrelevant to the assessment of some specific arguments, but relevant to the assessment of others. The obvious cases are those in which one or more premises in the argument have to be taken on the word of the arguer. Similarly, if the arguer puts herself forward as an expert to vouch for the truth of a premise, then it will not be a fallacious Ad Hominem to point out that the arguer lacks expertise. If the arguer cites other genuine experts instead, of course, it will be irrelevant and hence a fallacious Ad Hominem to dwell on the arguer's lack of expertise.

Poisoning the Well

The Fallacy of Poisoning the Well is quite a subtle one, related to Ad Hominem. A statement poisons the well if it is a general attack on the worth or reliability of an arguer's utterances; if successful, this can have the effect of destroying the very conditions required for the rational dialogue.

To dismiss an argument on the grounds of the speaker's criminal past—whether or not they have one—is probably just an Ad Hominem fallacy. To dismiss an argument with the claim that, for example, the speaker is really just conditioned to say that sort of thing is to poison the well: it taints everything the speaker might then say and, if generalized, undermines the whole conversation. After all, *everyone* might only say what they say because they've been conditioned that way.

A common example of well-poisoning, familiar to many young people, is the dismissive observation, "Oh, I used to think that when I was your age." When one discussant is older than the other, this sort of comment is often used not as a mere report of the older discussant's former state of mind, but as way of a devaluing any view the younger person might espouse in opposition to the older. The insinuation is that the younger person has some general lack of insight or knowledge compared to the older person—hence the connection to Ad Hominem. Well-poisoning is often pre-emptive, moreover, with the speaker attempting to delegitimize an obvious or predictable objection for which there is no good reply:

> "Everyone knows that all Scots are cheap. But just wait for the radical politically correct crowd to start whining about sweeping generalizations! They love to hide in hair-splitting when reality itself offends their tender sensibilities."

If we reply that the initial claim really is a fallacy of Sweeping Generalization, we seem only to confirm the speaker's dismissive opinion. Indeed, any clear and careful reply is likely to be characterized as "hair-splitting." In this case all we can do is point out the unwarranted claims and perhaps clarify our motives: not tender sensibilities, but a distaste for shoddy reasoning.

The Mrs. Lincoln Fallacy

The Mrs. Lincoln fallacy, so named by the philosopher Rolf George, is a species of evidential fallacy, but is interesting for procedural reasons. Its name stems from a slightly morbid joke referring to the assassination of American president Abraham Lincoln during a play in 1865: "Other than that, Mrs. Lincoln, how did you like the play?" The fallacy consists in ignoring clearly relevant factors and then treating subsequent inferences as significant.

To some extent this has to be acceptable. Most theories and explanations contain some degree of idealization, abstracting away from details that would be hard to factor in precisely. But in order for this practice to be benign, we must have a rational confidence that whatever is idealized away would not make a big difference to the outcome of our deliberations, were we to include it. When the factors being set aside are obviously significant, or when we simply have no idea at all what difference they would make, then little or no weight can be attached to the conclusions we reach by ignoring them.

It's an evidential principle that we ought to use all the evidence at our disposal when we reason—including, of course, evidence about what other bits of evidence may be safely set aside for current purposes. But the fallacy is best seen as procedural, because it proceeds by setting up a conversational situation in which it appears you are permitted to keep drawing conclusions, even as one potentially important factor after another is ignored.

The fallacy might also be called the Fallacy of the Romans, after a scene in Monty Python's film *The Life of Brian*. A group of aspiring revolutionaries are discussing their dislike of the ruling Roman Empire. "What have the Romans ever done for us?" asks their leader at first. But his colleagues point out a series of Roman contributions, in the spirit of fairness. After he grants these and sets them aside, his question ends up being "Apart from the sanitation, the medicine, education, wine, public order, irrigation, roads, a fresh water system, and public health . . . what have the Romans ever done for us?"

CONFUSIONS

Other procedural fallacies are a matter of setting up the discussion or the argument poorly. This can occur in many different ways, ranging from the set of presuppositions required for the argument to be coherent to the specific vocabulary one chooses in framing the issues.

Begging the Question, or Circular Argument

The term "Begging the Question" has now become so systematically debased by journalists and talking heads that it's safer just to use the term "Circular Argument." An argument is circular when it assumes the truth of what it purports to prove. The most direct way of committing the fallacy is for the conclusion of an argument to also be one of its premises. For example:

"I know that Jill was telling the truth. After all, she told me so herself."

How could we make this into an argument? We obviously have:

1. Jill said that everything she told us was true.
Therefore,
2. Everything Jill told us was true.

But as it stands this argument is of course not valid; the premise could be true and the conclusion false. How? Well, if Jill did not tell the truth about telling the truth. So to make the argument valid, we have to add another premise.

1.5. Everything Jill told us was true.

Now the argument works, after a fashion, but it's circular: Premise 1.5 is just what was supposed to be proved in the first place, so the argument *assumes* the truth of what it was supposed to prove.

A circular argument need not have a single conclusion functioning as its own premise. It can also be a matter of two propositions being used alternately as premise and conclusion. Suppose someone gave the following argument.

1. Ted said that smog is good for people.
2. Ted has reasonable opinions about air-quality issues.
Therefore,
3. It's reasonable to think that smog is good for people.

Naturally one might wonder about the truth of Premise 2, given Premise 1. Suppose we ask for a justification of Premise 2 and are given the following argument in reply.

1. Ted said that smog is good for people.
2. It's reasonable to think that smog is good for people.
Therefore,
3. Ted has reasonable opinions about air-quality issues.

Now we've been led in a circle. Jointly these two arguments commit the fallacy of Begging the Question: we try to prove two dubious statements by alternately assuming their truth.

This is an interesting fallacy, theoretically speaking, since a Circular Argument is always valid. Indeed, as long as the statement doing double duty as premise and conclusion is true, any argument of the form "P, therefore P" is not just valid, but sound! (Check the definitions of validity and soundness to confirm this.) Even so, there's obviously something wrong with a circular argument.

This returns us to the question of how we think of arguments; that is, whether we are pursuing the study of *arguments as logical objects,* or the study of *argumentation as a rational practice.* This is another occasion on which these two conceptions come apart, since the former conception does not explain what is problematic about a Circular Argument's having a true premise that serves also as its conclusion. The problem with a Circular Argument is just that it fails to provide a reason to believe its conclusion, irrespective of its validity or soundness. If one did not already believe the conclusion, a question-begging argument provides no reason to accept it. For this reason we could include question-begging among the evidential fallacies. But its more fundamental flaw is that it cannot be used to do what good arguments are for. It is a pragmatic fallacy.

False Presuppositions

As we saw in Chapter 2, presuppositions are propositions that one must grant or assume in order for a statement to make sense. It's predictable that any mechanism for getting one's audience to grant or assume things can be an instrument of misleading argument. The problem is that a statement's presuppositions may be false, in which case addressing the statement will commence with addressing its presuppositions rather than its explicit content. At best this is time-consuming. At worst, false presuppositions sneak substantial claims into a discussion without their being critically analyzed. Consider the following utterance:

> "The next time the global warming crowd gives you their arrogant theory, ask them to explain why everyone who looks at the data ends up rejecting the theory."

The statement itself might not even seem to make a positive claim; it really just looks like a piece of advice. But even as a piece of advice, it's only felicitous if the hypothesis of global warming really is inherently arrogant, and if everyone who looks at the data really does end up rejecting the hypothesis. Presented with this utterance, we ought to note that both presuppositions are false rather than admit them to an argumentative context without challenge.

Fallacies of Definition and Connotation

Another way in which assumptions or biases may find their way into a persuasive case without being explicitly represented in the premises is through the particular choice of words and the communicators' assumptions about them. For example, a fallacy that might be considered a lesser form of circular argument is the fallacy of **Slanting Language**. This fallacy is committed in its most general form when a speaker describes some situation in terms that already entail or suggest the desired conclusion. For example,

> "Abortion is immoral right from conception, because a baby has a right to life!"

Now, whatever one thinks about the moral permissibility of abortion, presumably one will recognize that the word "baby" is not a very natural or accurate description of (say) a 1-celled or 2-celled or 128-celled organism. The choice of the word "baby," with its connotations of an infant, biases the utterance in favour of the impermissibility of abortion from the moment of conception.

The choice of positive-connoting labels can go beyond strictly defined Persuasive Defini-tion. One American author discusses "greenwashing," the practice by which corporate or industrial conglomerates choose environmentally friendly names for organizations that exist mostly on paper, and whose function is actually to lobby for less restrictive environ-mental protection laws.

"The Citizens for the Environment (CFE), for example, has no citizen membership and gets its support from a long list of corporate sponsors who use the organization to lobby against the Clean Air Act and other environment regulations. The Environmental Conservation Foundation is a front group for land developers and other businesses opposed to wetlands regulations. The Evergreen Foundation is a timber-industry mouth-piece that promotes the idea that clear-cut logging is beneficial to the environment. Cit-izens for Sensible Control of Acid Rain is a front for the oil and electric industries that is opposed to *all* controls of acid rain."[5]

Sometimes it can be difficult to find completely or even mostly neutral terms to define some discussion. Different sides in a debate work hard to define the discus-sion in their own terms, trying to institute their own rhetorical devices and resist those of their opponents. This version of Slanting Language is the fallacy of **Persuasive Definition**: not simply describing something in question-begging terms, but attempting to *define* it in such language. Concerning the labels "Pro-life" versus "Pro-choice," and "Anti-choice" versus "Anti-life," the mainstream media seem to have settled on describing both sides in their own pre-ferred terms, while using neither side's term for the other. Media practices are rarely this carefully consid-ered, though: armed groups once known as *freedom fighters* may quickly become *terrorists* or *insurgents* if they switch sides—even without switching their methods. These choices are importantly linked to how it seems reasonable to think of some issue or group, which is why it is important to think past the labels.

A fallacy akin to Persuasive Definition is **No True Scots** fallacy, which is a kind of equivocation

FIGURE 4.1

Who Is This?

Is this a soldier, warrior, freedom fighter, guerrilla, terrorist, irregular, or insurgent? The labels we use for people and the conclusions we draw about them are powerfully linked.

Mohammed Ameen/Reuters/Landov

between an empirical claim and a definition. It takes its name from this famous example of dialogue:

> A: All true Scots eat oatmeal.
> B: But MacGregor doesn't eat oatmeal.
> A: Well, then MacGregor is no true Scot!

In this example, a claim that first seems to be offered as an empirical truth (All true Scots eat oatmeal) is saved from a falsifying counter-example by being converted into a stipulative definition (now "True Scot" is *defined* as "one who eats oatmeal"). This rules out counter-examples altogether, of course, making the claim necessarily true— but at the cost of triviality and equivocation, since that is not how "Scot" is more generally defined. If a true claim, it's not a true claim of English, but of the speaker's private idiolect. If the defining example above seems extreme, notice that the fallacy can come in stronger and weaker versions, too. I once had something like the following exchange with a Relatively Famous Professor of Philosophy.

> RFPP: All competent economists now admit that the New Deal actually prolonged and worsened the Great Depression in the United States.
> TK: Really? I have a hard time believing that [well-known economists X and Y] would accept that.
> RFPP: Oh, please. X and Y? I said *competent* economists.

Here it's possible that I did indeed unknowingly name two genuinely incompetent economists. But there's at least a whiff of No True Scot fallacy as well. The greater the evidence that the economists I named are competent, the more reasonable it is to diagnose the reply as strategic redefinition as a way of saving the initial claim— but at the cost of trivializing it.

Related fallacies of biased definition need not rule out counter-examples altogether, though. Consider a recent study that was touted as showing that a "faith-based" prisoner reform program was more successful than secular programs. The claim was based on the relatively low rate of recidivism—that is, re-offending— among the program's "graduates." But on a closer look, it turned out that the study recognized someone as a graduate only if they stayed off drugs and held down a job well after they left prison. It was still *possible* for such a person to re-offend (unlike the No True Scot case of completely defining the main claim as true). It's just that the biased definition of a graduate filtered out a large percentage of subjects who *tried* the program but nevertheless went back on drugs or lost their jobs—situations highly correlated with returning to a life of crime. This sort of fallacy and No True Scot are closely related; the biggest difference is the extent to which counter-examples are ruled out by the biased definition.

MULTIFACETED EXAMPLE

The prison reform program is a multifaceted example. An important related issue here is the concept of an "intention to treat" group in a scientific study. Reporting the results of all the cases to which we *try* applying a treatment is a scientific method that avoids the fallacy of trimming the sample. This example is discussed again in Chapter 9.

Finally, a very common procedural fallacy of definition is **Argument by Dictionary**. It may seem strange to include a reliance on dictionary definitions in a section that emphasizes *biased* definitions. Shouldn't dictionaries be the safest example of unbiased information? But dictionary definitions tend to be biased themselves: perhaps only rarely by the publisher's perspective on a topic, but always by the need for brevity and simplicity. Using a dictionary definition as an inflexible standard in an argument is therefore a likely way of producing a ham-handed argument that misses the subtleties of which most interesting issues consist.

This fallacy is committed when a speaker appeals to a dictionary definition as a means of settling a dispute. (That is, a dispute about something other than what that dictionary says.) A debate over the moral status of pornography will naturally include much discussion over what pornography *is*. Any such discussion is likely to aim at getting a thorough and refined definition of the key terms. A dictionary may be a place to start looking at definitions, especially if one is unfamiliar with the keywords at the outset, but dictionaries cannot be the last word. Dictionaries are not intended for, and are not suitable for, settling disputes between fine-grained interpretations of a term. They are too brief in their definitions, too dependent on uncertain relations of synonymy and too little with connotations and the overtones of words to settle any but the grossest kinds of terminological dispute.

For example, if a speaker claims that the word "fecund" means "having a very bad odour," then citing a dictionary definition is an acceptable way of showing that this claimed definition is utterly wrong. But suppose a speaker argues for a distinction between "weak atheism" and "strong atheism," where the former might mean simply lacking a belief in gods while the latter might mean positively believing that there are no gods. The response that some dictionary defines "atheism" as "believing no gods exist" would not suffice to show that "weak atheism" is a self-contradictory phrase.

Of course an arguer will sometimes use terms idiosyncratically. The most compelling criticism of the resulting argument, though, is to show that the word as used by the arguer does not have the consequences it would need in order for the argument to be substantial or interesting. Argument by Dictionary doesn't establish this; a bit more conceptual analysis is needed in presenting such a critique. In general, arguments do not arise over matters so simple they can be settled by consulting a dictionary. Citing the dictionary is therefore a way of missing the point, in most cases. For this reason an effective response to the Argument by Dictionary is to rephrase the point in a way that does not use the contested term. This retains the focus of discussion on the specific issue and not on the idiosyncrasies of one dictionary.

Fallacies of the Complex Question

The various fallacies that travel under this description are mostly unified by their involving subtle shenanigans with disjunction, of one sort or another. The most famous examples of the complex question are cases of **loaded questions**, in which some proposition is presupposed whether the answerer replies in the negative or the positive. (Hence this is also a species of False Presupposition.) Consider, for example, the question "Have you renounced your criminal past?" Either simple answer of yes or no seems to concede the presupposition that the respondent *has* a criminal past.

In other words, if the questioner (or the context) requires such a one-word answer, the question amounts to a version of the False Dilemma fallacy: it limits the options to two cases, one in which the respondent has a criminal past and has renounced it, and one in which the respondent has a criminal past and has not renounced it. Of course this excludes the obvious further options in which the respondent has no criminal past whatever. Answering *no* is strictly correct if one has no criminal past, but pragmatically gives the appearance of accepting what the question presupposes.

Other fallacies quite different from loaded questions also count as complex questions. One version hinges on the behaviour of disjunctions in evidential and group-decision contexts. Suppose, for example, that a jury of twelve people is considering the question "Is the defendant guilty of the charge C?" Suppose also that charge C is a complex disjunction. For simplicity's sake, let C have twelve disjuncts: that is, "The defendant committed crime 1, *or* the defendant committed crime 2, *or* . . . the defendant committed crime 12." Notice what can now take place. Because the correct answer to this complex question will be yes provided *any* of the disjuncts is true, it could occur that the jury's beliefs are eleven to one *against* guilt on every single sub-charge, but that for each sub-charge it's a different single juror who believes the defendant guilty. That is, each juror believes the defendant is guilty of one and only one sub-charge, and no two jurors agree on which sub-charge it is. Then, when the jury votes on an answer to the question "Is the defendant guilty of the charge C?" the vote will be unanimously in the affirmative! The verdict will seem to show an unreserved judgment of guilt, when in fact every specific charge met with an overwhelming assessment of innocence.

OUTLIERS

In Chapter 5 in the discussion of statistics, the notion of an outlying value, or an **outlier**, will become important: the term means something that is far from the norm or not easily categorized. We can use the idea here, too, since not all fallacies fit neatly into the three major categories above. What follow are some important and frequent fallacies that have no very tidy classification.

FALLACY OF FALSE ENCHOTOMY (FALSE DILEMMA, FALSE DICHOTOMY)

The Fallacy of False Enchotomy is a very common kind of fallacy that consists of the assumption that there are only a certain number of possibilities, when in fact there are more. The problem with an argument based on this assumption is that it simply contains a false disjunctive premise. This makes it hard to classify, since "argument with false premise" is not a very helpful category. Nevertheless, it is an easily identifiable pattern of unsound reasoning.

The term **False Enchotomy** is of my own devising; typically this fallacy is characterized as **False Dichotomy** or **False Dilemma**. These terms are overly specific, though, since the fallacy is not limited to cases of mistakenly considering only two options (which is what the "di–" indicates). Whenever we list three or four or five options and treat them as exhausting the alternatives—in particular, whenever we try to infer the truth of one proposition from the falsity of all the other listed options—it is incumbent on us to be confident that we really have listed all the live alternatives. We can commit false trichotomies, false pentachotomies . . . indeed, for any number n of options that we disjunctively list, we might commit the fallacy of false n-chotomy, if there are in fact $n+1$ or more (reasonable) options. To simplify the spelling of this appropriately general term, however, I will call the fallacy False Enchotomy.

To see the fallacy in its simplest form, recall the valid argument form of Disjunctive Syllogism:

1. P or Q
2. Not Q
Therefore,
3. P

Even though it is valid, the soundness of an argument having this form requires, of course, that the premises also be true. And we have seen that the truth of a disjunction like Premise 1 above requires that at least one of the two disjuncts be true. In other words, the two disjuncts must *exhaust the possibilities*. If they do not—if there are other possibilities not expressed by P or Q—then it's possible for both P and Q to be false, in which case Premise 1 is false and the argument is unsound. One reason this fallacy is easily committed is that it can reflect a "rush to judgment" from someone already convinced of the conclusion, so that one too hastily takes one's own position as the only remaining option, once some other view is falsified.

Here is an example of a False Enchotomy—a dichotomy, in this case.

> There are some problems with Darwinian theory. Therefore, it's most reasonable to believe the biblical Genesis account of the origin of species."

Now, like most poor reasoning, this example has more than one problem. There is the implicit attempt to move from "There are problems with Darwinian theory" to "We ought to reject Darwinian theory." As a general principle of accepting and rejecting scientific theories, this cannot be right, since there are (in some sense) problems with virtually every scientific theory, however powerful or useful. Yet it would be absurd to suppose we ought therefore to reject every scientific theory. A second problem is the imprecision of the term "Darwinian": does this strictly mean Darwin's actual theory as he originally presented it, or does it include any subsequent theory that incorporates elements of Darwin's insights? But never mind these problems, for current purposes. Even were we to grant that we ought reject Darwinian theory, there is a fallacy of false dichotomy committed here. For we can only get from

1. We ought to reject Darwinian theory.
to
2. It's most reasonable to believe the Genesis account of the origin of species.
if there is a further implicit premise in the background. Namely,

1.5. Either Darwinian theory is correct, or the Genesis account of the origin of species is correct.

But there are many, many other options, ranging from non-Darwinian naturalistic theories of speciation, to non-biblical creation stories. So this dichotomy is a false one. Under analysis it becomes clear that the original statement depends on the assumption that its two options exhaust the possibilities, when in fact they do not.

FALLACIES OF COMPOSITION AND DIVISION

The fallacy of composition and the fallacy of division are duals; some cases are equally well diagnosed using either explanation. Both fallacies are a matter of the relation between a whole and its parts. The fallacy of composition occurs when we say things of the form "The parts each (or mostly) have property X; therefore, the whole has property X." The fallacy of division runs the other direction: "The whole has property X; therefore, its parts have property X."

Any number of examples serve to show that both directions of inference are invalid. All the best players do not necessarily make the best team; the compositional inference fails. Nor does the best team necessarily have all the best players; the divisional inference fails as well. By the same token, a profit-oriented company need not comprise only employees who are profit-oriented. The secret of many successful companies is to employ some people who never worry about profit. So on one hand the inference from profit-minded company to profit-minded workers is fallacious, and on the other hand the inference from profit-minded workers to profit-minded company also fails. For if each person or unit in a company is working at cross-purposes, the company as a whole may be directionless, in spite of the fact that each person or unit is trying to maximize profits.

REASONING FROM SIMPLIFICATIONS OR CLICHÉS

Two wrongs don't make a right. In a democracy, the majority rules. The ends don't justify the means. Everyday talk is larded with these and similar sayings and platitudes, often encoding a message that seems too obvious to doubt. Sometimes, however, a piece of alleged wisdom can attain the status of commonsense even though it is easily misapplied or even a gross oversimplification. They are easily remembered and easily invoked, but reasoning from such slogans can be highly misleading. Clear communication and effective argument analysis require thinking beyond bumper-sticker slogans and questioning their applicability when they are presented as authoritative.

Consider the first example just listed. What is the *point* of asserting that two wrongs don't make a right in a discussion? Notice that, for the most part, this platitude is said to (or said about) someone who doesn't think the act in question wrong at all, given that some previous wrong has been committed already. So the point in dispute ought to be whether that act is wrong, not whether two admittedly wrong acts amount to a right act. For example, to someone who believes in retributive justice (i.e., putting someone in prison as a form of punishment, and not just for rehabilitation or to protect the public) there is no point in explaining that depriving

CHAPTER 4   *Fallacies: When Arguments Turn Bad*

someone of their liberty is wrong, and that even though a criminal has committed a wrong, two wrongs don't make a right. That person's position, after all, is that depriving a convicted criminal of liberty, at least for a time, is *not* a wrong. So the cliché is simply irrelevant. The advocate of retributive justice doesn't believe that two wrongs *do* make a right; she believes that an act of retributive justice is right. Saying to this person that two wrongs don't make a right really amounts to a way of saying, "This act is wrong, whatever you may think." But that pronouncement doesn't carry any of the satisfying weight of folk wisdom that the cliché seems to possess! A substantial argument in such a situation will focus instead on the speaker's reasons for thinking that the act in question is wrong, rather than on a slogan that simply presupposes this.

If we consider the second example, by contrast, there is at least a basically correct definition underlying the claim that democracy means majority rule. The problem is that this is such an extreme simplification that the claim is useless for many contexts of application. There are so many ways for the broad concept of democracy to be implemented, and so many reasonable constraints on the will of the majority in every nation called a democracy, that appealing merely to the idea that the majority rules is practically pointless on its own. For example, someone might argue, "Polls show that 58 percent of Canadians think that police should be able to hold suspected terrorists indefinitely, without laying criminal charges. In a democratic society that settles it." This (fictional) example overlooks that Canada is not a "democratic society" in *that* particular sense of the phrase; the momentary popularity of an idea or policy with a majority of the population is not sufficient grounds to enshrine it in Canadian law. Indeed, no nation calling itself democratic has such a system, partly because it would be enormously difficult to implement, and partly because most nations are (or at least purport to be) based on a constitution and the "rule of law," rather than the direct will of the majority. In Canada the Charter of Rights and Freedoms powerfully constrains even what the country's system of representative democracy can directly decide, especially with respect to basic rights. Appeal to an oversimplified conception of democracy would not be a cogent argument for overriding the legal rights of some people.

Similar examples are not hard to find in everyday discourse. Arguments that seem to rest on such platitudes may well be open to reformulation in better terms; perhaps people use clichés or catchphrases as shorthand for more detailed reasoning that they can't be bothered to demonstrate at the time. But in order to recognize the argument as a good one, it is the detailed reasoning and not the sloganeering that we need to see.

There are many, many other fallacies, some of which we will introduce in subsequent chapters as the context requires. For now, however, this suffices to introduce the basic concept of a fallacy, some major divisions among them, and some of the keys to recognizing them and diagnosing them.

CONCLUSION

Fallacies are recognizable patterns of unreliable reasoning and argumentative practice. We can categorize them by reference to their logical invalidity, evidential weakness, or communicative or pragmatic errors, though there are important fallacies that do not fit neatly into any one category. Fallacies often are committed by sheer carelessness or oversight, but can be committed as deliberate attempts to deceive, mislead, or obstruct; the procedural fallacies in particular are likely to be of this sort. Many examples of poor reasoning include more than one fallacy and implicate issues besides fallacies as well.

By learning to recognize fallacies we enhance our ability to avoid committing such errors in our own work and in our communication more generally. We can also more easily diagnose unreliable reasoning when we encounter it. Still it is important to bear in mind that fruitfully diagnosing a fallacy is a matter of accurately interpreting the argument from the outset, and especially in the case of evidential fallacies the error need not be all-or-nothing. In these cases, what matters is getting a good sense of the degree of cogency of the argument, rather than deciding whether the argument is definitely fallacious or definitely not.

REVIEW QUESTIONS

1. List, label, and explain the differences between Modus Ponens, Modus Tollens, Denying the Antecedent, and Affirming the Consequent.
2. Explain the conditions under which Appeal to Authority is not a fallacy.
3. Choose three clearly different fallacies discussed in this chapter and find one instance of each in a major Canadian newspaper from the past month. Any city newspaper will do, and the online editions are acceptable. Make sure to explain precisely why the example you've chosen counts as an instance of that particular fallacy.

NOTES

1. "How to Identify Misinformation," International Information Programs, United States of America State Department, http://usinfo.state.gov/media/Archive/2005/Jul/27-595713.html.
2. Review of Ray Monk, Bertrand Russell, *The Ghost of Madness 1921–1970. Los Angeles Times Book Review,* April 8, 2001.
3. Statement by character Daryl Zero in the movie *Zero Effect,* written and directed by Jake Kasdan (Castle Rock Entertainment, 1998).
4. *Wiltshire Evening Advertiser,* story first published June 28, 2001; from "Trail of Coincidences" (http://archive.thisiswiltshire.co.uk/2001/6/28/215077.html).
5. R. Kennedy, Jr., *Crimes Against Nature* (New York: HarperCollins, 2005), pp. 27–28.

CHAPTER 5

Critical Thinking about Numbers

In fall 2000, the city council of Waterloo, Ontario, voted to accept a lease deal for a large recreational and park complex. The wonderful thing about the deal, from the city's perspective, was a low annual interest rate on the money needed to finance the park: 4.73 percent over 30 years, costing the city around $113 million in total. The problem with the deal, again from the city's perspective, was that nobody did the arithmetic correctly. Well after the vote was taken and the deal signed, the financial corporation that purchased the lease (from the brokers who had arranged it) contacted the city to explain that, according to the formula given in the contract the city had signed, the interest rate would turn out to be more like 9 percent. The real costs would be around $228 million, roughly twice what the city had believed. *Oops!* It almost always pays to be careful when working with numbers. Sometimes it pays a lot.

One of the great intellectual advances of humanity was the set of discoveries that enable the precise **quantification** of facts, situations, or data: that is, using numbers and numerical concepts to characterize things. In its most basic form this process began with the invention of number systems, enabling us to reason in the abstract about counting and measurement. In modern terms, it includes conceptual and technological tools for subtle statistical analysis.

Careful and appropriate quantification of data can greatly assist our understanding of complex situations. In fact, certain sorts of complex correlations become visible through quantitative analysis, which would be difficult or impossible to detect through any informal comparison of people's reported observations. Associated with numerical reasoning, however, is a substantial class of fallacies; as usual there are more ways of doing things badly than there are of doing them well. Applied inappropriately, numerical reasoning is just another way of reasoning badly—with perhaps the added problem that poor reasoning couched in the mathematical language nevertheless conveys a sense of precision and certainty to many people.

One of the fundamental problems in this domain is the interaction of two phenomena: **innumeracy** (the arithmetical equivalent of illiteracy), and the belief that innumeracy is intellectually acceptable. It is quite common to hear an otherwise educated person breezily say something like "Oh, I'm no good with numbers.

In calculating the cost of their recreational and park complex, the City of Waterloo's treasurer and other council members didn't just accidentally make an arithmetical mistake; they seem to have misinterpreted their own calculations, owing partly to the apparent trust and friendship established by the lease broker. This example is discussed again in Chapter 8.

I just don't understand all that math stuff. I never really got it." Few people think this is an outright *good* thing, of course. But that it happens at all is remarkable. Sometimes the way people talk about mathematics even suggests a belief that numeracy is incompatible with being artistic, literary, or creative. In this way some people may be inclined to read a virtue of sorts into the weakness of their arithmetical abilities. Even if this attitude is relatively rare, few people regard innumeracy as a major impediment to their being generally competent critical thinkers.

This is a mistake. Increasingly, the attempts at persuasive reasoning that we encounter from every source of information exploit quantitative reasoning, in particular in claims about rates, percentages, averages, and other statistics. To be unable to understand these claims critically is to be caught in a dilemma: either to trust claims that are framed in mathematical terms we cannot evaluate ourselves, or to generally reject them *because* we can't evaluate them ourselves. With the first strategy, we will certainly be victimized by the shoddy or unprincipled use of mathematics; with the second, we lose access to extremely important and useful information.

The attitude itself could never be generalized to literacy, moreover. Consider: "Oh, I could never really be bothered with learning how to read and write. All those word things? I never really got them." This is simply not a widespread social attitude that could be generally greeted with the understanding nodding of heads. One might wonder whether this is a good analogy, of course. Literacy is, plausibly, more important than numeracy for getting on in society, so it may be understandable that illiteracy is less cheerfully admitted and accepted than innumeracy. But innumeracy is increasingly a barrier to personal and professional success and hence an increasingly important critical thinking skill. Fortunately, the level of numeracy required for accomplished critical thinking is very basic. Earlier I defined numeracy simply in terms of *arithmetic*. The idea is not that one needs to have mastered calculus, nor even advanced algebra, but rather that one needs to employ basic arithmetic *generally* and *automatically*.

In his book *Damned Lies and Statistics*, author and numeracy advocate Joel Best reports reading a Ph.D. prospectus that included the claim "Every year since 1950, the number of American children gunned down has doubled."[1] The sort of numeracy we ought to aim for is that roughly sufficient to ensure that we do not just read over a claim of this sort without seeing a red flag, and the sort to ensure that upon thinking about the claim for a moment, we understand why it cannot be correct.

The quote given by the graduate student was in fact accurately taken from a 1995 issue of an academic journal, Best discovered. The author of the journal article in turn cited the Children's Defense Fund's *Children Yearbook* from 1994. What the

CDF *Yearbook* said, however, was that the "number of American children killed each year by guns has doubled since 1950." The author of the journal article somehow transposed this as "Every year since 1950, the number of American children gunned down has doubled." And neither the referees and editors of the journal, nor the student who eventually used the quote, stopped to reflect on what exactly the truth of this statement would involve.

The Children's Defense Fund statement is at least reasonable. It says that if there were n deaths in 1950 then there were $2n$ deaths in 1994; the annual number of deaths had doubled since 1950. But as Best observes, the truth-conditions of the journal article's claim are utterly fantastic. The difference in word order makes an enormous difference, amounting to the assertion that if there were n deaths in 1950, then there were $n \times 2^{44}$ annual deaths by 1995. That's 2 multiplied by itself 43 times. What does this mean? For the sake of simplicity, assume that only 1 child was killed by guns in 1950. Then in 1951, 2 children were killed; in 1952, 4 children; 8 children in 1953, then 16, 32, 64. . . Because each year the number is bigger, the effects of doubling it the next year are correspondingly bigger. By 1995 there would 2^{44} annual deaths; that is over 17.5 trillion deaths per year—far more deaths than in all of human history! If all one does is think of the first several doublings, it might seem unbelievable that the number could get so big so fast. But a basic familiarity with the arithmetic reveals that it does. That, essentially, is the requisite numeracy: to understand those basics, and, just as important, to apply them automatically in all domains of discourse.

This is not, however, a book that aims to teach arithmetic. If you don't recall or never really learned its basics (the latter, sadly, is a genuine possibility even for secondary school graduates), there are books that can help. My own approach, since I am not mathematically gifted, is to buy a used mathematics textbook every couple of years, the kind with lots of problems and a detailed answer key in the back, and work through it by doing a few problems each week. A used high school text or introductory university-level text in applied mathematics will work well for this purpose. This approach will not make you a great mathematician, but it will give you all the skills you need for critical thinking. It's one approach to (re-)acquiring numeracy. This chapter, however, assumes that you know at least the basics, in order to focus on the idea of a representative number.

The most common uses of numerical reasoning in popular discourse involve percentages, rates, and simple averages. What these uses have in common is that each is a way of taking some complex state of affairs or state of information and reducing it to a single **representative number** that is supposed to encode what's important about that information. In the case of the gun-deaths claim, the relation between the number of deaths at one time and the total at another time is given in terms of the number 2 ("doubling"). Used correctly, representative numbers of the three sorts listed above are extremely convenient ways of simplifying reasoning that would otherwise be slow and complicated. But, as the example shows, there are pitfalls by which we can wind up numerically *mis*representing affairs—for instance, taking the number 2 as the factor relating each year's deaths to the previous year's, rather than as the factor relating the total change over all the years. In this chapter we will examine some of the ways in which reasoning from representative numbers can go wrong.

PERCENTAGES

A good place to begin understanding the potential pitfalls in numerical reasoning is with claims and arguments involving **percentages.** "Percent," of course, just means "out of one hundred." When it is not an instrument of confusion, this is a very handy notion.

Percentages are useful mostly because they are a way of considering ratios in terms of a common standard: the ratios we might get as we consider various sets of data can be converted into percentages and then compared on the same footing. For example, suppose we have three boxes of apples. If 12 out of 39 apples in Box 1 are rotten, along with 70 out of 413 in Box 2 and 21 out of 151 in Box 3, we might find it difficult to quickly compare the proportion of spoiled apples in the three boxes. But if we frame these results as 31 percent, 17 percent, and 14 percent spoiled apples in the three boxes, the proportions are effortlessly compared. A complex bit of information like *70 out of 413* gets converted to the single representative number 17; even the *percent* aspect fades into the cognitive background.

This intuitive and flexible practice is fraught with possible confusions, however. The most obvious problem involves the **loss of information** about the data—that is, the loss of important contextualizing information that was carried in the absolute numbers we started out with. This loss of information accompanies the conversion of an initial ratio into a percentage. If all we are told is that 50 percent of all accidental injuries in Leaf Rapids, Manitoba, in 1994 were caused by nasal pencil insertion, we have no way of knowing what on earth this could mean without knowing the absolute number of accidental injuries in Leaf Rapids for that year. (Or without knowing the absolute number of accidental nasal pencil insertions. The 50 percent figure lets us calculate either number given the other.) Obviously in this case we would suspect, or certainly hope, that the percentage figure is an artifact of some very low number of total injuries; the simplest case would be two injuries in total, with one being a pencil up someone's nose. But the percentage figure is at least *consistent* with any number of pencils up any number of noses. In less unusual (and less fictional) examples, it can be genuinely unclear how much significance we should attach to percentage claims, given that the absolute numbers are not known to us.

When we are talking about changes over time in terms of percentages, for instance, the concern about absolute number is a matter of the base values involved. The significance of saying that some phenomenon has increased or decreased by 50 percent can vary enormously depending on the initial amounts. In a small town, a 100 percent increase in burglaries over one year might simply be a matter of having 2 burglaries last year and 4 this year, a trivial change likely to be a "blip"—an unusual but essentially random change. But a 10 percent increase in thefts over a single year in a nation of 30 million people could cash out as more than 50,000 additional crimes and is likely a sign of some serious social factors. (A sample so large is quite resistant to merely random blips of any great size.)

To take another example, consider this excerpt from the abstract for a talk:

> According to the 2001 census, the number of Muslims in Canada rose
> over the previous decade by 129%, Buddhists by 84%, Sikhs by 89%,

and Hindus by 89%. Clearly, new waves of immigration have changed the Canadian religious landscape.[2]

Now, there is a weaselly interpretation of "changed" on which the latter claim would be true provided any change whatever had occurred. We can assume that the speaker did not intend us to read the abstract in this trivial way. Yet if we take the claim to be that "the Canadian religious landscape" has changed in some fairly significant way over the past ten years (that is, worth giving a talk about), then the figures cited do not show it as clearly as the abstract suggests. Hopefully, the speaker made the argument more convincing by examining the absolute numbers in the actual talk, because, unless we know both the absolute numbers of followers of each religion and the absolute number of the wider population in which they live, we have no way of concluding from these percentage figures that the change is socio-religiously significant. Notice also that the first sentence leads off with the highest percentage change, as if to emphasize its extremity. But again, the large percentage figure may, for all we are told, have more to do with the relatively small number of Canadian Muslims in 1990 than with the significance (relative to the total Canadian population) of the change in the interim. The point is not that the abstract for the talk (still less the talk itself) is deeply mistaken, but rather that a straightforward appeal to percentage comparisons can make an inference seem clear despite not providing enough information to justify it.

COMBINING AND COMPARING PERCENTAGES

Doing simple arithmetic with distinct percentage figures is a delicate matter, for reasons that ought now to be obvious. (If they weren't already.) For example, because each percentage figure from our rotten apples example represented only a ratio *within* each box, we can't go adding or subtracting, or, perhaps more temptingly, averaging those percentages. Only by returning to the absolute numbers can we meaningfully combine the data.

To see this, look at the results we get if we attempt to average the percentages of rotten apples in the three boxes. Suppose we added the three percentage values and divided by 3, hoping to get the average (mean) percentage.

$$(31 + 17 + 14) \div 3 \approx 21$$

Someone using this as a way of figuring out the average percentage of rotten apples in all three boxes, then, would conclude that in total 21 percent of the apples are rotten. But this can't be right. (In particular, if the boxes are of different sizes.) When we go back to the initial data, we see that we have $39 + 413 + 151 = 603$ apples altogether, of which $12 + 70 + 21 = 103$ are rotten. But 103 out of 603 translates into 17 percent rotten apples, not 21 percent.

What went wrong? By combining the percentages as if they were all equally significant, we made the "data points" (apples, in this case) from the smaller boxes count for more than the data points from the larger boxes. Notice that if we had a fourth box with only two apples, one rotten and one not, this would change only our absolute numbers of rotten apples and total apples to 104 out of 605—still

17 percent, if we round off to the nearest whole number. But if we were to factor this 50 percent box into the faulty calculation over the percentages, it would distort the result still further, producing a mistaken average of 28 percent rotten.

$$(31 + 17 + 14 + 50) \div 4 \approx 28$$

To put the problem itself in percentage terms: those two apples in the fourth box, and the distribution of rottenness among them, would be counting as fully 25 percent of our information (1 of 4 percentage figures) despite being only 0.33 percent of the actual data (2 apples out of 605). It is a mistake to calculate percentages from other percentages, so any suggestion that a figure has been derived in this way is an immediate red flag. When in doubt, go back to the absolute numbers. Go back to the data yourself, and make sure the arithmetic works.

We'll discuss similar issues when we discuss averages below. First, however, it's worth noting that faulty reasoning about percentages does not require the comparison of different samples. Changes over time in a single measured group must be handled carefully too, if they are represented by percentages. The real danger in making such comparisons is that we may too hastily overlook what the percent claim *means*.

Everyone understands that if an amount first doubles and is then halved, it has returned to its original value. But careless reasoning about percentages may overlook the fact that a 100 percent increase followed by a 50 percent decrease is the same sequence of operations. There may be some temptation to add and subtract these figures as if they were simple numbers. There is even an old joke to this effect, about a man who has ten dollars and then finds another ten on the sidewalk. Unfortunately the found money falls out of his pocket on the way home, but he consoles himself that having increased his wealth 100 percent when he found the ten-dollar bill, and having decreased it by 50 percent (from $20 to $10) when he lost it, he must somehow still be ahead by 50 percent. That such a mistake is very basic only highlights the importance of basic numeracy to coherent reasoning about the most common ways of presenting quantified data. Really the error is just another example of overlooking absolute numbers; the 50 percent decrease is applied to a number twice as large as the 100 percent increase had been.

NON-LITERAL USES OF PERCENTAGE FIGURES

The concept of a percentage has become so widely employed that it has assumed a non-literal conventional meaning in some contexts. To see one example, first consider the practice of making wrong answers count for more than right answers on a multiple-choice examination. This policy is intended to counterbalance the presumed rate at which students guess when they don't know the answers. If there are four answers on every question, three of which are wrong, then on average students will be right in one out of every four wild guesses. To prevent them from benefiting by guessing, some instructors subtract one-third of a mark for every wrong answer. That way, for every three incorrect answers students will lose four marks total—thus cancelling out the one correct answer in four achieved by guessing. Sometimes, moreover, a teacher will simply subtract the number of wrong answers from the number of right ones on a test or quiz. The idea is to emphasize errors on what is judged to be an easy task.

CHAPTER 5   *Critical Thinking about Numbers*

On either approach we end up with a percentage grade that does not actually reflect how many answers out of one hundred are correct, hence doing some violence to the concept of percentage. The latter policy especially seems to hinge on some independent conception of what particular numerical grades mean within that evaluative system (i.e., "Anyone who gets 10 of *these* simple words wrong isn't a 90 percent student!"). More broadly, some grading systems altogether abandon the traditional meaning of a percentage while continuing to use the terminology. The Ministry of Education's grading guidelines in Ontario, for example, are based on a set of formulas that represent different facets of a student's individual assignments and tests, along with her performance over time, according a non-numerical set of descriptors—that is, summary guidelines for assigning a level to the work being assessed. For the sake of familiarity to students and parents, however, and to enable comparisons with other educational systems, school boards may elect to frame these levels in percentages at the final stage, based on a pre-arranged understanding of how percentages ought to match up to the aggregate effect of the descriptors. The resulting numbers, though framed in percentages, are unlikely to represent any information about the proportion of work that a student did correctly. Wherever possible, it is worth confirming that a claim phrased in a percentage really bears the proper relation to a ratio of 100. Applying any sort of arithmetical analysis to a purely conventional percentage claim is likely to lead to a false sense of precision and representativeness.

Sometimes percentage claims are meaningful only if understood metaphorically. The most common example is the sports interview cliché of giving "110 percent." Of course there is nothing wrong with talking about percentage values greater than 100 if we are comparing two things. We can say that this year's student enrolment is 110 percent of last year's—meaning simply that there are 10 percent more students this year. In the latter context, though, there is no suggestion that 100 percent denotes the maximum *possible* amount, while in the sports context there is such an understanding. To "give 100 percent," presumably, means to try your utmost. So to give 110 percent must mean something metaphorical; for instance, to try exceeding what you *thought* you could do at your best—in order to come closer to *actually* giving 100 percent, in other words.

RATES AND PERCENTAGES

One of the most common uses of percentages is to express not just changes but rates of change. Again this can be an extremely useful way of framing rates, especially as a way of keeping track of changes in the rates themselves. But it should now be particularly clear that as absolute amounts change, and as base rates change, the potential for confusion in comparing percentage rates is substantial.

One source of reasoning errors about rates and percentages is the fact that some apparently simple claims about rates are subject to ambiguity. We just saw the example of this year's student enrolment being 110 percent of last year's enrolment, meaning a 10 percent increase: all of last year's number (i.e., 100 percent), plus 10 percent more. This is a very different claim than that this year's enrolment is up 110 percent, though. The latter claim amounts to more than doubling last year's amount—the increase itself is 110 percent. We have to be careful, both in interpreting others and expressing ourselves, to distinguish between percentage figures of these two different kinds.

A further set of logical pitfalls associated with reasoning about rates derives from the difficulty of keeping straight what level is being described whenever we consider claims about higher-order rates—that is, rates of rates. Think about monetary inflation: the rate at which the overall price of goods increases (calculated as a per annum percentage). Suppose we are evaluating the following claim:

> "Under Premier Binkley's leadership, this province saw the first negative inflation in thirty years!"

There is the potential for ambiguity here: this might be about deflation—the claim that the overall price of goods decreased during Binkley's tenure. But it might also be about disinflation—the claim that the rate of inflation decreased, so prices are still going up, but not as quickly as before. All the previous cautionary notes about reasoning with percentages are compounded here by the need for care in distinguishing these possible interpretations of the level at which the term "negative" is intended to apply.

Similarly, a political campaign might see assertions like the following.

> "Under Premier Binkley's leadership, this province saw a 50 percent decrease in the rate of inflation growth!"

This falls into a category of utterance we've already discussed: things that can be said quickly and easily, but have to be understood slowly and carefully. Notice how the different quantifications stack up. Inflation is the basic rate here: the rate at which consumer goods, or a representative sample of them, go up in price over one year. So the rate of *growth* of inflation is a distinct higher-order rate. It is the rate at which the rate of inflation gets higher over a year. Finally, the claimed 50 percent decrease is a higher order again, since it applies to the rate of growth of the rate of inflation.

As a quick "soundbite," this claim suggests a very positive situation, but when these levels are all parsed the claim is at least consistent with some pretty negative outcomes. Suppose the basic rate of inflation was 1 percent two years before Binkley took office, and 2 percent over the year before he took office. Then the 1 percent increase in the rate of inflation amounts to a 100 percent rate of growth to the rate of inflation. Now suppose that the rate of inflation continued to climb in the year after Binkley took office, going from 2 percent to 3 percent. Since 1 is roughly 50 percent of 2, this can be described as a 50 percent rise in the rate of inflation. So the rate of increase in the rate of inflation can be said to have gone from 100 percent to 50 percent—a decrease of 50 percent, just as advertised. This strictly and literally licenses the claim of a 50 percent drop in the rate of increase of the rate of inflation. But the effects of absolute numbers are felt here: the 50 percent increase applies to a larger base number than the 100 percent increase the year before. In the most straightforward description of the situation, the inflation rate has continued to rise at the same pace: namely an additional 1 percent in the year before and the year after Binkley took office. Of course, this has few of the positive connotations that the original claim had, which is why it would be a less likely press release.

Linear Projection: Assumption of Constant Rates

An evidential fallacy that frequently arises in reasoning about rates is **Linear Projection.** This species of Hasty Generalization is the assumption that a rate observed over some specific duration must extend into unobserved territory as well—either the past or the future. So, for example, a large business might see a million-dollar increase in annual profits by cutting one hundred jobs. It would be a mistake to conclude merely on this evidence that for every hundred jobs cut, another million dollars of profit will be gained. Depending on the details of the mechanisms relating to size of work force and business profits in that particular case, the extra profits might be lower or even higher still for the next hundred job cuts and will obviously decrease sharply, even to the point of becoming financial losses, if critical jobs are cut (or if the remaining work force is demoralized by the process).

Similarly, the discovery that the moon is currently receding from Earth at around 3.8 centimetres per year does not entail that it has always receded at the same rate; it would be a hasty generalization to calculate its distance from Earth n years ago simply by multiplying 3.8 by n and subtracting the total from the current distance. In fact the moon receded more slowly in the past—the recession rate is thought to have been less than 2 centimetres per year around 650 million years ago—so for the distant past the linear projection would lead us substantially astray.

A more complicated set of issues is raised in an example employed by one writer opposed to gender-based affirmative-action policies. Dr. Grant Brown approvingly cites "one researcher" as claiming that, in Quebec,

> in 1990–91, 70.2% of girls entered college, compared with only
> 52.9% of boys. . . . [I]f you were to project these [educational] trends to
> the year 2050, you would eliminate boys and men from the work force.[3]

Taken at face value, this quote is an example of the fallacy of Linear Projection; it projects a constant rate into the distant future for no very clear reason. In this case, the projection is partially implicit, since there is no real numerical trend over time that is identified—only a single number for both males and females. We're left to infer that either Brown or Jocelyn Berthelot, whom Brown is apparently quoting, is appealing to some common knowledge that the percentages for males and females were suitably different in the past. In any event, however, the correctness of the mathematics itself is no great virtue if its application to reality is unclear.

It may well be mathematically true that extending that particular trend through to 2050 would have the claimed consequences; the question is why we should take that 58-year extension very seriously. Think of the trends in education that were occurring 58 years in the *past;* from 1992 (the time of the original quote) this would take us back to 1934. Is there any reason to be surprised that trends from the year 1934 had ceased to apply by the year 1992? For example, from 1955 to 1958 the

Grant Brown's citation is also an example of **misquotation,** a problem discussed in Chapter 4. Just as the statistic about child deaths from guns provoked Joel Best to go back to the original source, the quote given in Grant Brown's article presents a claim extreme enough to be worth investigating. What we find is that Jocelyn Berthelot, the researcher cited by Brown, did not really say what the quote attributes to him. In fact, the first sentence of the quote belongs to *Montreal Gazette* writer Janet Bagnall, not to Berthelot, and comes from several paragraphs *later* in Bagnall's newspaper article than does the second sentence.[5] The second sentence in the quote is indeed a partial quote from Berthelot, but the absence of quotation marks erases the boundary between what he said and what Bagnall wrote. Moreover, since the two sentences are from completely different contexts, the pronoun phrase "these trends" did not apply to the figures about college enrolment, as it appears when the sentences are stuck together in this way by Brown. Rather, Berthelot was discussing high school educational trends. Brown's version not only *adds* the word "educational" in order to generalize Berthelot's remark to college enrolment, but it also eliminates both the context and a key qualifying word. The original *Gazette* article first attributed to Berthelot the view that the "potential for controversy around this issue is enormous," then directly quoted him as saying, "If you were simply to project these trends ahead to the year 2050, you would eliminate boys and men from the work force." The context seems to show that Berthelot was *explaining* why these statistics can figure in controversy, rather than offering a worry about the year 2050 as a conclusion from his research. And the important term "simply" just disappears without any ellipses (". . .") in the mangled version of the quote. That word is significant because it suggests that Berthelot is aware of the naïveté of this projection; it is an additional indication that the original point was that too simple a use of the statistics can lead to controversy.

The issue this raises is one already familiar: that critical thinking frequently requires a willingness to directly confirm the data when there is a red flag about it—for example, when it seems inherently strange or is presented in a context making it likelier that the line between a rhetorical flourish and an outright distortion might have been crossed.

---

ratio of males to females in Quebec college undergraduate programs went from 5:1 (male:female) to 6.1.[4] Extending that trend 50-ish years into the future would have had the 2005 ratio of male undergraduates to female undergraduates in Quebec sitting at roughly 20 to 1—which, obviously and unsurprisingly, it isn't. For that matter, consider any two-day period in a given year comprising the day before payday and the day after payday. Overnight we could see a trend in my bank account that, if extended through every day until 2050, would see my total earnings clocking in at over $50 million. The extension of that overnight trend is arithmetically accurate, but bears no relation to reality since, alas, payday is not a permanent state for me. It's no more likely that the measured trends in male education and employment are permanent, either, so the eye-popping claim is at best a strained rhetorical device. Alarmist linear projections are red flags, obliging us to look carefully at the context to determine whether the assumption of a fixed rate is a reasonable one.

Sometimes factors are related in a fixed linear manner, but they might also be related exponentially, in irregular and more complex ways, or even chaotically (that is, unpredictably). It all depends on the details of the mechanisms relating the factors, and those details can vary greatly at different times and different levels. A line plotting the relation between two factors given only a few "local" measurements might begin as a tidy and straight one, but, once past some crucial "tipping point," in the words of author Malcolm Gladwell, might change its shape altogether.[6] In other words, some factors are related in a linear fashion only above or below certain thresholds. In epidemiology, the study of diseases, small but steady increases in the rate of new infections can correspond with surprisingly fast growth in the infected proportion of a population, while small increases in the infected proportion can, if they push the infected proportion past the tipping point, result in massive increases in the rate of new infections. This is true even of *closed* systems—meaning, nothing new gets in or out of the system—that have the right sort of complexity. (Human populations aren't closed, but even if they were, disease could still spread in the manner just explained.) Once we consider open systems, in which things enter and leave the system, we really don't even need any interesting sort of internal complexity in order for the linear assumption to fail.

If Canadian universities increase the number of medical doctors they train, for example, will the nation's population reflect a directly proportional increase in (i) the number of doctors or (ii) the percentage of the population who are doctors? Not necessarily. For nations are not closed systems: the answer to the question depends on how many people immigrate to or emigrate from that nation, what the specializations of the immigrants and emigrés are, and so forth. If more doctors enter Canada than leave it, or if young doctors graduate faster than old ones retire (or die), or if the reverse of either occurs, then changes in the numbers or rates of doctors trained will not accurately reflect changes in the numbers or rates of doctors in the population.

RATINGS AND RANKINGS

PERCENTAGE VERSUS PERCENTILE

As we have seen, percentages are not raw or absolute scores, unless the raw data happen to be out of 100. But percentages are at least representations of the absolute scores: 70 percent represents a raw score of, say, 21/30 on a quiz, while a 20 percent increase in a student's course grade is relative only to that student's course grade—not to any others in the class.

Percentile, by contrast, is a term often used to numerically rank values by how they compare to other values. To score in the 90th percentile on a test, for example, is to have a raw score better than 90 percent of the class. This might involve getting either more or less than 90 percent on the exam, though. On a very difficult test (or in a group of underachieving students) a grade of 65 percent might be in the 90th percentile, while on a very easy test (or in a group of outstanding students) a test grade of 95 percent might put one only in the 80th percentile. So even though the terms sound and look similar, the difference between them is crucial. Percentiles are inherently comparative within a group.

FIGURE 5.1	PERCENTAGE CHANGE IN INCOME BY DECILE FOR CANADIAN FAMILIES, 1990–2000[7]

It is important to know what information is actually being presented in a chart such as Figure 5.1. For example, the bars showing the income increase for the lowest and highest deciles of families over ten years indicate percentage changes that apply to different absolute amounts in the two deciles.

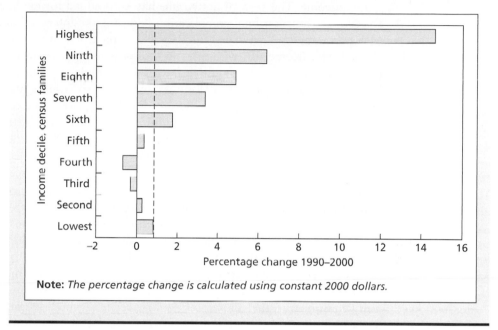

Note: *The percentage change is calculated using constant 2000 dollars.*

Source: "Income deciles, census families," from the Statistics Canada publication "2001 Census: Analysis Series, Income of Canadian Families, 2001 Census," Catalogue 96F0030XIE2001014, May 13, 2003, available at: http://www12.statcan.ca/english/census01/Products/Analytic/companion/inc/charts/chart1.cfm.

The idea of an *n*-ile ranking can be more coarse-grained than percentiles, as well. Instead of listing where some value falls relative to others on a scale of 100, we can instead break down a set of things (ranked by some measure or other) into quartiles: four even groups. Or quintiles: five even groups. The claim that a tax cut will give the greatest benefit to people in the second income quintile means that we are taking the population of income earners and ordering them from lowest income to highest, then dividing them into five groups of equal size; the first quintile will be the fifth of the population with the lowest income, the second quintile will be the fifth of the population with the next highest incomes, and so forth. (We count first, second, third *n*-iles starting from the bottom up, not from the top down.) Putting it another way, the second quintile for income is the group comprising the 21st through the 40th percentiles of income-earners.

Partly this is important because dividing up a group of values in this way can make for some surprising problems. (For an example, see the section on Simpson's Paradox in Chapter 6.) Partly it's important just because it can be easy to confuse one concept for another when percentages and percentiles are combined. In the graph shown in Figure 5.1, for example, we have deciles (a division into ten even groups) arranged vertically, and percentage changes represented by horizontal bars. Stacked vertically are equal-sized slices of the population, 10 percent in each group, at least when carved up by family. Horizontally we have percentage changes in family income. The vertical dotted line has been added for explanatory purposes.

Notice the additional complication here, for the interpretation of percentages: each percentage change represented by a horizontal bar in the graph is relative only to the 1990 income *of that decile*. So the sizes of the bars do not indicate changes that are proportional to the other bars. For example, the bar showing the income increase for the lowest decile of families over ten years is something like one-fifteenth the size of the bar showing the increase for the highest decile of families. It would be easy to misinterpret the graph, written by experts with little regard for public consumption, as showing that the incomes of lowest decile families grew by an *amount* roughly one-fifteenth the amount by which highest decile family incomes grew. But like the case of the man who had first a 100 percent increase then a 50 percent decrease to his net worth, these bars indicate percentage changes that apply to different absolute amounts in the two deciles.

The lowest decile of families saw roughly a 1 percent increase to their already-low incomes between 1990 and 2000—in absolute terms, a very small increase—while the highest decile of families saw roughly a 15 percent increase to their already-high incomes over the same period. In absolute terms, this will be a much larger increase; indeed, the portion of the increase for the sixth through the tenth deciles that is *spatially* equivalent to that shown for the first decile, denoted by the dotted line, represents a progressively larger absolute increase for each higher decile. Suppose for ease of calculation that the lowest decile's average annual family income in 1990 was $10,000, for the ninth decile $100,000, and for the highest decile $200,000. Then the 1 percent increase for the lowest group would amount to an extra $100 each year, while a 1 percent increase for the ninth decile would be an extra $1000, and 1 percent for the highest group would amount to an extra $2000 each year. The full 15 percent increase for the highest decile would then be an extra $30,000 annually—300 times as large as the lowest decile's increase in absolute terms.

THE SIGNIFICANCE OF NUMERICAL RANKINGS AND RATINGS

If you were being ranked in comparison to others in your class, at your job, or on your team, would you like to be ranked first? Most people would. After all, first means best, and it's nice to be the best at something.

But as simple as this seems, the use of definite numbers to rank people, institutions, or products can be unprincipled or highly misleading. I work at a university that has consistently been ranked first by the annual *Maclean's* magazine report on Canadian universities (in the "Comprehensive" category—meaning, in effect, major universities without a medical school). In fact it *is* an excellent university. If it were lower in the rankings, though, would this show it not to be excellent? Many universities suffer in various ways for receiving a low ranking in this biggest-selling annual issue of *Maclean's*; most universities bemoan its influence, though the ones at the top of the rankings tended (until recently) to bemoan it rather quietly. So it is worth asking what these or other numerical rankings really mean.

Whenever we assign some objects a rank ordering, we are again dealing with a representative number, with all the loss of information that this implies. In the case at hand, a vast amount of information about a university's location, faculty, funding, student body, enrolment standards, application pool, alumni employment levels, reputation, and many other factors are reduced to a single ordinal number. (**Ordinal** means first, second, third, and so forth; **cardinal** numbers are one, two, three. . . .) Whenever we look at a comparison of ordinal rankings, the potential for reading too much into the numbers is particularly strong.

Consider Artemis, a runner who finishes eighth in a race. Is she a slow runner? On one hand, the eighth-place designation sounds unimpressive on the face of it. We tend to think of such sports results in terms of gold, silver, bronze, and then everyone else, with eighth being well into the "everyone else" category. On the other hand, virtually every piece of information and every definition that we need to answer the question meaningfully is missing.

For instance, we need to know the size of the group of racers: eighth in an eight-person race is one thing, while eighth in a major marathon involving five thousand runners may be another thing altogether. But in our university example we know the total number of schools being evaluated; suppose we are looking at the eighth-ranked university out of eleven in the "Comprehensive" category. In 2005 eighth place was a tie between Carleton University and Concordia University. Does that tell us that these universities, so near the bottom of the ordinal ranking, are poor institutions? Does it tell us at least that they are not excellent? *Does it even tell us that they are not as good as the schools at the top of the list?*

In fact the ranking in itself tells us nothing of the kind, no more than Artemis's eighth-place finish tells us that she is slow, even relative to the rest of the racers. We may simply be dealing with a close finish. In principle, and sometimes in practice, every runner in the race can end up virtually tied for the win, so that careful analysis is required to tell which runner actually crossed the line first. But with sufficiently precise photography an ordering can be determined, so that a finish that initially looked like a perfect tie to the unaided eye can be sorted into first through eighth positions. When we *know* that this has occurred, naturally we don't think of eighth place as a poor finish. The conventions of a competitive race normally require an ordering of finishers (even when those in a tight group are assigned the same race time, as in cycling races) but in some circumstances it is obvious that the real differences between the race run by each runner are, for any *non*-ranking purpose, trivial. Practically speaking, they all ran equally quickly. When we are given only the ordinal rankings, we don't know whether this is what happened. But the numbers themselves may bias our judgment toward the conclusion that the eighth-place finisher did significantly worse than the winner (see Figure 5.2, page 138).

Of course, in competitive racing the whole point is to establish a winner and an ordinal ranking. The position in which a racer finishes a race is not treated as *evidence* for some independently important virtue for which medals are awarded. Being first across the finish line is itself the virtue being sought. In the case of university rankings this is (one fervently hopes) not the case. Ranking universities, unlike awarding Olympic medals, ought not be an exercise in picking winners even in cases where the differences between them are practically trivial. The rankings in

FIGURE 5.2

What's the Difference Between First and Last?

If the results of university rankings could be seen in the same way that we can see the finish of a track race such as this one, how might we think differently about what it means to finish first or last?

Jason Reed/Reuters/Corbis Canada

this case really are supposed to measure some independently valuable properties of universities. So we need some reason to think that the differences between universities with respect to those properties are ones that *make* a genuine difference to the ability of universities to accomplish their independent aims—independent, that is, of doing well in the *Maclean's* ranking. We need, in short, an independent definition and measure of genuine differences in good-universityness, and we need to know whether the distinctions by which the universities are ranked in *Maclean's* correspond to those differences.

In the absence of this information, the ranking of universities from first to worst tells us nothing about how bunched up or strung out the universities are in objective terms. For all the *Maclean's* ranking tells us, it is perfectly possible that every ranked university in Canada is objectively excellent (in some respect or other; more on this below), and the rankings a largely arbitrary ordering among practically indistinguishable institutions. To know otherwise, we would need some argument establishing that University A's being ranked ahead of University B overall on account of, say, receiving a higher "reputation" rating in a poll is a meaningful distinction. Such an argument would have to establish, first, that reputation (in the sense measured) is an important element in a university's mission; and second, that the difference in reputation between A and B is a practically significant difference with respect to the role that reputation is supposed to play. It would have to be shown not just that reputation matters, in other words, but that it matters to the degree actually separating A and B.

If it turns out that what really matters is having a reputation greater than n (on some means of quantifying reputation) and B has reputation $n+1$ while A has reputation $n+2$, then the overall ranking of A ahead of B will be vacuous. It will be a distinction that indicates no difference. Whenever we are given an ordinal ranking there is a danger of just this kind of thing occurring: that both the position of an entry on the list and the use of seemingly hard numbers to frame the statement will convey the sense of a major difference where there is little or no difference in reality.

Finally, given that the rankings make sense only if we have some objective sense of how measured properties relate to the proper aim or function of a university, we need to know whether there can be *more than one* such aim or function. In fact it's quite obvious that there is more than one when it comes to universities, which can be excellent at different combinations of research, teaching, affordability, distance education, hands-on experience for students, and the like. The philosopher Aristotle argued that there is not much sense to the idea of just plain free-floating *goodness*. Instead, goodness has to be understood as applying to specific things. But what makes something a good saddle is not what makes something a good horse, and similarly for a good film, a good lover, or a good slap shot. By the same token there can be more than one *way* of being good at something; some films are good because they have brilliant characterization, while others are good because they have exciting action. A single numerical ranking of any group of things having more than one standard of goodness presumes that there is some way of sorting these standards out into a single ordering: either reducing them to a more basic standard or taking some combined measure. Realistically, any such attempt is going to be some variety of fudge or other. Often it will be plainly silly.

Suppose we are asking what car is the best one to buy. Will it be a half-million-dollar sports car? A fuel-economical city car? A tank-like off-road vehicle? A plush luxurious land-yacht? Each of these vehicles has something to recommend it, given a distinct set of purchasers' needs, abilities, or desires. We might draw up a short-list of cars worth buying on the basis of these various needs and desires, but is there some way of deciding which one is the best overall? If we go by affordability, it is trivial that the cheapest will win; if by speed, it will be the fastest. If we choose a mixture of these things, some mid-range car may come out on top. But by what principle do we designate our choice of any such standard of evaluation as indicating the best car *all things considered*? The sensible conclusion may be simply that there is no single "best car"—just cars suited to different purposes.

Inventing a criterion to force the list into an ordered ranking may well be meaningless. Having a way of sorting items into a well-ordered list doesn't make that ordering sensible. We could probably take our cars and rank them clearly—no ties, no inconsistencies, first to last—on how well each stops a rifle bullet, or how quickly each sinks when dropped into a lake. But the neatness and numerical nature of the ranking would not mitigate the fundamental pointlessness of those ordering criteria. (Barring a buyer's having very unusual needs in a car, that is.)

MEANINGLESS OR CONFUSED QUANTITATIVE RANKINGS OR COMPARISONS

As we saw, a substantial component of one annual ranking of Canadian universities is reputation. But the quality and extent of a reputation is a nebulous thing indeed. How does a number get assigned to it? In the *Maclean's* ranking, reputation is measured by sending questionnaires out to a range of people, primarily university officials, high school guidance counsellors and principals, and assorted business figures like CEOs and corporate headhunters. On the basis of their replies a numerical value for each university's reputation is calculated. The numbers are sharp and well-behaved. But can the same be said about the phenomenon the numbers are supposed to represent?

It would be nice to think that in reality all the people in the listed groups are highly informed about all or most Canadian universities and moreover are scrupulously honest in how they report their knowledge. But let's imagine a fictional country—call it Shmanada—in which this isn't entirely true. In Shmanada, high school guidance counsellors and principals are mostly preoccupied with student problems unrelated to choice of university and have relatively local educational backgrounds themselves. Partly for these reasons they have only a passing knowledge of the various universities in their immediate region and at most sporadic knowledge of institutions nationwide. CEOs and headhunters in Shmanada are neither trained in nor interested in giving really systematic thought to relative strengths and weaknesses of universities nationwide; their opinions may simply date back to their own university days or may be based on a few idiosyncratic experiences they've had with relatively tiny samples of graduates from specific institutions. So their opinions too will be inclined to reflect regionalism and other demographic accidents among their employees. More importantly, both groups may get their only (purportedly) systematic information about relative quality nationwide from published rankings! This creates a self-perpetuating cycle of high and low reputation, as each year the magazine's survey largely detects the effects of its last annual issue.

Shmanadian university officials, moreover, are subconsciously swayed by partisanship to rank their own universities highly. Indeed, they may be quite consciously tempted to regard the whole reputation survey as a political exercise. So not only do they rank their own institutions highly, but they go out of their way to rank universities they see as non-competitors—those far away and in different categories, unlikely to lure away prospective students—more highly than those they see as competitors. Respondents at both Shmaterloo and McShmaster universities are thus given a completely political reason to rate, say, the University of Shmethbridge over each other. The Shmanadian universities that are clustered together in higher-population areas tend to pursue this strategy of low-balling their neighbours. One aggregate effect is to push up the rankings of some regionally isolated institutions perceived as "unthreatening."

It's unclear to what extent Canada resembles Shmanada in these respects. But even if the resemblance was total, the survey would still generate objective-looking numbers that could be calculated into overall rankings with all the appearance of precision, even though the phenomena being quantified were an unprincipled hodgepodge. Nor is this practice of shoehorning potentially undisciplined data into a single statistical measure particularly rare. A nice example, still on the topic of measuring the relative quality of universities, occurred in the *Globe and Mail*'s "report card" on universities in October 2002. The newspaper's assessment was based on student feedback from each university, with students who visited a website voluntarily rating their own university on over sixty measures. These ratings generate numbers, and the numbers can then be combined, averaged, and compared with the appearance of clarity and objectivity.

The voluntary questionnaire was certainly a way of measuring *something*. Whether that something was university quality, student preferences, or student ignorance, however, is much less clear. For example, when rating the quality of off-campus entertainment, students at Wilfrid Laurier University gave their school the twelfth-highest grade of all the universities, while students at the University of Waterloo gave theirs the twenty-fifth-highest rating. Such an apparently large gap suggests a serious difference in the wider community of these two institutions, which is surprising, since Wilfrid Laurier University and the University of Waterloo are roughly 150 metres apart at the edges of the two campuses. I and other University of Waterloo faculty were also impressed that our students rated our law school as top ten nationwide—given that in fact we have no law school at Waterloo. (Nor a medical school, with which the survey also credited us.) Now, these may seem like mere hiccups, but they indicate that among the things measured by this or virtually any questionnaire is *how much the respondents know*. Students may not actually know a great deal about the university they attend, in which case no mathematical manipulation of their rating responses will make it suited to rank institutions. The tidiness and coherence of numbers themselves does not mean that the phenomena being quantified are tidy or coherent.

The problem of confused or incoherent quantification extends to the comparative uses of different **metrics**, or measuring systems. Even when the metrics are individually well-defined and familiar, comparing them may be meaningless. Ask yourself which is greater: the mass of the sun or the distance between Earth and Neptune? Of course, each of these phenomena can be numerically quantified, but this does not entail that the resulting numbers can be compared to any intelligible effect. That is, the numbers do not themselves amount to a common metric.

Similarly, we could quantify the average change in household income over ten years—suppose it's +$2000. And we could quantify the average change in number of preschool children per city block over the same time—suppose it's +10. Yet it would be nonsense to say, "Over the past ten years, average household income has increased two hundred times as fast as the average number of preschool children per city block." This claim presupposes that we have some common unit of measure for both the children and the income. But we don't. All that the distinct units of measure have in common is the fact that numbers can be applied to them, which is insufficient for an intelligible comparison.

Moreover, sometimes a numerical scale fails to make much sense even on its own terms. I might rank paintings on aesthetic goodness using a scale from 1 to 10, where what I am quantifying is how the painting struck me on the particular occasion I viewed it. If the same painting gets very different ratings from me on different occasions, and starkly different paintings often get the same rating, it would be entirely unclear how the numerical scale was illuminating or quantifying anything at all. Presented with such a subjective system of rating, it is worth asking for clarification about the principles on which it is based.

FALLACIES OF NUMERICAL REASONING

PSEUDO-PRECISION

As we have noted, claims can gain rhetorical power through the use of numerical expressions, piggybacking on the perceived clarity and certainty of mathematics. One way of exploiting this effect is to state a numerical claim in highly precise terms, heightening the perception that a great deal of research and care underwrites the statement. Of course, sometimes this is an accurate perception. But sometimes the claim could not possibly be warranted to the degree of precision it displays. Such claims are merely **pseudo-precise**.

This can include framing a statistical statement in terms more precise than the "noise"—like rounding off numbers, and so forth—make reasonable and overstating the numerical precision of calculations based on measurements known to have been much more coarse-grained. With a tape measure, a starter's pistol, a stopwatch, and a flag, any two people can go out on large area to empirically calculate the speed of sound at that altitude. One person fires the pistol while dropping the flag; the other person, a measured distance away, starts the stopwatch when the flag drops and stops it when she hears the sound of the pistol. After only a few trials, the average of the times might run on to many decimal places, but presenting the result to the thousandth or millionth of a second is obviously silly, given how rough the measurement process is in the first place. Human reaction times in coordinating the flag and the pistol, and in starting and stopping the watch, make the experiment inherently sloppy. To give an average time to ten decimal places would be to impute a precision to the results that we know they can't have.

Pseudo-precision also includes statements like "We've overseen the creation of 8,422 jobs in Nova Scotia this month." The creation of a job is a process spread out over time. At both the beginning and the end of any precisely demarcated period, there will be job-creation processes for which it is unclear whether they should be included in that period even if their creation is known immediately. So framing the claim precisely down to the last single job is unwarranted; the most precise claim for which one could reasonably have evidence would be pitched at the level of tens, possibly hundreds, of jobs.

GRAPHICAL FALLACIES—THE MISREPRESENTATION OF QUANTITIES/RATES BY MISLEADING GRAPHS OR CHARTS

We saw in the chart showing income changes to Canadian families that the interpretation of a chart or graph can be a somewhat tricky business, even when the graph is competently constructed and not (deliberately) deceptive. There are, however, a range of visual tricks that can be employed in the presentation of data through a chart or graph, amounting to visual rhetoric. Without strictly lying, one may present graphed information so that it inherits the overtones of definiteness and objectivity that quantificational claims often have, even though the style of presentation makes the graph at least powerfully misleading.

FIGURE 5.3 | TAX CUTS AND PRISON INCARCERATIONS

Figure 5.3 demonstrates several common pitfalls of graphical reasoning, including a carefully limited range of values on both vertical axes and vague or weaselly definitions of what is plotted.

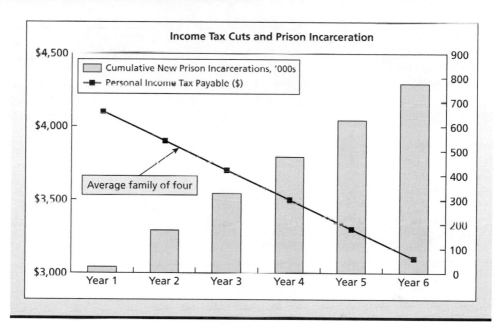

To see some of these tricks in action, consider the fictional example in Figure 5.3. We might have needed several graphs in order to see all the fallacies, confounds, and deceptive practices helpfully included in this single case! (If this example seems too obviously misleading to be a real-world example, you might consider a graph produced by the Ontario Ministry of Finance having some of the same properties as our sample here, yet plotting "job creation" against "income tax cuts.")[8]

Now, just looking at this graph it is clear what argument it is intended to communicate. The obvious implicit message of this chart is that income tax cuts have coincided with an increase in prison incarceration, inviting the conclusion that the tax cuts have *caused* prison incarcerations. In fact, the graph gives us no reason to believe this, when we inspect it carefully. Indeed, the graph appears to give evidence that the conclusion is false! The picture demonstrates several common pitfalls of graphical reasoning.

1. Carefully limited range of values on both vertical axes

There are two vertical axes on this graph, representing tax on the left and jobs on the right. At a minimum this requires us to pay special attention to which element of the chart is to be read against which axis. (For example, read in the usual left-to-right way, the line that stands for tax rate may seem to swoop down toward zero; in fact the numbers on the right have nothing to do with that line.) More to the point, the ranges of values for each axis have been chosen to produce the visual appearance of the largest changes. The right axis begins at zero, producing the largest possible representation of job creation, while the left axis goes from roughly

FIGURE 5.4 | VISUAL IMPRESSIONS CREATED BY CHOICE OF SCALE

These two graphs present the same information, but the large scale used in Graph A seems to reveal almost no change while the small scale used in Graph B seems to reveal a substantial change. Choice of scale affects the graphical information conveyed.

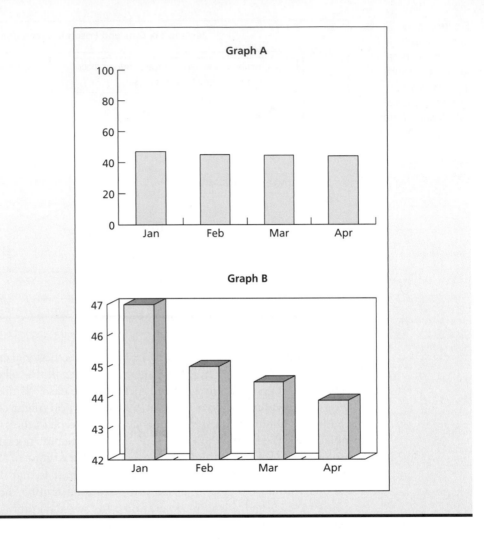

3000 to 4500, producing the largest possible representation of changes in tax rate. If the left axis were plotted from zero as well, the decrease would be barely perceptible; the line would be nearly flat.

For example, the two graphs in Figure 5.4, about a fictional company's sales over the first four months of a year, represent the same set of numbers entered into the graphing software that created them, but Graph A conveys a sense of stability—in fact, it's not clear from this chart that any change has occurred—while Graph B conveys a sense of disaster. All that differs is the range of the vertical axes: one runs from zero to 100, the other from 42 to 47. There is no saying which is less informative or more likely to mislead without knowing the details of the situation. Maybe no fluctuation smaller than 20 sales per month is significant, in which case Graph A is more useful; maybe the interval between 40 and 50 sales per month makes the difference between bankruptcy and wild success, in which case Graph B is by far the more illuminating.

With little independent reason to choose one scale over another, the grapher in Figure 5.3 aims to maximize the perception that the tax cuts are large by using that particular scale on the left axis. The effect is also to suggest that the tax cuts coincide with prison incarceration in some tidy intuitive way: the rising imprisonments and falling taxes seem to make a large X of straight-ish lines centred on the graph. If the range of values on the axes were not carefully chosen to create this effect, it would not appear.

This is a general issue with the interpretation of charts: the range of numbers chosen for the axes can make all the difference between changes that are barely noticeable and changes that look alarming and sudden. Just as a tabletop that is smooth to the touch will appear mountainous under a powerful microscope, a narrow range of values on a chart's axis can function as a kind of microscope, making small fluctuations appear large. Conversely, by choosing an outrageously large scale one can make changes that are significant by some independent standard appear trivial.

2. Vague or weaselly definitions of what is plotted

Probably the greatest absurdity on the graph in Figure 5.2 is the term "cumulative" on the right axis and what it signifies about the size of the vertical bars as we move from left to right. A quick look at the graph suggests that the increasing size of the "incarceration bars" indicates an increasing *rate* of incarceration. In fact these bars indicate, for each year, the total number of imprisonments *going back to Year One*, the first year shown on the graph. The word "cumulative" essentially means that each vertical bar includes the one before it.

It is hard to imagine a charitable explanation for the decision to choose a cumulative measure of prison incarceration, when it would be no harder to graph and vastly easier to understand bars that showed *only* new incarcerations from each year or even changes in the incarceration *rate* expressed as a percentage. The only obvious explanation for the cumulative measure is that it produces the highly suggestive march of upward-trending bars from year to year—in short, because the visual representation of the cumulative number has the considerable potential to mislead a reader into thinking that the tax cuts are causing more imprisonments. In fact, while the bars lend the appearance of a steadily increasing incarceration rate, the actual rate information is encoded not in the size of the bars, but in the amount by which each bar is higher than the one immediately before it. Looking at the graph, we can see that this amount is constant from year to year. What this means is that, other things being equal, the graph is actually an argument for the conclusion that the prison incarceration rate was unaffected by the tax cuts!

Relative to the intended conclusion, the information plotted against the right axis is also crucially incomplete. Obviously every year some people are imprisoned and others are released from prison. Data on new incarcerations alone tell us nothing about *net* changes to incarcerations. (The net amount is the overall amount when both gains and losses have been factored in.) In other words, the information in this graph is perfectly consistent with an overall *reduction* in the number of people in prison every year, if releases, which are not shown on the graph, happened to outstrip incarcerations.

A final thought to bear in mind about charts and graphs is simply that they can be vehicles for the display of most pitfalls in reasoning and communication discussed in this chapter. For example, a graph that used fixed spacing to indicate ordinal rankings (first, second, third . . .) would visually mislead us into inferring a substantial difference between first and worst, in just the way we saw allusions to ordinal rankings may do on their own. For the most part, if there's a way to mislead or draw mistaken inferences about numerical matters, there's a way to do it more vividly and more persuasively using a graph.

AVERAGES AND REPRESENTATIVENESS

Several times in this chapter we have had to appeal to the notion of an average, including in the analysis of the graph in the previous section. What exactly is an average? The concept is inherently probabilistic and statistical; for this reason it makes a natural transition into the next chapter.

As with the uses of numerical reasoning already examined, the basic idea behind giving an average value for some sample—the average consumer, the average bear, the average grade—is to give a representative number. The term "average" is triply ambiguous between the three interrelated concepts of the **mean**, the **median**, and the **mode**. For each definition, the average is supposed to be a single case or single value that can represent the sample well enough for the rational purposes at hand. Since there are different kinds of representativeness, there are different conceptions of an average.

The arithmetical mean represents a set of values as a ratio between their total value and the size of the set: it is calculated by adding up the values of a sample and dividing the sum by the number of elements in the sample. For example, if the total annual wages paid to 25 employees is $918,750, then the mean annual salary is $922,000 \div 25 = \$36,880$. When someone refers to an average without further qualification, they very often have the arithmetical mean in mind.

The median represents a group of data points by indicating the midpoint of its distribution. The median value in the group is the one that has as many elements greater than it as are less than it. In the following list of the number of flyers distributed by nine advertising assistants on one day, the median is 14; four numbers are lower and four higher. Coupled with the fact that the mean is 129, much higher than the median, this tells us that the numbers higher than the median deviate from it more than the numbers below it.

Group One: 5, 9, 12, 12, 14, 15, 24, 70, 1000

If there is an even number of values, and hence no single midpoint element, the median is taken to be the arithmetical mean of the two central values.

The mode is representative by way of being the most commonly occurring value in the set. In the above example, the mode is 12 since no other number occurs twice. In the set of observations below, the mode is 7.

Group Two: 4, 4, 7, 7, 7, 23

Depending on what we are interested in measuring, or depending on the point someone is trying to convey, these different conceptions of a representative value can be used to very different effects. Consider the case of the Great Western Spatula Corporation.

Salary structure at the Great Western Spatula Corporation:

CEO: $200,000

Executive manager: $80,000

2 Regional managers: $55,000

Marketing manager: $40,000

3 Marketing assistants: $31,000

4 Administrative assistants: $29,500

Factory supervisor: $29,000

12 Spatula makers: $21,000

Suppose the question is whether the Great Western Spatula Corporation pays its employees a decent wage. "Absolutely," replies the executive manager. "Our average wage is almost $37,000. It's not top dollar, but it's far from exploitation."

Of course this is a reference to the arithmetical mean—in this case, $36,880. But here again we see one way that stating an average can omit crucial information about the overall data: outlying values can badly skew the mean so that it tells us little about the bulk of the data points. The CEO's salary is so much larger than everyone else's that it drags the mean upward substantially and therefore makes it unrepresentative in a fairly obvious sense. Since the median is insensitive to the range of such outliers—they just count as one more value above or below the midpoint, and how far above or below doesn't figure into things—we can learn more by also considering the median. In this case, that's $29,000, the second-lowest salary (twelve people make more than that, twelve make less). In this sense, the average is substantially lower than that offered by the Executive Manager. But we also get relevant information by considering the mode, which is the lowest salary.

All things considered, the most revealing way to consider the question is to look at all the data, especially when it is ordered according to the basic concepts of statistics and probability. We rarely have the time or opportunity to seek out the raw data, of course, but at a minimum we can tailor our confidence in claims about averages by reflecting on the various data sets consistent with the claim. Practice with examples like the Spatula Corporation helps us to see just how wide the possibilities are. It is for reasons very much like this that the old saying exists, "Figures don't lie, but liars can figure." Equally importantly, people explicitly or implicitly using these broadly statistical concepts can confuse them by mere carelessness or incompetence, rather than by any intent to deceive. Here's an example from the *New York Times*, caught by Bob Somerby at thedailyhowler.com:[9]

> Perhaps most important, [the coming campaign] gives Al Gore a chance to present himself in human terms—he will talk a lot about himself and his family—and to try to overcome the perception that he is a wooden

technocrat, or, in the word that most people said in a Pew poll was the one that immediately came to mind when asked about Mr. Gore, "boring."

The Pew Research Center had surveyed 1786 people. Of all these people, only 66 chose the word "boring" when asked for one word about Gore. Still, no other word was chosen more often, so "boring" counts as the mode in the sample. That is, the word most often chosen by people to describe Gore was "boring." But compare:

The word most often chosen by people was "boring"
versus
The word most people chose was "boring."

The *Times* journalist uses the latter construction, which has a very different meaning than the former. And in this case, the latter is catastrophically false where the former is straightforwardly true, since the most-chosen word was "boring" but fewer than 4 percent of respondents chose it. Going back to the data to check for this sort of error is only rarely practical, but that is what we should do before basing any serious judgment on a claim involving statistical concepts, even in such common contexts as the reporting of polls. As is discussed in more detail in Chapter 10, a journalist or columnist can report on a poll without having much competence with the statistical concepts it implicates.

FROM AVERAGES IN A SAMPLE TO AVERAGES IN A POPULATION

Averages can be used and abused even in contexts where all the information is in our possession. The case of the Great Western Spatula Corporation employed averages in the reasoning even though the absolute numbers, all the salaries, were available. But most domains of information are much larger than this, and getting all the information would be expensive, or worse, impossible, or worse yet, hard work.

In these cases, therefore, we instead examine a **sample** drawn from the larger group that we want to know about and then take our conclusions about the sample to apply to the whole population. Of course, this raises a family of extra problems regarding whether any such mean, median, or mode is representative. We already had the concerns that arose in the Spatula Corporation case—basically, worries about whether one or another kind of average is representative of the sample—but now we also have concerns arising from whether the sample itself is appropriately representative of the wider population. For instance, quite apart from the confusion about interpreting modes in the case of the Pew poll on Al Gore, there is a further question of whether the responses of the particular 1786 people surveyed should be considered an accurate reflection of what United States citizens in general thought about Al Gore at that time.

Really this is just a standard inductive problem: we're trying to infer the unobserved from the observed. There is, for example, some precise mean height of Canadians at any given time. But at any given time the best we could reasonably do in trying to learn what that mean height is in the population is to sample *some* Canadians for their heights and then calculate the mean of the sample. The question is how we can have confidence in the conclusions we draw through such methods; indeed, how we can have confidence in cases where our information is partial, imperfect, or open to revision. Since this is a very large proportion of our reasoning, it is crucial to reflect on the best methods for making sense of its strengths and weaknesses. Those methods are expressed in the concepts of probability and statistics.

CONCLUSION

Numerical claims and arguments are pervasive in persuasive and informative communication. Moreover they are widely taken to have a particular authority and objectivity. Interpreting them with competence requires both the willingness and the basic ability to work through simple calculations and confirm that the numerical claims mean what they are presented as meaning.

Many numerical claims and arguments make use of representative numbers of some sort. These are devices of great convenience, but always involve the loss of information existing in the original data. Ways in which such information might have been lost amount to ways in which subsequent arguments using those numbers might be unsound. Moreover, the use of numbers to quantify any feature or property depends on the existence of a sensible metric, or measurement system, that the numbers can meaningfully represent. A subjective or nonsensical metric is not made rigorous or objective simply by assigning numbers to it. Rankings, comparisons, and mathematical charts are all of this sort: potentially useful reasoning tools that are commonly and easily the ingredients in reasoning errors.

REVIEW QUESTIONS

1. Explain two distinct interpretations of the claim that knitting is the fastest-growing hobby in Canada, corresponding to two ways of measuring growth. Which measure is clearer or more illuminating in your view, and why?
2. Politician A says, "Under our proposed tax reforms, Canadian families will save an average of $1000 per year." Politician B says, "Under A's tax reforms, the average Canadian family will save less than $200 per year." Without worrying about the details of Canadian tax law, discuss how both utterances might be broadly correct given different interpretations or applications of the term "average."
3. Scan some recent newspapers looking for charts and graphs and choose one. (The Business section is likeliest to have some.) Using the observations from this chapter, your independent knowledge, and your reading of the story accompanying the graph, assign the chart or graph a percentage grade. Justify your grade based on the chart's clarity, informativeness, accuracy, and honesty.

NOTES

1. J. Best, *Damned Lies and Statistics* (Berkeley: University of California Press, 2001).

2. P. Bramadat, Abstract for "Christian Canada No More?" St. Jerome's University lecture, Waterloo, Ontario, 2004.

3. G. Brown, "The Politics of Preference: A Catalogue of Criticisms of Employment Equity." Society for Academic Freedom and Scholarship website: www.safs.ca/meritdiversity/catalogofcriticism.pdf, November 25, 2005.

4. Statistics Canada, "W340-438. Full-time University Enrolment, by Sex, Canada and Provinces, Selected Years, 1920 to 1975," at http://www.statcan.ca/english/freepub/11-516-XIE/sectionw/W340_438c.csv.

5. Brown sources the quote in turn from an article by Katherine Young in *The McGill Reporter* (October 7, 1992), but cites it as deriving from the *Montreal Gazette* (June 6, 1992). The *Gazette* article, "Our Lost Boys," was written by Janet Bagnall, (pp. B1–2).

6. M. Gladwell, *The Tipping Point: How Little Things Can Make a Big Difference* (New York: Little, Brown, 2000).

7. Statistics Canada, "2001 Census of Canada; Analysis Series," at http://www12.statcan.ca/english/census01/Products/Analytic/companion/inc/charts/chart1.cfm.

8. The *2000 Ontario Economic Outlook and Fiscal Review*. E. Eves (Ontario Ministry of Finance) "2000 Ontario Economic Outlook and Fiscal Review" (Toronto: Queen's Printer for Ontario, 2000). Available at http://www.fin.gov.on.ca/english/economy/ecoutlook/statement00/. (This example was brought to my attention by Justin Podur, who wrote a critical treatment of a different version of the graph at http://www.zmag.org/instructionals/logstats/logstats17.htm.)

9. Bob Somerby (http://thedailyhowler.com), quoting Katherine Seelye, "The Unbuttoning of Al Gore: Act 1," *New York Times*, June 15, 1999, p. A20.

Probability and Statistics: Reasoning from Incomplete Information

A public-service advertisement in a magazine aimed at young women advises: "Don't be foolish. If you have unprotected sex, you have an 85 percent chance of getting pregnant within one year." Now, suppose a woman had unprotected sex once this year, on January 5. It's now the middle of November and there are no signs of pregnancy. Should she still be worried for six more weeks?

Clearly some information is missing from the advertisement. Its underlying message is entirely reasonable—don't have unprotected sex unless pregnancy is one of your immediate life goals—but it's given us a numerical measure of *how worried we should be,* without making much sense of it. If once per year is not enough unprotected sex to make that particular figure intelligible, how much is enough? Once per week? Per minute? The advertisement offers an assessment of risk, in the form of a probability, without explaining the risky behaviour upon which the probability depends. On what statistics is the prediction based?

Increasingly we swim in a sea of claims like this one: assertions about risks to our health, our environment, our society; statistics regarding things from the reliability of cars to the alleged traits of every socially identifiable group of people; probabilities that a marriage will end in divorce, that a tornado will strike, that a major earthquake will occur. Some of these claims, like this advertisement, partially encode an important truth. Many are utterly bogus. Either way, most are grossly incomplete and rely on the audience to be easily impressed with authoritative statements about likelihood, especially when these are couched in numerical terms.

BASIC STATISTICAL CONCEPTS

REPRESENTATIVE SAMPLING

Besides the need to make decisions, weigh risks, and predict outcomes, we use probability and statistics as powerful investigative tools that can reveal correlations and causes among various events or conditions. This is what the graph showing tax cuts and job creation purported to do in Chapter 5: compare statistics based on two socio-political phenomena in order to show that changes in one play a role in changes in the other. Similarly, we are interested in examples like the average height of Canadians not just because we're curious, but because this is a statistically measurable trend that might be linked with other measurable trends in some sense worthy of our attention. For this reason among others, we need to be confident of our ability to say what the averages and trends are in the first place.

We left off the treatment of averages in Chapter 5 with the problem of moving from the calculation of averages in domains where we have all the data, or at least can get it if we need to, to the calculation of averages for domains that go beyond—perhaps far beyond—the data at our disposal. Naturally, the way to do this is to obtain the data for a sample drawn from the broader population of people, objects, or events. We can then apply various statistical concepts, calculating averages and searching for trends and correlations within the sample data, and apply the results of this reasoning to the broader population: inductive reasoning in action.

The general problem, though, is that we can easily pick an **unrepresentative sample** from the population at the outset. If this happens, then no matter how careful our reasoning about the sample, it will be misleading with respect to the population. There are two broad ways in which this can happen: by incorporating some bias into the selection of the sample, and by being unlucky.

Consider first the idea of a **selection bias** in picking a sample. Suppose, for example, that a university wanted to know whether its graduates believed they had made a good decision in choosing that school, even years and decades after they'd graduated. The obvious thing to do is to survey those graduates for their opinions. But how could they be tracked down now? One thing the university might try is just randomly sampling the population at large to find graduates of their institution. But that would be a difficult way of finding any but a relatively small sample, since the proportion of any university's graduates in a population is quite low. "But wait!" says the university's vice-president of external affairs to herself. "I have to stop talking to myself. But first, I should contact the alumni donations office. They have a mailing list of graduates who donate money to the university. We can send out the questionnaires to that mailing list and get a large set of replies for our study."

Our general knowledge of how people think and behave is sufficient to reveal what's wrong with this idea. If the study is supposed to measure what *all* the university's graduates think of their experience at the school, the donations list is very likely to produce a biased sample. Why? Because all other things being equal, someone who thinks fondly of an institution is likelier to donate money to it than is someone who hates or resents it. So the donations list is likely to seriously underrepresent both the graduates who didn't enjoy the university and those whose opinion is roughly neutral, and to over-represent the people who feel positively about the university—at least, positively enough to donate money to it. Hence such a study would plausibly demonstrate a selection bias.

A selection bias commonly occurs in informal polling—and sometimes in "serious" polls—whenever the sample is simply drawn from the people who want to be heard on that particular issue. Having your say on a radio or television call-in show devoted to some issue usually involves some time and effort: dialling the number, waiting on hold for several minutes, describing one's intended question or comment to the staff whose job it is to screen out people likely to use profanity or, worse, intelligence, and then saying one's piece to the host. In general people don't go through all this only to say, "I don't really care one way or another" or "I think the most moderate position is probably reasonable." Usually when a news organization or website runs an informal poll on what people think of some issue, this is what they mean by saying in the small print that it's not a "scientific" poll. They are pointing out that their results might only indicate who was sufficiently motivated to volunteer their opinion. For call-in programs, the screeners themselves might filter opinions for the sake of getting a more even split among callers—the whole point of such shows often being to foster a controversy and not to sample a population.

Sometimes, moreover, a sample exhibits a bias because it was chosen for that very purpose. This is an effective, if deplorable, way of manufacturing the appearance of a significant phenomenon or story. Anyone who follows sports will be familiar with journalists who can create winning or losing trends out of thin air, simply by trimming the number of past games to fit the story. For example, consider how quickly a sports team's fortunes can change, according to the *Sun* media chain:

> *Wednesday February 18 2004, Sun Newspapers*: "Tensions ran high in Montreal, which is mired in a four-game losing streak."[1] (Previous 10-game record as of February 18: 4 wins, 6 losses.)

> *Thursday February 24 2004*: "Montreal is 4–1 in its last five games."[2] (Previous 10-game record as of February 24: 5 wins, 5 losses.)

By choosing the right number of past games on the right dates as the data set, the writers can take a team basically winning half its games and depict it either as red hot or ice cold. The practice is common far beyond sports journalism, too. It is important to bear in mind that any claimed trend might just be an artifact of such a **trimmed sample**; certainly a sample range or time period that isn't a conventional round number is a red flag. In the absence of some special explanation, a statement that begins "Did you know that since 1973 . . ." or "Statistics show that over the past 17 years . . ." is just begging for an analysis of the original data. At least as important to bear in mind is just how obvious this sort of reasoning can seem to us when we produce it ourselves. Other people do this for largely the same reason that you or I will: because visible streaks or trends in data strike us as intuitively significant. It takes an effort—or must be a habit—to stop and think whether the events or data would still count as a trend or streak if we considered a more principled sample size. Chapter 7 examines this problem in more detail.

A large component of any science of measurement within a particular field (e.g., biometrics, econometrics, psychometrics) is the study of how to get non-biased samples in light of the challenges specific to that field. Often the best tool one can use is one's general knowledge and imagination, since selection biases can be complex and subtle; it's useful to be able to think creatively about how the selection method *might* be biased. Clearly a poll conducted over the Internet on the usefulness of computers has the potential to be badly biased, but how might a telephone poll on the health of one's lifestyle be biased? What time of day do polling companies typically try to call? Are people who are frequently out in the evenings likelier to have a healthy lifestyle? What possible biases lurk in standard polling methods?

CHAPTER 6 *Probability and Statistics*

However, even if we do find a relatively unbiased way of sampling a population, we might just get unlucky anyhow. Choosing a sample for our height survey, we might do everything right but still just happen to get a group that's substantially taller or shorter than the real national average. Mostly this is a matter of the size of the sample, though. In the most extreme case of a small sample, we would just observe a single randomly chosen person. Obviously any single person's height could deviate from the true population mean height by a wide margin. It's also possible for a sample of two to deviate from the true mean just as widely. And three, and four . . . but the more people we sample, the more likely it is that we'll get a proportional representation of the population. So the average height of our sample will approximate the average height of the population ever more closely as the size of our sample increases—always assuming, that is, that there are no hidden biases in our selection method.

PROPERTIES OF A NORMAL DISTRIBUTION

One of the main lessons of our earlier examination of averages was the extent to which a mean, even when properly calculated, can hide important information about the sample over which it is calculated. Consideration of the median and mode can partially remedy this by revealing further information about the sample, as we saw. But it would also be very useful to know how *spread out* the sample is. The measure of spread in the sample data is called the **standard deviation** of a sample, a term you are sure to encounter in various information sources that offer you statistics.

The standard deviation is not quite an average, but it is another sort of representative number. The smaller the standard deviation, the more tightly grouped the data is around the mean. For example, recall the small data sets Group One and Group Two:

Group One: 5, 9, 12, 12, 14, 15, 24, 70, 1000

Group Two: 4, 4, 7, 7, 7, 23

In Group One, the single large value of 1000 will be represented in a large standard deviation, revealing that for a sample of such a small size, the data points span a wide range. (We won't worry about the formula for calculating standard deviations; the concept as just explained is enough for our purposes.) The standard deviation in Group One is approximately 327—but if we dropped the value 1000 from the sample, the standard deviation would be roughly 21 among the remaining data points. Again, this means that the average difference between the elements in the sample and the mean is 327 and would be just 21 if the outlying value was dropped. Which is just what we sometimes do, if it looks like the outlier was really just a freak occurrence. Choosing principled ways to make this decision and investigating whether somebody else left out some data in a principled way are important problems in any kind of statistical reasoning.

Among other things, the standard deviation lets us make useful comparisons between sets of data, telling that while they might have the same mean, they can have very different spreads of data from which the mean is drawn. Perhaps the easiest way to see this is pictorially, using the so-called **normal curve**, or "**bell curve**."

The area under the curve indicates how the data in a sample are distributed: for reasons that will become clear in the following section, the area under the curve is 1. The mean is the centre line (zero, that is) and the number of data points tails off symmetrically as values are farther from the mean. A vast range of natural and social phenomena produce data sets that have this shape, or at least can be mathematically massaged into this shape: the height example, for instance, works well here. Most adults cluster around a mean with respect to their height, with the number of people taller and shorter than the average dwindling symmetrically. Rather than dealing with the mean height value itself, we can conventionally think of the mean height as the zero value on the graph's horizontal axis, and then just quantify the various data points based on how far above or below the mean they are.

The application of the bell curve to student grades is quite familiar; a mean and median of 68 to 70 percent is a fairly common standard for first-year classes in many disciplines. But there are different curves having this general shape that share, or can be manipulated to share, the key properties of the example given above. A normal curve can be taller and skinnier than the one in Figure 6.1, or flatter and wider (holding the units of the vertical axis constant, that is). In each case, it will have the same mean and an area under the curve of 1. The standard deviation basically tells us the shape of the curve: a small standard deviation means a narrower

---

FIGURE 6.1 | A BELL CURVE

A normal curve or "bell curve" is a pictorial representation of the standard deviation of a set of data. The standard deviation defines the shape of the curve: a small standard deviation means a narrower curve (the data cluster together in the centre), and a large one indicates a flatter curve (the data spread out relative to the mean).

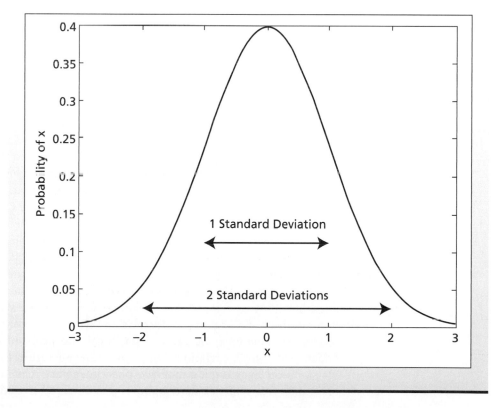

CHAPTER 6   *Probability and Statistics*

There is even a statistical theorem of sorts, called the **Fuzzy Central Limit Theorem,** which states that properties affected by lots of independent random factors (as height is affected by diet, genes, exercise, and posture) are approximately normally distributed, meaning that they can be made to fit a normal curve when a large sample is considered.

curve (the data cluster together in the centre), and a large one indicates a flatter curve (the data spread out relative to the mean). Whatever its particular shape, if the data—or, in the probabilistic case, the possible outcomes—fit a normal "bell" curve, then approximately 68 percent of the cases fall within one standard deviation of the mean, while approximately 95 percent of the cases fall within two standard deviations of the mean, and 99 percent fall within three standard deviations. (So the labelled arrows on the diagram should be understood to say "standard deviations *from the mean*"; the arrows actually *span* two and four standard deviations.)

The importance of knowing the standard deviation for some statistics should be clear. Suppose we were wondering whether any socially significant conclusions are suggested by data regarding changes in average incomes over time. For example, we might learn that the mean Canadian income has increased appreciably over ten years. Does this tell us that people in general are better off? Not by itself. Relevant information missing here includes not just possible changes in median income, if any, but also the standard deviations of the earlier and later income distributions. The mean income could increase while the difference among incomes grows; roughly, the curve might just get wider while also sliding to the right. The rich could be richer and the mean income could go up, while nevertheless more people dropped below (and further below) whatever line we designate as indicating poverty. This is the kind of information that a difference in standard deviation can indicate.

CORRELATIONS AND THE NULL HYPOTHESIS

One of the reasons people are so interested in assembling and comparing statistics is that they have the potential to tell us not just averages, not just *that* trends and changes occur, but *why* things are the way they are. We don't just want to know how tall Canadians are; we want to know how their average height has changed, and we're interested in what other things have changed along with it. We might be independently interested in how many Canadians smoke cigarettes and in how many Canadians suffer from heart and lung diseases. Particularly important, though, is the prospect of discovering that correlations hold between such things—between height and diet, between birth weight and literacy, between smoking and lung disease. Or, for that matter, that correlations do not hold between factors that strike some people as intuitively correlated. When we speak of **correlation**, we mean two phenomena or variables that "move together," that is, they co-vary in predictable ways across different circumstances. By looking at correlations (or their absence) and theorizing about possible explanations, we can use statistical and probabilistic reasoning not just to understand complex relations but to intervene and affect them.

If one starts off by assuming that two phenomena are related, it is particularly easy to over-interpret evidence that supports this assumption and often difficult to find positive grounds to overturn the assumption. Such an approach moreover violates the rationale of starting off by suspending judgment in a neutral state of information. For these reasons, when scientists do experiments to explore how phenomena interrelate, they begin with something called the **null hypothesis**. The null hypothesis is the assumption that any correlation observed between the phenomena is purely random or accidental. Its character as an assumption is crucial; if the evidence does not force the rejection of the null hypothesis, the response is not to *conclude* that there is no real effect. The only conclusion is that the null hypothesis is undefeated. That is, at the level of individual studies or experiments, scientists and statisticians usually distinguish between absence of evidence and evidence of absence, unless the study is particularly large and very thorough. For the reasons discussed in Chapter 4 regarding arguments from ignorance, the stronger conclusion that there really is no effect or no correlation normally requires looking at a series of studies, all or most of which fail to reject the null hypothesis.

A simple sort of correlation is co-occurrence, or just being found together. Suppose that 20 people meet once per week to play "pick-up" hockey. Playing pick-up means that there are no ongoing teams from game to game. Instead, once people are sitting down to put on their hockey equipment, teams are chosen just by the order in which people are seated: starting at one end of the room, players alternate between dark and white jerseys. Obviously, we should expect that any two players—take George and Bill, for example—will sometimes be teammates and sometimes opponents, as the weeks pass. But will there be any interesting trends? The null hypothesis is that George and Bill will be on the same team only by chance, and since there are only two teams (assuming that they both show up for all the games) a random team-sorting process should result in George and Bill being on the same team for half the games, and on different teams for the other half. If a pattern emerges in which they are on the same team disproportionately often, then they are **positively correlated** with respect to team membership. If they are on different teams disproportionately often, then they are **negatively correlated**. The question is how we decide whether this is so, and what the judgment of correlation really means.

Of course George and Bill might randomly happen to be on the same team for the first two weeks, or the first three weeks. Indeed, they *might* randomly end up on the same team every game for 10 weeks. It's just that the odds of this happening are low: for reasons explained later in the chapter, the probability of this outcome is $(1/2)^{10}$, or 1 in 1024. That is, we should expect such an outcome by sheer chance fewer than once in any thousand 10-week stretches that we examine. So if we notice

DETAILS MATTER

More precisely, in discussing the pick-up hockey example, we should describe the null hypothesis as holding that *as more weeks pass*, the ratio of teammate games to opponent games among George and Bill will *approach* 1/2. After all, even if the process is random we shouldn't expect that the numbers will be precisely equal after every even number of weeks have passed. Just the opposite, in fact. If they alternate like clockwork between teammates and opponents from week to week, that is powerful evidence of a pattern, the opposite of randomness.

that George and Bill are always on the same team for 10 weeks (or even 7 or 8 weeks), we would have good reason to think that the null hypothesis is false. It would be very probable that some explanation besides chance exists for that same-team correlation, especially given the independent plausibility of various non-random explanations.

How good do our grounds need to be for rejecting the null hypothesis? In order to err on the side of caution in giving up our initial state of suspended judgment, the normal scientific practice is to make it easy for the null hypothesis to "win." The term **"p-value"** is used to denote how probable it is, given a particular sample, that you would get a sample that far from the null hypothesis if the null hypothesis were true. For most scientific purposes, the value of p is pretty low: 5 percent or 1 percent are usual minimum p-values for claiming statistical significance. The null hypothesis is regarded as undefeated as long as it has even a 5 percent (or 1 percent) probability of being correct in light of the evidence, which essentially means that the probability of a non-random correlation between two phenomena, given the observed data, must be 95 percent (or 99 percent) before it can be said to hold with the appropriate confidence. By this standard, in the case of George and Bill it is clearly rational to reject the null hypothesis, which has less than one chance in a thousand of being correct.

On a more serious issue, people have thought it worth exploring whether cigarette smoking causes lung cancer. The null hypothesis in this case is the assumption that any tendency for lung cancer to occur in smokers will just be a matter of chance variations—that lung cancer won't occur in smokers at any higher rate than in non-smokers. If the observed correlations are too improbable on the assumption of pure chance, we reject the null hypothesis and conclude that there is a genuine connection between the two factors—smoking and cancer, in this case. In other words, the null hypothesis fails when the correlations we observe are highly likely *not* to be merely random.

Just as in the case of George and Bill, rejecting the null hypothesis when the data in our sample suggest a positive correlation between smoking and cancer is not the same as knowing what the connection is. Any specific attempt to explain such a correlation must rule out a wide range of **confounds**: alternative explanations for the observed data. We can conclude that there is some non-random explanation for the coincidence in George and Bill's team membership, but which explanation is it? A cynic might leap to the conclusion that the selection process is deliberately rigged somehow. George might be an outstanding player, so Bill chooses to sit an even number of spaces away from George in order for the counting process to place them on the same team. But this hypothesis has various confounds. Maybe various players arrive habitually at specific times, so that every week Bill arrives first, then someone else (call him Ken), and then George. They end up sitting down in that order, and Bill and George hence end up on the same team (and Ken on the other team). Or maybe Bill is fond of sitting at one end of the room, and George likes the other end of the room, but Ken always comes in late and squeezes in between George and the wall. Such combined accidents of seating preference trends and arrival time trends might also explain the correlation. Until they are explored and ruled out, the cynical hypothesis has outstanding confounds.

Similarly, even if smokers statistically suffer from cancer more frequently than non-smokers, if that is all the information we have, then the explanation that smoking directly causes cancer is confounded by the prospect of indirect connections between the two. The sheer number of studies on smoking and cancer is in part the result of trying to rule out such confounds with further information. The classic example of a confound for a causal explanation is a **common cause**. That is, X and Y may be correlated because they are both caused by Z, and not because X causes Y or vice versa. From October to January in Saskatchewan, an increase in average household heating costs is genuinely correlated with an increase in the average total weight of people's outdoor clothing. But neither of these things causes the other; they are both results of the onset of winter. In the smoking case, it may be that people predisposed to smoke are independently predisposed to get cancer; it is (barely) conceivable that some single genetic trait increases the odds of both. In that case smokers would indeed disproportionately suffer from cancer, but it wouldn't necessarily be *because* they smoked. Or maybe handling cigarette packaging leads to cancer. Here again smokers would be at higher risk, but not strictly because of the smoke itself.

We can control for these possibilities by observing people who want to smoke but don't, in the first case, or by tracking the information of people who handle cigarette packaging but do not smoke, in the second case. If we find any correlations in these tests, we basically factor them out of any overall correlations we observe between smokers and cancer victims. In practical explanatory terms, we infer some variety of causal connection between X and Y when there are observed correlations between them that cannot be deflated by appeal to indirect connections, and when we can furthermore appeal to some sort of mechanism that implements the causal relation.

Rejecting the null hypothesis does not in itself mean inferring a particular efficient-causal explanation of the data. It only means that the observed correlation is genuine, that it ought to be regarded as predictive of future situations that are relevantly similar. Hence it is much more common for statisticians to speak cautiously about correlations, rather than claiming to have discovered causal relations in as many words.

SIGNIFICANCE AND MARGINS OF ERROR

When we draw (non-deductive) inferences from some set of data, we can only ever be confident in the conclusion to a degree. **Statistical significance** is a measure of the confidence we are entitled to have in our probabilistic conclusion. It is, however, also a function of how precise a conclusion we are trying to draw.

In one sense, confidence is cheap. We can, after all, always be 100 percent confident that the probability of some outcome is somewhere between 0 percent and 100 percent inclusive. But that claim is so imprecise that we'd be placing our confidence in a complete triviality. After all, we can say of any proposition that it is

---

DETAILS MATTER

When an apparent correlation between X and Y exists by the virtue of Z's being correlated with them both, as when Z is a common cause, we say that Z **screens off** X from Y.

either necessary, or impossible, or somewhere in between. Any substantial claim will have a far more restricted **confidence interval** or **margin of error**. The confidence interval is the range of values within which we can be statistically confident (to some specified degree) that the true value falls. Alternatively, the margin of error is half that range, expressed relative to the midpoint of the confidence interval. Based on some poll of voters' intentions, we could say that we are 95 percent confident that 50 to 60 percent of voters will support Candidate A (the confidence interval), or, equivalently, that we are 95 percent confident that 55 percent of voters will support Candidate A, +/−5 percent (the margin of error).

As soon as we consider more precise claims, with smaller margins of error, we are less entitled to confidence in their truth unless we improve our state of information by considering more evidence. So we can swap confidence for precision, and vice versa, but we can't improve them both without more data. The smaller a margin of error we want to have in framing our conclusion, the more data we need in order to have high confidence in it.

Hence, when we are given some statistic based on some sample, we need to know both the margin of error—that is, how precise the conclusion is—and the significance of the result. This is why polls report having, for example, "a 3 percent margin of error 19 times out of 20." This means that we can be 95 percent confident of getting a result within 3 percent of the reported value. (Notice that this means 3 percent above or below the reported value; a result of n with a 3 percent margin of error means a 6 percent range with n in the middle of the range.) A statistical conclusion always represents a compromise between the precision of the claim and our confidence in its truth. We could, if we wished, convert our 95 percent confidence in some conclusion into 99 percent confidence. But nothing is free; we would either have to increase the margin of error or get much more data in order to increase our confidence.

In short, a set of data typically permits you to be confident, to a degree, in some statistical conclusion that is precise, to a degree. Understanding a statistical claim requires knowing both degrees. Using fixed standards of significance is the most common way of simplifying the interpretation of statistical correlations; 5 percent and 1 percent are standard significance levels for many scientific publications (though some fields demand much higher levels and some scientific journals used to publish results with confidence as low as 90 percent). To say that an observed result is significant at the 5 percent level is to say that over the long run such a result will show up at most 1 time in 20 if the effect isn't real—that is, if the null hypothesis is true.

One consequence of there being a specialized sense of "significance" in the realm of statistics is that an ambiguity may arise when the term is popularly applied to a scientific claim. News stories often include phrases like "Scientists reported that the new drug significantly lowers the risk of disease." To many readers (and perhaps to the reporter) this will activate an interpretation of "significant" meaning something like "substantial" or "worth acting on." But it might just mean significance in the statistical sense, which is consistent with the drug's having only a tiny advantage over other treatments (or even over no treatment). As long as that tiny advantage is detectable 19 times in 20 according to the data of the study, the result will be

FIGURE 6.2 | TYPE I AND TYPE II ERRORS

Errors in Judging Whether a Correlation or Condition Exists	No Correlation	Genuine Correlation
Don't Reject Null Hypothesis	Correct	Type II Error
Reject Null Hypothesis	Type I Error	Correct

significant in the statistical sense. The drug's effectiveness might still be insignificant according to the common meaning of the term.

ERRORS IN REJECTING THE NULL HYPOTHESIS

Of course we can and will make errors no matter what practical compromise we make between confidence and precision. Broadly speaking, there are two ways to go wrong in assessing whether two phenomena are correlated or whether some condition exists. These are called **Type I** and **Type II** errors. We can get the idea behind this distinction in diagnostic terms: if you go to the doctor and you are healthy, but the doctor decides you are sick, that is a Type I error. If you go to the doctor and you are sick, but the doctor pronounces you healthy, that is a Type II error. Figure 6.2 lays out the possible combinations of facts and judgments in a table.

Type I errors are sometimes called **false positives**, Type II errors **false negatives**. But if we think of the difference between a false alarm (Type I) and a failed alarm (Type II), it is easier to understand why Type II errors are sometimes taken to be an importantly different *kind* of mistake than Type I errors. The idea is that a false alarm is a matter of genuinely making a judgment about what has happened, while the failure of an alarm is strictly speaking the absence of a judgment rather than a false judgment.

Type I errors in an experimental situation amount to incorrectly rejecting the null hypothesis. But (in theory) we don't *assert* the null hypothesis when our results are indecisive. We just fail to find grounds to *reject* it. So when our results are mis leadingly indecisive, we're really just missing out on an opportunity to learn something by rejecting the null hypothesis. We don't regard a silent fire alarm under normal conditions as continuously giving us, hour after hour, day after day, the positive information "There is no fire!" So neither should we take it to falsely give such

LINK

Specific issues involving false positives and false negatives in the scientific literature are raised in the Discussion section of Reading 3, Chapter 11.

a message if it remains silent when there really is a fire. Hence it may be something of a mistake to call Type II errors false negatives; they are not genuine assertions of false negative claims, but rather are non-assertions of positive claims when a positive claim would be warranted.

However, we saw in Chapter 4 that it is sometimes reasonable to regard an absence of evidence as genuine evidence of absence. And for practical reasons, if nothing else, we sometimes have to decide things like whether to keep people under quarantine, if it is suspected that they have some contagious but untreatable illness. In such a case there is no practical action that corresponds to our merely suspending judgment; we have either to keep people under quarantine or to let them go. So in practical terms a Type II error will be a genuine false negative in such circumstances, since in the absence of evidence of illness, we will (eventually) treat a person as healthy. If we are mistaken, we will release a genuinely contagious person on the grounds of observing no positive evidence of illness. The distinction between judging the person *healthy* and judging the person *not proven unhealthy* collapses. In short, there are stronger and weaker Type II errors that can be made, depending on how strong a conclusion we wish to draw, or just how we have to act, in light of evidence that suggests no positive result.

BASIC PROBABILISTIC CONCEPTS

PROBABILITY, RISK, AND INTUITION

One of the most important things that emerged from our earlier introduction to arguments was the point that a great deal of our reasoning is based on partial or incomplete states of information, relative to the topic at hand. By the standards appropriate to deductive arguments, *any* ampliative argument counts as strictly invalid, leaving us with the problem of how to distinguish good inductive arguments from invalid arguments that amount to plain old bad reasoning. In other words, how can we distinguish between inductive reasoning that nevertheless reliably supports its conclusion, and reasoning (inductive or not) that is not merely deductively invalid but non-cogent in a broader sense? This is really the point of probability and statistics: together they are the science of confidence under imperfect knowledge. Since imperfect knowledge seems to be our lot in life, the main concepts of probability are relevant to most of our reasoning.

We use probability judgments for many purposes, broadly under the headings of prediction, explanation, and rational decision-making. If we want to know what's going to happen under certain circumstances, we can often form reasonable expectations about a range of options by considering how things have happened before in similar circumstances (as well as our theoretical knowledge, among other things). But we can also use similar reasoning retrospectively, as a measure of the likelihood of some explanatory hypothesis. Events whose occurrence is likely if the hypothesis is true, or whose non-occurrence is unlikely if the hypothesis is untrue, count as confirming that hypothesis to some degree. Probabilistic concepts provide a measure of that degree of confirmation. Together the possession of predictive tools and good explanations enables us to choose actions most likely to lead to some desired results.

It might not be clear what the distinction between probability and statistics amounts to. Actually the two are intimately related in fundamental respects. Probability is primarily about prediction and explanation, or conditioning our expectations on the basis of observed data. Statistics is primarily about analyzing observed data correctly. Both skills are crucial components of critical reasoning. No doubt this has always been true, but increasingly our informational environment consists of statistical and probabilistic claims: statements about polls, about risks, about statistically expressed problems, and about the likelihood of various solutions. To be incapable of critically analyzing such claims is to be vulnerable to all manner of distortions of the data, and to be disqualified from meaningful engagement with a great deal of public discourse and informed political judgment.

So competence in probabilistic and statistical reasoning is very important. The problem is, virtually all of us are quite bad at it, in the absence of specialized study. Our "factory settings" when it comes to reasoning about odds and risk are made up of mostly implicit or unconscious **heuristics** of various sorts—that is, rough and ready rules of thumb. For example, there is a tendency to think an event is more probable or a more serious risk simply on the basis of how often one hears about it. Sometimes heuristics like this can produce judgments that are approximately accurate, or at least better than nothing. In many circumstances, though, they are flatly misleading. Correcting and counterbalancing these intuitions is something that can be accomplished by coming to understand the basic concepts of statistical and probabilistic reasoning, but this itself is not a trivial matter. As usual, we have to work at applying these concepts *habitually,* since our heuristic reasoning is intuitively compelling, and correct probabilistic reasoning can be deeply counterintuitive.

The problem is not simply that we are bad at arithmetic. Arithmetical incompetence can make probabilistic reasoning that much harder, but the core problem is something else. The problem is something noted in Chapter 2: that we are not naturally good at recognizing the relevance of information to the truth of a proposition, and in particular we very often do not see how changes to our state of information should affect the way we think about a situation.

THE MONTY HALL PROBLEM

A nice illustration of this point is found in the so-called Monty Hall Problem, a puzzle that gained notoriety when magazine columnist Marilyn Vos Savant's (correct) explanation of it ended up surprising even some professional statisticians and probabilists. The puzzle involves an imaginary scenario loosely modelled on the final segment of a famous television game show. Suppose you are the contestant, and you are given three doors from which to choose. You are told (and have no reason to doubt) that there is a car behind one door, and nothing behind the other two. If you choose the door with the car, you get to keep it. (And if you choose a door with nothing, you get to keep that.) Having no further information at your disposal, you arbitrarily choose Door One.

At this point the game show host intervenes and tells you that, since he is in a very good mood that day, he is going to do you a favour. He is going to open one of the two doors you did not pick—specifically, a door having nothing behind it. That is, if you've already chosen a losing door, he'll open the other losing door; if you've already chosen the winning door, he'll open one of the losing doors at random. Suppose he opens Door Three, revealing that the car was not behind it. Now, he says, you can choose either to keep your original pick of Door One or switch to Door Two before the location of the car is finally revealed. The question is this: do you have any reason to switch doors?

It is common for people considering this problem to reason as follows: "Now it's down to two doors, so my odds of getting the car have gone from 1 chance in 3 to 1 chance in 2; the odds are 50–50. So I don't gain anything by switching my picks; the odds are the same no matter whether I keep Door One or switch to Door Two." Many people find this reasoning intuitively clear and compelling.

It's wrong, though. In fact you double your chances of winning, from 1/3 to 2/3, by switching your pick.

If you don't already understand why, it may help to consider the problem this way: first, what are the odds that you got the car with your first pick? Obviously, 1 in 3. Indeed, we can represent this by considering how often you would get the car if you ran this scenario over and over; in the long run you would get the car with your first pick in 1/3 of the cases.

So what are the odds that you *missed* the car with your first pick? Well, only two things can happen, given the right description of the situation—you get the car with your first pick or you don't. If the odds that you get the car with your first pick are 1 in 3, then the odds that you missed the car with your first pick have to be 2 in 3; that is, the remainder of the possible outcomes.

Now, you'll lose the car by switching doors only if you got the car with your first pick. So, in 1/3 of the cases you lose the car by switching. But again, only two things can happen: either you get the car or you don't. So if you *lose* the car 1 time in 3 by switching, that means you *win* the car 2 times in 3 by switching. You double your odds by switching your pick.

Still not convinced? Think of a parallel scenario where there are a million doors, and a car behind one of them. You randomly pick Door 1, and then the host opens every door except the one you chose and one other door, say, Door 643,551, showing you nothing behind each of those other doors. So either the car is behind the door you first picked randomly out of the million, or it's behind that one other door that's still sitting suspiciously closed, *wayyyyy* down the long line of doors. What are the odds that you managed to pick the right door with your first choice? It's literally one in a million. Now the decision is a no-brainer—*of course* you would switch your pick. You would do much better than doubling your odds of winning in this case; they would go from 1 in 1,000,000 to 999,999 in 1,000,000. (In general, for the n-door case of the problem described this way, your odds go from $1/n$ to n-$1/n$ when you switch picks.)

The interesting thing about this example, for our purposes, is that it's arithmetically trivial. The most mathophobic person knows that 2/3 is twice as much as 1/3. So the problem isn't hard because math is hard. Rather, the tricky bit is understanding how we gain relevant information from the host's opening a non-car door. In this case our state of information is improved because the description of the problem makes clear that the game-show host is *deliberately* opening a door with nothing behind it. That is, he knows what's behind the various doors and is choosing which one to open based on that knowledge. So even though we don't know where the car is, we can use the fact that *he* knows to improve our chances. This is especially clear in the million-door case, where the fact that the host knows the car's location obviously leads to the conclusion that he's left Door 643,551 closed either because the car is actually in there or because you got the car with your first pick. The latter case occurs only if you've randomly chosen correctly with your first 1 in 1,000,000 guess, though. For all practical purposes you can ignore that possibility.

BASICS OF PROBABILITY

Now we can see how these concepts lead into probability theory. We've been getting a feel for the process of calculating representative values and statistical correlations. We can use these values to understand the raw data better, but we can also use them to make predictions and to test hypotheses about the nature of the apparent correlations in the data. Calculating a mean height for Canadians tells us something general about Canadians, but in the process it also gives us insight into the probability that a randomly selected Canadian has a height that falls within a particular range. This is part of the traffic between probability and statistics.

The purpose here is not simply to memorize a bunch of theorems; the idea is to get a fundamental sense of what we're doing when we think probabilistically. We might be thinking about risk, weighing alternative explanations, or deciding how reasonable some belief is in light of the imperfect evidence at our disposal. In any such circumstance, a grasp of the basic concepts is very useful and sometimes essential.

The probability that an event e occurs can be written as "$P(e)$." This is not a "tensed" notion, as we will use it—that is, we are not inherently talking about the future or the past or the present. We might mean something predictive, as in "The probability that the dollar will fall in value within the next month is .8," or we might be talking about an event that has already occurred (or failed to occur), as in "The probability that Julius Caesar went prematurely bald is less than .5." In each case it just means " . . . given our statement of information." We'll also use "$\neg e$" to mean "not-e"; that is, any outcome in which the event e does not occur. So "$P(\neg e)$" will be read as "the probability that e does not occur." A fundamental theorem is that $P(e) + P(\neg e) = 1$: the probability that some event occurs plus the probability that it doesn't occur equals 1.

But what does this or any other such number mean, probabilistically? Earlier we described significance and p-values in terms of percentages, with 5 percent and 1 percent being the most common p values required for the scientific publication of a study. In fact these values are rarely presented in this way; more often they would be framed as .05 and .01, in accordance with the basic axioms of probability theory.

A basic axiom or definition of probability is that the probability of any outcome or event can be assigned a value between 0 and 1, inclusive. That is,

Axiom 1. $0 \leq P(e) \leq 1$

A necessary event has a probability of 1, while an impossible event has a probability of 0. Everything else has a probability somewhere in between; the higher the number, the likelier the event. The usual idea is that these numbers are to be understood in terms of *relative long-run frequency* of events. To say that an event has probability .9 is more or less to say that if the situation so-described were repeated many times, the event would occur in nine-tenths of the outcomes. A fair coin toss has even odds of coming up heads or tails, for example, which we express by assigning heads and tails each a probability of .5 (ignoring the tiny but pesky possibility that it lands on its edge and balances there, Figure 6.3). This doesn't mean, of course, that in every sample of coin flips half will be heads and half tails. It just means that the larger a randomly chosen string of coin flips, the more likely we are to approximate an even split between heads and tails.

The second basic axiom is that necessarily some member of the set of possible events occurs. Necessarily, something or other happens.

Axiom 2. Where S is the set of all possible outcomes, $P(S) = 1$

FIGURE 6.3

Neither Heads Nor Tails

We ignore the tiny but non-zero probability of this outcome of a coin toss when we say that heads and tails each has a 50/50 probability in a fair coin toss.

Derek Capitaine Photography

Some infinite domains need, and get, a different treatment. This won't come up for our purposes, but you should be aware of the limits of our approach.

Alternatively, this says that there are no outcomes outside S. This may seem painfully obvious, but it shows something important: namely, that the probability we calculate is only as well defined as the set of outcomes S. The less we know about how things *might* turn out, the less reliable our calculation of probability based on what we do know. Other things being equal, if we overestimate the number of possible outcomes, we will underestimate the probability of any particular outcome, and if we underestimate the size of S, we will judge any particular outcome more likely than it really is.

This second basic axiom is also what lets us invoke and understand the theorem mentioned above, that the probability of an event plus the probability of its negation is 1. This means that S can be divided into two classes of outcomes for any event *e*: the outcomes on which *e* occurs and the outcomes on which *e* does not occur. These exhaust all the options, so it's a certainty that either *e* occurs or it doesn't. And this in turn makes it possible to reason about what *does* occur based on what we know about what does *not* occur, and vice versa. That is,

$$P(e) = 1 - P(\neg e)$$

Or, the probability that *e* occurs is 1 minus the probability that it does not occur.

For most practical applications, the probability of an event is given by

Number of relevant outcomes ÷ Total number of possible outcomes

Suppose, for example, that we place a dartboard on the floor and randomly drop a dart somewhere onto it. There are four sections of equal size into which the dart might fall, one of which is shaded, as in the enlightening visual aid, Figure 6.4. So the probability of the dart landing in the shaded area is 1 ÷ 4, or 1/4, or .25.

What counts as a relevant outcome, and how do we count possible outcomes? In both cases the answer is partly a matter of the facts themselves and partly a matter of what we're interested in measuring. The easiest way to see this is through some varied examples. For instance, on a single throw of a fair six-sided die, what is the probability of rolling a 3? ("Die," by the way, is the singular form of plural "dice.")

It's a fact about a normal six-sided die that there is only one 3 on it, and in this case it's the "rolling a 3" outcomes that we're interested in. So there's only one positive outcome. And obviously there are six possible outcomes (provided we again ignore the possibility that the die will balance on one of its corners or edges). So the probability of getting a 3 in a single roll is

Number of outcomes that count as being a 3 ÷ Number of possible outcomes = 1/6 ≈ .167

(Again we can use the squiggly "≈" to mean "approximately equals.") But suppose instead that we wanted to know the probability of rolling any odd number on a single throw of a fair six-sided die. Now there are not one but three different ways

FIGURE 6.4 | ENLIGHTENING VISUAL AID

The probability of a randomly dropped dart landing in the shaded area is 1 ÷ 4, or 1/4, or .25.

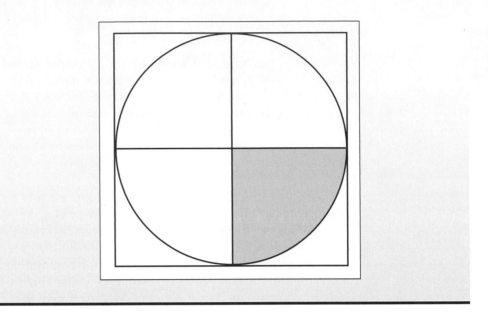

for the die to come up that will count as a positive outcome. So now our reasoning runs as follows.

Number of outcomes that count as being an odd number ÷ Number of possible outcomes = 3/6 = .5

While this example is quite simple, a large part of formulating good probabilistic explanations and predictions in complex situations consists of finding useful ways of individuating outcomes—that is, carving up possible events into relevant outcomes.

The same reasoning applies in more complicated cases; suppose we are considering the outcome of rolling two dice, which we imaginatively name A and B. If we want to know the probability of getting a roll in which the dots showing on dice A and B add up to four, we have to figure out how many outcomes satisfy that description, and how many possible outcomes there are in total. These kinds of questions are answerable quickly and conveniently using formulas for *permutations and combinations*, but we can see the idea quite intuitively without the formulas too. We could simply list the outcomes, for instance.

```
A1B1   A2B1   A3B1      . . .
A1B2   A2B2     .        .
A1B3   A2B3     .        .
A1B4   A2B4     .        .
A1B5   A2B5     .        .
A1B6   A2B6     .      A6B6
```

Statisticians often use the word "event" to mean a set of outcomes. On this way of speaking, we are asking for the probability of the *event* of getting a roll that adds up to three. The answer is supplied by considering what proportion of the total number of outcomes fall into the set of outcomes matching that description. Here there are 36 possible outcomes, of which the three outcomes A1B3, A2B2, and A3B1 satisfy the description "the dots showing on dice A and B add up to four." So the probability of this event is 3/36, or 1/12.

Notice that in the latter two examples we have grouped different kinds of outcomes (rolling a 1 and rolling a 3, for instance) into an event defined by some higher level description: *rolling an odd number*, say. In this sense, events have an implicit complexity. We could get the same correct answer by considering the probability of each more specific kind of outcome separately, and then calculating the overall probability of getting one or another of them. In order to calculate the probability of complex events, however, we need more theorems than those we've introduced.

PROBABILITY OF COMPLEX EVENTS

To begin, a symbolism note: for disjoint events (A or B, at least one event occurring) we use ∪ to mean, roughly, "or." Indeed, it's the *inclusive or*, as discussed in Chapter 1. For conjoint events (A and B, all the specified events occurring) we use ∩ to mean, roughly, "and." Now we have all the pieces to spell out the probabilities of complex events.

Probability of Two Disjoint Events

Often we need to know the likelihood that at least one of two or more events will occur. What are the odds that my car will break down *or* run out of gas on the way to work? From my immediate perspective it may not matter which of these things occurs; I'm worried about either occurring, so the probability that interests me is the disjunctive one.

$$P(A \cup B) = P(A) + P(B) - P(A \cap B)$$

Here's one way of reading this formula in English: the probability that A or B occurs is the probability that A occurs plus the probability that B occurs, minus the probability that both A and B occur. Maybe that sounds complicated, but we'll quickly see that it isn't.

First, think of the simple case in which A and B are **mutually exclusive**: that is, they can't both occur. When a patient undergoes surgery, surviving and not surviving are both possible outcomes, but they can't both occur. They are mutually exclusive, whereas surviving and having a finger amputated are not—they could both happen. In short, if A and B are mutually exclusive then $P(A \cap B)$, the probability that they occur together, is 0. So the last part of the equation, the bit after the subtraction sign, can be dropped for the special case of mutually exclusive events. We end up with this:

$$P(A \cup B) = P(A) + P(B)$$

And this just says that $P(A \cup B)$, the probability that A or B occurs, is the probability of A plus the probability of B.

A cautionary tale regarding the individuation of outcomes

Suppose you are indoors working on an assignment and can't join your three childhood friends in playing some basketball. But you can hear them playing out in the driveway. Your three friends are each wearing green jerseys and are shooting baskets along with your other friend, Steve Nash, who has stopped by for a visit and is wearing a white shirt.

Now, suppose you know (having compiled statistics on their play together) that each of your three friends has a .2 probability of coming up with the ball and sinking a shot on any given play, when that group of four players is together. Nash, who is twice as good, has a .4 probability of getting the ball and scoring on any given play. You hear someone sink a shot, and you ask yourself: did the scorer have a green shirt or a white shirt?

Obviously, since you weren't looking, this is a probabilistic question. But which question is it?

A: What colour shirt was it most likely that the scorer was wearing?

B: What colour shirt was the most likely scorer wearing?

The interesting thing is that the two questions have different answers. As you first asked it ("Did the scorer have a green shirt or a white shirt?"), the relevant question is A.

We'll trust your ability to detect a successful shot by sound alone, so we can say that the probability that *somebody* scored is 1. The probability that it was one or another of your green-jerseyed friends is

$$P(f_1 \cup f_2 \cup f_3)$$
$$= (0.2 + 0.2 + 0.2)$$
$$= 0.6$$

(We could also have calculated this as 1 minus 0.4, the probability that the scorer was Nash.)

So the answer to Question A is Green: there is a .6 probability that some green-jerseyed player or other scored, and a .4 probability that the sole white-jerseyed player scored. The answer to Question B, though, is White. The individual player most likely to have scored is Nash, and he is wearing a white jersey. Word order, and in general how we individuate outcomes by describing them, makes a huge difference to the meaning of probabilistic questions and claims.

This should be intuitive. We're asking for the chances that at least one of these events occurs. Any one of them will satisfy this description, so adding the chances of each tells us the chance that at least one occurs. The addition of each individual probability retraces an idea covered when we discussed the truth-conditions of disjunctive statements: that it's normally *easier* for a disjunctive statement to be true than for a simple sentence or a conjunctive statement, since the "or" statement casts its net wider. (Strictly speaking, it is *at least* as easy; in the case where the probability of B is zero, the probability of [A ∪ B] is just the probability of A.)

On reflection it ought to be clear that the single die-rolling example is a mutually exclusive disjoint case, since on any given roll only one number can come up. Whatever number occurs, it excludes the prospect of any other number coming up on the same roll. Any one of a 1, 3, or 5 will be sufficient to count as rolling an odd number, so we can use the simple version of the formula above, adding a third mutually exclusive event. The probability of getting an odd number on a single roll is just the probability of rolling a 1, plus the probability of rolling a 3, plus the probability of rolling a 5.

$$P(A \cup B \cup C) = 1/6 + 1/6 + 1/6 = 3/6 = 1/2$$

Of course we already knew this, but now it should be clear why we add the probabilities in the case of disjoint complex outcomes—that is, outcomes defined as one thing *or* another thing happening.

In the more complicated case where A and B are compatible, though, we need the whole formula $P(A \cup B) = P(A) + P(B) - P(A \cap B)$. What does the extra bit of the formula mean? In effect it's there so we don't count probabilities twice. After all, if A and B can occur together—not necessarily at the same time, but on the same outcome—then some A-events are also B-events. This means that if we just add the probability of an A-outcome to the probability of a B-outcome, we're counting some outcomes twice—the ones where *both* A and B occur. To get the correct value, then, we have to subtract $P(A \cap B)$, the probability that A and B both occur.

The three-variable non-exclusive case may look nasty, but it is harmless once you see that it's just an extension of this basic idea.

Probability of Three Disjoint Compatible Events

Of course the range of options is rarely limited to two, and the calculation of probabilities must be sensitive to this. I will only briefly indicate how the reasoning becomes more general.

$$P(A \cup B \cup C) = P(A) + P(B) + P(C) - P(A \cap B) - P(B \cap C) \\ - P(A \cap C) + P(A \cap B \cap C)$$

In English: The probability of A or B or C occurring is the probability of A plus the probability of B plus the probability of C (so far this is just the formula we used in the mutually exclusive case of rolling an odd number with a die), minus the probability that A and B occur together, minus the probability that B and C occur together, minus the probability that A and C occur together (again, in each case so we don't count the overlapping outcomes twice), plus the probability that A and B and C occur together. Putting things visually in Figure 6.5, the disjoint probability of the three outcomes is represented as the total area of the figure—that is, its outer border tells us the size of the set of outcomes that count as A or B or C. To calculate this probability given the probabilities of each sub-outcome, we first add the three probabilities together, in effect adding the areas of all three circles. This number is clearly too great, though, because the circles overlap—we're counting some outcomes more than once. So wherever any two circles overlap, we subtract one instance of the overlap. But because the region right in the middle is part of three overlaps—A and B, A and C, B and C—it gets subtracted three times, leaving a "gap." So that area, common to A, B, and C, gets added back in.

The two main conceptual points central to understanding the probability of disjunctive claims can be summarized, then, in the following way: first, if we want to know the probability of either A or B occurring, we add up the probabilities of A and B. Second, if A and B might occur together, we then have to subtract the

FIGURE 6.5 | P(A ∪ B ∪ C), PROBABILITY OF A TRIPLE DISJOINT EVENT

We get the joint probability of A or B or C, analogous to the area of this figure, by adding the areas of circles A, B, and C; subtracting the overlap (so that those areas are not counted twice); and adding the area of the centre (since it was subtracted three times and must be accounted for).

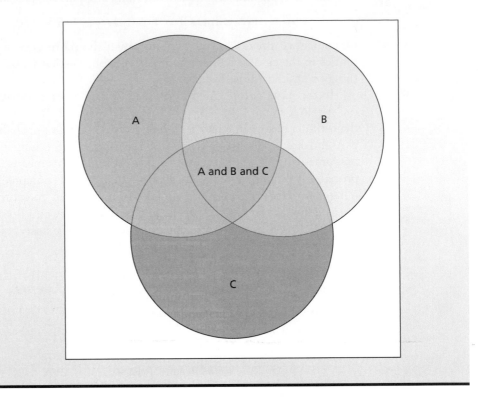

probability that they occur together, in order to avoid overestimating their disjoint probability.

This presupposes that we know how to figure out the probability of two events both occurring, of course. So we now turn to the question of how to think of **conjoint** probabilities—the probability of A and B both occurring. For this we need a different theorem.

Probability of Two Conjoint Events

The probability of *both* A and B occurring is the product of their probabilities: you multiply the probabilities. Since we are dealing with numbers less than or equal to 1, this means that normally we'll get a lower probability for the conjoint event than for the individual events; at most it will be equal to one event's probability, if the second event is necessary and hence has a probability of 1. As in the disjoint case, this mirrors the workings of conjunctive truth-conditions. We saw that conjunctive statements, all other things being equal, have more demanding truth-conditions than simple statements, because *all* of the conjuncts must be true in order for the conjunction to be true.

There are two kinds of cases of conjoint events, with different theorems describing them. In the cases where A and B are **independent**—that is, whether A occurs is not affected by whether B occurs—the conjoint probability is the simple product of their individual probabilities. For example, consider two events like my eating toast for breakfast and rain falling in Burkina Faso. Unless the world is even stranger than previously imagined, whether I eat toast for breakfast is independent of whether it's raining in Burkina Faso. The chance that either of these events occurs is completely unaffected by the occurrence of the other.

Independent A and B

$$P(A \cap B) = P(A) \times P(B)$$

When we ask for the probability of conjoint events A and B, we are asking about the overlap between the possible A-events and possible B-events. Multiplying the probabilities tells us the likelihood that an event will count as both kinds.

Obviously, though, not all events are independent. Sometimes the probability of a B-event will be affected by whether an A-event also occurs and vice versa. In this case we say that A and B are **dependent** events. Whether the Vancouver Canucks win a particular hockey game is not affected by whether my cat sleeps in the sink on that day, but is affected by whether their best player plays in that game. To calculate the conjoint probability of dependent events of that sort, we need to factor in the extent to which one event's occurring is conditional on the other event's occurring. This requires our last piece of formal symbolism: the vertical line in "P(A | B)" indicates a **conditional probability**, and is read as "the probability of A given B."

Dependent A and B

$$P(A \cap B) = P(A \mid B) \times P(B) \text{ [And, equivalently, } P(A \cap B) = P(B \mid A) \times P(A)]$$

What is the underlying difference between the dependent and independent theorems? Again, think of independence: the probability that a randomly selected playing card is a diamond is independent of whether it's a seven. One way to think of this is to note that if we wanted to know whether the card is a diamond, learning that it's a seven would not change our state of information in any relevant sense; we would know that there's one chance in four of it being the seven of diamonds, but then, we already knew that any randomly drawn card has a $13/52 = 1/4$ chance of being a diamond. So if we want to know whether a randomly drawn card is both a diamond and a seven (whether it's the seven of diamonds, to speak more naturally) we can treat the two probabilities as fixed independently and just multiply them: $1/4 \times 1/13 = 1/52$. Which is exactly right: there's a 1 in 52 chance of randomly drawing the seven of diamonds.

On the other hand, the card's being a diamond is not independent of whether it is red. If we're wondering whether a card is a diamond, and we learn its colour, this improves our state of information greatly either way. The chances that it's a diamond become zero if it's black and improve to $13/26 = 1/2$ if it's red (since there are 26 red cards of which half, 13, are diamonds). When we consider the probability that a randomly drawn card is both a diamond and red, then, we can't just take the two probabilities in isolation and multiply them. Why not? Because the probability that the card is a diamond is *affected* by whether it's red. (And vice versa, obviously!) If we just multiplied the probability that a randomly drawn card is a diamond by the probability that a randomly drawn card is red, we would have $1/4 \times 1/2 = 1/8$. But that's clearly wrong. We can see intuitively that the probability of a card's being a diamond and red is simply equal to the probability of its being a diamond—namely, 1/4—because being a diamond logically implies being red. (Logical implication is obviously a powerful statistical dependence relation; if A implies B, then the occurrence of A raises the probability of B to 1.)

When we use the dependent formula, and thus take into account the way that one condition's obtaining affects the odds that the other obtains, this comes out right:

$$P(C \text{ is a diamond} \cap C \text{ is red}) = P(C \text{ is a diamond} \mid C \text{ is red}) \times P(C \text{ is red})$$

$$= 13/26 \times 26/52$$

$$= 1/2 \times 1/2$$

$$= 1/4$$

Or, equivalently,

$$P(C \text{ is a diamond} \cap C \text{ is red}) = P(C \text{ is red} \mid C \text{ is a diamond}) \times P(C \text{ is a diamond})$$

$$= 1 \times 13/52$$

$$= 1/4$$

Finally, it should be clear that the formula for dependent variables is in fact the general case. To say that A and B are independent, after all, is really to say that $P(A \mid B) = P(A)$; B's occurring doesn't make any difference to the probability that A occurs. So when the variables are independent, the second formula reduces to the first.

CONDITIONAL PROBABILITY

So far, we've been treating conditional probability as if it were entirely obvious, by choosing cases in which it *is* obvious—like the probability that a card is red given that it's a diamond. Now we can explore this topic in slightly more detail. Conditional probability, again, is the probability that an event will occur, given that another event occurs.

$$P(A \mid B) = P(A \cap B)/P(B)$$

This says that the probability of A given B is the probability that A and B co-occur divided by the probability of B.

Suppose that my daughter and I each have toast for breakfast 20 days out of the year, on average. Then the probability that both I and my daughter have toast for breakfast on a given day is $20/365 \approx .055$. Suppose too that the total number of days per year my daughter has toast for breakfast is 65, on average. Then the probability that she has toast for breakfast on a given day is $65/365 \approx .18$. What, then, is the probability that I have toast for breakfast, given that my daughter does? The theorem tells us that

$$P(\text{I have toast} \mid \text{my daughter has toast}) = P(\text{I have toast} \cap \text{my daughter has toast})$$
$$\div P(\text{my daughter has toast})$$

$$\approx .055/.18$$

$$\approx .31$$

In other words, since roughly one-third of my daughter's toast days are also my toast days, randomly choosing one of her toast days gives approximately a 1/3 chance of thereby choosing one of my toast days too. Specifically, given that she has toast for breakfast there's a .31 probability that I have toast too.

Conditional probability is one of the key concepts of reasoning from states of information. Conditionalizing our knowledge is a matter of making our state of information explicit, as we've been seeing in a wide range of cases all along. Think of the difference between fallacious and non-fallacious Arguments from Missing Evidence: what I need to know is the significance of my lack of evidence, *given how hard I've looked for it*. The strength of an Argument from Authority is conditional on the expertise of the authority. In general, the way that changes to our state of information affect the confidence we should have in some proposition is a manifestation of conditional probability. In the next chapter we will examine some common biases that lead people to overlook conditional probability in evidential reasoning.

Effective probabilistic reasoning often hinges on distinguishing conditional probabilities from **categorical probability**, as the basic relative frequency of an event is known. For example, think of how to read the series of advice and observations made in this newspaper interest story on storm-related hazards:

> Seek safe shelter if the gap between flash and rumble is less than 30 seconds. Then wait 30 minutes before heading back outside.

> The chances of being struck by lightning run about one in a million. Yet lightning strikes cause more weather-related deaths in Canada than tornadoes, wind, hail and rain combined.[3]

The way this is written suggests that the probability offered here should be relevant in the situation described. But if "the gap between flash and rumble is less than 30 seconds," can you at least console yourself with the thought that "the chances of being struck by lightning run about one in a million"? The writer is no doubt just sticking together some facts here, in the manner typical of a terse news article. But the effect is to suggest that the .000001 probability of being struck by lightning is one that applies *within* the situation described. In fact, that probability is almost certainly categorical, derived by dividing the number of lightning strikes on people by the number of people in Canada, or whatever population it's based on. When the described circumstances exist, what's needed is a conditional probability: the odds of being struck by lightning, *given* that you're outdoors, in a thunderstorm, with lightning striking relatively near.

This distinction can be crucial to understanding an assessment of probability or risk when it is presented. Returning to the birth control theme that began this chapter, consider Figure 6.6, a table of success rates for various birth control methods compiled by the United States Food and Drug Administration.[4]

Without the concepts of categorical and conditional probabilities, it is difficult to make sense of this table. What exactly do the two columns of numbers mean?

The "Typical Use" row is more or less a categorical probability. It tells you how successful people are overall in using that method to avoid conception. But using a

FIGURE 6.6 | CATEGORICAL AND CONDITIONAL PROBABILITIES OF PREGNANCY

Method	Typical Use Rate of Pregnancy	Lowest Expected Rate of Pregnancy
Sterilization:		
Male Sterilization	0.15%	0.1%
Female Sterilization	0.5%	0.5%
Hormonal Methods:		
Implant (*Norplant*)	0.09%	0.09%
Hormone Shot (*Depo-Provera*)	0.3%	0.3%
Combined Pill (*Estrogen/Progestin*)	5%	0.1%
Minipill (*Progestin only*)	5%	0.5%
Intrauterine Devices (IUDs):		
Copper T	0.8%	0.6%
Progesterone T	2%	1.5%
Barrier Methods:		
Male Latex Condom[1]	14%	3%
Diaphragm[2]	20%	6%
Vaginal Sponge (no previous births)[3]	20%	9%
Vaginal Sponge (previous births)[3]	40%	20%
Cervical Cap (no previous births)[2]	20%	9%
Cervical Cap (previous births)[2]	40%	26%
Female Condom	21%	6%
Spermicide:	26%	
(*gel, foam, suppository, film*)		
Natural Methods:		
Withdrawal	19%	4%
Natural Family Planning	25%	1–9%
(*calendar, temperature, cervical mucus*)		
No Method:	85%	85%

1. Used without spermicide
2. Used with spermicide
3. Contains spermicide

Source: United States Food and Drug Administration

method (of anything) is not the same as using it *well*. The second column, "Lowest Expected," offers a conditional probability: the odds of getting pregnant while using each method, given that you use that method as well as it can be used. Two things ought to leap out from this example: first, the very large differences between typical and best success rates for some of these methods; and second, the fact that *either column's figures* could correctly be presented as an effectiveness rate for each method. If all we are given is a percentage or probability, we therefore have to inquire whether it is categorical, and if it is not, we have need to discover on what it is conditional.

Is either of these measures better than the other? It depends what use is to be made of them in the context. For the birth control example, if I am investigating these methods for my own use, I'll need an accurate self-assessment of my abilities to follow the protocols of each method. If I rightly take myself to be conscientious and disciplined, I might be able to count on approximating the lowest expected rate. If I know myself to be about as forgetful or slapdash as people are on average, I should expect my results to be roughly as good as the average person's—so the typical rate of success will apply to me. And of course if we are recommending methods for general policy or social purposes, it is the typical rates that matter since it is the typical person whose use of the method we are considering.

Good conditional reasoning is often just a matter of taking one's best evidence into account. For example, suppose that *Staphylococcus* infection responds to penicillin treatment in 92 percent of cases. Then the probability that Jane recovers, given that she has a *Staphylococcus* infection and is treated with penicillin, is .92.

J = Jane has a *Staphylococcus* infection
A = Jane is treated with penicillin
R = Jane recovers

$$P(R \mid J \cap A) = .92$$

However, suppose also that there is a resistant strain of *Staphylococcus* that responds to penicillin in only 8 percent of cases, and that Jane has this strain (call this situation J*). Although it is still true that she has *Staphylococcus* in this situation, so we *could* still just represent her predicament as J—although events of the kind J* are also events of the kind J—our first calculation would be a misleading way of reporting the situation. The calculation most relevant to the case once we acquire this more specific information is this:

$$P(R \mid J^* \cap A) = .08$$

This shows why we must be **maximally specific**, relative to our state of information regarding an event's properties, in order to derive a useful conditional probability calculation. As we saw with the phenomenon of implicature in Chapter 3, it is often insufficient merely to say something true—we have actually to make the most relevant observation we can, given what we know.

Crucially, we also have to take account of background information when using conditional probabilities. A **Base-Rate Error** is made when we neglect broader statistical or probabilistic information (or overlook the fact that such information is required) in favour of immediate or local information that is either incomplete or

L I N K

Base-rate errors are often cited as examples of failures that arise from our tendency to reason *heuristically,* via implicit shortcuts and approximations. This point is taken up again in Chapter 7.

irrelevant. Suppose, for example, that we are told that the raccoons in the park are four times more likely to have rabies than the other mammals. We know that animal control officers have caught a mammal with rabies in the park. What is the probability that it's a raccoon? Many people will leap to the conclusion that the probability is quite high—certainly greater than 1/2.

This mistaken judgment is the manifestation of a bias caused by the apparently decisive information that raccoons are four times likelier to have rabies. In fact the question can't be answered, not even approximately, without knowing the proportion (the base rate) of raccoons among the mammals in the park. If there were 220 mammals in the park, 20 of which were raccoons, with a rabies rate of 10 percent among the raccoons and 2.5 percent among the rest of the mammals, then there would be 2 raccoons with rabies and 5 other mammals with rabies. The probability that an arbitrary rabies-infected mammal is a raccoon, then, would be 2/7—far below 1/2.

THE PROBABILISTIC AND STATISTICAL FALLACIES AND PITFALLS

THE GAMBLER'S FALLACY

It seems to be a peculiarly tempting line of reasoning among gamblers to suppose that, since there is a certain distribution of wins and losses over the long run in random events like dice-rolling or card-dealing, a short-term run of losses must be balanced out by a short-term run of wins. The fallacy, in effect, is to think that if a series of independent events has the conjoint probability p, then the probability of any single event in the series is somehow dependent on the probability of the series as a whole. For example, the probability that in five flips of a fair coin all five come up heads is $(1/2)^5 = 1/32$. But if the first four flips come up heads, the antecedent improbability of the series occurring does not attach to the final flip. It's just an independent event with probability 1/2.

Hence it is a fallacy for the gambler to think, "I've been losing all night, so I must be *due* to win." It might have been relatively improbable at the start of the night that she would lose all night, but given that she has lost up to that point, the chances that she will lose all night have actually gone up enormously—since that probability reduces to the probability of losing the shorter series between that point and the end of the night. And the chances that she'll lose any given game remain the same no matter what has happened in previous games, provided it is a fair game of chance.

The Gambler's Fallacy is not just committed by gamblers. A broader version of it occurs whenever we take the odds of a single event to be conditioned by (or just identical to) the odds of the series of events of which it is a part. For example, in

2004 the Montreal Canadiens had been trailing 3 to 1 in a seven-game playoff series against the Boston Bruins. The following sports article was written after the Canadiens had won the next two games, tying the series at three games each, but before the seventh game that would decide the series:

> The Montreal Canadiens will attempt to become only the 12th team in NHL history to come back from a 3–1 series deficit to win a seven game series. The odds are certainly against them with just under 10 percent of teams in this situation emerging victorious.[5]

The claim, then, is that the odds in the upcoming seventh game were decisively against a Canadiens' victory. Why? Because winning the seventh game would *complete* a low-probability event: a comeback from a 3–1 deficit. But this confuses the probability of a series of events with the probability of one event in the series, in a sort of mirror image of the Gambler's Fallacy. It ignores crucial information that has been added: namely, that part of the initially low-probability event had already been settled. The Canadiens had already won two of the three consecutive games they would have to win in order to complete a comeback. Conditional probability in action again: the odds of completing three straight wins given that no games have been played are very different than the odds of completing three straight wins given that two wins are already in the bag.

COMPARING PROBABILITIES

Imagine that you are not feeling well and are trying to decide which of two hospitals to attend. You learn that, over the years, General Hospital has a better track record than St. Elsewhere Hospital at curing cancer-related illnesses: the former has a .8 probability of curing a patient, the latter .75. Investigating further, you learn that General Hospital also has a better history of treating all *non*-cancer-related illnesses than does St. Elsewhere Hospital: .6 to .5, in this case. There is no trick of some illness falling into neither category. Now, you don't yet know whether your malaise is cancer-related or not, but the information at your disposal seems to cover all the possibilities. Obviously, General Hospital must have the better track record overall.

Like many obvious things, this is wrong. The conclusion simply doesn't follow, a fact so surprising that it is called a paradox: **Simpson's Paradox**. If oncology and non-oncology exhaust the possibilities, and if General Hospital has better average success on both counts, how could it not be better overall? As always, the explanation lies in going back to the data.

Suppose that General Hospital treated (over the relevant time period) 100 patients for cancer-related illness, of whom 80 were cured. St. Elsewhere treated 400 cancer-related cases, of whom 300 were cured. This provides the grounds for regarding their respective probabilities of success as .8 and .75. Now suppose that General Hospital treated 400 non-cancer-related cases, of whom 240 recovered, while St. Elsewhere Hospital cured 50 out of 100 non-cancer-related cases. Thus we have General Hospital again with the advantage: .6 over .5. But now look at the overall numbers in Figure 6.7.

FIGURE 6.7 | SIMPSON'S PARADOX

Hospital	Cancer: cured/treated	Non-cancer: cured/treated	Total
St. Elsewhere	300/400 (.75)	50/100 (.5)	350/500 (.7)
General	80/100 (.8)	240/400 (.6)	320/500 (.64)

General Hospital has treated 500 patients altogether, of whom 320 have been cured. This gives us grounds to regard their overall probability of curing a patient as

$$320/500 = .64$$

But St. Elsewhere Hospital has also treated 500 patients, with 350 being cured. So their probability of success, by the same standards, is

$$350/500 = .7$$

Surprising though it may be, comparisons that hold within all partitions of the set of possible outcomes do not necessarily hold for the set as a whole. The general lesson is one first emphasized in Chapter 5 with the example of the apple boxes: information can be lost when we represent data sets of different sizes using single numbers. The lesson specific to Simpson's Paradox is that an apparent correlation in a set of data may actually be *reversed* within each subset of the data when it is partitioned in a particular way. In this case, the administrators of General Hospital can give a reasonable causal and arithmetical explanation for the overall results, consistent with their claim to have outperformed St. Elsewhere Hospital. They can observe that the non-cancerous illnesses were the harder ones to cure (in both hospitals), and that they encountered a higher proportion of those cases. In other words, a far higher proportion of St. Elsewhere Hospital's patients than General Hospital's patients were in the category that was easier to cure. So even though General Hospital did better within that category, the overall proportion of St. Elsewhere Hospital's patients that were cured was higher. Unless one is informed about the ways in which such apparent correlations can be misleading, it is easy to overlook the occurrence and relevance of such "Simpson's reversals" in a statistical argument.

REGRESSION FALLACY

Pride goes before destruction, and a haughty spirit before a fall. On its face, this ancient proverb sounds like an interesting empirical generalization, one that describes a tendency of pride to *cause* downfalls. No doubt pride does lead directly or indirectly to some people's own misfortunes in some specific cases. But a little reflection suggests that this saying might be based more on randomness than on any real insight about pride. After all, if you're already on top of the world, how can things get much better? And of course it's when people are doing very well that they are likely to be noticeably proud of themselves. Even if the changes in people's lives are essentially random, therefore, people for whom things are going as well as

FIGURE 6.8 | BELL CURVE ILLUSTRATING A REGRESSION EFFECT

If the first randomly chosen point is actually in a tail of some distribution of possible experiences (such as where the box is), the trend toward the mean as our experience grows can easily strike us as calling for some correlational or causal explanation, rather than as a trend entirely consistent with randomness. The Regression Fallacy is really a statistical analogue of the Post Hoc Ergo Propter Hoc Fallacy.

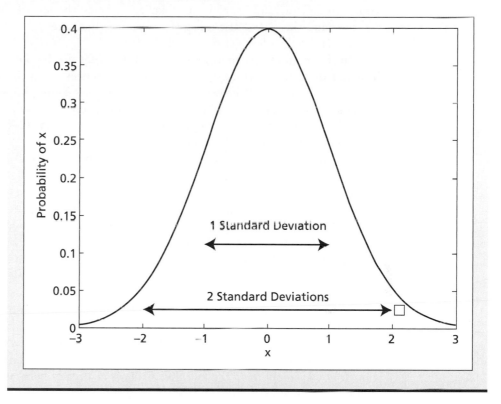

possible—that is, people likely to be proud—naturally will be subject to large downward fluctuations much more than large upward fluctuations. This need not be because they are proud, but simply because downward is the only direction in which large fluctuations can take place. So we may see plenty of cases that seem to fit the proverb, yet which are perfectly consistent with the null hypothesis that such downfalls are only randomly related to pride. One commits the **Regression Fallacy** when one confuses a pattern in random events by overlooking such **regression effects**.

What is a regression effect? This is another idea that's easy to see using a picture, so let's drag out our bell curve again (Figure 6.8).

Regression is a label for the almost trivial fact that a random sample within a normal distribution tends toward the mean. In other words, if you randomly pick a bunch of points under that curve, the odds are that most of them will be at or near the mean. Why? Because by definition, that's where most of the points *are*. So even

MULTIFACETED EXAMPLE

Pride goes before destruction, and a haughty spirit before a fall. This sort of proverb is also likely to seem more highly warranted than it is because it will activate a range of *confirmation biases*. It is discussed again in Chapter 7.

though the first point you pick might happen to be out near one of the "tails" of the distribution—where the box is, for instance—it's a matter of statistical necessity that your subsequent random picks are likelier to be to the left of the box than to its right. Again, this is because most of the points there are to randomly select are to the left, and only a few are to the right.

But from an experiential perspective, this might not be obvious. If we start off in a tail of some distribution of possible experiences, then the trend toward the mean as our experience grows can easily strike us as calling for some correlational or causal explanation, rather than as a trend entirely consistent with randomness. To make this mistake is to commit the Regression Fallacy. It is really a statistical analogue of the Post Hoc Ergo Propter Hoc Fallacy.

Imagine two children, Artemis, who is behaving very badly, and Basil, who is behaving very well (each relative to how that child *could* behave). Artemis's parents punish her, and Basil's parents reward him. What happens next? Suppose Artemis's behaviour improves somewhat while Basil's behaviour declines somewhat. Naturally both sets of parents will be inclined to conclude that their rewarding and punishing actions played a role in this. Artemis's parents may conclude that she just needed to be taught a lesson, while Basil's parents may conclude that they spoiled him. In fact, parents often find these very conclusions irresistible. But are they warranted by the evidence?

Well, suppose that the changes in the children's behaviour are more or less random. Then, while it's *possible* that Artemis's behaviour could stay the same or get worse, and it's *possible* that Basil's behaviour could stay the same or get better, what's *probable* in both cases is the children's behaviour will shift toward the mean. This follows simply from the fact that Artemis is already behaving very badly, relative to the range of behaviour that it's realistic to expect of her, and that Basil is behaving very well, relative to the range of behaviour that it's realistic to expect of him. There's just not much room for Basil's behaviour to improve—what can he do, start his own charity foundation? And similarly, what might Artemis do to behave worse—launch a military coup? The hypothesis that the changes in their behaviour are random and exhibit only a regression trend seem largely to account for the observed trends. Of course, punished children tend to behave better and rewarded children tend to slacken off: *if* their behaviour is going to change at all, it will tend to change toward the centre. But this is a fact about statistics, not about the effects of reward and punishment. Much of the evidence that parents take themselves to possess regarding the usefulness of punishment and the dangers of reward is confounded to some extent by unrecognized regression effects.

CONCLUSION

The basic concepts of statistical and probabilistic reasoning inform us in ways that are crucial to critical thinking. In part this means extending the notion of a representative number to include different kinds of averages, the probabilities themselves, and properties of the data we are considering (such as standard deviation).

But it also means illuminating the evidential relations between statements about correlations or causes and specific events or specific bits of data.

We must first have data that will reliably reflect unobserved cases, meaning that we must collect our data in the least biased ways possible. Using the conceptual tools of probability and statistics, we can then clarify the importance of randomness or chance as a potential explanation of any apparent tendency, trend, or correlation in the data. Concluding an explanation other than chance—that is, rejecting the null hypothesis—is an evidential judgment qualified by both a degree of precision, or margin of error, and a measure of confidence, or *p*-value. The lower the *p*-value, the less chance that the apparent effect is a mere accident, given the data. Different sciences have different fixed *p*-values to conventionally denote a statistically significant result.

The basic axioms of probability reveal how the likelihood of outcomes depends on the events that make them up, and upon the probability of other outcomes. A particular and ubiquitous problem here is understanding how some occurrences are conditional on other occurrences, and recognizing this when it is the case. Moreover, probabilistic and statistical reasoning are susceptible to a range of characteristic fallacies, such as the Gambler's Fallacy and the Regression Fallacy, that are hard to spot without an understanding of the basic concepts. Having seen what these broadly evidential fallacies are, we will go on to consider the many ways in which our intuitive judgments are biased toward committing them, and under what circumstances.

REVIEW QUESTIONS

1. What is the null hypothesis, and under what circumstances do we reject it?
2. I identified one way in which Figure 6.6 presents conditionalized probabilities. Find and explain two other ways in which the table does this.
3. Consulting current and back issues of a local newspaper, find and explain a case of a claim based on poor sampling or an example of the Gambler's Fallacy. Easy version: any example is fair game. Harder version: no using the Sports section of the newspaper. Industrial-strength challenge: no using the Sports or Business sections.

NOTES

1. http://www.canoe.ca/Slam040218/nhl_mtl2-cp.html.
2. http://www.canoe.ca/NewsStand/LondonFreePress/Sports/2004/02/27/362439.html.
3. Christian Aagard, *Kitchener Record*, June 7, 2005, p. B1.
4. http://www.fda.gov/fdac/graphics/1997graphics/birthcon.pdf. Data adapted from R. A. Hatcher, J. Trussell, F. Stewart, et al., *Contraceptive Technology*, 17th revised edition (New York: Irvington Publishers Inc., 1998). Table prepared by FDA: 5/13/97.
5. "Habs Look to Complete the Comeback," TSN.ca. TSN Staff with files from Canadian Press 4/19/2004.

Biases Within Reason

It was years ago that I first noticed the effect I have on streetlights: when I am out walking or cycling in the dark, it often happens that a streetlight flicks off just as I pass under it.

This doesn't happen every day, nor even every week. But it happens often enough to seem very strange. After all, I virtually never see streetlights flicking off from a distance, nor when I'm *not* passing by. It seems to be a trend. So what special electro-magnetic properties of my body or mind cause this intriguing effect when I'm in relative proximity to a streetlight? And how might I package my electro-powers in the form of a bracelet that can be sold for twenty dollars apiece on late-night infomercials?

Really, the flicking off of streetlights as I go past is a noticeable effect for me; the sense of *It's happening again!* when a light flickers out is powerful and immediate. Yet the strength of this feeling does not give me good reason to believe that the flickering of streetlights has anything to do with me. There are two main reasons to say this. First, there is no plausible account of how I could be having such an effect on streetlights. (In particular it would be hard to explain how I could fail to have a similar effect on other kinds of lights to which I stand much more closely every day.) And second, there is a range of plausible explanations for why these events might subjectively *seem* to add up to a regularity, even if they don't. The first sort of reason falls under the broad heading of causal reasoning, and can be understood in terms of Mill's Methods (discussed in Chapter 2). The second sort of reason is one of the main topics of this chapter.

A range of psychological biases almost certainly creates the illusion of a pattern or special regularity in my perception, interpretation and recollection of streetlight-burnout events. But it is a strong and intuitively convincing illusion. Thinking critically about judgments that seem intuitive and natural, like this one does, is an important part of understanding how my own reasoning and that of other people can be unreliable. It may seem obvious that I am not causing streetlights to switch off or burn out, but precisely parallel reasoning underlies many widespread beliefs about everything from cold remedies to pick-up lines to economic policies. A good deal of immediate or intuitive evidential reasoning is no better than the rationale for concluding that I have special electro-magnetic properties. We need a new perspective and some new diagnostic tools to understand and respond to these critical thinking issues.

FROM FALLACIES TO BIASES

Up to this point we have been mostly concentrating on forms and styles of argument and explanation, looking at the distinctions between reliable and unreliable reasoning in a range of domains. We have seen many examples and applications of the key concepts, all essential to a well-rounded set of critical thinking skills. Our focus so far has been on explicit reasoning of one sort or another: arguments, their functions, how they can succeed, and how they can go wrong.

What's characteristic of reasoning from that perspective is that it's *public* and focuses on *arguments*. Arguments and explanations are means of persuasion and discovery that can be studied over time. They can be put on hold while we check the truth of premises, and they can be revisited by different people to confirm that the advertised conclusions really do hold. So argumentation has a privileged place in the study of good reasoning. It is what we do when we wish to participate, or at least be seen to participate, in rational exchange. On the other hand, as critical reasoners we want not only to produce good arguments when these are called for, and to analyze arguments correctly when they are given to us, but more generally to *believe reasonable things*.

A great deal of our reasoning is *not* publicly displayed in the form of arguments. We don't reach conclusions solely on the basis of reasoning from premises. In fact that's probably a rare special case. In forming beliefs we often simply make judgments, settle on interpretations, and consult our intuitions; we perceive, notice, and remember. But these psychological activities, unlike argumentative practices, typically happen quickly and *implicitly*. It's not just that we don't display this kind of thinking to other people in the form of arguments. We are rarely even aware of what goes into these processes ourselves. Daniel Gilbert writes: "[O]ne of psychology's fundamental insights is that judgements are generally the products of nonconscious systems that operate quickly, on the basis of scant evidence, and in a routine manner, and then pass their hurried approximations to consciousness, which slowly and deliberately adjusts them."[1]

These cognitive processes are often characterized in terms of **heuristics**: these are problem-solving methods that trade some accuracy for simplicity and speed and are usually reliable for a limited range of situations. Our brains are superbly adapted to perceiving certain sorts of patterns at all levels, through biases and heuristics oriented toward certain circumstances. As we will see, however, these biases and heuristics can lead us astray in a range of ways. They can sometimes generate the powerful impression that a trend, pattern, or significance exists even when the data are ambiguous or random. The disposition toward positive pattern judgments also tends to favour one end of the frequency spectrum, so to speak. We are not well equipped to informally or intuitively detect and track genuine patterns that are spread out in time and space beyond the usual span of our attention or that consist of genuine but low-frequency trends. Our pattern-recognition biases deliver false positives, errors like the superstition of bad events happening after a black cat crosses one's path. But they also lead to false negatives, like a failure to detect slightly but definitely elevated frequencies of disease associated with some diets, habits, or policies. Similarly we may heuristically overuse recent or local information about rates and probabilities, rather than the background statistical information that is most relevant, when assessing probabilities and risk. A family of problems illustrating this is base-rate errors, discussed in Chapter 6.

From this perspective on human reasoning, knowing the standards for a good argument and being able to categorize fallacies when one notices them doesn't amount to a full set of critical thinking skills. What's needed in addition is a sense of how our implicit reasoning, and that of other people, may be going astray under the circumstances. Not only does this enable critical thinking about cases where no argument is really occurring, but it deepens our understanding and diagnosis of fallacies when arguments *are* in play. When we indulge in circular reasoning, for example, it's unlikely that we are doing so because we are momentarily under the impression that "P, therefore P" is a wonderful argument-form. Much more likely is that we're finding some bias-driven way of *not realizing* that our reasoning actually has a question-begging form. In order to more generally understand, recognize, and avoid unreliable reasoning, we need to understand the biases that underlie it.

For example, one of the least subtle cognitive biases affecting the way credibility is assigned to a statement is the tendency to believe statements that one hears repeated many times. This could be called the **repetition effect**: the tendency of people to judge claims they hear more often as likelier to be true. The effect is experimentally measurable under a wide range of conditions—including, surprisingly, when subjects are warned that they will be hearing falsehoods when the statements are introduced.[2] Think of watching some television show and seeing the same advertisement again and again. Televised movies and sports seem particularly bad for this; over the course of a hockey game one can see the same ad for a truck or the latest nine-bladed razor anywhere from ten to twenty times. Viewers' attitudes toward these commercial spots, when they notice them at all, typically range from boredom to annoyance. If the advertisers' intention were to *convince* viewers of the virtues of the products, then, this would be a poor approach—not least because the ads themselves rarely contain the kind or quality of information needed to build an argument. We would stretch the notion of an implicit argument quite far to suppose that an argument is expressed by a fifteen-second clip of a man who shaves with his new nine-bladed titanium razor and is then mobbed by beautiful women who seem to have lost something valuable inside his shirt.

Yet large companies are not (normally) in the business of losing money. They spend money on advertising presumably because it works. It just doesn't work by giving arguments and hence not by giving fallacious arguments. Repetition isn't a *fallacy*; it's just something to which our belief-formation and decision-making processes are sensitive. Repetitive advertising aims at directly modifying a viewer's beliefs and desires. Thinking critically about your own reactions to advertising, then, is a matter of taking seriously how it can directly bias your judgment and behaviour. This requires paying attention to some details of human cognition.

To the extent that we want to minimize our false or unwarranted beliefs, then, we have to consider not just how to recognize fallacious arguments—whether offered by others or by ourselves—but also how to recognize the wide range of cognitive biases and social forces that dispose us to settle on unjustified beliefs. This will explain why many fallacies are effective at persuading us, and it will illuminate the large class of judgments and decisions that we reach without any process usefully described as argumentative. The following two chapters offer an introduction to this aspect of critical reasoning. We will cover perceptual, cognitive, and social biases that can render our fast and implicit judgments unreliable. In this chapter, we will deal primarily with biases of perception, judgment, and memory, while the next chapter considers social aspects of reasoning and social effects on reasoning.

These perspectives enable us to recognize that some ways of being irrationally persuaded are traditionally viewed as fallacies even though they do not fit the mould. They make much more sense when they are viewed through the lens of psychology, sociology, history, or the sciences more generally. Most critical thinking texts discuss the fallacy of **Argumentum Ad Baculum**, for example—Argument from Threat of Force. The basic idea of this supposed fallacy is *Believe that P or suffer the consequences*.

But how often does this ever happen? And to the extent that it does happen, is it a manoeuvre that amounts to a fallacy? Imagine having a gun pointed at you and being told, "I order you to believe that you are in Viking, Alberta, or else!" It would be not merely unwise but completely off-topic for you to respond with "Ah, I see the fallacy in your argument." (If the example makes no sense, it may be because you are currently in Viking, Alberta. If so, drive to Camrose immediately and re-read the example.) The relation between the threat or use of force and changing people's beliefs is, plausibly, more purely a matter of causes and not a matter of reasons—not even *bad* reasons. When the relation holds, it holds more by first forcibly changing people's practices; it may occur most clearly over generations.

The historical use of force in compelling people to convert from one religion to another, for example, does not take the form of a fallacious argument that one person offers another. Rather it involves the long-term suppression of existing practices and the imposition of new ones. Over the longer term people—many of them, at least—do come to adopt the new belief system, perhaps by working aspects of the old one into it. And for their children the new beliefs may be all they are ever exposed to, and are hence taken for granted. But this is a matter of the psychology and sociology of belief change and belief fixation. Understanding how threats and uses of force can shape the beliefs that seem obviously right in a cultural context hence implicates a broader perspective than the study of arguments and fallacies alone. Identifying and critically analyzing beliefs that are intuitive or widespread for reasons other than their correctness are projects that benefit from taking that broader perspective seriously.

What do I mean by "bias"? In most informal contexts, the term denotes some sort of prejudice, especially a personal prejudice based on something like race, gender, or ethnicity. Hence it tends to have a strongly negative connotation. Even though we too are analyzing biases in terms of the critical thinking problems they can pose, the specialized sense of the term should carry no such inherent negativity.

CHAPTER 7 *Biases Within Reason*

Some longstanding fallacy types can be understood as intermediate between fallacies and biases. The Fallacy of Slanting Language, discussed in Chapter 4, can be seen as a style of reasoning that attempts to bias its audience through word choice. Another widely cited fallacy is **Appeal to Emotion.** Here too the idea is to bias the audience toward a conclusion, by exciting some powerful emotion that will lead them to jump directly to the desired conclusion—without noticing the lack of reasonable grounds to believe it. For example:

"Is Ericson guilty of murder? Well, let me tell you how sick I am of seeing innocent people cruelly killed, their families sentenced to lifetimes of anguish and depression. Their killers get a life on easy street, though: three square meals a day, and a TV to watch while they sit with their feet up in comfortable prison cells. And that's if they get convicted at all! These vicious monsters walk away free as birds, and who speaks for the victims? Who has the nerve to say: 'Stop!'? Enough is enough. Let's not let Ericson walk away from this crime."

Clearly this passage can be diagnosed in terms of the Fallacy of Appeal to Emotion. Nothing between its initial question and its final answer provides any real rationale for the conclusion; instead it just aims to create a sense of outrage, counting on the audience to accept the conclusion as a means of indulging or satisfying that outrage. It's both a fallacy of irrelevance and an exercise in evoking a biased response.

A **bias** in my sense just means a disposition to reach a particular kind of endpoint in reasoning or judgment, being skewed toward a specific sort of interpretation. There is no question that biases in this sense are very often integral to our reasoning. They contribute to our ability to make fast judgments using incomplete information. And they are in any case inevitable. The idea is not to get rid of biases in human cognition, but rather to understand how and when these biases can over-apply, or be "spoofed," or otherwise lead to unreliable reasoning.

PERCEPTUAL BIASES

Few thoughts or utterances communicate a greater sense of rational entitlement than "I saw it with my own two eyes" or "I heard it with my own two ears." We are all aware that illusions, hallucinations, and other kinds of misperceptions are possible, of course. But in practice it is tempting to treat a particularly clear or vivacious perception as unimpeachable—a completely reliable source of information: "Raise whatever theoretical issues you want, but *I was there*; I saw what I saw, heard what I heard, and that's the end of it."

Yet we are all familiar with a wide variety of perceptual illusions that show how our senses can mislead us in certain circumstances. Two circles of the same size can nevertheless appear different, if one is surrounded by smaller circles and the other by larger circles. Apparently our visual judgments of an object's size are not absolute, but are influenced by other objects in our visual field. Depending on the context, straight lines can seem curved, motionless drawings can seem to rotate, and grey photographs can seem coloured. In themselves these might seem small worries from a critical thinking perspective, but they provide a starting point from which to consider illusions on a grander scale—perceptual and otherwise—that amount to much larger concerns.

Now, on one hand the point is not to suggest that we should *generally* reject the evidence of our senses. There are ancient philosophical questions about the force of such broad sceptical worries—for example, *Is there really an external world corresponding to the evidence of our senses?*—but these questions are not our current focus. After all, to treat our perceptions as generally reliable is not to treat any *particular* experience as accurate. The issue at hand is how to think critically about particular perceptual experiences, whether our own or those reported to us by others. If our perceptions are being skewed by one or more biases, other contextual evidence and background knowledge should indicate this—provided we are habitually open to noticing such red flags. In order to have a reasonable sense of when other contextual evidence *should* weigh more heavily than the evidence of our senses (or the evidence of someone else's senses, delivered via their testimony), we need to gain a sense of two things: the sort of biases that can affect our perceptions, and the sort of circumstances under which it is reasonable to worry that they are having an effect.

LOW-LEVEL BIASES

Some biases are built into our perceptual "hardware" while others are effects on perception of beliefs, expectations, and emotions. Each sort of perceptual bias can have startling effects that are significant in critical reasoning contexts, but they also serve as vivid analogies for how biases can operate at higher stages of psychological processing. Just as perceptual biases can give rise to powerful and unexpected perceptual illusions, so can biases that operate on judgment and memory subject us to powerful cognitive illusions. These colour the way we think in virtually every situation and can lead us significantly astray in the absence of effective measures for self-monitoring.

Some perceptual biases are largely the result of the basic structure of our perceptual and neurological mechanisms. The detection of visual edges, for example, is enhanced by the layout and interaction of neurons within the eye itself. These factors combine to take patterns of activation in visual receptors that are fuzzy but edge-*like* and enhance them into sharper lines. We could think of this as a very low-level bias of the visual system in favour of edge-detection, one that serves us very well in most situations. A more complex visual bias is that in favour of detecting faces. A great deal of important social information about the people around us, both their identities and their moods or attitudes, can be gleaned from their faces. Also, noticing faces is a way of noticing that someone else is noticing *you*. So a great sensitivity to facial detection and recognition is unsurprising for developmental, social, and evolutionary reasons.

An effect of this face-detection bias, however, is that we are quite easily spoofed into seeing faces in visual information that is ambiguous or just plain random. It seems like it ought to be relatively easy to see a knee, for instance, in an ambiguous visual situation: think of all the things that could look like a stick-drawing of a knee in an abstract wallpaper pattern, when waving tree branches cast shadows on it at night. Compared to a relatively complex pattern like a face, seeing a knee or an elbow in this situation ought to be much easier. But who ever looks at abstract patterns, or at clouds in the sky, and sees a knee or a forearm? Lots of people see a face in the moon; few seem to have noticed an elbow. We have no appreciable bias toward the detection of elbows and knees, while we do have such a bias in the case of faces.

One particularly nice illustration of the strength of this perceptual bias is the **Hollow Face Illusion**. The example shown in Figure 7.1 is of an Egyptian burial mask.[3] Figure 7.1a shows the mask from the outside, as it was meant to be viewed. Figure 7.1b is a picture of the very same mask, but taken from the *inside*. The nose in the picture on the right is actually concave, projecting away from you. Your brain, however, is not particularly built to see something having virtually all the visual cues of a human face, but seen from the inside. With that much face-like information in the input, your visual system simply jumps to the perception of a face—a normal face, that is, projecting out toward you.

Perhaps the most compelling aspect of the illusion when seen in person is that the inverted face will seem to move, turning to follow you as you walk past it. To get a (rough and simplified) idea of why this happens, think of what *ought* to

FIGURE 7.1

The Hollow Face Illusion

The burial mask of the Swansea Museum's 2000-year-old Egyptian mummy, Hor, seems to defy natural laws: the outside and inside each seem to face out toward the viewer. The illusion results from perceptual bias in how the brain processes the shapes and shadows of the mask.

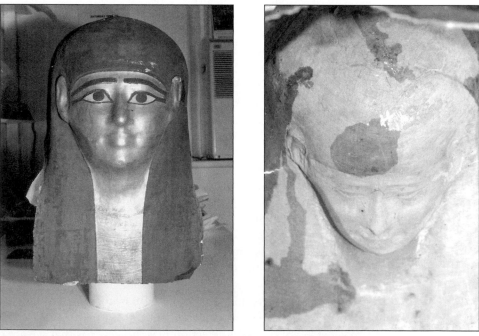

Courtesy of Swansea Museum, photographs supplied by Richard Jaeschke

happen as you walk past a face. If you are standing in front of a person and you move to your left, you ought to lose sight of the right side of the person's nose and cheek (the side to your right, that is) and get a more direct look at the left side. But of course you can't get a better look at the left side of the nose on an inverted face as you move to the left, because there really is no nose protruding. So the perspective doesn't change in the way it ought to, if your brain's working assumption about the face were correct. So what would normally explain your not getting a different perspective on a face as you walk past it? The answer is plain: if the face turned to follow you as you moved past, your perspective on it would not alter. Your brain, having leaped to the "normal face" perceptual judgment, now has to make a second leap to preserve that judgment: the face must be turning to follow you. Do you see it with your own two eyes? There is no arguing with the *clarity* of the perception; the vivacity of the experience seems beyond serious doubt. (You can get this effect with a cheap plastic Halloween mask placed backwards on a window sill or ledge, provided you experiment with the lighting a bit.) Yet the experience is delusive.

From a critical reasoning perspective, this is a respect in which self-monitoring becomes significant. If it is ever an important question whether I have seen a face when I had only a fleeting glimpse, when no independent confirmation is available, and when a great deal hangs on my judgment, then I must be prepared not to place much trust in even a quite clear recollection of my perceptual experience. And if there is positive evidence that *no* face was there—if other witnesses did not see one, for instance—then the knowledge that my brain is naturally on something of a hair-trigger for seeing faces should lead me to revise my confidence in my own experience downward. The specific instances in which this is an issue may be rare, but the phenomenon serves to introduce a broader lesson: judgments and experiences that seem clear and obvious can simply be the result of biased information-processing. When there are red flags about the truth of some such perception, the clarity of the perception or the judgment cannot be taken to automatically override such concerns.

Such biases can operate in profoundly convincing ways, illustrating that our brains can "edit" reality quite heavy-handedly provided that the right conditions hold. One perceptual bias that drives this point home is the **McGurk Effect**. This illusion is **multi-modal**, meaning that it involves more than one sensory system. The effect can be elicited by recording a video clip of the face of a speaker uttering a sound, and playing the recording back with a different speech sound in the audio track. Confronted with visual input of a person making one sound and audio input of a different sound, what the audience often experiences is the perceptual judgment of some third sound. That is, what you hear is neither the sound it looks like the person is saying, nor the sound actually recorded, but something else altogether! For example, video footage of a person clearly articulating "gah" combined with a superimposed audio track of someone saying "bah" produces the widespread judgment in the audience that the person is saying "dah" or "thah." To speak metaphorically, the brain reaches a compromise solution, below the level of conscious awareness, on data that don't quite fit with expectations: the subjects just hear "dah."

In 1954 the Bank of Canada released a new currency series. The new money replaced a 1937 design featuring King George V with an engraving of the new monarch, Queen Elizabeth II. Yet within only two years the Bank of Canada was revising the currency again—replacing the 1954 picture of the Queen with a new picture. The problem with the original 1954 issue, it turns out, was demons.

No, really. The problem was demons. Some people claimed to see the face of a demon in the whorls of hair behind the Queen's left ear in the original picture. Rather than risk committing an ongoing monetary *lèse majesté*, the bank decided to begin replacing the bills with a new series (the detail in the hair removed by darkening), though it did not remove the old bills from circulation. Yet the original engraving was based on a photograph, making it very unlikely that any such image had been deliberately placed there. It was almost certainly a particularly expensive example of people imposing an interpretation on ambiguous visual information. To this day, the entire original 1954 series of bills is called the "Devil's Head" series.

A similar lesson is found in the **Cutaneous Rabbit,** a somatosensory illusion (that is, involving our sense of touch). When a series of rapid taps to the same spot on the wrist are followed by one near the elbow, subjects report feeling a series of evenly spaced taps that "hop" up from the wrist to the elbow.[4] That this represents some innate or acquired perceptual bias is plausible, since it makes sense to be on alert for the feeling of something crawling up your arm! But it is clear that considerable "editing" is going on in the construction of this perceptual experience, given that there is no way for the brain to know that the first few taps should feel like they had marched up the arm, until after the last tap is administered at the elbow. It appears that subjects' tactile processing systems quickly rewrite recent history after the final tap, assimilating the inputs to a perception toward which they are biased. Again, examples like this help to shake up our common-sense intuitions about the connection between the clarity of an experience and the confidence we should place in it, all things considered.

TOP-DOWN EFFECTS ON PERCEPTION

Biases operating on perception become more interesting when we consider cases of top-down effects. If we think of raw sensory input as the bottom level of psychological processing, with explicit conscious reasoning residing at the top level, then it's natural to think of perception as mostly a "bottom-up" process. In other words, it's natural to think that what we perceive is just a matter of the information coming in through our senses. This is only a partial truth, though. It turns out that our perceptions can be partly determined by what we already believe, desire, expect, or remember. The old saying goes "Seeing is believing." Yet in many cases it's more accurate to say that believing is seeing.

Consider, for example, the widespread concern over secret backwards messages in rock music. In the early 1970s the idea began to spread that there were secret messages recorded backwards in some popular music; one story circulated widely that Paul McCartney of The Beatles had died, and that the words "Turn me on, dead man" were a hidden clue to this fact, audible when a portion of one of the band's songs was played backwards. Within a few years, and lasting through the 1980s, many variations on this backwards messages idea had spread and mutated, especially in some circles of North American culture, into the conviction that rock music contained backwards messages of demonic origins, which could have a sub-conscious or "subliminal" effect on the listeners' beliefs and desires.

This is a quite improbable thesis or, more accurately, a collection of improbable theses. Yet part of the reason that it was widely repeated and believed was that it seemed directly confirmable. On radio shows and religious television shows, self-described experts on music (or demonology) would explain specific backwards mes-sages that could be heard in specific songs when played backwards. When vinyl records were the primary means of playing music in the home, it was quite a simple matter to reverse the music oneself. So anyone hearing or reading about the alleged messages could try it out personally, provided they owned the record. And in many, many cases, they discovered they really could hear the backwards mes-sages—sometimes eerily distorted, sometimes shockingly clear.

The effect was a top-down bias introduced by creating the expectation that the particular phrase would be heard, and then exposing the audience to ambiguous sounds that loosely approximated the phrase in question. By having read, heard, or just thought about the alleged secret message, each such living-room experimenter was primed to hear that message in the sounds. That this effect can be easily induced is not terribly surprising, since human voices still sound like human voices when played backwards, and naturally we are inclined to look for meaningful patterns in human voices. The expectation of a hidden message, and especially the exact words given for it, is just the sort of nudge that can put our speech interpretation faculties on a hair-trigger, ready to interpret any roughly suitable input as the message in question. The resulting "message" that is heard can sound very clearly spoken, moreover. It is a stark example of how our expectations can shape the content of our very perceptions.

Notice too that we are using the term "expectations" in a very broad sense. One need not *believe* that the effect will occur; indeed, one can actively doubt that words will emerge from the sounds after priming takes place. It's enough that the priming information (e.g., what the hearer is told to expect) is *salient*. Just having those words in mind, even as part of a general scepticism, is often sufficient to elicit the top-down effect. This is a crucial point: being subject to top-down biases of belief, expectation, or memory does not require that one be strongly convinced of the out-come toward which one is biased. The phenomena are not limited to fanaticism or pathological self-deception; biases can operate within an otherwise moderate, neu-tral, or sceptical mindset.

Another top-down effect is the orientation of our attention. This can give rise to one of the more spectacular phenomena of our quirky cognitive tendencies: **inattentional blindness**. When even competent, calm, normally sighted people are

The effect of apparent backwards messages is easy to create yourself, if you like, by using digital audio editing software (some of which is available online as freeware) to reverse short sections of almost any song containing lyrics. While listening repeatedly to various samples of backwards music, you can brainstorm phrases or whole sentences that might sound vaguely like the warbling nonsense you are hearing. Once you've come up with something that's close enough to a phrase matching sounds in a clip (even a non-sense phrase will do, but try to make it at least vaguely meaningful), you can try it out on an audience. First play the backwards clip without any comment. Then ask your audience to listen for the particular phrase you came up with. In many cases they will be shocked at how clearly the message can be heard when you play it again. You may be surprised, too, and find it hard to believe in retrospect that it took you some time to think up a phrase that would fit the sound. It is an interesting challenge to try going back to hearing the clip as mere nonsense, once the "hidden message" has been heard. Most people will find this impossible.

concentrating on one task, it is possible for grossly irregular events to occur right in front of them and not be noticed. To some extent we are all familiar with it. For instance, we have probably all walked or driven right past a friend or family member, who smiled and waved at us while seeming to make eye contact under good visibility conditions, yet failed to recognize them or respond. More striking examples are easy to generate, however. In one experiment, Daniel Simons and Christopher Chabris filmed a mixed group of white-shirted and black-shirted people, with each group throwing a ball around to people with the same colour of shirt.[5] Subjects were shown the film and were given the task of counting how many passes were made by one set of people. Partway through the video, however, came the surprise: a person in a full gorilla suit sauntered right through the two groups of ball-throwers. (In one version the gorilla-impersonator actually stops, faces the camera, and does some chest-thumping before continuing on.)

Astonishingly, nearly half the subjects did not report seeing the gorilla. By the simple expedient of asking them to pay attention to events surrounding the gorilla and even overlapping it, Simons and Chabris were able to render their subjects temporarily gorilla-blind. Yet how would any of us react to the suggestion that someone in a gorilla suit might have wandered through our field of vision without our knowing it? The producers of television prank or gag shows have already cottoned onto this trick, playing it for laughs by constructing real-world cases filmed by hidden cameras. An actor will strike up a conversation with a stranger, but the conversation will soon be interrupted by a distraction—most conveniently, by two more actors passing between the speakers while carrying a large sheet of plywood. When they pass by, the original actor sneaks off behind the plywood, while yet another actor, who had been concealed behind the wood, is left standing there. With surprising regularity the stranger will fail to notice the complete change in conversation partner. Again, it is tempting for us to over-idealize our perceptual capacities and habits. Distractions or our own focused attention can leave us far less informed about events and our environment than our intuitions might tell us.

The top-down effects of expectation and belief can extend to judgments of taste or preference as well. Recently I found a container of frozen soup in my freezer, while looking for a quick lunch. I could not remember what kind of soup it was, but my wife called from another room to tell me it was chicken with rice. When I defrosted the soup, though, I discovered that it had gone bad. *Really* bad. It had turned green, and the rice had dissolved into mouldy unidentifiable mush. It looked disgusting, and the thought of eating it was revolting. Then my wife called again from the next room.

"Actually," she said, "that container might have been split pea soup." And just like that, the soup no longer looked disgusting; as split pea soup goes, it looked just fine. It no longer looked rotten or spoilt at all. Phenomena like this blur the idealized boundary between perception, tastes, and judgment, and illustrate how top-down effects can apply to more than just propositions of fact.

COGNITIVE BIASES

The most psychologically distinctive feature of humans is not our sensory capacities, but our cognitive capacities. Our rich mental lives are characterized by the fact that we have beliefs and desires, suspicions and fears, anticipations and recollections, cautious optimism and dejected pessimism. Largely the same biases as those introduced in connection with perception apply to these cognitive processes as well, along with a range of further biases that raise serious critical reasoning issues in some contexts.

As critical thinkers we ought to be fundamentally concerned with the (apparently) uniquely human psychological activities of judging, thinking, planning, deciding, and remembering. While it may be unclear just how often a bias in favour of perceiving faces will be the key issue in some piece of reasoning, it is perfectly clear that a bias in favour of forming or holding on to a particular belief will very often amount to uncritical reasoning. Having introduced some key concepts and phenomena through perceptual examples, we can now apply and extend those concepts by looking at the effects of various biases on how we think, what we think, and what we remember.

CONFIRMATION BIASES AND EVIDENCE

Harvey Mansfield, a professor of government at Harvard University, wrote a book called *Manliness*, claiming (among other things) that women are the weaker sex, and that important manly virtues have been threatened by recent social moves toward gender equity. Interviewed in the *New York Times Magazine*, Mansfield was asked about an incident involving Harvard president Lawrence Summers, who had mused during a speech that women might be inherently less able than men to do science. Mansfield defended this statement, claiming that Summers "was taking seriously the notion that women, innately, have less capacity than men at the highest level of science. I think it's probably true. It's common sense if you just look at who the top scientists are."[6]

It should be clear just how disastrous such reasoning is, in light of the material covered in Chapter 6 and throughout this book so far. An appeal to "common sense" is normally a red flag, and in this case the worry is immediately increased by the suggestion that one need only "look at who the top scientists are" in order to realize the inferiority of women in the relevant respects. Depending on the reader, this may simply be an invitation for people to canvass their own preconceptions about whether the stereotypical scientist is male. Who, after all, is one to think of as a top scientist?

What Mansfield seems both to demonstrate and to invite with the last sentence of the quote is a **confirmation bias**. This is really a blanket expression for a family of biases, a wide variety of ways in which beliefs, expectations, or emotional commitments regarding a hypothesis can lead to its seeming more highly confirmed than the evidence really warrants. (Technically, some people refer also to **disconfirmation biases** as well, by which is meant biases that overstate the evidence *against* a hypothesis. But for our purposes we can just think of these as a subcategory of confirmation biases—those applying to the negation of a hypothesis.) The idea applies to any way of gathering, noticing, interpreting, or remembering evidence so as to make one overestimate the evidence for one sort of conclusion.

In this case, thinking of top scientists is for many people a matter of thinking of *famous* scientists—but fame itself may be badly confounded evidence, for instance by lagging behind demographic changes in science by years or decades. The fame of scientists like Einstein, or Watson and Crick, dates from an era before the increased opportunities for women even to have careers in science. And even supposing that current "top scientists" were predominantly male, it would be an obvious statistical and causal fallacy to infer a sex-based explanation from that correlation alone. A parallel argument about women and their fitness to be doctors would have been just as applicable in the 1960s, but in the meantime, the removal of societal and attitudinal barriers to women doctors has substantially undone the male domination of the doctoring profession, indicating that innately gendered abilities were never a very good explanation for the earlier predominance of men among doctors.

Again, all these are factors that should be clear upon just a little reflection. The example is useful precisely because it is so unlikely that a professor would be *generally* inclined to reason so dubiously about data or evidence. Mansfield would presumably reject the suggestion that one could "just look" at who the world's top hockey players are and conclude that Australians are innately less capable of skating. No doubt he would recognize that this pattern of inference, this *method* of supporting a belief, is unreliable in domains removed from the issue of "manliness." Cognitive biases, including confirmation biases, need not and probably do not in general indicate a broad incompetence or poor grasp of reasoning skills. They often work piecemeal, shepherding particular bits of poor reasoning through our cognitive self-policing, when personal convictions, attitudes, desires, and expectations are on the line.

Creating Evidence

Confirmation biases can take the form of top-down effects on perception akin to those discussed earlier. Thomas Gilovich mentions a partially perceptual sort of confirmation bias: that of seeing resemblances between a newborn and its parents.[7] Believing that an infant is the biological child of someone with whose features we are familiar, we can find it deceptively easy to see resemblances between them. This doesn't mean that there never are such resemblances, but their frequency and degree may be much less than they would have to be in order for all those grandparents to be right in saying, "Oh, she looks just like her mother!" (Still less when saying "She looks just like her mother did when *she* was born!") Expecting to see resemblances may lead us to see resemblances—whether or not they're really there. In this case the bias creates an unwarranted impression of evidence for a claim or hypothesis by actually helping create a perceptual judgment of similarity between infant and parent.

Beliefs, expectations, and emotions can also induce confirmation biases by shaping how we categorize events. For example, a friend of mine once told me that he was taking cold prevention pills on a daily basis through the winter. The results were impressive indeed: he hadn't missed a day of work due to a cold in the whole winter. Normally, he said, he would have missed at least a few days. Of course, the pills weren't *magic* or anything. He still got sniffles here and there, and a sore throat once, and he had a bit of a cough back in January. But as for a real *cold*—no, nothing like that! From his description of events, it seemed quite plausible that the only effect of the cold medication had been to elevate my friend's standard of what counted as a cold, biasing him in favour of the belief that the medication was effective.

Confirmation biases are more typically considered to involve the acquisition and interpretation of evidence rather than its manufacture. We can think of this family of issues in three broad divisions: **situational** or **structural biases** that systematically affect the availability of evidence for or against a hypothesis; **attentional biases** affecting the degree to which we examine and remember evidence even if it is available; and **interpretive biases** affecting the significance we assign to evidence that we do examine and remember.

The Accessibility of Information

The notion of a confirmation bias is usually applied to people and their psychological dispositions, but can be meaningfully applied also to situations themselves. Situations may be structurally biased to deliver only information that supports or information that undermines a hypothesis. Any situation in which we are given a biased sample, as discussed in Chapter 6, is likely to fall into this category. In other words, one reason I might end up with too strong a sense of evidence supporting a hypothesis and too little sense of evidence undermining it is that only or mostly evidence supporting the hypothesis is provided to me.

Consider, for example, an idea suggested in Chapter 4: that even though police officers in one sense have expertise on issues involving illegal drug use, their experience of the phenomenon might be skewed by seeing it disproportionately often in the context of connections to a wider criminal lifestyle—the sort of thing that especially calls for police investigation. So they may be over-disposed to see an inherent causal connection between drug use, on one hand, and more serious or more generalized lawlessness on the other hand. The sense that this inference is reasonable may stem from encountering a preponderance of confirming cases and only a small number of countervailing cases (where a countervailing case is something like an illegal drug user who is scrupulously law-abiding in every other respect). The notion of a situational confirmation bias allows us to see in more fine-grained detail what might be going on with this example. In such a case it need not be that a police officer has any *personal* bias toward finding a connection between drug use and broader lawlessness. It might simply be that the facts of her job conspire to present her with data that systematically over-represent apparently confirming evidence.

In fact, Lita Furby and Baruch Fischhoff noted a similar phenomenon in their research on useful advice for women on dealing with sexual assault situations.[8] Law-enforcement workers tended to advise that physical resistance to rape was inadvisable. Yet Furby and Fischhoff discovered at least tentative evidence that physical resistance was the better strategy. One explanation for the incongruence is that law-enforcement staff (including police) encounter a disproportionate number of rape victims who unsuccessfully resisted their attackers and suffered further injuries in the process. Why? Because victims who resist make better witnesses in court, and obvious injuries are often easier to prove in court than the forced sexual contact itself. In other words, the process of selecting cases for prosecution seems biased toward cases with sexual assault victims who resisted unsuccessfully and suffered further injury; these victims are over-represented in the investigative and trial processes. (There is a further question of whether victims who resist are also more likely to report the crime.) So law-enforcement personnel may be faced with biased data, making it seem to them that physical resistance to assault is correlated with a failure to escape the attackers or a failure to minimize the harm suffered in the attack.

For another illustration, suppose that a university wants to raise its standards for the teaching skills of new faculty. Are there any ways of predicting, before someone is hired, whether they will be a good instructor and not just a good researcher? In fact, many departments at many universities require that prospective faculty teach a sample lecture to students during the hiring process. The students' feedback is then taken as a relevant consideration when a decision is made about whom to hire. Suppose the University of Moose Jaw considers making this a university-wide requirement, but it first asks the Department of Chemistry, which has been using this method for some time, to report on how successful *they* think it's been in filtering out job applicants with lower teaching skills. The chair of the Chemistry Department says to herself, "Let's look at the people we've hired using this method. They all have pretty good teaching evaluations over several years; one of them, in fact, has won a teaching award. So I'd have to say that having job applicants give a sample lecture has been effective in filtering out poor teachers."

The problem, though, is that the chair lacks a crucial sort of information: namely, how well the applicants who *didn't* get the job are teaching. More specifically, she doesn't have the information regarding how well the unhired applicants would teach over several years at the University of Moose Jaw. A really thorough study would involve giving that opportunity to a number of applicants, including those who did poorly in the sample lecture, and seeing whether they were worse teachers over the longer term. But job openings are few and costly; the university can't run such an expensive experiment (still less justify an experiment that would treat students as guinea pigs). So just by the very structure of the situation, a potentially disconfirming kind of information is systematically unavailable. If it so happens that most of the people still up for consideration once a job competition has got down to the interview stage are in fact good teachers, then even a purely random method of whittling the applicant pool down to one will result in the hiring of good teachers. In that case, the only data available will seem to support the hypothesis that teaching a well-rated sample lecture is a useful tool for discriminating better instructors from worse ones, even if this is false. In general, when evidence seems to be accruing with respect to some claim or conjecture, it is important to think about the structure (in a broad sense) of the situation, in order to gauge the likelihood that one sort of evidence is being filtered out by contingent circumstances.

One more class of structurally biased problem cases consists of events that don't happen. It may seem strange to talk about such events, but they play a very important role in much of our reasoning and decision-making. If some policy or program succeeds in reducing the rate of teen suicides, for example, this would be taken as a good thing precisely because we understand there to be a set of events that can now only be specified **counterfactually**, that is, as events that could have happened but didn't. Obviously, it is very difficult to acquire evidence regarding things that don't happen, though. For the most part we learn about them statistically, by noticing changes in the number of events of that sort over time.

For this reason, when we consider actions or policies that are intended to prevent certain kinds of events, it is important to remain sensitive to the relative invisibility of their successes. For example, many universities have "speech codes" intended to foster an atmosphere of tolerance, by imposing constraints on forms of speech that are typically racially offensive, sexist, bullying, or otherwise oppressive in some degree. The aim is to create a learning environment that doesn't marginalize or intimidate particular groups through hostile speech. Yet in some cases this has created procedures for complaints and discipline that lack transparency and fairness, punishing or embarrassing people over minor infractions or simple misunderstandings. It's predictable that these negative outcomes will be particularly salient because the purest success cases of these policies, if any, will occur when someone *refrains* from saying something genuinely racist or sexist or harassing, without themselves feeling that they have been silenced on an academically important matter—for example, when someone decides against telling a racist joke.

But when this is the case—when *nothing* happens where something unpleasant might otherwise have done—obviously there can be no report of it. This is not because *people* are biased in what they report. It's because there simply is nothing to report on a case-by-case basis. By their very nature the worst failures of such policies will be specific knowable events, while their successes, if any, will be nonevents. Any positive effect will be visible only to statistical analysis over time (if this information has been tracked). Of course, in itself this does not mean that the policies do more good than harm. It just means that we should expect event-based evidence about them to over-represent negative cases, even if they are positive measures overall.

Finally, the content of a claim or the definitions of its key terms may inherently create a bias for the appearance of supporting evidence. The Elizabethan poet Sir John Harington quipped, "Treason doth never prosper: what's the reason? For if it prosper, none dare call it treason." Living under an absolutist monarch who was not afraid to imprison, exile, or execute dissidents, Harington's point was that whether events get *defined* as treasonous, as opposed to acts of liberation or of righteous resistance, has much to do with who is in power after the fact. Queen Elizabeth I's grandfather Henry Tudor could be said to have acquired his crown by committing treason, in warring against King Richard III—at least, this could easily be said *now*. To have said it during Elizabeth's reign would have been very unwise. So a potentially disconfirming bit of evidence about the thesis "Treason doesn't prosper" would have been papered over by the way events were categorized.

A somewhat similar effect arises from temporally open-ended predictions or prophecies. Suppose I predict, "Someday a man in an orange and blue shirt will stand atop a hill and shake a hand-crafted tambourine while yodelling a selection of movie theme songs." Provided someone cares enough about my predictions to write them down—me, in this case—this prediction will remain on the record into the indefinite future. Every day that passes *without* the prediction being fulfilled of course fails to falsify it; after all, I didn't say *when* this would come to pass. Virtually the only evidence that will seem relevant to it will be a confirmation, if and when that eventually happens. Just by its content, such a claim is biased in favour of supporting evidence. Such vague or open-ended predictions or prophecies, therefore, are a red flag. Their apparent confirmations, should they occur, are likely to seem intuitively more significant than they are.

Noticing Evidence

Even when the situation does not make one kind of evidence hard or impossible to find, confirmation biases of the more usual cognitive sort can result in a failure to consider countervailing information. Such attentional biases can take many forms, ranging from simple perceptual-behavioural phenomena, like how long someone looks at something, to complex patterns of biased information-gathering. Just as the focus of attention can lead to our missing extreme changes to our immediate environment through inattention blindness, so can a belief lead us simply to overlook evidence that would count against it.

Life is short and busy. With many demands on one's time and attention, there are always decisions to be made about what to bother thinking about or investigating. In the normal run of events, then, one reason for not paying attention to some bit of information might be that it looks like evidence against a proposition that one already believes. It's not that one *must* dismiss such evidence. It's just that it can seem like a waste of time to dwell on evidence regarding some matter one regards as a settled question. Even when countervailing evidence is available in a context, it's a further question whether it really gets considered. The expectation that some view is correct can function (often quite rightly) to minimize the attention paid to evidence that threatens to count against it.

Aspects of emotion, preference, or desire—"motivation," as psychologists put it—can also play an important top-down role, both here and in confirmation biases more generally. If I would rather not have my belief undermined because, say, I am especially emotionally attached to it, this can lead to my giving contrary evidence little notice. As we all well know, when there is something we would rather not do, it is usually easy to justify finding something else that needs doing instead. When a course assignment is due, the laundry may suddenly seem a much more pressing task, for instance. In much the same way, we may never quite get around to consulting the information sources we suspect are likely to give the best arguments against some view we hold and cherish.

All of these factors can make themselves felt in complicated and diverse ways that amount, in practical terms, to the creation of a structurally biased situation. Already believing that P may lead us not only to *ignore* evidence suggesting that not-P, but also to *stop looking* for evidence once we have data supporting our prior belief. That is, a confirmation bias can be manifest in the information-gathering methods we employ. Broadly this stems from decisions we make about what is attention-worthy. But as a result it determines what information is available in a situation. For example, having decided early in the year to subscribe to one newspaper rather than another, I have to some extent constrained the content and emphasis of the news information and commentary I receive for the remainder of the year.

Hence this phenomenon can go beyond the all-or-nothing question of *whether* we look for information, and become a matter of *how* we look for information. Naturally one way of inflating the evidence supporting a belief already held is to go about looking for evidence in a way that is particularly likely to find results favourable to the belief. Behaviour of this sort overlaps with the Multiple Endpoints Fallacy, discussed in Chapter 4. A common way for a confirmation bias to be present in our search methods is for our beliefs, desires, or expectations to affect which facts to focus on, out of a potentially very wide range of facts, just as in Multiple Endpoints. More generally, the books we read; the news media we read, watch,

ANOTHER EXAMPLE

Newspaper columnist Mark Steyn wrote:

"These days, whenever something goofy turns up on the news, chances are it involves a fellow called Mohammed. A plane flies into the World Trade Centre? Mohammed Atta. A gunman shoots up the El Al counter at Los Angeles airport? Hesham Mohamed Hedayet. A sniper starts killing petrol station customers around Washington, DC? John Allen Muhammed. A guy fatally stabs a Dutch movie director? Mohammed Bouyeri. A terrorist slaughters dozens in Bali? Noordin Mohamed. A gang-rapist in Sydney? Mohammed Skaf."[9]

The crimes mentioned by Steyn range over six years (2000 to 2005) and span three continents. In some of them, the named person acted alone; in others he was a participant. Some targeted groups; some targeted individuals. Most were murders; one was not. Nothing ties them all together except the name of a criminal.

Clearly this list is based not on some analysis of the relative frequency of names in crimes worldwide, but on a search (of Steyn's memory, if nothing else) for people with the name "Mohammed" who have committed crimes. The search, in other words, is tailored to produce the conclusion—a particularly gross example of a confirmation bias. One could choose almost any common name that one was already convinced indicated a criminal mindset—"Mark" would certainly work—and effortlessly compile a list of murderers bearing that name, drawn from the same time period and regions as Steyn's examples. Searching for evidence to *confirm* a belief, rather than to *test* the belief, is a large red flag in reasoning.

and listen to; the experiments we design; and the sort of questions we ask can all be chosen in a way that makes it more likely that supporting information and arguments will be presented and less likely that countervailing information or contrary arguments will be encountered.

Notice how psychologically roundabout or indirect this sort of top-down effect can be, if we engage in complex actions that limit our access to data in confirmation-biased ways. Being well-informed, getting an accurate sense of the evidence on some issue, can be a matter of going out of our way to consult information sources that our gut feelings tell us to dismiss or distrust. Those gut feelings may simply be confirmation biases at work.

Another powerful way for confirmation biases to affect how we notice evidence occurs when it is only or mostly the confirming instances that *remind* us of the hypothesis in question. Consider the old cultural stereotype that Scots are particularly frugal. If you believed this, then the cases in which you saw someone you believed to be Scottish doing something to save money would strike you as particularly significant; in fact, these might be the only occasions on which the stereotype came to your mind. Hence, every time you end up thinking about the stereotype, it would seem to be confirmed.

Yet this wouldn't be because Scots are frugal—not even within your experience. It would only seem this way to you because the cases in which you encountered Scots spending freely, and for that matter the cases in which you encountered non-Scots being careless or carefree with money, didn't call the stereotype to mind. The stereotype might never have to survive contact with countervailing evidence, in your thinking, because countervailing evidence fails to make you think about the stereotype. Parallel remarks apply to the saying "Pride goes before a fall," discussed in Chapter 6. Once we are aware of the saying, it is far likelier to come to mind when we see a case of a proud and successful person suffering a major setback than when we see someone already doing badly who ends up doing worse. Confirmation biases on how we notice and remember information are likely to make such a platitude seem more supported by evidence than it really is.

Remembering Evidence

Memory is also implicated in confirmation biases that create the unwarranted perception of a trend or regularity, when chance occurrences of a kind of event remind us of the other events of that kind that we have experienced. One example of this is the sudden sense of having dreamed about an event that is occurring (sometimes called *déjà vu*) and coming to believe on the basis of such experiences that one's dreams are prophetic. Many people believe they have had this experience; each instance may call to mind the earlier instances, while the large numbers of unfulfilled dreams and of significant but undreamed-of events are never recalled.

Another example is the phenomenon of picking up the telephone to call someone, only to find that they are already on the telephone calling *you*. This eerie experience can seem trend-like when it occurs, as memories of earlier occurrences come to mind immediately whenever the next instance occurs. But the sense of a trend pops out of the data because so much of the disconfirming data fades away in retrospect. When I pick up the telephone, get a dial tone, and dial normally, there is no reason for me to open the subsequent conversation by saying excitedly, "You'll never guess what just happened! I just went to call you and *you weren't already on the phone!*" The sheer volume of such countervailing cases, suggesting the randomness of the eerie cases, does not come automatically to mind when an eerie case is encountered; indeed, it's difficult to guess at the number of normal cases even if we try. Again, the disconfirming evidence in this sort of situation may never be applied to the relevant belief, simply because it fails to get one thinking about the belief at the right time.

In these cases too we don't even really need a belief, commitment, or motivation for the effect to occur. The mere relevance or significance of a hypothesis may be sufficient. Consider the sorts of superstitions that are widely known even though few people believe them any longer. Even if you're entirely convinced that walking under a ladder does not bring about (non-ladder-related) misfortune, just being aware of the superstition's existence can make a misfortune seem more noteworthy if it happens right after you walk under a ladder. Similarly for misfortunes that happen to follow breaking a mirror, spilling salt, or having a black cat cross your path: your confidence that these are merely superstitions does not prevent your familiarity with them from making the seemingly confirming instances more noticeable and more memorable.

We will see further biases involving memory later in this chapter. For now an important point to emphasize is that such effects can not only reinforce existing unwarranted beliefs and expectations, but can introduce new unwarranted beliefs as well. Someone who sends on a chain-letter that promises good luck might be doing so purely out of curiosity at that point, open to the idea that it works but not committed to the idea. This alone can be sufficient to get the disproportionate confirming effect, though. I might cooperate with the chain-letter's instructions on Tuesday in a moment of whimsy and forget that I've done so within a matter of hours. But then a sudden bit of unexpected good news on Wednesday is likelier than a completely uneventful week to remind me of having done so. Confirmation biases don't just make believers into stronger believers; they can make seekers into believers.

Interpreting and Assessing Evidence

Another kind of confirmation bias is active when the existence of an expectation or motivation leads one to place disproportionate credence in evidence supporting a belief or hypothesis. Suppose that the situation presents me with a representative sample of information relevant to some hypothesis, and suppose also that this information is drawn to my attention in roughly representative proportions. In other words, there is neither a situational confirmation bias nor a bias in the extent to which I notice the evidence that's available. Nevertheless I may be subject to a range of confirmation biases in favour of the belief. Such biases are felt when the supporting evidence is judged to be disproportionately significant or weighty, in comparison to the apparently countervailing evidence also in my possession.

Consider, for example, the situation in which two expert opinions are known regarding some question—one supporting a claim, the other denying it. Someone who believes the claim may have access to both opinions and may have paid attention to both opinions, yet still be subject to a confirmation bias in the form of an intuition or gut feeling that the expert whose opinion supports the belief is the more reliable or competent. This sort of thing amounts to giving a "free pass" to seemingly supportive evidence: that is, not really questioning favourable evidence, or not making the cognitive effort to explore potential tensions or contradictions between various pieces of evidence. We have seen that one form of confirmation bias in favour of a proposition is to pay little attention to evidence weighing against it. It is perhaps surprising, then, that another form of bias is to pay especially close attention to countervailing evidence. Yet how could it ever be a reasoning error to pay very close attention to evidence?

Again the answer has to do with the difference between how evidence for and against the belief is treated. Just as I might casually accept arguments that support a belief while ignoring arguments that undermine it, so might I accept supporting arguments uncritically while raising every conceivable challenge against opposing arguments. This is made explicit in cases of an evidential **Double Standard**, in which one holds the opposing position to higher evidential standards than one's own beliefs. For example:

Arynn: I hear they did a study proving that kids who watch more television are also more violent.

Bianca: Well, Professors Yosh and Stan at Harvard University did a study on that question in 1989, published in the *Journal of Higher Televology*, that showed no such correlation. I can give you the reference if you'd like.

Arynn: Wasn't there a major scientific fraud case at the Harvard Medical School? I think we shouldn't go believing willy-nilly everything we hear from Harvard researchers.

Of course Arynn is right that "we shouldn't go believing willy-nilly everything we hear from Harvard researchers." But that's not what Bianca was suggesting. More to the point, Arynn ends up suddenly demonstrating a level of scepticism about reported studies that would, if applied consistently, be far more damaging to her own evidence of a nameless study by nameless researchers than it is to Bianca's more precise and apparently confirmable evidence.

SELF-FULFILLING PROPHECIES AS CONFIRMATION BIASES

From gambling to consultancy to personal financial investment (if there is a difference), one of the most highly charged and nerve-racking things we do is try to predict what the future will bring when our information is equivocal. People who demonstrate an ability to do this—to predict what the markets or the government or the weather will do in the future—are respected and valued for their insight and even, sometimes, for their alleged supernatural powers.

The question of how predictions can come true, or be perceived as having come true, is large and multifaceted. But one class of predictions of particular interest is that of **self-fulfilling prophecies**: predictions that come true not simply because the predictor foresees how events will unfold, but because the prediction itself has an effect on how things unfold. That effect can apply to the events themselves, in the case of self-fulfilling prophecies, or to the *perception* of the events in a related sort of case.

In the self-fulfilling case, the prediction gives rise to an expectation that the prophesied event will occur, and this expectation leads to actions that bring about the event. This doesn't indicate that the predictor had any real insight into the future, however. For example, suppose a palm-reader tells Ted that his hockey team will win their next game, against a much better team. Such a prediction may seem unlikely to come by sheer chance, making it an impressive feat of prediction to get it right.

But now suppose that it's this very act of prediction that gives Ted extra confidence and focus, which he wouldn't otherwise have had. This leads him to play an unusually strong game, and his team wins as a result. While it's true that the prophecy turns out to be correct in such a case, there's no reason to put this down to any predictive (as opposed to *motivational*) abilities of the prophet. That's the straightforward sort of self-fulfilling prophecy; the existence of a plausible means by which the prediction could have contributed to its own fulfillment counts as a

CHAPTER 7 *Biases Within Reason*

red flag for the claim that the predictor had some special insight or predictive powers.

Another way in which predictions can be judged correct as a result of their own effects is by their affecting perceivers' judgments themselves. A prediction is just the sort of thing that can introduce a powerful confirmation bias at the levels of perception, cognition, and memory, by leaving an observer with the expectation that an event will occur, or simply by making the possibility that it will occur more salient.

Suppose that our palm-reader tells Ted that he will play a better game than usual. If this leads Ted to play a better game than usual, it's a simple self-fulfilling prophecy. What might also happen, though, is that even though Ted plays normally, he perceives his normal play as being better than normal, and each of his good plays strikes him as particularly significant in light of the prediction. When his shots fail to score, he interprets them as having been promising efforts that were only frustrated by bad luck or excellent play from the other team, when he would usually regard them as poor shots or not dwell on them at all. He also notices his (real or perceived) good plays more during the game and recalls them more clearly after the game, while overlooking or minimizing his average or poor plays. So he believes he has played better than normal and regards the prophecy as confirmed, owing to the effect of the prediction upon *him* rather than on the outcome itself. For that matter, Ted might overlook or forget other predictions that were clearly not fulfilled, either because he is motivated to believe in the predictive powers of the palm-reader, or because only confirming instances remind him of the various predictions he was given.

The genuine sort of self-fulfilling prophecy discussed first amounts to a situational confirmation bias, with respect to evidence for the prophetic abilities of the predictor. By causing a situation likely to produce confirming evidence, the prediction biases the evidence in favour of itself. Of course this doesn't change the fact that the prediction ends up being *true* in such a case; it just means that it turned out accurately because it was made, rather than being made because it was accurate. The merely apparent sorts of self-fulfilling prophecy, on the other hand, have the appearance of accuracy due to a range of psychological biases. These may include effects on perception that seem to confirm the prophecy; effects on the interpretation of evidence in a way that supports the prophecy; and confirmation biases on both one's decisions about what to count as having been a prediction, after the fact, and one's memory of what predictions were even made.

These sorts of self-fulfilling prophecy may occur together. For example, consider someone who takes *Echinacea* (a herb widely believed to have health benefits) in order to recover more quickly from a cold. On one hand, simply taking the *Echinacea* may lead her to believe that she will recover more quickly, and this, by instilling a positive frame of mind, might somehow boost her body's recovery systems—not least by acting as a reminder to eat healthily, drink often, and get rest. On the other hand, she might simultaneously misinterpret random or independent daily fluctuations in how she feels as signs of early recovery or underestimate the severity of her symptoms in comparison to earlier colds she remembers experiencing. The net effect would be a genuine accelerated rate of recovery, subjectively enhanced by the misperception that she was recovering still more quickly, all consistent with there being no genuine medical effect of *Echinacea* on colds.

The intertwined self-fulfilling prophecies in this example are both forms of the *placebo effect,* the apparent or actual improvement in someone's health that arises merely out of their belief that they are being medically treated. This is discussed in detail in Chapter 9.

EGOCENTRIC BIASES

If you watch or read enough news, you will encounter reports on the sole or few survivors of tragedies in which large numbers of people died. What is revealing about such cases is the frequency with which the survivors will explain their survival in terms of fate, or destiny, or some divine will. "It wasn't my time yet," they might say, or "Somebody had a plan for me." From an objective perspective, the survival of a single person out of an entire busload of people seems quite a good candidate for a random outcome. But from that person's perspective, the fact that one person survived is far less striking than the fact that it was *them*. The point is quite general: we have a tendency to read special significance into the events that involve us and into our roles in those events.

Self-Serving Attributions

Partly this is due to the fact that we have so much more information about our own case—our own thoughts, history, and intentions—than we do about anyone else. So it is natural that our place in the events we experience seems particularly significant. But there is also a frequent element of motivated inference in egocentric reasoning. Most people like to see themselves as basically decent and rational, and this provides a powerful motivation to reinterpret events and actions in a way that fits these emotionally attractive preconceptions. One area in which egocentric biases come to the fore is **attribution theory**, an approach to studying how people ascribe psychological states and explain behaviour—including their own.[10] There are different dimensions of explanation proposed by the theory; for example, I may explain a failed action in terms of either my own abilities or the effort I put into it. My emotions, desires, expectations, and personality may combine to produce a **self-serving bias** toward one of these explanations over the other, depending on whether (oversimplifying, of course) I would rather think of myself as talented but lazy, or modestly gifted but hard-working.

A more fundamental distinction, however, is between explanations in terms of internal factors, which would include both abilities and effort, and external factors—aspects of the situation, other people's actions, history, and other environmental contingencies. A great deal of social psychology research reveals a tendency for people to explain successes internally and failures externally. "Victory has a hundred fathers," runs an old saying, "but defeat is an orphan." This tendency to own success and disown failure is not just a matter of what people will publicly admit, regarding their culpabilities and merits. It extends to our actual self-perception, where it is more than a quirky weakness in our self-knowledge. On one hand it can cause us to underestimate the need to change our own ability and effort levels as a response to failure, and on the other hand it can lead us to devalue and hence fail to maintain the social or situational factors that lead to our successes. A red flag attaches to any situation in which one needs to explain one's own success or failure. To reason accurately in such contexts may require making an effort to identify internal causes, in the case of failure, and external causes for success.

Optimistic Self-Assessment

The **Lake Wobegon Effect** is one of the best-known examples of an egocentric bias. Also known as **optimistic self-assessment**, the effect takes its more folksy name from the fictional town of Garrison Keillor's novel *Lake Wobegon Days*, in which "all the children are above average." This rather gentle poke at parental pretensions is a good metaphor for a general truth about our self-evaluations: at least in North American culture, and probably more generally too, most people tend to rank themselves as above average with respect to certain virtues. While it is logically possible for more than half of a sample to be above the mean (though not the median, obviously), to have a large majority of people ranking themselves far above average is a powerful indication that people are ranking themselves unreasonably highly relative to other people. For example, one survey of over 800,000 American high school seniors found that all of them ranked themselves above average with respect to getting along well with others, and fully one-quarter of them ranked themselves in the top 1 percent. *Somebody* must be mistaken!

As with motivated inference more generally, optimistic self-assessment is not unconstrained. We don't find people wishing they were good at structural engineering and hence simply *believing* that they're good at it. The effect seems to be limited to virtues that are more vaguely defined and that are not frequently or publicly measured or compared. It would be difficult for a radical misconception about one's abilities at doing mathematics to survive in the face of evidence from one's math tests in school. But less well-defined and seldom-compared properties like cooperativeness or leadership skills are more amenable to over-interpretation and tend to show a Lake Wobegon Effect.

Hindsight Bias

One manifestation of **hindsight bias** is sometimes called the Historian's Fallacy, the error of supposing that past events were predictable and should have been foreseen as the consequence of the actions that precipitated them. The ancient Greek proto-historian Herodotus recounts an anecdote about a high-ranking Persian soldier who predicts to his Theban host over dinner that the entire Persian army is soon to be destroyed by the Greeks. Since Herodotus is writing after this has already occurred, such a story has considerable appeal; it makes an event that was no doubt contingent and unpredictable in advance seem foreseeable, even inevitable, in retrospect.

At the personal level, hindsight bias does not just consist of past events coming to seem inevitable and foreseeable. It manifests as unreliable memory, an overestimation of one's own earlier confidence that events would happen as they actually did. That is, hindsight bias isn't just a matter of saying, "S should have known that

X was a bad idea"; it's also a matter of saying, "I knew that X was a bad idea before S tried it."

Hindsight bias is an extremely important critical thinking issue when it has this egocentric aspect. This is not simply because it leads to particular false beliefs about our past assessments of evidence. The bigger problem is that these false beliefs undermine our motivation for considering alternative methods of gathering and evaluating evidence and of making decisions. This is a quite general worry and an illustration of the dictum that critical thinking is partly a matter of learning not to trust yourself. As Justin Kruger and David Dunning put the problem, reporting on their study of how ignorance and incompetence diminish one's self-perception of the need to improve: "[W]hen people are incompetent in the strategies they adopt to achieve success and satisfaction, they suffer a dual burden: Not only do they reach erroneous conclusions and make unfortunate choices, but their incompetence robs them of the ability to realize it."[11] The first step in deciding to improve our ways of reasoning is to discover that the ones we are currently working with are flawed. Hindsight bias is one of the ways in which our sense of these flaws is minimized, by rewriting our memories of what we thought and why we acted as we did. (It may well be that we find people who say, "I told you so!" obnoxious not so much because they are smug, but because [that is, when] they are *right*. Being reminded of the details of our past assertions, beliefs, and decisions brings us face to face with the errors that hindsight bias would otherwise whitewash.)

The point is perhaps sharpest when we consider certain kinds of professional judgments. For example, we want to think that medical doctors are continually updating and improving their diagnostic methods, depending on how accurate those methods prove to be. Hindsight bias is likely to impede this learning process to some extent, though.[12] Yet one needn't be a medical doctor to feel the force of the worry. The issue of knowing when to reconsider our problem-solving, decision-making, and belief-forming practices goes to the heart of the critical thinking project. It is obviously important that we remain sensitive to the possibility that we are mistaken in our judgments.

There is some evidence that the hindsight bias is one of cognitive availability—that one's knowledge of the actual outcome makes one's memories of the particular prior evidence that was *relevant* to that outcome more available to recall. Strategies for reducing the bias include rehearsing possible explanations for alternative outcomes. Speaking in 2005 about the 2003 invasion of Iraq, a long-standing opponent of the invasion might display a degree of hindsight bias in saying, "I was pretty sure in 2003 that there were no longer any chemical weapons in Iraq." A debiasing strategy for that person might be the self-prompting question "What would I have said had it turned out that there *were* chemical weapons discovered in Iraq?" By drawing her own attention to such alternative outcomes, and, presumably, the reasons for opposition to the war that she would have retained in those circumstances, the speaker may come to a fuller and more nuanced (though perhaps less self-flattering) recollection of her reasons for opposing the war in the first place. This would be a reduction of hindsight bias. More effective still, perhaps, would be to actually review what she had said (more particularly, what she had written) at the time.[13] Often there is no such objective record of our thoughts after the fact, of

CHAPTER 7   *Biases Within Reason*

course. Yet in principle keeping such a record in the form of a diary dealing with contentious issues and consulting earlier entries after events have unfolded is a means of ingraining the lesson that our judgments are often more tentative and less accurate than our memory tells us they were.

BIASES OF LANGUAGE AND COMMUNICATION

Continued Influence Effects

If I told you, on some day in December, that I'd seen a weather forecast calling for a blizzard the next day, you would (other things being equal) then come to believe that a blizzard was likely to occur the next day. But suppose I then came back to you and said I had been mistaken—that I'd wrongly looked at the forecast for another part of the world altogether or had actually glimpsed a flashback-style report on a storm that had happened ten years earlier. What should your expectation of a blizzard be, at that point? If you were inclined to believe me about the blizzard in the first place, then presumably you should be equally willing to believe my *retraction* of my original claim. In retracting it, I've undone my original assertion, so any belief that you based on that assertion should now be given up.

In 2005 a group of psychologists headed by Stephan Lewandowsky published the results of a study on the psychological effects of *corrections* and *retractions* in the mainstream media.[14] The same reasoning should apply more generally in the case of the media and our responses to it. Sometimes the news media will get a story wrong, and sometimes they will even announce that they've done so, retracting the story after the fact. A reasonable expectation is that a rational audience will continue to believe the initial story only to the extent that they do not see or hear the retraction. If I accept a news source as sufficiently reliable to justify my belief in their testimony, my trust surely ought to extend to believing their corrections and retractions as well.

But that's not what Lewandowsky and his colleagues found. To continue with the example discussed as a potential hindsight bias: in the fall of 2003 Lewandowsky's researchers questioned nearly 900 subjects from three countries on whether they believed a range of statements regarding the invasion of Iraq, which took place in March 2003. Some of these statements were false ones that had been initially reported during the invasion, but were subsequently retracted. Later, without permitting the subjects to re-examine the answers they'd already given, the psychologists showed the subjects the same statements and asked whether they could recall retractions being issued for any of them. The reasonable expectation is that remembering a retraction would be inversely correlated with judging a story to be true. That is, when subjects remembered seeing a retraction for a story, they should be *less* likely to have marked that story as one they believed in the first place. Remarkably, though, in one large group of subjects this was not the case: for these people, an ability to remember a retraction simply did not influence the credence they placed in the statement!

Who were these subjects? At first glance they were just the American subjects in the experiment. (As groups, the German and Australian subjects demonstrated the predicted inverse correlation between recalling a correction and believing the statement.) But the deeper explanation turned out *not* to be nationalistic; it had to do with whether the subjects were initially cautious about the rationale for the invasion of Iraq. Subjects of *all* nationalities who were the least sceptical of the publicly proposed reasons for the war were also least likely to update their beliefs in light of their knowledge of the retractions.

This has been called the **continued influence effect,** a term denoting the way that information continues to influence our judgments even after we know enough to conclude that it was actually *mis*information. In another example, Hollyn Johnson and Colleen Seifert had subjects read a series of reports that first described a man as a suspect in a crime, and then later explained that the man was no longer a suspect, his alibi having been accepted by police.[15] The latter information ought to have exonerated the accused in the eyes of readers, since it was attributed to the same source as the original accusation. Yet the subjects tended to continue thinking of the man as probably guilty. Once again, what they read first was sufficient to plant a belief, and what they read subsequently was insufficient to extinguish that belief—even though in theory it negates the rationale for the belief.

Plausibly this sort of bias relates to a problem noted in Chapter 2, in particular the difficulty we often have in dealing with neutral states of information. Having felt briefly entitled to take a position on the question of who committed the crime in such a series of reports, subjects are reluctant to go back to a state of "I just don't know." In order to abandon the belief that one person is guilty, they require more than just the removal of the evidence to that effect; they require another suspect to substitute for the original one (as Johnson and Seifert found in a variation of their experiment). One lesson is that we have to take special care to regard retractions as red flags, consciously working out the implications of a retraction when we encounter one. Treating it merely as one piece of information among others is apt to lead to its getting lost in the shuffle, never modifying established beliefs in the way that it should. A second and more fundamental idea, suggested by Lewandowsky's results, is that the initial adoption of a general critical thinking attitude toward reports prepares us to use new information when it comes along. Uncritically accepting a report at the outset may make it particularly difficult for us to update our beliefs rationally later on. This reflects the importance of the idea that critical thinking should be habitual, rather than something we decide to exercise case by case.

Framing Effects

Some of the fallacies and red flags discussed in Chapters 3 and 4 hinge upon the effects that different word choices can have in an argument or assertion. As noted about the Fallacy of Slanting Language, for example, our reactions to particular claims about people may be very different depending on whether they are described as soldiers or as insurgents. Such lexical choices, and still subtler differences in language and communication, can have astonishingly strong effects on the judgments we reach and even on the contents of our memories. The informal notion of "spin" reflects a broad psychological truth: the way a situation is described can have a powerful influence on our thinking about it. These influences are called **framing effects.**

Daniel Kahneman and Amos Tversky, who pioneered much of the "heuristics and biases" approach to cognition, demonstrated framing effects in a famous experiment testing subjects' responses to a fictional scenario.[16] In this scenario 600 people are sick. There is only enough medication either to give an under-dose to everyone, in which case there is a two-thirds chance that everyone will die, or to give a full dose to 200 people, in which case they will live and everyone else will die.

According to decision theory of the sort that informs basic microeconomics, these two outcomes ought to have the same "expected utility"; they should be judged equally desirable if people reason in accordance with (the simplest versions) of microeconomic theory. So it was an interesting and important result that Kahneman and Tversky's subjects preferred the sure gains of saving 200 people over the merely probabilistic alternative by a proportion of 72 percent to 28 percent. But at least as interesting was this: when the scenario was described differently, as "400 people will die" rather than "200 people will live," and when the alternative was described as a one-third chance that nobody would die, the subjects' preferences were reversed. Only 22 percent favoured giving full doses to 200 people when the scenario was described in these terms, with 78 percent choosing the one-third chance that everyone survives. Yet these seem to be just two ways of describing the same situation. The descriptions themselves, and what they emphasize—sure gains versus the probability of complete loss on one hand, and sure losses versus the probability of full gains on the other—seem to have an enormous effect on what people judge to be the best action.

Framing can also affect judgments that are more perceptual in nature. Elizabeth Loftus and John Palmer studied the effects of different descriptions of a car accident on the judgment of subjects who had witnessed the accident.[17] To recognize the significance of what they found, it might be useful to begin by considering the following list of words that could be used to describe the physical interaction of two cars in an accident, and ranking them according to how much physical force they suggest.

hit
bumped
contacted
smashed
collided

Loftus and Palmer showed their subjects video footage of cars running into each other, then asked them to estimate their combined speed at the moment of impact. They framed the question differently to different groups of students, however. Some subjects were asked how fast the cars were travelling when they *hit*; others, when the cars *collided*; still others, when the cars *smashed*; and so forth. Figure 7.2 summarizes the results.

The somewhat boring result was that subjects were not very good at estimating impact velocities no matter how the situation was described: whether the true speed was 20 mph or 40 mph, the average estimate was in the high 30-range. More interesting, though, is the way their inaccuracy varied with the terms used to describe the impacts, as Figure 7.2 indicates. The more force or violence suggested by the word, as these words would be ranked by most people, the higher the impact speed was

FIGURE 7.2 | SPEED ESTIMATES FOR VERBS USED IN EXPERIMENT

Verb	Mean Speed Estimate (mph)
Smashed	40.5
Collided	39.3
Bumped	38.1
Hit	34
Contacted	31.8

Source: Reprinted from *Journal of Verbal Learning and Behavior,* Vol. 13, Elizabeth F. Loftus and John C. Palmer, "Reconstruction of Automobile Destruction: An Example of the Interaction Between Language and Memory," pp. 585–589, Copyright 1974, with permission from Elsevier.

judged to be, on average. (The milder terms did not lead subjects to underestimate the speed, but this aspect of the Loftus and Palmer experiment may not generalize.)

In short, the effects of fallacies like Slanting Language and Persuasive Definition can be very strong and can also range beyond the scope of argumentative fallacies. Any careless or imprecise description of a situation, deliberate or not, has the potential to bias our intuitive reactions or reasoning about the situation. One potential strategy for avoiding such a bias is to monitor claims and questions for terms with strong connotations, and to consider how such claims and questions would look with more neutral (but still strictly correct) terms substituted for them. If one's response is substantially different when the loaded terms are weakened somewhat, a framing effect might be creating a problematic bias.

BIASES OF MEMORY

I remember very clearly how I learned about the explosion that destroyed the space shuttle *Challenger* on January 28, 1986. I was just finishing a Grade 12 Physics final examination, when a gentle knock came at the door. My teacher answered it quietly and slipped out into the hallway for some quiet murmuring. When he returned, his head was bowed. He paused for a few moments, then wrote on the board that the space shuttle had exploded, and that no survivors were expected. I could add more details to the story; the memory is exquisitely clear to me.

Yet for all that, I would not bet a great deal on the accuracy of this memory. It's just too easy to be wrong. Memories of traumatic or famous events are sometimes known as **flashbulb memories**, a reference to the frozen-moment photographic quality that they often subjectively possess. The classic examples are of the "I remember where I was when I first heard that . . ." variety. Beginning with the assassination of American president John Kennedy it has become something of a cultural theme for people to discuss their recollections of how they first learned about such defining events. No doubt this is a way for us to personally relate to momentous events and to share our reactions to them. Yet there is a tempting mistake lurking in the popular conception of such memories, to the effect that the trauma or significance of the event results in a particularly sharp, clear, and reliable memory.

Memory can be very frail, and the nature of its frailty is that the reliability of memories may be starkly at odds with their vividness and intuitive accuracy. Ulric Neisser and Nicole Harsch made a study of people's memories of the *Challenger* disaster, asking them where they were when they heard about it, and then two years later asking the same question.[18] Setting aside the question of whether the subjects' initial reports were accurate, it turns out that the average score for accuracy between the first answer and the follow-up answer was less than 3, on the 7-point scale Neisser and Harsch employed. People's confidence in their second answer was affected by the vividness of the imagery they associated with the memory—but not by its accuracy. A similar effect has been observed in people's recall of their location and actions when they heard the news of the attacks of September 11, 2001.[19] One study even noted that American president George W. Bush seems to be subject to erroneous flashbulb memories of that event.[20] How does this happen, and how might we be on guard against it?

How to Manufacture Broken Glass

The Loftus and Palmer experiment described earlier serves as a useful transition to critical thinking issues involving memory and judgments based on memory. In that experiment, the choice of words to describe a car accident had a measurable effect on the speed at which subjects judged the collision to have occurred. That is a framing effect on judgment. But the experiment had an additional component.

In a follow-up protocol, subjects from the "Hit" group and the "Smashed" group were questioned about their memories of the videos one week later. Without seeing the video again, both groups were asked specifically whether they could remember witnessing broken glass in the crashes. (There wasn't any.) Neither group was very likely to mistakenly claim to have seen broken glass, but the Smashed group was twice as likely to say this than the Hit group: 16 percent to 8 percent. Moreover, this effect was not simply a function of the higher speed estimate, since it persisted even in the elements of the two groups that overlapped in their speed estimations. That is, the people in the Smashed group who estimated a lower speed of collision were still likelier to attest to broken glass than people in the Hit group who guessed a higher speed of collision. This is evidence that the words used to ask about a past event can fairly directly affect the "visual" contents of the memory being accessed.

For critical thinking purposes, these experimental framing effects on memory show that the way a memory is elicited—the particular wording or implicatures of a question about how some past event occurred—can have a powerful effect on what gets remembered. Important details can disappear from memory, and entirely false ones can be confabulated, depending on how an inquiry is framed and how it interacts with the subject's state of mind. As in the case of perceptual biases, the lesson is *not* that memory is uniformly or even broadly unreliable. If it were, then one's memory of these psychological studies couldn't be evidence for it! Rather, the lesson is that when a memory, even a clear and compelling memory, is inconsistent with independent evidence, the memory becomes only one piece of evidence among others.

Extending the theme of Loftus and Palmer's experiment, suppose that the eyewitness to an accident recalls seeing broken glass at the scene. Nothing we've seen here makes it reasonable for such a witness to believe from the outset that this memory is dubious. But if the police report indicates that no broken glass was found, the fallibility of memory should immediately be recognized as a serious issue—including by the eyewitness. It would then become an important question just what questions were used to elicit the eyewitness's initial report, when this initial report was taken, and to whom the eyewitness had spoken in the meantime. Depending on what information, if any, is available about these events—and often this sort of information is impossible to collect with any confidence after the fact— the evidential weight of the memory might be substantially reduced, relative to other information that suggests the memory is mistaken. This openness to scepticism isn't a natural attitude for us to take toward our own clear memories, nor toward the sincere memory-based testimony of normally reliable people. An acquaintance with experimental results and case studies of the sort we've examined, and the habit of bearing them in mind in relevant circumstances, are key components of a willingness to distrust one's own judgment when independent evidence speaks against it.

False Memories

One way for memories to acquire misleading details after the fact, then, is through descriptions containing loaded terms. Other mechanisms exist as well. In the case of the apparently mistaken memories of George W. Bush, the mechanism seems to be the post-event insertion of some later memory. Bush repeatedly stated that he saw the footage of the first airplane hitting the World Trade Center tower before going in to speak to some schoolchildren, then learned of the second attack while he was in the classroom.[21] Yet no footage of the first crash was available that quickly. Declining the more exotic theories alleging Bush's responsibility for the attacks, the obvious charitable conclusion is that he was misremembering in a quite familiar way: his seeing footage of the first attack after the fact could easily have inserted this additional element into his memory of the day itself.

The prospects for false memories go well beyond even these quite strong effects, though. Not only can aspects of memories be added or changed, but entire vivid memories can be implanted by circumstance or by design. For example, one highly controversial form of therapy (and, to an extent, activism) through the 1980s and 1990s was intended to awaken *repressed memories* during counselling. The idea was that many traumatic events, especially from childhood, and especially of a sexual and violent nature, would become hidden from the victims of the attacks. These memories would cause psychological problems, but would not be explicitly accessible until the patient or client submitted to therapy intended to draw them out.

This therapy tended to involve visualization exercises and the repetition of narratives in role-playing, over long periods of time and against the background assumption that *not* discovering such memories represented a kind of therapeutic failure. The problem is that these conditions have been experimentally demonstrated to enable a therapist or researcher to implant entirely false memories. The rehearsal of a narrative seems to be an effective way of inducing such false memories, especially those purporting to be based in childhood.[22] Using this method and mixing the false narrative in with (apparently) accurate narratives for each subject, Elizabeth Loftus was able to induce memories of being lost in a mall in many adults. Ira Hyman and colleagues were able to create a false memory of a hospitalization or a birthday party with a clown (having confirmed with parents that neither had occurred) in roughly 20 percent of the college student subjects, in another study using essentially the same approach. In some of these cases, moreover, the subject took the initiative in adding contextual details to the false memories, fitting them into other memories and integrating them with general facts about the subject's life. The evidence is strong that imagining events as if they happened, and talking about them as if they happened, is a reasonably effective way of producing potentially very vivid memories of the events happening. Memories that could have been instilled in this way—say, seeming memories of early childhood that might have been told as stories by friends or family members—should be regarded as red flags. If independent evidence suggests that the event did not happen, or did not happen in the way remembered, the clarity of memory cannot be taken to outweigh such evidence automatically.

CONCLUSION

Biases and heuristic reasoning operate at the level of perception, judgment, and memory. Some of them just seem like structural quirks of our cognitive architecture, but others also stem from the effects of what we already believe, desire, and expect. A thinker's existing state of mind, as well as external factors like the choice of words by which information is conveyed, can have powerful effects on the outcome of our reasoning. One of the most powerful and common effects is to reinforce what we already believe, even though the evidence may not really support this conclusion.

It may all seem a bit pessimistic: we can't trust our senses, our judgment, our motives, methods, or memories. But this would be to misinterpret the fundamental lesson. There is no good reason to suppose that we are generally deluded in perceiving, interpreting, and remembering events. It's just that we can be mistaken in ways that are surprising and moreover invisible to our intuitions. That is, the mistakes in question are not necessarily accompanied by a sense of uncertainty. The most difficult ones to detect are those that seem like the most incandescent common sense. And if these errors are not pervasive, neither are they as rare or exotic as one might think, prior to studying how easily they are induced. The lesson is not pessimism, however, but a kind of cautionary note. This is what it means to develop the habit of not trusting oneself: to be alert for situations that can make one's own biases worse; to monitor the situations and reasoning of other people and judge their claims accordingly; to listen to one's own words for signs that would lead one to judge that someone else was unduly biased, given the circumstances; and so forth.

REVIEW QUESTIONS

1. List and explain the biases in this chapter that could help explain the opening example of a seeming trend: the streetlights that switch off as I pass by. Then describe any similar incident or phenomenon that happens, or has happened, to you. What biases might explain your experience?

2. Scan newspaper editorials or opinion columns for examples of framing effects: claims whose plausibility is greatly diminished merely by replacing loaded terms with more neutral terms. Avoid inserting question-begging terms of your own, even if you believe them accurate. Instead, try to use words that people on all sides of the issue would accept as accurate (even if they wouldn't find them perfectly precise).

3. Prepare a longer-term critical thinking project. As proposed in the discussion of hindsight bias, look at the current news and try to identify three or four issues regarding some future events, which are likely to be settled within the next two to four months. Based on your reading of the news, jot down what you think the likeliest outcomes are for each issue, your confidence in these predictions, and your reasons for thinking so. Set a reminder for yourself (by marking it on a calendar or using scheduling software) to check out the issues four or five months from now to see how they turned out. When this date arrives, look at the actual outcomes without at first re-examining what you'd written. Record your perceptions of how close to accurate your predictions were (including, if you think you were wrong, the reasons you might have been wrong). Finally, go back and compare your recollection of your predictions with the predictions you actually wrote down. Hindsight bias may be reflected in an inability to remember evidence that you originally noted, bearing on outcomes that did not occur, and the ease of remembering and overestimating evidence supporting outcomes that did occur. Describe any signs of hindsight bias you might see. Finally: could you be confirmation-biased in favour of detecting a hindsight bias?

NOTES

1. D. Gilbert, "Inferential Correction," in *Heuristics and Biases*, T. eds. Gilovich, D. Griffin, and D. Kahneman, 167 (Cambridge, Mass.: Cambridge University Press, 2002).

2. A. Brown and L. Nix, "Turning Lies into Truth: Referential Validation of False-hoods," *Journal of Experimental Psychology: Learning, Memory, and Cognition* 22, no. 5 (1995): 1088–100.

3. For more images of the Hor mummy mask and the Hollow Face Illusion, go to http://dragon.uml.edu/psych/hor.html. This Hor mummy web page is part of David Landrigan's Illusions Gallery website at the University of Massachusetts Lowell Psychology Department.

4. F. Geldard and C. Sherrick, "The Cutaneous 'Rabbit': A Perceptual Illusion," *Science*, 178, no. 4057 (1972): 178–79.

5. D. Simons and C. Chabris, "Gorillas in Our Midst: Sustained Inattentional Blindness for Dynamic Events," *Perception*, 28 (1999): 1059–74.

6. D. Solomon, "Of Manliness and Men," *New York Times*, Magazine Section, March 12, 2006, p. 15.

7. T. Gilovich, *How We Know What Isn't So* (New York: Free Press, 1991), 60.

8. Reported in B. Fischhoff, "Giving Advice: Decision Theory Perspectives on Sexual Assault," *American Psychologist* 47, no. 4 (1992): 577–88.

9. M. Steyn, "Racism Is Bad—So Is Self-Delusion," *The Telegraph* (http://www.telegraph. co.uk/opinion/main.jhtml?xml=/opinion/2005/12/20/do2002.xml), December 20, 2005. Accessed January 4, 2006.

10. D. Miller and M. Ross, "Self-Serving Biases in the Attribution of Causality: Fact or Fiction?" *Psychological Bulletin*, 82 (1975): 213–25.

11. J. Kruger and D. Dunning, "Unskilled and Unaware of It: How Difficulties in Recognizing One's Own Incompetence Lead to Inflated Self-Assessments," *Journal of Personality and Social Psychology* 77, no. 6 (1999): 1121–34.

12. H. Arkes, R. Wortmann, P. Saville, and A. Harkness, A "Hindsight Bias Among Physicians Weighting the Likelihood of Diagnoses," *Journal of Applied Psychology* 66 (1981): 252–54.

13. U. Hoffrage, R. Hertwig, and G. Gigerenzer, "Hindsight Bias: A By-Product of Knowledge Updating?" *Journal of Experimental Psychology: Learning, Memory, and Cognition* 26, no. 3 (2000): 566–81.

14. S. Lewandowsky, W. Stritzke, K. Oberauer, and M. Morales, "Memory for Fact, Fiction, and Misinformation: The Iraq War 2003," *Psychological Science* 16 (2005): 190–95.

15. H. Johnson and C. Seifert, "Sources of the Continued Influence Effect: When Misinformation in Memory Affects Later Inferences," *Journal of Experimental Psychology: Learning, Memory, and Cognition,* 20 (1994): 1420–36.

16. D. Kahneman and A. Tversky, "The Framing of Decisions and the Psychology of Choice," *Science*, 211 (1981): 453–58.

17. E. Loftus and J. Palmer, "Reconstruction of Automobile Destruction: An Example of the Interaction Between Language and Memory," *Journal of Verbal Learning and Verbal Behavior* 13 (1974): 585–89.

18. U. Neisser and N. Harsch, "Phantom Flashbulbs: False Recollections of Hearing the News about *Challenger*," in *Affect and Accuracy in Recall: Studies of "Flashbulb" Memories*, eds. E. Winograd and U. Neisser (New York: Cambridge University Press, 1992): 9–31.

19. J. Talarico and D. Rubin, "Confidence, Not Consistency, Characterizes Flashbulb Memories," *Psychological Science* 14, no. 5 (2003): 455–61.

20. D. Greenberg, "President Bush's False 'Flashbulb' Memory of 9/11/01," *Applied Cognitive Psychology* 18 (2004): 363–70.

21. E. Loftus, "Creating False Memories," *Scientific American* 277, no. 3 (1997): 70–75.

22. Loftus, "Creating False Memories."

CHAPTER 8

The More We Get Together: Social Cognition and the Flow of Information

Recently I was on my way to a round of golf with a friend and two other acquaintances. Since we all live in the same general neighbourhood, one of them offered to drive all of us in his car. During the drive, one of my acquaintances told a racist joke. It was a little long, but it culminated with people from several different racial minorities ("immigrants," as the joke went) standing around on the street of some Canadian city and talking about how great life in Canada is, until one of them asks where all the "white people" are. "Oh," replies another in the punch line, "they're all working!"

Now, on one hand, I didn't laugh. Nor did I even smile politely. Neither did one other fellow in the car. But the joke-teller himself laughed heartily, as did the fourth person, though (it seemed to me) rather less heartily than the joke-teller. On the other hand, you may wonder how many people in the car made a point of actually saying, "Not funny" or "I guess we know different immigrants" or "Wow, that was really offensive and stupid"? The answer, I confess, is zero. Not even a mild or indirect form of explicit disapproval was expressed—including from me.

Besides unburdening my conscience, what is the point of this confession? It illustrates something that may well be familiar to many people from their own experiences: that in many, many social contexts there are powerful pressures that work to prevent challenging and debunking dubious beliefs, or even known falsehoods. As a result, there are propositions that continue to circulate despite being unjustifiable—in this case, the unwarranted and offensive proposition that non-white immigrants to Canada typically live a life of happy indolence.

Most of us are familiar with the experience of biting our tongues rather than embarrassing a friend, annoying a family member, or being seen as unpleasant company. Unfortunately, the minority response (laughter) and majority response (silence) were both likely to have led the joke-teller of my story to assume that his attitudes are commonly regarded as sensible, at least among his peers, and that jokes of that kind are actually funny. This is a problem that we, as critical reasoners, must bear in mind when we consider how attitudes and beliefs can become prevalent or at least common in social groups. The many social communities to which we all belong function as (among other things) channels for the communication of vast quantities of information. Episodes like the racist joke-teller drive home the importance of social biases on individual reasoning and collective transmission of information. What sorts of information persist and spread through social channels of communication? What gets filtered out? And how should the answers to these questions affect our evaluation of information in context?

THE EFFECTS OF SOCIAL CONTEXTS ON COGNITION

Our private and public lives are largely constituted out of our relations with the people around us: family members, friends, employers and employees, business contacts, teammates, and co-participants in cultural practices of every sort. They are the immediate sources of much of our information about a vast range of topics. Some of this information is mundane and specific to passing situations, but some is broadly applicable and colours our reasoning more generally. Moreover, much of our reasoning is specifically *about* these people: what they have done, what they think, and what they will do.

In some respects this indirectly reflects reasoning about ourselves, since we may want to know not just what others are thinking, but what they're thinking about *us*. Moreover, a person's interest in how others are acting is often a matter of deciding what is rational for the person herself. Cases of cooperative action are good examples. For example, each person in a village may aim to benefit personally by cutting as much firewood as possible from a nearby forest, but if everyone does this the forest will be destroyed before it can renew itself. (This sort of case is often called "the tragedy of the commons.") When deciding whether it is reasonable to cooperate by voluntarily limiting the amount of wood one takes, though, a key question will be whether other people are also cooperating. If all or most of the others continue to take all the wood they can, then the only person who tries to act cooperatively loses both in the short term and the long term, since the forest will be destroyed anyhow. Any analogous situation requires both evidence-gathering and thinking about what the other people are doing, or will do in the future, in order to decide one's own best course of action.

Even when we are not thinking about other people explicitly, their presence and our implicit attitudes toward them can powerfully influence the way we think about the situation at hand. For example, a substantial body of research (and occasional tragic news stories) indicates that when someone witnesses a person in distress, their response tends to depend on whether other people are present (and known to be present) at the time. A lone witness to someone in distress is more likely to assist or intervene than a group of witnesses; the presence of the other witnesses seems to leave each person feeling less obliged to help—or less culpable for doing nothing.

In general the social groups in which we are embedded have an enormous influence on what we believe and the inferences we draw from our beliefs. These social groups may be defined along many different dimensions; there is a sense in which everyone who has read this book can be said to belong to a community defined by that fact. People interact over the Internet; by telephone, television, and radio; and in many other ways besides, with each form of interaction presenting additional ways of belonging to social groups. But the most obvious determinant of social groups throughout history, and probably still today, is physical location. We see the effects of this at the largest scale when we consider the social effects of local culture on individuals' beliefs of various sorts. For example, many religious believers take themselves to hold their beliefs as the result of a carefully considered weighing of the evidence. Yet most people who believe themselves to have reasonably inferred the truth of Christianity live in predominately Christian cultures, while most people who believe themselves to have reasonably inferred the truth of Islam live in predominately Islamic cultures—and similarly for other major religions. Since it's hard to see how mere geographical differences could influence which belief seems the most reasonable, the plausible conclusion is that the social contexts in which this reasoning is performed are having a strong influence on it.

At a much finer level of detail, too, we can see social factors emerging as crucial to our evaluation of information. We are all familiar with the basic worry of having to decide whether to accept some information in light of concerns about the reliability of the source. The fact that so much of our knowledge comes to us through testimony raises reliability issues that might not be immediately obvious, until we take stock of how information flows through social groups and how various biases may conspire to hide the problems from us. In this chapter we will examine the effects of social contexts on human reasoning, first as a means of revealing biases that can be anticipated in our own thinking and that of others, and later for the purpose of seeing how information that spreads through a group can be affected by individual and collective properties of the people in the group. The project of believing reasonable things involves paying attention to the qualities of these information channels, and noting the extent to which they are inclined to preserve truth and weed out falsehoods.

REASONING ABOUT OTHER PEOPLE

Our reasoning about the people around us occupies enough of our time and mental resources to pose characteristic problems of its own. Whether we are explicitly attempting to fathom someone's motives or implicitly reasoning about them in light of our perceptions of their gender, race, or age, we can easily make systematic and predictable errors stemming from biases of various sorts.

SOCIAL STEREOTYPES

A **social stereotype** is a cluster of associated characteristics attributed to people of a particular sort. Beliefs or perceptions about a person of that sort—i.e., that sort of gender, race, height, hair colour, etc.—can activate the automatic assumption that the whole cluster of characteristics applies to that person. One result to emerge from social psychology is the discovery that fast, intuitive judgments about people may be significantly influenced by prevailing social stereotypes, even in subjects who sincerely take themselves *not* to accept such stereotypes. Indeed, even people who are the objects of negative stereotypes may think, feel, and act in ways that suggest an implicit acceptance of the stereotype.

A difficulty in coming to understand the extent and effects of social stereotypes is that people are unlikely to admit to having stereotyped attitudes. Partly this is because it is socially discouraged to admit having prejudices in many (though not all) contexts, but partly it is because someone might be unaware of having the prejudice in the first place. As we saw many times in Chapter 7, we are normally unaware of the biases affecting our reasoning. So our evidence for the significance of social stereotypes tends to be indirect and statistical.

One way of examining the nature of social stereotypes and the connotations that constitute them is by the Implicit Association Test. This is a test that indicates how strongly people associate two concepts or categories, by measuring how difficult they find it to categorize objects under time pressure when those two categories are split apart. To use an example from a study cited below, suppose you are given the task of pushing one button if you are shown a male name and a male face, and another button if you see a female name paired with a female face. You would likely perform these button-pushes in response to the stimuli much faster (say, in two-thirds the time) than if you were asked to push one button when a male name appeared with a female face and another button if a female name appeared with a male face. The fairly obvious explanation is that for most people names and faces are psychologically very closely associated under the categories of male and female. When we implicitly associate concepts, categorization schemes that separate them make judgments more difficult, and this is reflected in the extra time it takes us to make them.

This is at least a suggestive diagnostic tool for measuring implicit biases, because it permits graded results—that is, it's not all-or-nothing—and it need not rely on subjects' conscious statements about their prejudices or lack of prejudices. Experiments indicate that implicit racial biases are detectable through this test. For example, Anthony Greenberg and his colleagues studied responses to racial categories and observed that subjects found it substantially easier to categorize words into the frameworks of "White or pleasant" and "Black or unpleasant" than to categorize them using "White or unpleasant" and "Black or pleasant."[1] This suggested a common implicit association of Whiteness with positive connotations and Blackness with negative connotations among the subjects. (Researchers sometimes use capitalization to distinguish the concepts of race from mere colour concepts.) Perhaps most significantly, these results did not correlate with the subjects' own statements about their racial attitudes. It looks like one can have racial biases that tinge one's responses and judgments, despite having the conviction that one's attitudes are quite unbiased.

Of course, any one such experimental result may be confounded in various respects. But other results support similar conclusions. Travis Dixon and Keith Maddox tested how people's reactions to a video news story about a murder varied according to how dark the skin of the reported perpetrator was.[2] They found that, on average, the emotional distress viewers felt in watching the report was greater with a darker-skinned reported perpetrator. Viewers also found the perpetrator more memorable when his skin was very dark than when it was white or only

A striking feature of the Dixon and Maddox study was the observation that heavy news viewers reported the greatest emotional distress at a darker skin tone for the perpetrator. Coupled with independent evidence that the news media over-represents darker-skinned people as perpetrators of crimes,[3] this illustrates the prospect for a "feedback loop" between the media and viewers: in reporting what viewers consider worrisome, hence newsworthy, the media may both reflect and ingrain such stereotypes. This theme is taken up in various ways in Chapter 10.

somewhat dark, and reported a more positive view of the victim (whose race was not mentioned) when the perpetrator's skin was very dark. Again, it looks like a stereotype was activated in the subjects by their perceptions of race, which influenced both their emotional and cognitive responses.

Studies also suggest a similar stock of social stereotypes regarding gender. One of the earliest investigations of the question, published in 1968, found that women themselves tended to rate a piece of writing as better (i.e., more persuasive) if it was attributed to a male author than if a woman was listed as the author.[4] By using a single piece of work and changing only the alleged author's name, experimenters clearly seem to isolate the biasing effects of social stereotypes on people's evaluations of the work. This bias against academic and professional work perceived as performed by a woman has been confirmed many times over (in a North American context, at least), with both male and female subjects. The effect seems to occur even if evaluators only suspect that the author is female—for example, when the author's name is initialed, but readers have contextual information suggesting a female author.[5] It occurs for adults and children and can arise from information as weak as handwriting that is perceived as feminine.[6] To be blunt: the odds are good that you and I would intuitively rank the same piece of work more highly if we thought it was written by a man than if we thought it was written by a woman—and our explicit attitudes on the equality of the sexes might not have much to do with this.

What critical thinking lesson can we extract from the evidence, of various kinds and strengths, indicating that stereotypes affect our reasoning about other people? Further evidence suggests the existence of similar stereotypes regarding height, weight, tone of voice, baldness, and many other properties that may be implicated in the formation of first impressions. But if socially stereotyped reasoning is this pervasive, what can we do about it? The answer, like the problem, is one of degree. There is no tidy way for any of us to eliminate social stereotypes from our reasoning, but the first step is to be aware of the problem case by case and to think about how it could be affecting us in a given context. For example, the policy of having university students identify themselves on assignments and examinations only by their student numbers can be seen as critical thinking on an institutional scale: forewarned of the kind of biases that commonly affect an evaluator's reasoning, we can take steps to minimize those biases by keeping names out of the equation altogether. In this way we get academic grading that is uninfluenced, or less influenced, by the graders' perceptions about the students' personal characteristics.

When making judgments in situations where we do have information likely to activate some social stereotype, though, it is important to be prepared to self-consciously counteract implicit biases. Once the genie is out of the bottle, and I know that I'm dealing with someone likely to fall under some social stereotype—positive or negative—I need to monitor my own reactions in light of the understanding that my initial responses, gut feelings, and dispositions may be influenced by that social stereotype. Taking this concern seriously could involve using a kind of "benefit of the doubt" principle: if negatively stereotyped Alice and positively stereotyped Bruce both seem like roughly equivalent job candidates, I might choose Alice on the grounds that implicit gender biasing would have led to her abilities, accomplishments, and interview performance being implicitly under-rated throughout the process. Or I might seek feedback from a reliable third party after having removed the stereotype-identifying information from the candidates' files. Whatever measure one employs, the idea is to use our knowledge of how such biases can affect our reasoning, in order to forestall or minimize those effects.

THE FUNDAMENTAL ATTRIBUTION ERROR

One of the reasons we spend so much time and energy thinking about other people is that their motives and character generally mean at least as much to us as the consequences of their actions. As Daniel Gilbert and Patrick Malone remark, "Two equally rambunctious nephews may break two equally expensive crystal vases at Aunt Sophia's house, but the one who did so by accident gets the reprimand and the one who did so by design gets the thumbscrews."[7] But even when the consequences of people's actions are clear, their motives can be hard to calculate.

As we saw in Chapter 7, social psychologists use attribution theory to explain certain egocentric biases. But attribution theory is more generally applied to explaining our social interactions, in particular how we assign psychological states to other people, rather than the construction of our self-image. Investigating and

FURTHER REFLECTION

Other people's intentions are crucial to our understanding of their actions. Indeed, one of the basic principles of the philosophical study of Action Theory is that actions are individuated by intent; the best description of *what you did* is typically determined by *what you meant to do*. For example, we would normally describe a particular action as "turning on the light," and not as "exciting the flow of electrons in some nearby wires." The physical movements that make up the action will have both consequences, but if your goal was to make the light come on then that's the best way to characterize your action. The connection between intention and action is hence so deep that it can be difficult to discuss actions without simply presuming an attribution of intent.

theorizing how we go about attributing beliefs, desires, motives, and character traits to other people is a major research project, results from which shed light on a range of critical thinking issues associated with our reasoning in social contexts.

One social bias illuminated by this research is so common and powerful that social psychologists flatter it with the name "the **Fundamental Attribution Error**." This is a bias in favour of explaining someone's situation or behaviour in terms of their personality, character, or dispositions while overlooking explanations in terms of context, accidents, or the environment more generally. Suppose that while standing in the checkout line at the grocery store, in the middle of the week, I overhear Ted saying, "I did absolutely nothing yesterday." I think to myself, "Yesterday was Tuesday! Must be nice to laze around instead of working." In the absence of more specific information about Ted, I commit the Fundamental Attribution Error if I judge that Ted has a lazy character rather than taking seriously the range of alternative explanations. There are innumerable alternatives, but a few reasonable ones include that he was sick yesterday; that it was his first day off work in two weeks; that he was just laid off; and that he does shift work.

The truism that first impressions are critical to the opinions people form of one another turns out to be quite correct, but that's nothing for us to be happy about from a critical thinking perspective. The general point is visible to most people through an honest self-appraisal: despite being aware that I can occasionally be rude or thoughtless just because I'm "having a bad day," I do not tend to assume that someone who is rude or thoughtless to me at a first meeting is merely having a bad day or even just a bad minute. The temptation is to attribute a character disposition instead, to come away thinking, "What a jerk!" Or worse.

A classic experimental demonstration of the Fundamental Attribution Error was published in 1967 by Edward Jones and Victor Harris.[8] At that time, the regime of Fidel Castro in Cuba was a particularly hot topic in American politics, and subjects were given essays that argued for or against Fidel Castro's government. But they were also informed that the authors of those essays were *instructed* to take the positions they argued. That is, the pro-Castro essays were written by people who had been given no choice but to write a pro-Castro paper, and the same went for the anti-Castro essays. The sensible conclusion ought to have been that the essays really didn't give any useful information about the authors' attitudes toward Castro. Nevertheless, the subjects tended to attribute pro-Castro sentiments to the authors who wrote pro-Castro essays, and anti-Castro sentiments to the authors who wrote anti-Castro essays. The relevant information that the authors were given no choice of what to write about could not outweigh the bias in favour of reading general attitudes into single instances of behaviour.

The Fundamental Attribution Error has particular significance for the existence of social stereotypes of various sorts. It is apt to prop up the idea that if someone is poor, ignorant, unemployed, homeless, or otherwise disadvantaged, it must be owing to her personal disposition to be that way. Whether through choices or abilities, from the perspective of the Fundamental Attribution Error a person's circumstances stem from something internal to them.

Yet both the rich, privileged, and powerful on one hand, and the poor, deprived, and powerless on the other hand, may owe their situations partly or wholly to external factors. This is easily overlooked when our immediate reaction is to think that situations and behaviour primarily reflect attitudes and abilities. Indeed, we might see links between our intuitive reasoning on such matters and certain cases of the Naturalistic Fallacy, as discussed in Chapter 3. A fallacious inference from the non-moral statement "Ted is poor" to the morally loaded statement "Ted *deserves* to be poor" might be eased along by the heuristic judgment that a person's circumstances are explained primarily in terms of their character and choices.

In fact it is unclear whether anything about a person's character, personality, or general beliefs can be reliably inferred from single instances of behaviour. This worry arises in part because, as we have seen, social stereotypes have a tendency to do some of the work in such snap judgments. Moreover, the terms we use to categorize character traits tend to be unhelpfully vague. To call someone *honest* is not yet to say very much, if this label does not distinguish between a reluctance to tell *any* lie, a reluctance to swindle, and a reluctance to commit thievery, among other things. (And similarly for calling someone *dishonest*.) Some thieves are honest in their personal relationships; some inveterate liars would not cheat family or friends out of their savings; some swindlers would not shoplift. None of them is honest, period, yet each displays some honesty.

Besides the stereotype problem and the general terminology problem, there is a specific empirical problem, too: the sorts of behaviour that strongly tempt us to attribute character, beliefs, and attitudes may have very little to do with any of these dispositions. Various experiments suggest that the features of the immediate situation are a surprisingly strong determinant of a person's behaviour, leaving it unclear how great a role is normally played by character dispositions. Alice Isen and Paul Levin published an intriguing study of the phenomenon in 1972, including an experiment in which people who had just finished using a public payphone encountered someone who "accidentally" dropped a sheaf of papers. But the apparent accident was part of the study; the experimenters wanted to see whether a situational factor as minor as *finding a dime in the payphone* could make a difference to the caller's immediate behaviour. There were 16 dime-finders, of whom 14 helped collect the papers. Yet of the 25 non-dime-finders, only 1 helped to pick up the papers.[9] This result prompted a number of follow-up studies of varying results, mostly confirming the general effect, though also suggesting that a range of factors is implicated.

The following year another landmark study, this one by John Darley and Daniel Batson, took religious seminary students as its subjects.[10] The students were told that they had to hurry to another room to give a short speech. Some subjects were told they had a few minutes to spare; others were told that they were late to some degree. Also, some subjects were told that they had to speak on the topic of getting a job in a seminary, while others were told they would be speaking on the parable of the Good Samaritan—that is, a biblical story about the importance of helping strangers. On the way from one room to the other, the students passed a deliberately placed actor who lay slumped as if unconscious or hurt. Fewer than half the students offered any kind of help, but among those who were told they had a few minutes to spare, over 60 percent helped while those who were in the greatest hurry only helped 10 percent of the time. How rushed the subjects felt clearly had a powerful influence on whether they would help the apparently distressed person. Yet the topic of the speech they were considering did not have an effect; subjects pondering the Good Samaritan were no likelier to help than were those contemplating job prospects. Indeed, some of the "Good Samaritan" subjects actually stepped over the actor without stopping to help!

Results like these cast further doubt on our intuitive attributions of personality, intent, character, desires, or innate ability on the basis of briefly observed behaviour or the circumstances in which we find someone. A person's action or situation at any given moment may have far more to do with immediate environmental factors than with their personality traits. Reasoning about other people based on small samples of their behaviour is therefore a red flag. The problem with reasoning from limited behaviour to deep personality traits might be obvious on evidential grounds, but what we need to bear in mind is how intuitively tempting we find such inferences in the social realm. A willingness to treat momentary behaviour as a "one-off" can help us to form more accurate impressions of the people around us—or, at a minimum, help us not to form inaccurate impressions.

FALSE POLARIZATION EFFECTS

Discussions on controversial topics that have established stereotypical positions can follow an unfortunate pattern: as soon as a speaker voices one idea that's broadly characteristic of one stereotype or extreme, the audience takes her to hold that stereotypical view on every aspect of the issue. This tendency to impose an unjustified sharpness on the perceived positions in a discussion is a species of Hasty Generalization. It is facilitated by the use of labels to lump potentially diverse views into a single fuzzy category: terms like "liberal-left" and "neo-conservative" are often used to produce this convenient and tempting polarization of issues.

Suppose, for example, that Artemis says, "I think some sort of work-for-welfare program isn't a bad idea." Hearing this expression of support for a policy typically associated with socio-political conservatism, Bruno, who disagrees with work-for-welfare programs, judges Artemis to be a stereotypical conservative. That is, he immediately perceives her as holding stereotypical versions of conservative views on a wide range of topics. His recognition that she has voiced support for a position he opposes can bias him in favour of overestimating the extremism of her actual view. In Bruno's reckoning of Artemis's perspective, her reference to work-for-welfare may overshadow her qualifications of her support for such policies: that she thinks *some version* of the program *isn't a bad idea*, specifically. Because Artemis is subject to the same sort of bias toward Bruno, once it becomes clear that he disagrees with her, we have a recipe for a disagreement based on substantial misunderstandings. Artemis and Bruno may generally share core values and beliefs, and may not even be far apart in the views on the specific topic under discussion, and yet each sees the other as holding a stereotypically opposing view.

The **False Polarization Effect** is the tendency to overestimate two things: the extent to which the views of others resemble the strongest or most stereotypical positions of those sorts, and the difference between one's own view and the view of someone who disagrees. The idea is conveyed graphically in Figure 8.1.

FIGURE 8.1 | THE FALSE POLARIZATION EFFECT ACTUAL VIEWS: TRIANGLE'S PERCEPTION: "THEM" "US" CIRCLE'S PERCEPTION: "US" "THEM"

These diagrams illustrate the False Polarization Effect, which is the tendency to overestimate two things: the extent to which the views of others resemble the strongest or most stereotypical positions of those sorts, and the difference between one's own view and the view of someone who disagrees.

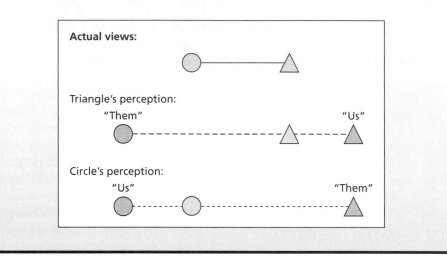

Source: From Emily Pronin, Carolyn Puccio, and Lee Rose, "Understanding Misunderstanding: Social Psychological Perspectives" in Gilovich, T.; Griffin, D.; Kahneman, D. (Eds.), *Heuristics and Biases,* p. 651. © Cambridge University Press 2002. Reprinted with the permission of Cambridge University Press.

This bias may be an artifact of the difference in the availability of reasons between oneself and others. The (apparent) availability to each person of her own reasons for holding a view on some issue makes it relatively easy for her recognize the respects in which that view deviates from the stereotypical versions.

Someone who believes that abortion is morally problematic, for example, might state that she does not favour the widest possible access to abortion. Yet she could still believe that abortion at the earliest stages of pregnancy is not particularly wrong, or that abortions should definitely be available to victims of rape. Knowing this about her own views, she will locate herself on the more moderate side of the most extreme anti-abortion position one could hold. Yet under the influence of the False Polarization Effect she may still be inclined to interpret someone who voices support for wide access to abortion as holding the sharply defined position of "pro-choice" advocate. Again, the same bias can operate in the other direction at the same time. Hence a debate between two people who would actually agree on propositions like "The fewer abortions the better, all other things being equal" and "Late-term abortions are more morally problematic than early-term abortions" can get bogged down in the mistaken assumption from each discussant that her opponent is a dogmatic ideologue or has a greater burden of proof than is actually the case. The overall effect is a misleading sense of sharp differences between simplistic positions, where the real viewpoints may have both commonalities and nuances.

Social thinking that entrenches these misunderstandings is directed toward both the group that agrees and the group that disagrees with one's perspective. When among others of broadly similar sympathies, we may feel it would be hostile to voice

A pattern of thought related to False Polarization is found in reasoning like this on some contested issue:

"People at both extremes on this issue disagree with me, so my view must be relatively innocent of bias or axe-grinding. The fact that the extremists on both sides disagree with me is evidence that my view is neutral and reasonable."

This kind of inference may well be biased toward the self-perception of reasonable neutrality. It is a red flag to find yourself reasoning in this way, since it is a line of thought subject to confirmation biases at more than one level.

First, deciding who *counts* as an "extremist" is an opportunity for biased personal definitions to creep in, perhaps influenced by a prior Lake Wobegon-style judgment that you are an unbiased judge. For if you already thought that your judgment was neutral, then what located others toward the biased extremes relative to you, in your assessment, would be nothing other than their disagreement with you on one side of the issue or the other. Any such effect of pre-existing bias on your categorization of who counts as an extremist will amount to a means for the bias to confirm itself.

Your perception and recollection of the disagreements that you notice can also be skewed here. As long as *somebody* voices a more extreme view than you on one side of the issue, you might over-interpret their difference of opinion to make it seem the evidential equivalent of the dissent of everyone on the other side. The number of dissent-events on both sides might seem roughly equivalent due to biasing effects on your memory, for example, or you might simply be dealing with a biased sample of opinions in your personal experience. If we can think of the spectrum of views on some issue as varying from heavily biased toward the pro-side to heavily biased for the con-side, with some relatively unvarnished understanding somewhere in the middle, you might actually be far over to the pro-side and yet have all the materials you need to run through the reasoning sketched above. Even though you very well *might* hold a relatively neutral view, your intuitions about who disagrees with you are not a good reason to believe this.

the differences that distinguish our view from theirs, or we may worry that this would be perceived as disloyal somehow. On the other hand, in our interactions with those broadly unsympathetic to our views, we may also worry that it will be thrown in our faces or taken as weakness if we express any scepticism about the stereotypical version of the view we support or about other views that are characteristically associated with it. Both kinds of concern act to suppress the open expression of variety in our beliefs and attitudes that might help to curb False Polarization Effects. Influences of this sort of social cognition on communication is discussed later in this chapter.

REASONING AFFECTED BY OTHER PEOPLE

Following up on a theme first raised in the Introduction, we saw in Chapter 4 that critical thinking about numerical claims is very often a matter of actually doing the calculations yourself or confirming them through some independently reliable source. The example at the start of that chapter concerned a borrowing contract recommended by the treasurer of the city of Waterloo, Ontario, and subsequently approved by the city council. The contract was announced as having a total cost of around $113 million, but turned out to cost roughly twice that amount. Yet perhaps the strangest aspect of that example was not simply that the mistake was made. The curious question is *how* the mistake came to be made.

Kevin Crowley, the local newspaper business reporter who broke the story, explained: "I took out a pencil and a calculator and worked my way through the formula . . . the total cost was about $200 million."[11] But when Crowley contacted the city's financial officer to ask why the reported formula didn't match with the reported cost, he got a truly astonishing reply: "He said he and his staff had come up with a similar total when they first did the calculation. But it turned out they had done it incorrectly, he said. . . . So, who showed you the right way to do the calculation? I asked. [T]he salesman who arranged the lease-style loan, [he] replied." The reporter went on to explain that the final contract had only been sent by the loan negotiating company just before the meeting of the city council to approve it. The treasurer did not check to ensure it added up; he just trusted the salesman and recommended that the city council approve the deal.

It might seem incredible that someone in such a position of responsibility would recommend the contract to the city council without having read it through, and without working out its details, with over $100 million on the line. Yet that strangeness pales in comparison with the treasurer's decision to continue placing such trust in the salesman *after having reached a different answer in his calculations.* What could explain such remarkable decisions about what to believe and what to recommend to others?

These decisions become intelligible when they are seen as judgments affected by social pressures. Throughout the previous year, the main company salesman had nurtured a social relationship with the treasurer. As Crowley noted, the loan brokerage "treated him and other city officials to golf games, charity balls and other events,"[12] such as tickets to the Canadian Open golf tournament, which the men attended together, and then a second trip to golf at the same exclusive club. In short, there was an extended period of time during which the salesman did the sort of things that a very rich and very generous friend might do for his pal. So when the pressure was on and it became a matter of either trusting his own arithmetic with an admittedly complex formula or unquestioningly accepting the explanation offered by someone who had done so many nice things for him, the city treasurer seemed to go with the relationship rather than the calculations. Setting aside the question of whether anyone was deliberately misled in this episode, this much still seems obvious: without the social factors of trust and perceived friendship, the costly and mistaken deal would not have been made. We don't just think *about* other people; other people change the way we think about everything.

JUMPING ON THE BANDWAGON

In earlier days of American politics, election campaigns would sometimes see the candidates organizing parades through neighbourhoods to drum up support and increase their profiles. Often these would include a musical band being drawn along on a wagon, playing festive music. The idiom "to jump on the bandwagon" arose as a metaphor relating to this practice, alluding to the people who would get sufficiently caught up in the excitement to jump on the wagon for the ride and the music without having known or cared much about the candidate beforehand. The idiom has come to have a definite negative connotation, since it suggests that the bandwagoner is uncritical and easily swayed by popular opinion. Human social cognition being what it is, there is no shortage of opportunities to use this saying.

One of the simplest and most general respects in which social contexts affect our judgment is just the **Bandwagon Effect**: the tendency for our beliefs to shift toward the beliefs we take to be widely held by those around us. When it occurs it is almost certainly a result of many cognitive, motivational, and social factors working together. Social psychologists suggest that bandwagoning can be partially explained by the appeal of certainty and the costs of holding an unpopular view. The idea is that it's easy and pleasant to have one's beliefs confirmed. One way of arranging this—not, typically, as a conscious decision—is to mould one's beliefs to fit the (local) consensus. On the other hand, to hold and to express a position that runs against the consensus can be socially and cognitively expensive. A minority view will be challenged more often, requiring its holder to have and to produce an argument for it, whereas someone who voices the consensus view is less likely to have to defend it. And in social groups that place a high value on sharing particular beliefs, not accepting those beliefs can lead (or be expected to lead) to the social exclusion of the dissenter.

These explanations of the Bandwagon Effect are largely in terms of motivated inference; that is, they appeal to what it is personally advantageous or preferable for an agent to think. But situational biases and other cognitive biases are also likely to play some role. Almost by definition popular perspectives are likely to be the most repeated and most frequently endorsed within that group; this will bring the Repetition Effect into play as well, skewing individuals' judgments toward the popular view in a self-reinforcing way. Whatever the explanations, the phenomena are quite clear: from fashions to fads to beliefs, many things become more popular for little reason other than that they are already popular.

Of course, the Bandwagon is highly sensitive to context. It is not always the simple (perceived) majority that shapes the attitudes of the individual; often there is some preferred sub-group that acts as the bandwagon that the individual wishes to join. The initial stages of a spread in belief or fashion may be driven by different factors—the emulation of a celebrity, as with some fashions, or an attempt to identify with perceived trends among the wealthy, a factor in trends of the names that parents tend to give their children. Once the trend is established, however, aspects of bandwagoning can arise. For example, once it becomes more work (within one's social group) to explain why one *doesn't* wear bell-bottom jeans, or own a Che Guevara shirt, or have a tattoo, or support a war, than it is to explain why one *does*, a Bandwagon Effect is likely to be exerting some pressure on one's judgment. While it is every bit as unreasonable to adopt an unpopular position merely for the sake of holding an unpopular position, being aware of the Bandwagon Effect enables us to self-monitor for signs that we are dismissing or marginalizing minority perspectives without giving them careful consideration.

The case of the racist joke lets us see some of the complexities that arise in actual contexts of communication. Had we been on our way home *after* the round of golf when the joke was told, my friend and I would (I submit) have been much likelier to voice a direct challenge to it. Why? Because the social consequences of the challenge would have been greatly reduced if we were minutes away from going our separate ways anyhow—especially since these acquaintances were not people with whom I interact daily. (For instance, I wouldn't see them the next morning at work.) On the way *to* the golf course, however, there was still a five-hour stretch of shared company and conversation ahead of us. I recall thinking about that very point as I silently debated whether to risk blowing the afternoon over the bit of nastiness in question. In what I would now characterize as a failure of moral nerve, I decided against saying anything. Others might consider that I showed social grace in biting my tongue; either way, by following some deeply ingrained social norms, I very likely perpetuated the joke-teller's sense that there is consensus in favour of his viewpoint among the people with whom he socializes.

The **False Consensus Effect** is the common tendency to overestimate the extent to which others share our beliefs and attitudes. This term was coined in the report of an experiment in which subjects were asked which of two somewhat unappealing actions they would choose to perform if they had to.[13] The subjects were asked to give some reasons for their choice and then were asked how they expected others to choose on the task. Most subjects predicted that most other subjects would make the same choice they did—no matter which choice it was. Unsurprisingly, the immediacy of one's own reasons for belief tend to override or prevent any consideration of reasons that others might have to hold a different view.

It is perhaps understandable that we so easily believe that others around us share our beliefs, since, by and large, those around us really do share our beliefs. But this is due to the fact that most of our beliefs are pretty obvious, even to the point of being trivial. We believe that water is wet, that dropped objects fall, that rain is correlated with clouds, that fire can cause burns, that our parents weren't robots, and so forth. What would it be like to even try communicating with someone who could not be taken to hold these or similarly mundane beliefs? Our social interactions typically *must* presume a large overlap of belief sets with our hearers, if we are ever to get around to saying something relevant with the expectation that it will be understood.

Of course, when we make a point of saying things like "My beliefs are important to me" or "What are your personal beliefs?" we almost always mean something more rarefied by "belief" than that water is wet. We mean to flag the relatively small subset of our beliefs that might not be shared after all, since they are foreseeably contentious: beliefs about politics, religion, ethics, and the like. But in some social contexts it is tempting to overestimate the extent to which these beliefs too are shared. This can be true even if the speaker recognizes that *generally,* in the population at large, there is substantial opposition to the view she is asserting. The reasoning may be that while *they*—other people, elsewhere—might doubt the obvious truth, *we,* here, of course all know that they're wrong.

One way in which the False Consensus Effect is implemented is by interpreting other people's *lack of objections* as evidence for their concurrence with one's own view. This was even codified in an ancient legal principle: *Qui tacet consentire videtur* (that is, whoever is silent is understood to consent). In this form the bias can be a two-stage process that actually entrenches one's expressed convictions: first I take other people's silence as evidence that they share my expressed belief or attitude, and then I interpret this imagined consensus as a validation of my belief. Rationally speaking such a conclusion is obviously a house of cards—if Argument from Popular Opinion is a fallacy, how much worse is Argument from *Imaginary* Popular Opinion?—but this does not make the effect any less real.

One of the general effects of False Consensus judgments, then, is to give us a misleading sense of the reasonableness of our beliefs and attitudes. But as a result, the bias can moreover lead to unpleasant surprises in many contexts. In a group decision-making situation, for example, your formal decision or vote on an issue might be the opposite of what I expected on the basis of our informal discussions. I may chalk this up to your fickleness or personal betrayal when in fact my expectation was based on the False Consensus Effect all along, and not on any overt expression of intention or belief on your part. In this way the bias can hamper our interpersonal relations, much like the False Polarization Effect does.

A curious thing about the False Consensus Effect, finally, is that it's often quite obvious to us when our own silence is permitting someone else to mistakenly believe that we agree, yet this prospect is much harder to take seriously from the other side of the informational divide. Even though we know the phenomenon from having been the silent dissenter, at least from time to time, it still does not come naturally to canvass possible reasons that those around us might be quietly demurring from views we've expressed. In this respect, the bias resembles other weaknesses in social reasoning that involve an asymmetry between the way we think about other people and the way we expect them to think about us.

SEEING OURSELVES THROUGH THE EYES OF OTHERS

Consider an entirely fictional person with an entirely fictional randomly chosen name—for example, the name "Dad." Dad has the condition widely known as male pattern baldness: his hair no longer grows directly atop his head, but continues to grow around the sides and back of his head. To sustain the appearance of having hair on the top of his head, Dad routinely performs the manoeuvre known colloquially as the Comb-Over (see Figure 8.2). Having allowed the hair on one side of his head to grow long, Dad combs this shock of hair over the otherwise bare patch atop his head and anchors it in the thatch of hair on the other side.

This operation is plausibly a foray into social cognition, an attempt at managing the perceptions of other people regarding the hair situation on Dad's head. What's curious about this example of an **interpersonal strategy** is (at least) the following: presumably, when Dad encounters another man who employs the comb over, *he isn't fooled.* He doesn't look at that man, at the thin parallel lines of hair raked neatly across the man's otherwise bare polar regions, and think to

FIGURE 8.2

The Comb-Over

What difference would it make if we could see ourselves as others do? The comb-over is an interpersonal strategy intended to create an illusion, but the question may be "Who is the *real* audience?"

Philipp Nemenz/Taxi/Getty Images

himself, "What a fine, vigorous head of hair that young fellow has!" Why, then, does he expect others to be any more convinced by his own comb-over? There is a gap between what Dad effortlessly reasons about others and what he expects others to reason about him in precisely similar circumstances. One explanation is that this gap in reasoning is covertly bridged by motivated inference. Dad's desire to appear non-bald affects his reasoning about his own case, but not his reasoning about other devotees of the comb-over.

The domain of interpersonal strategies contains many analogous examples of biased reasoning shoring up dubious conclusions. A family of interrelated strategies falls under the heading of **self-handicapping**: claiming that there are barriers to one's success, typically as a way of excusing failure or magnifying success. A familiar example is the student who before the exam loudly claims not to have studied for it. In the event of a poor showing on the test, there is an explanation available *other* than the explanation of insufficient ability. In the event of a good result on the exam, the success appears all the greater in light of the student's claim not to have studied.

Or so one might reason. In fact, self-handicapping of this sort is often just a more complex version of the social comb-over. In spite of the fact that we are rarely persuaded by others' attempts to minimize the perception of failure and maximize the perception of success through self-handicapping, we still indulge in it ourselves. Some people even engage in the genuine article, a sort of self-sabotage by which they don't merely claim that there are barriers to their success, but actually erect such barriers—perhaps preferring a sure failure that's explicable by poor judgment over the risk of failure that might be explained by a lack of personal ability. But in the more common and less serious cases of merely cultivating the appearance of barriers, something similar to the comb-over is at work. Projecting our desired view of ourselves into other people's judgments of us may be very important to us. This emotional importance seems to ease our believing in the effectiveness of strategies that we know, or ought to know, we do not find effective when we see them employed by others.

BIASES IN AGGREGATE

What happens when the various heuristics in reasoning and inferential biases that we have examined over the past two chapters come together in complex social contexts? We have already considered the prospect for a bias like the False Consensus Effect to affect a person's interaction with a social group, for example. In brief: there seems to be some tendency to assume that other people will share our preferences and judgments. This may interact with an additional tendency to regard an absence of explicit disagreement as a form of tacit approval. Hence the silence of one's hearers can seem like a genuine validation of the view one has expressed. This could amount to a potent mechanism for unwarrantedly entrenching one's own views. The worry becomes greater when we consider the wide-ranging and powerful social strictures against challenging someone's assertions or presuppositions—think back to the racist joke-teller.

To put it another way: if I tend to interpret other people's silence as agreement with my assertions, then the fact that many people in many situations resort to silence when they *disagree* will mislead me about the extent of consensus on my assertions. In most social contexts we are reluctant to say things like "That doesn't sound right" or even "What's your evidence for that?" when somebody makes some claim. Challenging the speaker on a claim, even one that is demonstrably false, is very often interpreted as a hostile social act, not only by the person challenged but by other witnesses. Rather than be seen as committing an act of social aggression, or as being nitpicky or a know-it-all, many people are content to let points of disagreement pass in silence. Indeed, this is often judged to be a social grace.

We all do this sort of thing on more or less a daily basis, though not necessarily in such morally freighted circumstances. The people around us make claims; frequently we disagree in silence—of our own accord or not. When a brief visitor to my house started explaining why her daughter's horoscope (cast at her birth by a friend of the family) had convinced her "there's really something to astrology," my wife elbowed me before I could even open my mouth. *Not worth it to me*, she was saying. So I said nothing (again!) and our visitor no doubt left under the impression that her views had been regarded as cogent.

In this latter sort of circumstance it seems quite reasonable to keep quiet. The reasoning presumably goes something like this:

> If I challenge this claim, no matter how delicately, I'm likely to offend the speaker without convincing her in any case. If I don't challenge this claim and just keep silent, this may have the effect of falsely encouraging the speaker, but at least I won't be *actively* encouraging her, and the social atmosphere will remain cordial.

The critical thinking point is not that this line of reasoning is inherently flawed; I am not claiming that we should all be *Star Trek*'s Science Officer Spock, dispassionately voicing scepticism when we feel it and relentlessly confining our own conversational contributions to those we recognize as highly warranted in our state of information. Rather, we should simply recognize and take seriously that statements making their way to our ears by transmission through social contexts like these *cannot* be regarded as earning any very interesting degree of trust. The temptation to think that people couldn't say it, couldn't repeat it, couldn't spread it, if it were demonstrably unreasonable is hopelessly optimistic in many contexts. For better or worse, the combined phenomena of hearers' keeping silent about disagreement and speakers' hearing silence as agreement add up to a context in which demonstrable falsehoods get repeated with increased confidence and can therefore seem reasonable to hearers who may lack the information undermining the claims.

Looking beyond this particular example of interacting social and cognitive biases, we can think more generally about the communicative processes by which an opinion spreads through a social group. These processes, it is important to note, may have far less in the way of filters or barriers to unjustified beliefs than we might like to think. Indeed, our socially functional ways of communicating—trying to be interesting, trying to be polite, avoiding challenges that could be perceived as aggressive—may actively encourage the spread of unwarranted beliefs and attitudes. There is clear connection here to the Fallacy of Appeal to Popular Opinion; what we have is a partial explanation for why an opinion's being widely held is not only no guarantee of its truth, but need not even carry much evidential weight at all.

FRACTURES IN THE BODY OF SOCIAL INFORMATION

Another family of cognitive biases discussed at the individual level in Chapter 6 is the behavioural confirmation bias on evidence-gathering: our attitudes and expectations can simultaneously be both causes and effects of the information sources we choose to employ. This topic arises again in Chapter 10, in light of the proliferation of increasingly specialized media sources that can be tailored to accommodate one's preconceptions. When this sort of phenomenon is aggregated in a population of people, an unusual situation can arise. The population can be fragmented along many different lines of informedness, even though everyone has access to the same information in some clear sense.

The fundamental point is that the gap between having access to information—including having it freely delivered to you over the airwaves, if desired—is not the same thing as being informed. Evidence that is freely available to everyone may be internalized to very different extents by various sub-populations, especially when contentious social, political, religious, or other sensitive issues are in play. Hence it is an error in reasoning, and can lead to other errors in reasoning, to think of populations as even generally homogeneous in their states of information.

For that matter, even within a social group there might be outright contradictory assumptions that are generally accepted. When a belief and its negation are both apt to play useful social roles, it is unsurprising to find both of them espoused by turns within a group. Historically, for example, many cultures had a rich practical knowledge of the workings of heredity, manifest in spectacular success at breeding domesticated animals into specialized sub-species. Yet in some cases this knowledge was long able to cohere with explicit fables and theorizing about heredity that got things spectacularly *wrong*. Consider the following two quotes; the first is from the Old Testament book of Genesis.

> Genesis 30:37–39: Jacob, however, took fresh-cut branches from poplar, almond and plane trees and made white stripes on them by peeling the bark and exposing the white inner wood of the branches. Then he placed the peeled branches in all the watering troughs, so that they would be directly in front of the flocks when they came to drink. When the flocks were in heat and came to drink, they mated in front of the branches. And they bore young that were streaked or speckled or spotted.[14]

The second quote is from a more obscure source, though one that was quite popular in its day. Published in various editions in the early and mid-eighteenth century, *The Works of Aristotle the Famous Philosopher* was not, in fact, a work by Aristotle, the famous philosopher. It was an anonymously authored contemporary piece, a compendium of folkish wisdom, muddled scholastic doctrines, medical guesswork, and a bit of racy biological detail, which could no doubt be read in public with a clean conscience, given the author's name on the cover. In one section, the book takes the idea suggested in the quote from Genesis and applies it to people in considerable detail. It's worth quoting it at length, to get a sense of both the elaboration of the underlying theory and its rather obvious functional appeal: specifically, that it blames the mother's weakness of mind for all blemishes and defects in a child, and that it licenses virtually limitless paranoia about cuckoldry for a man!

> *The reason why children are like their parents; and that the Mother's imagination contributes thereto; and whether the man or the woman is the cause of the male or female child.*
>
> In the case of similitude, nothing is more powerful than the imagination of the mother; for if she fix her eyes upon any object it will so impress her mind, that it oftentimes so happens that the child has a representation thereof on some part of the body. And, if in act of copulation, the woman earnestly look on the man, and fix her mind on him, the child will resemble its father. Nay, if a woman, even in unlawful copulation, fix her mind upon her husband, the child will resemble him though he did not beget it. The same effect has imagination in occasioning warts, stains, mole-spots, and dartes; though indeed they sometimes happen through frights, or extravagant longing. Many women, in being with child, on seeing a hare cross the road in front of them, will, through the force of imagination, bring forth a child with a hairy lip. Some children are born with flat noses and wry mouths, great blubber lips and ill-shaped bodies; which must be ascribed to the imagination of the mother, who has cast her eyes and mind upon some ill-shaped creature. Therefore

it behoves all women with child, if possible, to avoid such sights, or at least, not to regard them.[15]

It's fair to say that both of these sources enjoyed at least considerable popularity over a considerable time—the former, indeed, overlapping with the latter. But in both societies that gave rise to these stories (I will use the word "story" to include things like anecdotes, gossip, rumours, sayings, advice—broadly the kind of thing that can be told and retold), there were thriving domestic animal breeding programs. These were people who *knew* how traits get passed on from one generation to the next. They didn't understand genetics, but at the level of animal reproduction they clearly had the basic idea well worked out. The "what the mother sees" theory could not have been correct, given the information that was, in this clear sense, available to them.

Yet even individual people can hold mutually inconsistent beliefs. Such beliefs can cross one another's wakes many times without quite colliding, as when I think on various occasions about two appointments I have, scheduled for the same time, without realizing the incompatibility until the day arrives. In a social group it is much easier still for information to stay isolated in sub-groups and never really propagate through the whole community or to cycle between prominence and dormancy in the wider community while a contradictory belief does so on an alternating schedule. It takes an effort to pull such beliefs together at the same time and point out their mutual tensions. Over the long term it also takes dedicated institutions, a social context that tolerates such trouble-making, and a platform for disseminating the analysis. The two "packages" of information about heredity described above, one practical and one theoretical, were able to spread and thrive in the same social group over long periods. There just wasn't quite the right mix of people interested in making a stink about the fact that they couldn't both be true.

SOCIAL INFORMATION TRANSMISSION: UNFILTERED

Did you hear about the guy who made $70,000 in the first month he started doing home sales over the Internet? What about the guy who launched himself over his own house by pouring gasoline into a drainage culvert, then crawling in and lighting a match? Or did you hear about the guy whose girlfriend impregnated herself with a condom he discarded and then the court ruled he had to pay child support? Many of the stories circulating through our social contexts begin with "Did you hear about the guy who. . ." Framed in terms of some particular person, such stories take on a narrative quality and repeatability that would not attach to an otherwise equivalent utterance beginning with "Did you know that it's possible to. . . ." Personalized anecdotes like these can divert us, appeal to our fears, gull us, convince us of their literal truth, or serve as miniature morality lessons. It's not just that such-and-such could happen; there's *the guy* or *the girl* to whom it really did happen.

What these stories and others like them have in common is not that they are all false. Some of them are false, of course, but others are partly or even largely true. Calling stories like these **urban legends** is a common but somewhat misleading choice, therefore, since it suggests that all such stories are false. What might be fairer to say is that they spread irrespective of their truth or falsity. They spread by appealing to one or more widespread preferences for the stories we tell.

Certainly at least some of these stories do deserve the label of a legend or myth. Did you hear about the girl who looked back? This girl and her boyfriend were out for a drive one dark night when his car stalled on a deserted road. She thought her boyfriend was just playing a trick to get some extra cuddle time, so when he got out to fix the car and she heard some loud banging and yelling, she assumed he was just trying to scare her. But then an unfamiliar man's voice outside the car told her to get out and run, and not to look back. Terrified, she bolted from the car. But as she ran away, she glanced back . . . only to see a shadowy shape standing on top of the car, holding her boyfriend's severed head.

Yuck. But that is the point, after all: to shock and titillate, and maybe to frighten. Urban legends like this one often come in a few different versions, each of which might appeal to us in slightly different ways. The appeal of a story might stem from its use of irony, of coincidence, or of just deserts—as when somebody gets a well-earned comeuppance at the end. The reasons that various stories appeal to us need not even be mutually consistent. Some stories we accept and repeat because they are plausible, others we accept and repeat precisely because they are implausible.

If that itself seems implausible, it may help to think about the social assumptions and implicatures (discussed in Chapter 3) that situate many utterances. Suppose Jill tells me, with all the hallmarks of sincerity, something that seems quite outrageous. Then I may well reason in the following way: "If that were false, it would be so easily revealed as false that it would be virtually certain to be exposed. Nobody would say something so easily demonstrable as false if it were really false. So it must be true—or, at least, Jill believes that it's true, and she wouldn't believe it without sufficient evidence."

While the wilder urban legends may be too obviously unbelievable to pose much of a critical thinking concern in themselves, they illustrate something important about the nature of information transmission through social groups: truth, evidence, and reasonableness needn't have much to do with whether a statement or story gets widely repeated. In many situations we simply are not entitled to reason, "If this were false, nobody would dare to say it." Nor are we justified in thinking, "If this were true, I'd have heard about it already," which is at least as tempting a thought in many cases of encountering a surprising claim. The former reasoning presupposes a level of policing of claims that is untrue of most social contexts, while the latter presupposes that knowledge is fairly exhaustively distributed through a community ("coverage," as philosopher Sanford Goldberg puts this latter property of testimony).

Neither of these presuppositions is generally correct. Consider the first: the assumption that a statement is true because if it were false this would come to light. (For example: it's so crazy it *must* be true!) In fact, there are several non-exotic reasons why a disprovable statement may be presented as true. The obvious reason is that the speaker may believe it's true. Nothing should be less surprising than that someone can simply be mistaken—even on a matter the truth of which is fairly accessible. The more interesting reasons involve dishonesty, though. It's an idealization to think of lying as an extreme sort of act, when there are unsurprising reasons

CHAPTER 8   *The More We Get Together*

that someone might lie quite directly. In the words of philosopher Rolf George: "The most common fallacy is the fallacy of lying."

For example, someone might deliberately, publicly, tell an untruth despite its being provably false simply because she hopes that nobody will ever bother to check. More specifically, one might hope or expect that the people one wishes to convince won't bother to check. Knowing that some people will investigate one's claim and find it to be false is consistent with having a reasonable expectation that other people will neither investigate the matter themselves nor pay attention to the people who did. Finally, someone might assert a provable falsehood simply on account of not caring about the predictable consequences. The benefits of lying in a situation may simply outweigh the social (or the legal) costs of getting caught in the lie. This sort of situation sounds extreme from a naïve moral perspective on lying, yet to some degree it may be very common indeed.

Suppose Ted could get rich by lying, and that it's unlikely that Ted would lose his riches when caught. He might well reason that in the worst case he will be unmasked as a rich liar and decide to accept that risk. Or consider an orchestrated smear campaign during an election: it might not matter to a politician, lobbyist, or campaigner that her negative claims about an opponent would eventually be revealed as falsehoods, provided that the election was won in the meantime. The discovery of a deception rarely completely undoes whatever the deception was intended to do.

For example, consider the case of "Nayirah," a teenaged Kuwaiti girl who testified before the Human Rights Caucus of the United States Congress prior to the Persian Gulf war of 1991. Nayirah's real identity had to be kept secret, the caucus was told, because of the fear of reprisals against her family by the Iraqi military, who had invaded Kuwait in the summer of 1990. She testified to having personally seen Iraqi soldiers dumping babies out of incubators in the hospital where she volunteered, in order to take the incubating machines back to Iraq. Given that the decision to go to war was passed in the United States Senate by only five votes, this story, which was widely reported in the news media and mentioned repeatedly by President George H. W. Bush, may have been crucial to getting public opinion and politicians behind the idea of the first Gulf War. Yet it turned out, after the war, that Nayirah was actually the daughter of the Kuwaiti ambassador to Canada and the United States; that no evidence existed that she had left North America to return to Kuwait and volunteer in a hospital; and that she had been coached for her testimony by the world's largest public relations firm, which was being paid by the Kuwaiti government-in-exile to lobby for an invasion.[16] There was some slight political fallout from the discovery that this information, which would no doubt have greatly diminished the weight assigned to the testimony, was deceptively kept secret from the caucus. But this cost was trivial in comparison to the goal that was accomplished—aided, no doubt, by the Repetition Effect and the Continued Influence Effect discussed in Chapter 7.

The lesson? It is a red flag to find yourself thinking that nobody would deliberately mislead you under the circumstances at hand. It might be *probable* that a testifier has no discernible motivation to deceive, given the evidence available in that situation. But even if we do reasonably believe what we are told, after reflection, there is still a lasting value to having contemplated reasons the speaker might be lying. As we saw in a study on the Continued Influence Effect in Chapter 7, having considered such sceptical questions in the first place can make it easier for people to rationally update their beliefs when new relevant information comes in.

The second presupposition is active in the opposite sort of case, when I reason that some surprising claim must be false, because if it were true I would already have heard about it. Sometimes this is a reasonable response. But in many cases it can also be a serious over-idealization. The issue really comes down to the most obvious reason that provably false statements are asserted as well: ignorance. Bringing our background knowledge to bear on a claim, asking whether the claim squares with other things we know, is perfectly good practice. But the prospect always exists for random oversights or situational biases to have left one unaware of something confirmable, even easily confirmable. So it is important to bear in mind the number of occasions on which each of us makes surprising "late discoveries." Sometimes things become common knowledge, but somehow never register with me. Keeping this fact in mind can help me think more carefully about rejecting a surprising claim merely on the grounds that I would expect to already know it, were it true.

Consider that it has been over twenty years since the original scientifically robust discovery that peptic ulcer patients typically have particular sorts of bacterial infections. It's been over a decade since the United States National Institute of Health released its consensus judgment that ulcers are largely caused by bacteria, and not primarily by stress, which was long believed to be their main cause. And now consider this exchange between two informed, educated people, Alice and Bruce:

Alice: "I'm so stressed out, I'm sure I'm going to get an ulcer from it."
Bruce: "Actually, I think I heard that bacteria are more important than stress in most ulcers. I wouldn't worry about an ulcer just because you're stressed."
Alice thinks to herself: "If that were true, I'd have heard it by now."

Even though the connection between certain bacteria and ulcers is widely accepted by doctors, has been reported in the news media from time to time over the past years, and spreads somewhat by word of mouth, there are still people who haven't even heard of it yet. Reliable and uncontroversial information can just miss us sometimes. When this happens, the "coverage" assumption fails; just because I haven't heard of it yet doesn't mean it's not true.

What emerges, then, is the importance of taking seriously how few filters for falsehoods, and how little incentive for strict truth, can characterize a social context of communication. It is very often reasonable to believe what we are told, all things considered. Yet critical reasoning about a claim and the community through which it has travelled frequently requires us to consider whether its truth would explain its transmission, and whether its falsity would have prevented its transmission. The less reason there is to think so, the greater the red flag attaching to the claim.

ANECDOTAL EVIDENCE

The aggregation of social and cognitive biases also explains the relative unreliability of **anecdotal evidence**: the unmoderated "story-telling" sort of evidence that informal socializing largely provides. The norms of casual socializing, combined

In Chapter 9, several possible definitions of science are discussed. One additional way of thinking about science, though, is in a social context of communication. As you read about the hallmarks of successful science, you should think of how those characteristics combine to place an artificially high premium on accurate claims and to reward the identification and elimination of inaccurate claims.

with the operations of memory, are apt to over-represent certain kinds of information in the anecdotes that spread through a group.

Suppose, for example, that Artemis says to Bruce, "I'm thinking about trying herbal *Echinacea* to see if it will help me recover from this cold." As we saw in Chapter 2 regarding causal reasoning, and in Chapter 6 regarding statistical reasoning, the information relevant to Artemis's pondering relates to at least three groups of people. There are the people who took *Echinacea* and recovered from their colds more quickly; the people who took *Echinacea* and did not recover from the colds more quickly; and the people who did not take *Echinacea* and recovered from their colds more quickly. The first group is the most direct first-blush evidence of a causal role for *Echinacea* in curing colds; the second group is direct first-blush evidence against a causal role for *Echinacea* in curing colds; and the third group is evidence that any causal role suggested by the first group is misleading. That is, if as many people recover quickly without *Echinacea* as recover quickly with it, that's strong evidence that quick recovery is either random or is determined by some other factor altogether.

But now ask yourself: which sort of evidence is apt to be first remembered by a conversationalist and then willingly contributed? People who personally took *Echinacea* may be confirmation-biased to perceive an effect and, having perceived an effect, are likelier to want to share the good news. By contrast, who makes a point of reporting on a perceived failure, thereby entering information about the second group into the social stock of anecdotes that Bruce may have encountered? Even if some such stories are told, the tendencies to recall confirmatory evidence will tend to call these stories to Bruce's mind less effectively than stories about people who tried *Echinacea* and thought it worked. Finally, information about the third group, so crucial to determining whether apparently confirming stories are genuinely evidence, is simply invisible from the anecdotal perspective. There is neither a general cognitive reason to remember nor a social or conversational reason to report things that you *didn't* do, nor to correlate things that you didn't do with other things that happened to you. That information emerges only as part of a careful and deliberate accounting of factors, as in a scientific study or an experiment.

Of course, anecdotes are often the sort of thing that might lead us to study some phenomenon further; they are not *nothing*, after all. But the phenomenon in any such case is to be understood, in the first instance, as the mere fact that people relate similar anecdotes. The phenomenon to be explained should not immediately be taken as whatever people say it is. The trend of people saying that *Echinacea* cures colds is a datum to be explained; that *Echinacea* really cures colds is only one possible explanation for that anecdotal trend and is not automatically assumed. For reasons like these, and because anecdotal evidence is so intuitively persuasive when it comes to us from many different people, it is worth bearing in mind an old saying from the study of psychology: *The plural of "anecdote" is not "data."*

THE MUTATION OF INFORMATION: MECHANISMS AND EXAMPLES

"The tale grew in the telling," author J.R.R. Tolkien once wrote in reference to his lengthy fantasy writings, but this phenomenon is hardly unique to fantasy fiction writers. To understand and appropriately evaluate the information we receive from every sort of source, we need to think critically about how tales commonly grow, shrink, and simply *change* in the telling.

Much of our current understanding of how testimony is affected by retellings reflects the early work of psychologists Gordon Allport and Leo Postman, who in 1947 wrote an influential book on factors that explain and influence the spread of rumours. They noted two complementary phenomena that occurred in their experiments when they induced the social transmission of information through personal interactions: Allport and Postman called these phenomena **levelling** and **sharpening**. Levelling is the process by which the elements of a story that are perceived as minor or less central tend to get minimized or omitted over successive retellings. Sharpening occurs when some aspects of a story become exaggerated as the story is retold. This exaggeration can be a matter of the specific details getting enhanced, or it can simply be a relative matter of some details acquiring different significance or connotation, once the contextual details that would normalize or make sense of them are levelled away. Levelling is largely a matter of details simply disappearing from a story.

Allport and Postman's experiments typically involved a subject's memorizing a detailed picture showing many events, some of which were deliberately ambiguous. The subject who examined the picture would then summarize it verbally to another person, who would in turn describe the picture to a third, and so forth. These stories generally became shorter, indeed with most of the original detail getting levelled out, before reaching a sort of maximal compression—becoming so short that they could be passed on without further loss, almost as a matter of rote memory. But just what sort of thing got levelled was not constant from one of Allport and Postman trials to the next.

They discovered that some things are commonly levelled, for example, the non-human details of human interactions. If a scene shows two people kissing beneath a sign advertising soap, the price of the soap is likelier to be levelled than the fact that there are people kissing. But in a scene containing various elements that could be perceived as important, the content of the final compressed story is partly a contingent matter of what gets dropped in the early stages of the transmission process. Once eliminated from the story at any stage, the original details can't be recovered at any subsequent stage within that chain of transmissions. Similarly, while details likely to be levelled are correspondingly unlikely to be sharpened, what *is* likely to be sharpened can depend on contingencies about the particular testifiers and the circumstances under which they are reporting. Small differences of emphasis or word choices early in the transmission process can be sharpened into the key elements of the described situation within just a few retellings.

Of course, levelling is complicated when we consider non-experimental situations. The transmission of information is often characterized by multiple interactions between chains of testimony, for instance. We often hear about an event from more than one source, each representing a distinct chain of testimonial transmission. These distinct chains of testimony stemming from the same origin—either from the event itself or from some single report of it—might level different aspects of the original information. But if these streams "cross" occasionally during the transmission process, when someone hears about the events from two different sources, the interaction may periodically result in information that had been lost in one stream or the other being reunited in the story as that person goes on to repeat it. Hence levelling need not be a constant degrading of detail down to the rote memory point; an improved story-chain might result from the combination of two distinct comparatively degraded ones. However, this process can also compound sharpening errors that have grown independently in each chain of transmission by combining them as well.

Allport and Postman proposed the notion of *assimilation* to explain levelling and sharpening. The idea is that people repeating some story do not simply attempt to reproduce the words by rote nor precisely memorize the details. Instead they internalize the *point* of the story to some degree and then explain that point when they retell the story. But in so doing, they have to fit the report into their own theories, world views, and cognitive economy generally. The opportunities for top-down effects of all sorts are plentiful and obvious. Between the hearing and the retelling, the story gets modified.[17] For example, in one of Allport and Postman's protocols, subjects were asked to study the details of a complex drawing of a train or trolley car and its passengers. The drawing showed, among other things, a well-dressed dark-skinned man seeming to argue with a slovenly light-skinned man who holds a straight-razor or switchblade. By the sixth or seventh retelling, in a substantial proportion of the trials, the knife managed to find its way into the hand of the dark-skinned man. Allport and Postman posited that these narrated details were rearranged as a result of the assimilation of the information into the communicators' broader theories and attitudes, including those having to do with race. Maybe the hearer deliberately "corrected" what was taken to be a mistake on the speaker's part; maybe the shift was unconscious. In either case, the hearer's attitudes are incorporated into the story when it is retold.

In part because they are an amalgam of some of the powerful biases and effects already discussed, levelling and sharpening can lead to very radical changes to narratives in very few retellings. No general impeachment of honesty or competence is presupposed in the assimilation theory proposed to explain these data. It is perfectly reasonable for speakers to emphasize what is relevant to a discussion (or a casual visit, or a bull session). It is equally reasonable to minimize what seems marginal to the discussion and make the results as punchy as possible. And it is permissible, if not entirely responsible, to choose the more self-serving or entertaining from a range of honest (or not-dishonest) interpretations of some testimony, when it comes time to relay the testimony on to someone else. But clearly this just *is* levelling and sharpening. Indeed, to avoid levelling and sharpening altogether is exceedingly difficult; one nice case study concerns the simplified stories that social psychologists themselves have told about a classic experiment.[18]

Examples of how stories can mutate in retellings are not difficult to find, though chasing down the precise details requires some careful research. Documenting the shifts is difficult in any case, but nearly impossible for purely verbal examples of levelling and sharpening. The clearest cases include written statements with known dates. Consider the claim that "Eskimos" have some surprising number of different words for snow. (Many Inuit and Yupik people of northern Canada and Alaska reject the term "Eskimo"; I use it because the snow vocabulary claim almost always includes it.) This factoid is often presented as rather exotic (to the non-Arctic-dweller) evidence of some tight connection between concepts, language, and lived experience. Because Inuit and Yupik people, among others, have a long history of living in a snow-dominated environment and culture, runs the idea, they have more and richer *concepts* of snow. This richness is allegedly a function of the large snow-related vocabulary of their language, which is said to contain some improbable number of snow-words for which there are no English equivalents.

This is not true, or at least not in any interesting sense. Like many languages with very productive word-formation rules, Yupik can generate many *words* from relatively few *roots*. In English these words just become phrases, though. Comparing root words, there seems to be no deep difference in expressive powers regarding snow between Arctic languages and English.[19]

The snow-words myth has perhaps begun to fade recently, owing to the gradual snowballing effect of an analysis by Laura Martin.[20] In brief: Martin traced the fascinating academic history of the idea that Arctic dwellers have surprisingly many words for snow back to some innocuous written remarks by Franz Boas in 1911, who briefly noted four different Yupik terms for snow. Possibly taking his cue from Boas, Benjamin Whorf wrote in 1940 that there were five such terms, though if he was using Boas as a source, he translated the words differently. One widely read academic book from 1959 alluded to an apparently large number of Arctic snow-words, wrongly crediting the data to Boas. Another such book from 1958 cited Whorf but gave the number of words as three and overlooked many important linguistic distinctions in presenting what Martin called "a complex psycho-cultural argument based on cross-linguistic 'evidence'. . . with not a single item of Eskimo data in support."[21] A subsequent text cited the 1958 source, but swiftly moved from the claim that there are three words for snow to the claim that there are "many."

Since the story about "Eskimo words for snow" came packaged with the theoretical explanation that life in the snow produces a language enabling uniquely fine-grained thoughts about snow, the actual number of alleged snow-words could grow by leaps and bounds from one telling to the next. As the snow-words myth filtered from careless academics into the "Did you know?" files of popular writers and broadcasters and then into popular culture, the number of Arctic terms for different kinds of snow grew remarkably. Martin cites examples that confidently posit nine, fifty, one hundred (in the *New York Times*), and even two hundred Arctic words for snow.

There is no clear reason to think that any of these story-tellers lied. All that is needed to explain these shifts is a mixture of carelessness, attachment to a theory, and a willingness to give what is perceived as a ballpark estimate of a number that is pretty much accurate. Merely the desire to entertain or a commitment to the theory would explain why the actual claimed numbers would then shoot upwards,

CHAPTER 8   *The More We Get Together*

since they would be driven to the high side of the range of sharpenings that "ballpark" and "pretty much accurate" permit without a sense of outright dishonesty. Of course, this doesn't mean that dishonesty *never* played a role in the many mutations this myth has undergone. It just means that there are plausible mechanisms by which innocuous truths can become utter falsehoods *without* any single person in the process being a liar—nor even, necessarily, foolish.

Jeffrey Shallit traced another interesting example of a mutating factoid when he tracked down the source of a claim that began to appear with some frequency among defenders of the Intelligent Design movement.[22] Intelligent Design is a variety of creationism, the view that life (or the entire universe) shows signs of having been designed, probably by some supernatural agent(s). The claim that caught Shallit's eye was found in several variants, but the main idea was that the Smithsonian Museum in Washington, D.C., had many, many objects that were known to have been designed, even though their purpose was unknown.

This was thought to be important because it seemed to bear on whether the notion of design could be understood independently of a designer's abilities and purposes. This in turn mattered because, on one hand, if the alleged designer of the universe (or biological life) were taken to be godlike—to be omnipotent and to have inscrutable motives, for example—then any phenomenon whatever could be the product of design, and Intelligent Design would seem trivial. And on the other hand, if one did not wish to assume anything about the properties of a designer, it would have to be possible to identify design in nature without reference to what a designer could do (or would like to do). In fact, in the case of human-designed artifacts this is quite uncontroversial; we might identify features like tool marks on ancient pieces of stone and wood, which would reveal that they had been constructed by known techniques even if their function was not understood. Such human-designed examples therefore do not provide an accurate analogy for the case in which even the "construction methods" of a potentially supernatural designer are not known.

Yet Shallit's discovery is interesting for current purposes not because the Intelligent Design analogy fails, but because it illustrates how a story that *seems* useful can grow in the process of retelling. Between Shallit's investigation and a subsequent expansion by Nick Matzke, we can list a plausible genetic trail from an original claim in the museum's official magazine to some grossly inaccurate ones.[23]

1. "The final category [in the Exhibit], Unidentified Objects, consists of several items that no one can figure out." (*Smithsonian*, April 1980)
2. "The Smithsonian Institution has a collection of obviously designed human artifacts, concerning the purposes of which no one has a clue." (1998)
3. "There is a room at the Smithsonian filled with objects that are obviously designed but whose specific purpose anthropologists do not understand." (1998)
4. "For example, the Smithsonian contains thousands of intelligently-designed objects whose function, or intended function, is unknown to us." (2002)
5. "There's an entire wing in one of the museums in [Washington] D.C. that's dedicated to objects that we don't know what they are, but we know they're objects made by humans." (2005)

Notice that quote (2) is actually consistent with (1), which is the statement in the original magazine article. The phrase "a collection" perhaps over-sells the mere existence of "several items" but does not completely misrepresent it. At least, anyone who understood the original claim would see how the phrase "a collection" was faithful to it. But someone who didn't already understand (1) and didn't investigate the accuracy of (2) could easily be misled into applying a stereotypical conception of a museum collection. The result would be something like quote (3), which is now a thorough misrepresentation of (1). Yet (3) leads rather naturally to (4)—after all, mightn't it take thousands of articles to *fill* a room? Yet "thousands" could mean anything from 2000 to 199,999, if a reader considers (4) in isolation. Suppose one took a compromise interpretation of (4) to be that around 30,000 articles existed. Why, it would take an entire section of a museum to house them! So from (4) it might not seem an outrageous stretch to (5).

Again, without anything that one could confidently call lying—with only carelessness and a tendency toward the grandest and most favourable permissible interpretation—we get from *several items* to *thousands of items* in *an entire museum wing* in just a few steps! These examples show why scholars—and instructors—insist on the value of documenting and confirming sources. It's not because they have some conviction that hard work builds character; it's because second-hand assertions, even coming from sources who confidently present themselves as in the know, can become wildly misleading. It's unclear from the information presented whether each of (2) to (5) was based solely on the claim immediately before it—perhaps (4) and (5) both followed directly on from (3), or perhaps verbal chains connected some of these statements. But what is clear is that going back to the original source would have revealed the inaccuracy of each of (3) to (5). As we saw in the discussion of misquoting, in Chapter 3, critical thinking frequently consists of the determination to go back to the original source. This enables us both to discover inaccuracies that others are presenting to us and to avoid perpetuating and deepening those inaccuracies ourselves. In this case, four steps of sharpening created thousands of artifacts and built a new wing on the Smithsonian.

A final point on which to elaborate. Testimony does not just provide us with particular bits of information in the form of statements or propositions. The complexity of a social group includes the complexity of the manner in which such statements are presented to us. For example, we can hear or read something *often*—from the same source repeatedly, or from many different sources. Naturally the information tends to gain credibility as we are exposed to it from different sources, each of which plausibly provides a degree of independent confirmation for the other sources. Hence it is important that we are sensitive to the possibility that such apparent confirmations are not really independent.

The flow of information through a social group provides a great deal of opportunity for a single information source to influence many people. Each of these people might then independently relay that information to many other people. In this way, the number of people who have testimonial evidence for some claim can quickly become very great. Yet the sole authority for the assertion remains the original source, as long as no independent attempts to confirm the claim have been made along the individual chains of transmission. We can call

Recall the news story about the Two Lauras, discussed as an example of the Multiple Endpoints Fallacy in Chapter 4. A girl named Laura Buxton sent off a note attached to a helium balloon; a different girl named Laura Buxton received the balloon; and news stories spelled out many other similarities between the girls—many of which were spurious and could have been found between many pairs of people.

Yet our earlier treatment of the example neglected one of the most important aspects of the story: the balloon was actually found by someone else, not by the second Laura Buxton! Such a demystifying bit of context is an excellent candidate for levelling when the story gets retold, which is exactly what we find. Notice the difference between the first report below, which was both early and local, and the second report, which came out later, and was more sensationalized.

Early, local-interest source:

> The discovery of a deflated balloon in a hedge has sparked off an amazing series of coincidences for ten-year-old Laura Buxton from Milton Lilbourne, near Marlborough, and her namesake who lives 140 miles away in the Midlands.
>
> The tale of the two Lauras began when Andy Rivers, of Milton Lilbourne, was checking cows in a field and found a balloon in a hedge. Closer inspection revealed the balloon said "Happy 50th Birthday" and had a label on it with the name Laura Buxton and an address near Stoke on Trent.
>
> Mr Rivers knew his neighbours Peter and Eleanor Buxton had a daughter called Laura so gave the balloon to them.[24]

Later, mass-media source:

> The Two Lauras: Laura Buxton tied a message to the end of a balloon. It landed 140 miles away in the garden of another girl named Laura Buxton. And Believe it or Not, the similarities don't stop there![25]

The role of Mr Rivers, which so clearly reduces the aspect of an astonishing coincidence, has been levelled out of the retold version.

the subsequent critical reasoning problem **pseudo-independent confirmation**: apparently independent assertions of the same claim, which are actually dependent on a single (or at least very limited) information source. This might occur when a single observer reports an event, setting off the explosive growth of testimonial retellers. It might be a matter of a narrative "bottleneck"—an information source whose presentation, collection, or popularization of some claim ends up being the one from which most subsequent reports trace. Or maybe someone just makes something up.

Indeed, it may be all three together. For example, there is some reason to think that many of the persistent negative myths about the effects of masturbation (blindness, hair on palms, insanity, and the like) trace back to the appearance of an anonymously authored book called *Onania*, beginning in London in the early eighteenth century. Several editions of the book were published, in which the tract's author either invented or simply collected and organized reports of the most alarming symptoms ("Many young men . . . dry and emaciated, sent to their graves"). The tract served as such a seminal information source that for many generations its particular claims have been regarded as common knowledge in various societies. If one hears these claims today from dozens of different contemporary sources, without knowing that a single source explains them, one is subject to a particularly widespread case of pseudo-independent confirmation.

CONCLUSION

While it is empirically easiest and theoretically simplest to conceive of persons in isolation, and to study them in isolation, we are socially embedded throughout our lives. The social aspects of cognition are crucial to an understanding of critical thinking. This is true because so much of our reasoning is about other people; because our perceptions of other people have such a strong influence on our reasoning more generally; and because our social environment is the conduit for most of our information about the world. Hence we must understand the biases that operate on our reasoning about others, and the biases that our perceptions of others exert on our thinking. Critical thinking about ourselves includes a sensitivity to the prospect that social factors, including social stereotypes, are tweaking our intuitive judgments. Critical thinking about other people's claims and choices requires analogous monitoring of their social context for factors that will predictably pressure them in one direction or another. And we must also consider the effects that the sum of individual biases have on the information that reaches us through testimony in a population spread over space and time.

As with cognitive biases, social biases do not imply any general scepticism. There is no reason to conclude that testimony is universally or even typically unreliable, for example. But there are reasons to examine individual claims and stories when their contents, and our knowledge of the community through which they've travelled, suggest that they spread for reasons other than their putative truth.

REVIEW QUESTIONS

1. Describe a time when you held your tongue for social reasons, when a claim or attitude was expressed with which you disagreed. Explain the claim, why you disagreed with it, and why you did not voice your objection. Do you think your silence was mistaken for agreement?
2. Search through recent major Canadian newspapers for a news story illustrating the False Polarization Effect. Be sure to argue from the details of the story for the conclusion that an over-sharpening of the two positions was likely taking place.
3. Research and clearly explain two examples of urban legend, one of which sounds inherently plausible but is false, and one of which sounds inherently implausible but is true. Be explicit on what the plausibility and implausibility consist in.

NOTES

1. A. Greenwald, D. McGhee, and J. Schwartz, "Measuring Individual Differences in Implicit Cognition: The Implicit Association Test," *Journal of Personality and Social Psychology* 74 (1998): 1464–80.

2. T. Dixon and K. Maddox, "Skin Tone, Crime News, and Social Reality Judgments: Priming the Schema of the Dark and Dangerous Black Criminal," *Journal of Applied Social Psychology* 35 (2005): 1555–70.

3. T. Dixon and D. Linz, "Overrepresentation and Underrepresentation of African Americans and Latinos as Lawbreakers on Television News," *Journal of Communication* 50 (2000): 131–54.

4. P. Goldberg, "Are Women Prejudiced Against Women?" *Transaction* 4 (1968): 28–30.

5. M. Paludi and W. Bauer, "Goldberg Revisited: What's in an Author's Name?" *Sex Roles* 9, no. 3 (1983): 387–90.

6. J. King, "The Effects of Gender Bias and Errors in Essay Grading," *Educational Research Quarterly* 22, no. 1 (1998): 13–25.

7. D. Gilbert and P. Malone, "The Correspondence Bias," *Psychological Bulletin* 117 (1995): 21–38.

8. E. Jones and V. Harris, "The Attribution of Attitudes," *Journal of Experimental Social Psychology* 3 (1967): 1–24.

9. A. Isen and P. Levin, "Effect of Feeling Good on Helping: Cookies and Kindness," *Journal of Personality and Social Psychology* 21, no. 3 (1972): 384–88.

10. J. Darley and C. Batson, "From Jerusalem to Jericho: A Study of Situational and Dispositional Variables in Helping Behavior," *Journal of Personality and Social Psychology* 27 (1973): 100–108.

11. K. Crowley, "The Deal That Sounded Too Good to Be True." *Media*, Summer (2002). http://www.caj.ca/mediamag/summer2002/award-mitchener.html (Accessed March 18 2006).

12. Crowley, "The Deal That Sounded Too Good to Be True."

13. L. Ross, D. Greene, and P. House, "The False Consensus Effect: An Egocentric Bias in Social Perception and Attribution Processes," *Journal of Experimental Social Psychology* 13 (1977): 279–301.

14. International Bible Society *The Holy Bible, New International Version* (Grand Rapids, MI: Zondervan, 1984).

15. *The Works of Aristotle the Famous Philosopher*, http://www.gutenberg.org/etext/12699.

16. J. MacArthur, *Second Front: Censorship and Propaganda in the 1991 Gulf War* (Berkeley, California: University of California Press, 2004).

17. G. Allport and L. Postman, *The Psychology of Rumor* (New York: Henry Holt and Co., 1947).

18. L. Berkowitz, "Reporting an Experiment: A Case Study in Leveling, Sharpening and Assimilation," *Journal of Experimental Social Psychology* 7, no. 2 (1971): 237–43.

19. G. Pullum, "The Great Eskimo Vocabulary Hoax," *Lingua Franca*, June 1990, pp. 28–29.

20. L. Martin, "'Eskimo Words for Snow': A Case Study in the Genesis and Decay of an Anthropological Example," *American Anthropologist* 88, no. 2 (1986): 418–23.

21. Martin, "'Eskimo Words for Snow'," 419.

22. J. Shallit, "Anatomy of a Creationist Tall Tale." Posted at http://www.cs.uwaterloo.ca/~shallit/cw.html (Accessed January 20, 2006).

23. N. Matzke, "Kangaroo Court Transcripts Are Up." Posted on The Panda's Thumb, http://www.pandasthumb.org/archives/2005/06/kansas_kangaroo_2.html (Accessed January 20, 2006).

24. "Trail of Coincidences" *Evening Advertiser*. June 28, 2001. http://archive.thisiswiltshire.co.uk/2001/6/28/215077.html (Accessed September 12, 2004).

25. *Ripley's Believe It or Not*. May 1, 2002. Episode 303, http://www.sonypictures.com/tv/shows/ripleys/database/ep_303a.html (Accessed September 12, 2004).

CHAPTER 9

Critical Reasoning about Science: Cases and Lessons

In September 2001, there occurred an event having the potential to rock the major institutions of Western civilization to their foundations.

It is probably not the event that immediately leaps to your mind, however. The event to which I'm alluding was the publication of a study by Rogerio Lobo, Kwang Cha, and Daniel Wirth in Volume 46, Number 9, of the *Journal of Reproductive Medicine*, a prestigious medical science journal.[1] The study, two of whose authors were Columbia University medical researchers, claimed to present powerful scientific evidence showing that Christian prayers made from the other side of the world improved the likelihood of pregnancy among couples undergoing artificial *in vitro* fertilization, or IVF treatment, in South Korea. By the statistical standards of medical intervention, the claimed improvement was mind-boggling: an outright doubling of the odds, from 26 percent in the prayerless group to 50 percent in the group that was prayed for. If genuine, the result would have substantially restructured the space of possible scientific or causal explanations across the entire spectrum of disciplines. It would also have provided at least defeasible scientific vindication of Christianity specifically (as distinct from other major religions), introduced entirely new categories of scientific correlation and measurement, and justified any number of new programs of prayer-based health care, in a single pass.

You might have noticed, however, that the major institutions of Western civilization have *not* been rocked to their foundations on account of the IVF prayer study. In fact, you may not have even heard about it before now. What happened instead was that the study quickly became recognized as an important recent entry in the annals of failure in scientific practice. The story of the IVF prayer study illustrates a series of key critical reasoning issues for the interpretation of scientific evidence—or, perhaps more accurately, for the interpretation of scientific claims that come to us through various sources. How does the story end? I'll save that for the end of the chapter.

Instead I will discuss three other published studies on the medical effects of prayer, using this theme to illustrate observations about science and how it works. Since these three studies will come up repeatedly through this chapter, it is worth getting to know them from the outset.

The Byrd Study: One of the first studies suggesting the medical efficacy of prayer to appear in a reputable journal was led by Randolph Byrd in the early 1980s and published in 1988.[2] Byrd studied a large number of patients in the coronary care unit at San Francisco General Hospital. In addition to their normal medical treatments, some patients were assigned specifically to Christian believers who would pray for them, while other patients were part of an un-prayed-for control group. Byrd's article in the *Southern Medical Journal* reported a statistically significant advantage overall for the treatment (prayed-for) group in his study, based on a range of twenty-five different indicators of health.

The Harris Study: A follow-up to the Byrd study was led by William Harris in the late 1990s.[3] It too was based on a large group of heart patients, this time at a hospital in Kansas City. Published in the *Archives of Internal Medicine* in 1999, the Harris study concluded that a statistically significant benefit accrued to the treatment group—again, once the data from a wide range of health indicators were weighed.

The Sicher Study: Just prior to the Harris study, another study vindicating a therapeutic role for prayer was published in the *Western Journal of Medicine*. A 1998 article by Fred Sicher and others presented the results of their study on the effects of intercessory prayer and "psychic healing" directed toward AIDS patients.[4] Yet again, there was a statistically significant overall result in favour of the prayed-for group, though in this case the intercessors were not only Christians but faith healers from a range of religious and spiritual backgrounds.

Advocates of the therapeutic use of prayer often cite one or more of these four prominently published studies as evidence for the practice as a medical tool. Each received widespread favourable (and often uncritical) reports in the local, national, and international media at the time of its publication, and each continues to be cited favourably in newspaper special-interest stories, alternative medicine magazines, Internet articles, and some scientific journal publications. They have been taken as powerful, even decisive, evidence by many people who have been made aware of them.

But there are serious problems with each of these studies and with the conclusions drawn by their authors. By seeing in some detail how these studies fail to live up to the standards of reliable science, we can get a sense of how to distinguish reliable from unreliable scientific claims. This is a key critical reasoning skill, since while studies about prayer are a smallish and manageable topic that enables us to distill some important lessons, they are among the least of the critical thinking worries that beset medical science, still less science in general. The red flags that arise for the research discussed in this chapter are red flags that may arise with greater consequences for both human health and public costs, when one turns to consider larger topics like the conduct of pharmaceutical research or research into educational policies.

The broad goal is to understand the output of scientific processes, as it is made available to information consumers like us. Our critical thinking concern with science applies to the broadest conception of how information tagged with the label *scientific* comes into our possession, and how we ought to treat that information, depending on what we know about that process. Science, after all, is the single most important and trusted arbiter of factual questions and reliable methods in contemporary intellectual life. The prestige and authority of scientists and science mean there is a powerful rhetorical force to the vocabulary of science. But simply to say that a statement, argument, or method is scientific is no more enlightening than to call it reasonable. We need to know what it means to appeal to science, and under what circumstances such an appeal is both plausible in itself, and apt to confer greater plausibility on whatever is being called scientific.

Critical reasoning requires some insight into how science works, in order to evaluate the claims of scientists and the interpretations of those claims by non-scientists. That is the focus of this chapter. First we will consider what, if anything, sharply distinguishes science as a discipline or a body of knowledge; then we will look at a few hallmarks of successful or reliable science. With those observations in hand, we can return to the studies described above and draw some lessons about how good science ought to work.

SCIENCE AND NON-SCIENCE

Science, we might say, is based on evidence, observation, and experiments. It presents laws, theories, and hypotheses. Science teaches us the facts. Through rough and ready descriptions like these, we generally feel we at least know what science is and that it works. On the other hand, most of us also know what a flush toilet is and are confident that it works without having a very detailed conception of *how* it works. Science is rather more complicated than a toilet; the popular conceptions of what it is and how it works require some refinement if we are to think critically about the claims that are presented to us as validated by science.

Much of what characterizes science we have already studied in earlier chapters. Taking up themes in the order of chapters: science is both deductive and inductive in its reasoning methods, making heavy use of both logico-mathematical reasoning and evidential reasoning. Scientific thinking emphasizes defeasibility, inference to the best explanation, analogy, and causal arguments. Every contemporary science is deeply informed by statistical and probabilistic reasoning in its quantification of the data and in evaluating the theories that explain the data. Scientific protocols and conventions are constructed to filter out sources of perceptual and cognitive bias at all levels. The social context of scientific communication is intended to minimize rumour and to reward effective challenges to theories—even to accepted theories. There is a pretty good sense in which scientific reasoning just is a collection of refined and domain-specific versions of the domain-general critical thinking methods that we have explored. Still, this may seem imprecise as an account of what science really amounts to.

Much of the work that has gone into refining our definitions of science has occurred in the context of the debate over the dividing line between science and non-science or pseudo-science. But it's worth asking why anyone would want a way of sharply distinguishing science from non-science in the first place. After all, we don't suppose such boundaries to exist except in quite arbitrary senses when it comes to distinguishing between disciplines at a finer-grained level. Biology and chemistry are linked by (among other fields) microbiology and biochemistry, but these overlap in so many ways that no sharp dividing line would distinguish the two in an entirely intuitive way. The same goes for sociology and social psychology, economics and political science, urban planning and environmental engineering.

The difference in these finer-grained cases is this: it is quite rare for any significant issue to depend on whether some person, publication, practice, or claim falls into the category of (say) microbiology *rather than* biochemistry. But it often seems quite important (to many people, at least) whether something or someone counts as scientific overall. The judgment that something is scientific is widely taken as a positive evaluation, connoting reliability, honesty, and the overriding aim of achieving accurate explanations. These virtues, to whatever extent they really characterize science, should not be attributed to non-scientific claims and practices that do not possess them, or that possess them only to a far lesser extent, despite bearing a superficial similarity to science. In other words, much of the motivation for trying to say what *is* scientific has derived from the inclination to say that particular people, claims, and practices *aren't* scientific. The worrisome category isn't so much *non*-science as *pseudo*-science: non-science that masquerades as science, invoking the authority of scientific discourse without possessing its virtues.

The motivation of isolating and unmasking pseudo-science establishes a criterion for the success of proposals to distinguish science from non-science. The idea is that we have clear examples of scientific theories and practices, like the atomic theory of matter and peer-reviewed publication; and we have clear examples of unscientific claims and practices, like the healing powers of crystals and telling the future by looking at chicken entrails. What's wanted is a reasonably tidy definition of science that makes cases of both sorts come down on the proper sides of the line. But this, it turns out, is a surprisingly difficult definition to produce—especially if one is serious about the details of actual scientific practice, current and historical. Apparent cases of non-science and apparent cases of science can overlap in surprising ways, making the project of neatly distinguishing them quite problematic. This problem of finding a definition that precisely distinguishes science from non-science is often just known as the **demarcation problem**. It is a much-discussed issue in science and the philosophy of science, one having many subtleties. But even a brief discussion of the main proposals for demarcating science from non-science is useful, illuminating some of the breadth and complexity of scientific theorizing and practice.

JUST THE FACTS

It is sometimes said that science is a matter of "just the facts" or is built upon pure observation of data without preconceptions. The idea is to distinguish science from an activity like determining how many angels can dance on the head of a pin, since that there are pins is a fact in evidence, while that there are angels is not. Science is distinguishable from non-science, on this view, by its practice of starting from the facts rather than introducing doctrinal or theoretical commitments right from the outset.

It's true that a fundamental aspect of scientific endeavours is typically to explain some phenomenon or other. But it's implausible, and maybe even incoherent, to depict science as proceeding from facts in a theory-free or commitment-free fashion. For one thing, there is the question of which facts are the relevant ones. Any situation embodies a vast number of phenomena or facts, most of which are either too trivial or too arcane to be notable. But the standards of triviality and arcaneness depend on what is of explanatory interest to us in each situation. So our interests tend to exert a strong influence on our sense of what the facts are in the first place. Moreover, our theories and expectations play at least some role in how our very experiences get carved up and categorized into observations, facts, or phenomena. Over the course of a day, to choose a simple example, do you see the sun going around the earth, or do you see the sun enter and gradually leave your field of view as the earth rotates? How you characterize the phenomenon itself depends in part on your underlying theory of local celestial mechanics. But that theory in turn is likely to be a matter of your broadly scientific reasoning and beliefs. In sum, a careful look at the history of science, the psychology of observation, and the concepts of *fact* and *data* themselves, suggests that facts and data are **"theory laden"** or **"theory-infected,"** as it is sometimes put. This doesn't mean that there is no difference between theories and data, but it strongly suggests that science can't really be *defined* in terms of some conception of facts as independent of scientific theorizing itself.

DETAILS MATTER

Although there is some vagueness in their use even within scientific contexts, the words "law," "theory," and "hypothesis" have sharper scientific meanings than in ordinary talk, where they are often used as synonyms. A **law** is normally a generalization that describes some observed fact or tendency in mathematical terms; laws are broad, even universal, but normally apply to more basic or simple phenomena. A **theory** is a more complex construction, usually pulling together multiple phenomena and offering an explanation of one or more in terms of their interactions. Theories are the result of refinement and testing; unlike common usage, scientific usage does not equate a theory with a mere guess or conjecture, and the term should not be thought to convey the degree of uncertainty that a non-scientist might convey in saying, "That's just a theory." Even though we are practically certain that germs cause many diseases, for example, we still speak of a *germ theory of disease*. A **hypothesis** is usually more of an initial conjecture, a proposed explanation in the early stages of testing or development. We can think of hypotheses as proto-theories awaiting observational evidence, without going far wrong of normal scientific use, or just as conjectures about phenomena that aren't intended to become theories themselves. So, for example, one might *hypothesize* that (a certain type of?) prayer will correlate with improved outcomes for some medical procedure, without yet having *theorized* a connection that explains that alleged correlation in light of known *laws*. While the distinctions between these notions are blurry, even somewhat arbitrary, they can serve a useful purpose in letting us speak clearly about different kinds and stages of scientific inquiry.

THE SCIENTIFIC METHOD

The recent history of thought contains various more sophisticated proposals than this for defining science and for establishing a science pseudoscience boundary. One common line of thought identifies the **scientific method** as the defining characteristic of science. There are various popular ways of summarizing the scientific method for simple presentation. The following set of steps as written captures the content of most such summaries:

Scientific method:

1. Observe some phenomenon or problem to be explained.
2. Formulate a hypothesis which, if true, would explain the phenomenon.
3. Deduce the implications of the hypothesis, including its observational consequences.
4. Test the hypothesis by observation and experimentation.
5. Evaluate the hypothesis in light of the fit between its predictions and the results of testing it.
6. Repeat steps 2 through 5 as necessary, modifying the hypothesis to achieve accurate prediction and description of the phenomena.

It's fair to say that this set of steps describes something common to a great deal of scientific practice. So it's a perfectly good description of scientific method as far as it goes. The question is, how far does it go?

Notice first that the method itself does not insist that the phenomenon or problem mentioned in the Step 1 be discernible or describable *as* a problem, except through the lens of some pre-existing theory. So this conception of the scientific method does not presuppose a sharp distinction between theory and data; the question of the theory-infectedness of data is left open. Also left open are the questions of what counts as an explanation, an implication, a test, an observation, and accuracy in prediction. On each of these questions, we might find important differences between inquirers who accept steps 1 to 6 as written, but who disagree about the interpretations that make these steps correct. In different scientific disciplines there may be very different understandings of how to implement the scientific method. So the above summary of the scientific method is not as tidily definitional as it may seem. Its plausibility to many people might just arise from its amenability to equivocal interpretations.

Partly as a result of this vagueness, this sort of step-wise conception of the scientific method doesn't help much with the demarcation problem. Agreement on steps 1 to 6 does not settle, nor even very tightly constrain, what counts and fails to count as science. Moreover, a realistic look at how science actually works reveals that large swathes of work—entire projects, even careers—can take place within a subset of these steps, and perhaps even within a single step. To be sure, it may be that when we are confident that some broad project or result counts as scientific, we can look back on it and identify stages conforming to steps 1 to 6. But that doesn't mean we can take some disputed or unclear case currently in progress and decide whether *it* counts as scientific based on whether it satisfies steps 1 to 6. There may simply be no way, at the time, to know whether someone's work will eventually emerge as a sub-project of step 1 or step 3 or step 5, for some broadly scientific success story over the longer term. Certainly lots of people and lots of work that intuitively count as scientific will never seriously engage in some of the steps listed above. A theoretical physicist may never personally suggest, design, or conduct an experiment; a zoologist may have a valuable and respected career that consists entirely of publishing detailed reports on the behaviour of tortoises in the wild. Overall, appeal to the scientific method is not in itself a very compelling way of distinguishing science from pseudo-science.

NATURALISM

It's sometimes said that science is defined by its adherence to **naturalism** of one sort or another. In particular, many people have claimed that science is inherently limited to **methodological naturalism**, a concept typically defined in turn as the rejection of appeal to supernatural entities or processes in explanations. This is contrasted with **metaphysical naturalism**, the view that there are no supernatural entities. Methodological naturalism is the view that whether or not there are such entities, science cannot implicate them in its theories.

Allusions to the naturalistic character of science have become fairly common, due in part to the political and educational controversy over efforts to introduce the teaching of *Intelligent Design* in American public schools. This is the belief that certain features of the world, and especially of organisms, show signs of having been deliberately engineered by a creator. Opponents of the political efforts to introduce this account into school curricula have often countered with the charge that it is an attempt to smuggle religious doctrine into science classes. In this context many scientists have asserted that Intelligent Design is not scientific, on the grounds that it appeals to a supernatural entity while science is strictly naturalistic.

Quite apart from whether this is an accurate characterization of Intelligent Design, it is not a very useful description of science. One way to see the problem is to observe that the word "supernatural" is defined as whatever falls outside the natural. But now we can't in turn define naturalism as the *rejection* of the supernatural, or we would have no idea what either term meant. A way out of this problem is to identify naturalistic entities and processes as those detected, appealed to, or intervened in by science itself. However, the claim that science employs only naturalistic explanations then becomes the claim that science employs only explanations that science employs. This is true, no doubt, but thoroughly vacuous as an explanation of what's wrong with Intelligent Design or any other purported scientific theory.

There is little reason to think of any purportedly factual claim as beyond the relevant application of science, including claims about prayer, ghosts, or magic. Someone who calls statements about the healing powers of prayer unscientific, on the grounds that science is naturalistic, can't be correctly saying much more than that there is no good evidence for the healing powers of prayer. But that's not a matter of such statements falling outside the naturalistic scope of science; on the contrary, if true it's a way of saying on eminently scientific grounds that the claim lacks justification.

The failings of a hypothesis are best presented in specific terms. At best it's an unilluminating shortcut to allege that science has a commitment to something called naturalism, which excludes the hypothesis from its consideration. At worst it gives the mistaken impression that science is barred from considering entire classes of conjectures about causes and effects owing to some assumption of naturalism. This does not seem to follow from any plausible understanding of what naturalism might be.

VERIFIABILITY AND FALSIFIABILITY

Another line of thought from early twentieth-century philosophy of science takes **verifiability** as the feature that distinguishes science from non-science. This can seem quite plausible, if we start from the idea that science is about giving evidence for claims. For a claim to at least be a candidate for a scientific truth, then, we have to be able to say what evidence would verify it. On this proposal for solving the demarcation problem, statements having expressible verification conditions are scientific (though perhaps false), while statements having no such specifiable verification conditions are altogether non-scientific. (**Verificationism** in philosophy more broadly is the name of the view that this is the criterion not just for a statement's being scientific, but for its being *meaningful*.)

A serious problem with taking verifiability to distinguish science from non-science, however, is the ambiguity of the term "verify" itself. If we take it to mean *conclusive* verification, then vast swathes of genuine science (by anyone's reckoning) will be ruled out, since scientific evidence frequently falls short of conclusive demonstration. But if we weaken the notion just to mean having *some* evidential support, then many of the things that proponents of a demarcation were concerned to rule out in the first place will end up counting as scientific. There is at least preliminary evidence, however weak, for the existence of demons and ghosts, after all. In fact, it's unclear that this weakened notion would rule out any sort of minimally intelligible claim or conjecture. No very plausible middle path exists, again given the purposes for which a demarcation is usually wanted. For instance, a distinction between various (non-zero) amounts or degrees of evidence, and hence between degrees of scientific status, doesn't really seem likely to amount to the sharp division between science and non-science that was wanted in the first place.

A more subtle proposal for a demarcation criterion is **falsifiability**: the requirement that there be specifiable observations or experimental outcomes under which a theory or explanation would be judged *false* (or at least less probable). At first it may seem odd to see a theory's openness to being falsified presented as a virtue. Wouldn't a theory that couldn't be proved false be the best theory imaginable? But the basic idea is quite straightforward, when you think about it: a real explanation, or the theory it invokes, should have *observational consequences*. In other words, your theory should imply that if you test it by doing such-and-such, you will observe so-and-so. The theory enables predictions about what will happen in certain circumstances, and if that outcome does not happen under those circumstances, the theory must be regarded as false (or at least as less probable). If your theory is consistent with absolutely anything, if no possible outcome would be taken to lower its probability, then it's not really giving you any information.

For example, if I say that the weather is caused by the invisible levitating newts in my shower, but then I say that absolutely no test could reveal the existence of these newts, nor their mechanism for implementing changes in the weather, then it would be fair to say my explanation is inherently unfalsifiable and hence not a scientific hypothesis. For a theory or any other purported description of the world to have content, for it to say *The world is this way*, is for the theory to be inconsistent with the world turning out *not* to be that way; so if there's no way the world could turn out that would be inconsistent with an alleged theory, the theory doesn't really have any content—it doesn't tell us anything about the world. In the words of Karl Popper, the philosopher of science who first formulated falsifiability as a demarcation principle: "Irrefutability is not a virtue of a theory (as people often think) but a vice."[5]

Again, though, things are not quite as simple as that. It is clear that in a vast range of circumstances, we would not regard *apparently* falsifying outcomes as genuinely falsifying a highly confirmed theory, nor even as lowering its probability. Otherwise the atomic theory of matter would be falsified a hundred times each day by high school students across Canada, who use the theory to predict the observational outcomes of their various experiments, but get unexpected (and sometimes quite startling) results that differ from their predictions. Naturally we do not regard well-established theories as being less secure simply in light of these surprising results.

What this kind of example shows is that theories enable predictions partly on the basis of **auxiliary hypotheses**: assumptions and theories external to the theory being tested, which help "connect" it to empirical observation. When we do an experiment having the potential to test, say, the theory of valences, the theory itself doesn't tell us that the test tubes in any given trial are clean, nor that the experimenters are competent, nor that the chemical samples are pure, nor that no unusual local conditions hold. Those are all independent hypotheses. So if we get an outcome not predicted by the theory itself, it's always open to us to reject one of those auxiliary hypotheses instead of rejecting the theory. If the theory is highly confirmed and useful, that's what happens. In the case of high school science disasters, we immediately assume that one or more of the auxiliary hypotheses just listed is false—and all things considered that seems reasonable. When I, as a sixteen-year-old, tried to make banana esters in chemistry class, but instead made something approximating a moth reproductive hormone, my chemistry teacher quite rightly did not regard me as having experimentally overturned the foundations of organic chemistry. Instead he probably chose to reject the auxiliary hypothesis that I was a competent experimenter—a hypothesis that he was right to regard as tenuous anyhow. This decision surely wasn't unscientific on his part! Still less did it somehow make the bulk of organic chemistry unscientific, even though it was and is routinely insulated from such apparently falsifying results. For at least this reason, falsifiability will have to be refined and qualified if it's to be invoked as a demarcation criterion.

THE SCIENTIFIC ATTITUDE

Something importantly correct is broadly shared among these proposed criteria of demarcation. What they may be really getting at is the importance of a particular cluster of attitudes for good science.

What the appeal to naturalism in science gets right is that the class of alleged entities that are typically dismissed as inconsistent with naturalism are ones that have failed to be detectable, predictive, or explanatory. The clearest sense in which appeals to ghosts are unscientific is that it's not a proper scientific *attitude* or *method* to continue appealing to ghosts as an explanation of events, since ghosts have systematically failed to figure in any explanatory or predictive theory. But that has nothing to do with what we might call the *spookiness* of the concept of a ghost, if we can use that term to loosely mean whatever is spiritualistically common to explanatory appeals to gods, ghosts, magic, and other categories of concern to science defenders.

History provides a useful comparison. For a period in the seventeenth and early eighteenth centuries, scientists (or "natural philosophers," as they were known) speculated that combustion consists of the release of an element present in all flammable substances. They called this element **phlogiston** and appealed to it in various chemical explanations for decades. The really decisive refutation of the theory came when Antoine-Laurent Lavoisier carefully isolated and weighed the products of combustion and discovered that the solids weighed more after burning than they had before—though the air itself was lighter. This powerfully indicated that combustion was a matter of *adding* something from the air rather than *releasing* something into it. Lavoisier coined the term *oxygen* for this substance (which was co-discovered by Joseph Priestley, though he considered it to be "de-phlogistonated air"). So here we are today: there is no useful explanatory or predictive role for phlogiston; the very concept turns out to be ill-defined; and while there are unanswered questions about oxygen, as there are about everything in the domain of science, those questions don't seem to be well answered by appeal to phlogiston. Hence it would be a poor scientific attitude to continue invoking phlogiston theory. Yet presumably there's no temptation to say that phlogiston falls outside the naturalistic purview of science.

The falsifiability condition too might be more reasonably invoked to distinguish science from non-science, or at least proper from improper science, if understood not exactly as a property of theories, but as a property of theorizers' attitudes. Karl Popper observed that even some "genuinely testable theories, when found to be false, are still upheld by their admirers—for example, by . . . reinterpreting the theory *ad hoc* in such a way that it escapes refutation."[6] This, Popper claimed, resulted in "destroying, or at least lowering" the scientific status of the theory. But scientific theories are often changed to better accommodate new data; far from being an essential feature of pseudo-science, this is arguably a great strength of much successful science. Looking at actual scientific practice, it isn't always a bad

FIGURE 9.1

Scientific Attitude Affects Scientific Belief

The tenets of proper scientific attitude or method require acceptance, revision, or even refutation of theories as new information becomes available. In this engraving, French chemist Antoine-Laurent Lavoisier (1743–1794), centre right, shows fellow scientists his experiment that revealed the composition of air in 1776. Lavoisier identified oxygen gas and discredited phlogiston as the theoretical source of combustion. Proper scientific attitude enables scientific beliefs to change over time in response to ongoing research.

Science Photo Library

thing to reinterpret a theory and hold onto it in light of new data. So there can be no general scientific requirement not to do this, notwithstanding the appeal of falsificationism.

The phenomena Popper intended falsifiability to rule out of science (giving a few examples that irked him, like theories of Freudian psychology and Marxist history) seem more a matter of the attitudes and dispositions with which one weighs evidence than of anything inherent in the theories themselves. In effect the proper attitude is one that takes seriously the *defeasibility* of scientific claims, a concept discussed at length in Chapter 2. Good science need not consist in dropping an established or previously useful idea at the first sign of trouble. But it does require an openness to the prospect that new data, new theories, or new concepts will make it reasonable to reject the propositions we currently accept. In principle, any element of our best scientific account of the world could be falsified.

This alleged possibility of error may seem a very strong claim. Is it a genuine possibility that we could discover, say, that iron really has a higher atomic number than cobalt? At most there is a minimal sense in which the answer is yes, but a more serious possibility is that the entire theoretical framework within which the atomic numbers are meaningful could be replaced by another framework that classifies elements in a very different way. Such a framework is hard to imagine, perhaps, but then so is any theory that we don't yet have. Good science is characterized by at least a basic willingness to entertain alternative theories and a sensitivity to the potential for new data to reduce the credibility of our current theories.

Any sort of context of inquiry that requires and enforces a doctrine viewed as indefeasible therefore casts doubt on the conclusions that emerge from it. Returning to an earlier example, some organizations or institutions that present themselves as scientific opponents to evolutionary theory require that their members, employees, or researchers pledge their commitment to the absolute literal correctness of (in North America, typically) the Christian Bible. If an advocate of an Intelligent Design hypothesis works at such an institution, there is at least something to the charge that she is not free to have a proper scientific attitude toward her research. She would have to adopt powerful factual assumptions that are then not viewed as corrigible, guaranteeing that the evidence will always be reinterpreted to accommodate those assumptions without at least the principled possibility that new evidence could instead overturn them. This does not mean, however, that the hypothesis itself falls outside the bounds of science.

It is neither feasible nor desirable to go more deeply into these difficult issues here. The important lesson is just that the distinctions between science and non-science *are* difficult to spell out. No conception of critical thinking as just being scientific thinking can provide a simple recipe for believing reasonable things, for at least the reason that there is no simple recipe for recognizing science, as opposed to other less reliable or unreliable processes or bodies of beliefs. For current purposes, we should leave it at that. Rather than thinking of pseudo-science as something sharply distinguished from (something called) real science by its violation of some clear principle or method, we can think of unreliable science as a *syndrome:* a set of beliefs, claims, and practices presented as scientific, but which depend upon a mixture of prejudged conclusions, sloppy methodology, irreproducibility, and an unwillingness to give up a relevant conviction in the face of countervailing evidence. Poor science is characterized by the degree to which it relies on a range of the fallacious reasoning, dubious statistics, and perceptual, cognitive, memory-based, and social biases described in previous chapters.

Hence the difference between good and bad scientific practice is multi-dimensional, and each dimension is open to differences of degree rather than just all-or-nothing distinctions. Based on such a conception we can make reasonable evidential judgments about the credibility of claims put forward as scientific, without worrying about whether a given statement, theory, or method definitely counts as science or something else, nor even whether it definitely counts as good science. For both of these questions the best answers available in the present will allow for many uncertain borderline cases, and the clearest answers will be available only in retrospect, when the utility of the currently disputed example will have become a matter of record. As one of my colleague puts it: "If you want to know whether something is good science . . . wait three hundred years."

In the shorter term, we need to develop context-sensitive ways of seeing how various problems with scientific claims interact with each other and with our broader knowledge of the world. As a way of understanding both the operations of science and how activities that are represented as scientific can fail, we will now examine some hallmarks of reliable or successful science. Scientific theories, methods, or research can fail by degrees for each of these hallmarks. They can fail to display the hallmarks singly or in conjunction with others. Certainly lots of fertile, reliable, useful science will fall down to some extent on one or more of these standards. So this approach won't provide sharp dividing lines between science and pseudo-science, nor will it enable simple one-dimensional diagnoses of how science (or attempted science) goes wrong. But it may have the virtue of actually being accurate, and it is still consistent with the prospect of drawing some important distinctions between reliable and unreliable scientific reasoning.

SOME HALLMARKS OF RELIABLE SCIENCE

EXPERIMENTAL DESIGN

A study or experiment should attempt to measure the phenomena of interest as directly as possible. It should be only as complicated as the elimination of confounds requires—that is, any complications in its structure and methods should all specifically aim at distinguishing different kinds of results, selecting one hypothesis over another, or settling some question of fact. And a study or experiment should make use of recognized successful techniques for testing phenomena of that sort, unless there is a good reason not to. Pointless complexity, unaccountably roundabout measurement techniques, and a departure from reliable methods are red flags, raising the prospect of (possibly deliberate) opportunities for bias and confounds to creep into the study.

Basics of Experimental and Observational Methods

Things—objects, situations, chemicals, people—are complicated. They can change (or fail to change) in surprising and unforeseen ways. So whenever we conduct a study or experiment to measure the effects of some factor on whatever kind of thing we're examining, we are confronted with a serious problem: how can we discriminate the effects of the factor we experimentally introduced, or observed occurring in context, from the changes or lack of changes that the things would have undergone anyhow?

The answer to this problem is to introduce the distinction between a **treatment group** (or **test group**) and a **control group**. A test group is one on which some test is performed; the control group is one to which the test group is compared, to distinguish test-relevant effects from other effects. If we have a group of apple trees in an orchard, for example, and we want to know the effects of seaweed fertilizer on their fruit output, we first divide the trees into two sub-groups that are as similar as possible *overall* with respect to every property that might make a difference to the outcome of the procedure. Basically we want to be as confident as possible that anything that would happen in one of the tree groups merely on account of facts about apple trees and the general orchard conditions would also happen in the other tree group.

If we are dealing with large numbers of trees, a random assignment of trees into test and control groups ought to give us the desired similarity between the groups. The bigger the sample, as we saw in Chapter 6, the smaller the chance that we will get unlucky and draw a biased selection in one group or the other, relative to the broader population. If we are stuck with using a small sample, though, the chances of randomly getting a biased treatment-control division may be too high for any result to be statistically meaningful. In these cases we may have to give randomness a helping hand by employing some method or other that actively aims at getting an appropriate sample. For the medical studies we are mainly considering now, one such method is **pair-matching**, or dividing the subjects into two groups whose members are deliberately matched with respect to properties that we *suspect* could make a difference to the outcome. In the case of trees, these properties used for matching might include size, depth of roots, soil properties, quality of foliage, irrigation, average exposure to sunlight, proximity to beehives, and so forth. This explains why the larger studies by Byrd (393 subjects in total) and Harris (990 in total) used simple randomization to make treatment and control group assignments, while Sicher's small study (40 total) used pair-matching to organize subjects into most similar pairs according to age, blood cell counts, and medical histories. We know those things can make a difference to patient recovery, and with a sample as small as 40 patients, there's too great a likelihood that merely random assignments would place a majority of older, sicker, or weaker patients in the treatment or the control group. This would skew the results. Sicher therefore pair-matched his patients and split each pair between the treatment and control groups.

Of course, one thing that pair-matching cannot do is change the size of the sample. So any relevant factors that we *don't* know about stand a good chance of invisibly confounding our results. For at least this reason, scientists are particularly cautious about the conclusions drawn from studies with small sample sizes, no matter how carefully the research was conducted.

So, returning to our apple trees: we choose the two groups in the most non-biased way we can, all things considered. Then we apply seaweed fertilizer to one of those groups, but we observe both groups. The idea is this: if something happens to the fertilized group (the treatment group), but also happens to the unfertilized group (the control), then it probably isn't the fertilizer that explains it. But if something happens in the fertilized group that *doesn't* happen in the unfertilized group, then the fertilizer probably explains what happened. It's Mill's Method of Difference in action (discussed in Chapter 2).

Applied carefully and systematically, this approach helps remove the worry that any conclusions we draw will be based on *post hoc ergo propter hoc* reasoning. It's not just that something happened *after* we applied fertilizer to the trees; it's that it also *didn't* happen when we did not apply fertilizer to the other trees.

LINK

The discussion of Reading 5, Chapter 11, raises an important related point about an even smaller pilot study conducted by Sicher and reported in the same journal article. The pilot study seemed to suggest that prayer had a significant effect on AIDS patient mortality, but an error in the assignment treatment and control groups sufficed to explain this appearance.

We don't even need to have two groups in order to get the control group effect. There might not be enough trees to use only half of them in the test group and still get a statistically meaningful result—recall the point from Chapter 5 that using a small sample is likelier to generate apparent correlations that are really just due to chance. In this case we might get our two groups by dividing the single group over time. In such a **longitudinal study** we might first measure the fruit output of our trees for several seasons, again taking note of every characteristic that might end up being relevant to the fruit output over that period. Then we could add the fertilizer to all the apple trees, and see how their fruit output subsequently changed, if at all. One specific worry in this case is that we might really be measuring a change that all the trees would have undergone anyhow; we might not be able to control for things like age, if all the trees were planted at the same time. Another worry is simply that the past is gone, so to speak. If the possibility of some confounding factor occurs to us after we perform the test, if we begin to wonder about the possible effects of some property about the control group that we didn't measure at the time, there is no way to go back and get that data. By altering the control group we destroyed it as a source of further uncontaminated information.

A way of partially addressing such worries in a longitudinal experiment is to retain at least a small control group outside the treatment group. That way we get historical control information drawn from the entire group, but can still monitor at least some non-test cases in parallel with the test group. Experiments and observational studies frequently have to seek such compromises in order to strike a balance between practical or financial limitations of the situation and the need for effective controls. In the example just considered, it would be important to ensure that fertilizer applied to one tree does not just leach through the soil to affect the control group trees as well. A way to avoid this would be to use two completely different orchards, far enough apart that the fertilizer could not be spread by groundwater, but this would raise worries about having the appropriate similarities between test and control. Again, good science often depends on striking the best balance possible in the circumstances and then making clear in one's report of the experiment exactly what was done, and why. Fully understanding a scientific result requires examining this information to see just what balances were struck and how these might contribute to an unreliable outcome. Since few popular reports of a scientific experiment will contain this information, it is yet again a case of our going back to the primary sources to reach an informed judgment about a claim.

So far I have been using the terms "experiment" and "study" as if they were nearly interchangeable. To an extent they are, even in the scientific literature. But an important distinction is that between an experiment and an observational study. Normally when scientists refer to **experiments**, they mean an investigative technique involving a deliberately controlled intervention: actively introducing some factor into a situation, in order to see what results. For a whole host of reasons ranging from the financial to the ethical, however, it is often possible only to observe events in an uncontrolled (or less controlled) non-intervening fashion. This kind of inquiry is called an **observational study**. So, for example, if we want to know the effects on children of skipping the seventh grade, it would be unethical to intervene by randomly picking some kids and skipping them from Grade Six directly to Grade Eight.

CHAPTER 9 *Critical Reasoning about Science: Cases and Lessons*

We couldn't do such an experiment, since it may well lead to our harming some of our human subjects. Hence our curiosity must be satisfied with observational studies: we have to find the data that exist on past cases of children skipping grades, or we have to ask to be informed when a child is currently skipping a grade for independent reasons and then try to track the effects in whatever way is least likely to be obtrusive or harmful.

Observational studies are much better than no information at all, to be sure. But at the same time they are rarely as reliable as experimental studies. (They can also be more expensive; consider how many schools we might have to contact and track in order to get a large enough sample of children skipping grades.) Without the ability to positively control for confounds, the scientist is left to brainstorm about what possible confounds might be operating in each situation, and what degree of effect they might be having. Because the "data points" (schoolchildren and their performance, in the example given) have to be studied where and when they are available, there is no guarantee that one is quite comparing apples with apples. So observational studies tend to offer more suggestive than compelling conclusions. This is perhaps especially the case when what's being observed are people, for whom differences of background, dispositions, and attitudes can make up a vast set of possible confounds.

Now, think back to the four studies of the medical effects of prayer and consider the question of treatment and control groups for those studies. We could think of these as aiming to fall midway between observational studies and controlled experiments. The researchers could at least partially guide the element of prayer, in that they could ask people to pray for a group without being able to confirm either that the pray-ers had *actually* prayed for that group or that other people outside the experiment had not prayed for either group. But they could not impose even that much control over the medical treatments given to the subjects, who were already ill, had different doctors and nurses, may have had varying levels of medical insurance, and so forth. When we reflect on how these studies could follow the basic methods covered above, it quickly becomes clear that a complex set of assumptions underlies the prospect that prayer can be medically effective independent of a patient's attitudes. If the effect of the prayer is assumed to be mediated by the will of a god, for example, that in itself is an irremovable confound. For how might the will of the relevant god be acting on the situation *independently* of the number and kind of prayers being offered? The idea of a systematically testable effect has to treat the connection between intercessors and patients as a kind of passive linkage, albeit perhaps of a spiritual sort, rather than an active agency that might, for all we know, be taking a notion all its own and acting on the outcomes in unsurveyable ways.

Suppose we grant that all other things are equal, as far as the will of the god or gods goes, and accept a picture in which it just comes down to who's praying for whom (perhaps by conceiving of the relevant god as more or less taking orders via prayer, or by thinking of prayer non-theistically as a psychic instrument of some sort). Still it is entirely unclear how many confounds the wider world of praying people introduces to any attempt at conducting a controlled study. Again, dividing the subjects into treatment and control groups requires matching the groups as closely as possible along any dimension that might be relevant to the outcome of the experiment. But on the assumption that prayer *can* make a difference, how many such dimensions are there? The assumption that each patient receives the same default level of prayers from his or her family is very, very dubious; imagine testing a drug to control blood pressure merely on the *assumption* that each patient had the same blood pressure in the first place. Yet it's an assumption that must be made for any medical prayer study, since measuring each patient's level of personal "prayed-for-ness" is at least practically impossible and maybe impossible in a stronger sense. It would require not just rigorous investigation of the prayer habits of patients' families and friends, but also judgments about the relative quality versus quantity of prayers, about the expected effects of silent versus audible prayers, individual versus group prayers, and so forth, which are likely too ill-defined to even begin measuring.

Suppose nevertheless that we grant the same default level of personal prayer for each patient from their friends and family, as well. Still, there are a lot of people who pray in the world, and many of them pray for people they don't know. If groups of people around the world are praying for the well-being of those who are unloved, for example, this means that the treatment and control groups must be paired not only by similarity on health properties, but also by similarity on how *loved* each patient is. Otherwise we may randomly assign more unloved people to one group than to another, and that group will hence receive more prayers.

Do we have a measure for global belovedness, though? Certainly none of the prayer studies in question made any attempt to perform such a quixotic matching procedure. Now, how many other dimensions of comparison are relevant to getting a proper distinction into control and treatment groups, given the way that people worldwide conduct their prayers? Thinking back to Chapter 6, you might see that if there are relatively few such immeasurable ways in which unknown intercessors could be affecting patients, these would create a serious confound in just the way we've seen with belovedness. Perhaps counterintuitively, the *more* such points of unknown contact that existed, the greater the chances that their effects would statistically balance out across otherwise well-matched treatment and control groups, becoming a sort of constant background "noise." But we don't know how many ways there are for unknown intercessors to pick out patients with their prayers. Indeed the problem in essence is that, quite apart from not knowing how the treatment could *work*, we don't really have much of an idea what the treatment itself *is*.

Finally, many people worldwide may well specifically pray for those who don't have enough people already praying for them! Presumably these will count as praying disproportionately for the control group in such experiments no matter how the two groups are divided, making a rigorous control outright impossible. It makes the problem of dividing the trees in an orchard into control and treatment groups seem mild by comparison, but the extreme practical and conceptual problems with establishing a control group in the case of "distant healing" are stark examples of potential problems that any scientific study must confront.

The Placebo Effect and Single-Blinding

The term "placebo" is often used to mean a treatment or action that is inactive, one that has neither positive nor negative effect in and of itself. The idea is crucially important for controlled experiments involving human (and even many animal) agents. Part of having the control group match the test group as closely as possible is having the control group go through as many of the test procedures as possible. If we are experimenting to determine the effectiveness of some medicine that is taken in the form of a pill, and only the test group takes a pill, that amounts to a major difference between the test and control groups. Any subsequent differences between the groups might, for all we know, be due not to the contents of the pill but to the act of taking it. We can factor this out by giving a placebo—say, a sugar pill of roughly the same size and appearance—to the control group members on the same schedule and with the same routine by which the test group gets their medication.

The reason this methodology is so important is that the **placebo effect** can be extremely powerful. This is a complex and fascinating phenomenon: people who believe they are receiving a treatment often feel better as a result; indeed, they sometimes *recover* as a result. This is least surprising for cases in which having the illness and feeling the effects of the illness are not so different; some medical conditions are defined, or nearly defined, just in terms of the patient's feeling a particular way. But there are also more surprising cases in which it seems that even illnesses defined in terms of some symptom-independent underlying condition are mitigated or reversed due to the placebo effect.

FURTHER REFLECTION

There is a perspective from which the placebo effect might be taken to be a sufficient virtue of some treatment. A friend tells me that he takes one popular cold-avoidance treatment even though he's more than half-convinced it exerts only a placebo effect on his health. "If I can feel cold-free for $35 a week, it's worth it," he says. Feeling better is feeling better, after all. So what if you're buying ordinary tap water for $20 per bottle, convinced by an "infomercial" that Dihydrogen Monoxide reduces anxiety? By drinking it under the impression that it will work, you may come to feel much less anxious. Why should this be judged anything other than a success of "alternative" or "complementary" medicine?

Of course, one obvious problem is this: you're buying plain tap water at twenty bucks a pop, and ordinary tap water on its own doesn't do anything to reduce anxiety. In the best case, there may be little irrational about the actions of someone who buys Genuine Placebo Brand Anti-Stress Dihydrogen Monoxide (*"Accept no cheap imitations!"*), having found that drinking it reduces her anxiety. But that is perfectly consistent with its being immoral or irresponsible to *sell* Genuine Placebo Brand Anti-Stress Dihydrogen Monoxide, since in putting a product up for sale, one is presumably selling it not just to those who derive the benefit, but also to people who are not able to enter the proper state of mind to experience a placebo effect. If a treatment is to be sold to people it should have a measurable beneficial effect distinct from—that is, additional to—any benefit accruing from the user's state of mind in taking it. Of course, in the worst case the placebo effect will make a subject *feel* better (or convince her that she feels better, if there is a difference) while some underlying condition worsens in the absence of effective treatment, leading to serious illness or even death.

Thinking back again to the lessons of Chapter 6, and specifically the question of what it means to *not* reject the null hypothesis in an experiment, it should be clear that the placebo effect is something that should be cautiously attributed. After all, both the control and treatment groups in a human study might show the same improvement owing to some common external cause, and not simply because of their expectations, beliefs, or attitudes. The best evidence for a genuine placebo effect in a single experiment occurs when the experimental factors are already well-understood, and no common external mechanism for the indiscriminate effects on both groups is plausible in light of that information.

Similarly, we can attribute the placebo effect when blinded applications of the treatment consistently produce insignificant results and unblinded applications of the treatment frequently produce significant results. For example, there is independent evidence that patients who are told that they are being prayed for can be affected by this knowledge, though there is no tidy connection with the kind of effect experienced. (Another large recent study of therapeutic prayer led by Herbert Benson not only showed no difference between double-blind treatment and control groups, but showed a significant *negative* effect for a third group of patients who knew they were the objects of others' prayers![7]) If there are grounds to doubt any significant effect in the blinded studies—and the methodological problems with the very concepts of control and treatments groups give us one red flag, so far—and yet we observe significant effects in the non-blind cases, then prayer is reasonably (though defeasibly!) considered a placebo from a medical perspective.

The power of the placebo effect means that an experiment involving people, and especially one in which people are given treatments of some sort, must take special steps to ensure a proper control group. Obviously if the test group is given a treatment while the control group is not, there is a crucial difference between the two groups that will badly confound the results. The solution is to treat both groups the same, giving the control group a placebo in exactly the same way that the test group is given the treatment. That way, presumably, any effects due solely to the subjects' belief that they are being treated will occur equally in both groups. So any effectiveness of the treatment itself will be manifest as an *extra* effect, additional to the placebo effect. In order for this to work, however, subjects can't know which group they are in. If you know you're in the control group, you know you're getting a placebo rather than a treatment—eliminating or greatly reducing the placebo effect in the control, and hence confounding the results again. So the distribution of subjects between groups must be at least **single-blind**: the subjects cannot know whether they are genuinely being treated. An experimental design that allows information like this to filter down to the subjects is therefore compromised.

It is worth reflecting for a moment on just how demanding the requirements of effective experimental blinding can be. Think, for example, of your experience in taking pills like vitamins, analgesics, anti-inflammatory medication, or antibiotics. Each of these pills can have a characteristic (and usually unpleasant) after-taste—for instance, if you burp shortly after swallowing it. If you didn't notice any after-taste, as a subject in a clinical trial for some sort of medicine, or if it just tasted like sugar, you might correctly guess that you were in the control group. Or if the real medicine had a distinct after-taste, as in at least one study on the effects of Vitamin C on colds, you might correctly guess that you were in the treatment group just from a burp or two.[8] So, strangely enough, good experimental design requires putting a serious thought into the problem of making non-medicines taste like medicine, in order to prevent subjects from burping their way into knowledge of which group they're in and thereby creating an uneven placebo effect between control group and treatment group. And this is just one possible avenue of such information; in general, science puts enormous effort and creativity into the project of ruling out confounding explanations.

Scientists testing surgical procedures on animals, for example, must also make a point of conducting "sham surgery" as well, in which all the procedures short of the actual surgical intervention are followed—up to and including anaesthetizing and cutting the control group animals—just to ensure that none of those procedures could be causing any effect observed in the animals receiving the surgical treatment. Another entire family of potential "information leaks" is found in the experimenters themselves, who, if *they* know the members of the two groups, can behave differently toward them. Even if subtle and wholly unintentional, this differential behaviour can have differentiating effects. This is one of the reasons for wanting experimental designs that are still more tightly constrained than single-blinding in many situations.

E-bias and Double-Blinding

In many kinds of inquiry a major worry is the prospect of **experimenter bias** (sometimes just **E-bias**). This is really an amalgam of various more specific biases of the sort described in Chapter 7, especially confirmation biases of one kind or another. They are called E-biases in the context of an experiment or observational study, when the beliefs, attitudes, or emotional commitments of the experimenter influence the data recorded and the conclusions drawn from it.

A classic illustration of E-bias in science that deals with human subjects is actually drawn from an experiment not about experimental contexts but about classroom contexts. In the 1960s, the educational psychologist Robert Rosenthal ran a series of experiments on the effects of teachers' attitudes toward children on two things: how the teachers reported the children's performance, and how the children actually performed on standardized tests.[9] In one kind of experiment, Rosenthal and colleague Lenore Jacobson administered some standard cognitive and skills tests on the children in an elementary school class, but told the class's teacher that these tests enabled them to predict which children would soon undergo a "blooming" period—a kind of rapid intellectual development that would see them outpace their classmates academically. The teachers were informed which children they could expect to see blooming (in fact the children were selected at random). This procedure substantially resulted in the teachers reporting that the unusual blooming really did occur for the identified children. The teachers' expectations regarding what the children would do ended up playing a role in how they perceived and described the children's academic behaviour. Asked to make a note of any instances of children showing a creative or insightful response to class material or events, the teachers reported a disproportionately high number of such responses among the children who had been identified as likely to blossom. Perhaps even more striking was the result that these children subsequently showed disproportionate improvement on standardized tests as well—that is, tests *not* graded by their teachers. Apparently it wasn't just that the teachers' expectations led them to *interpret* the children as more creative, insightful, or generally gifted. The way they acted toward the children actually helped the children perform better on objective measures of cognitive abilities. It became a single instance of both a self-fulfilling and a confirmation-biasing prophecy, two kinds of prophecy discussed in Chapter 7.

What are the lessons? Experiments on E-bias illustrate how powerful top-down effects of expectation or motivation can operate on educated professionals in information-gathering contexts. Both perception and judgment are open to such biasing effects, as we have seen; there is nothing about one's scientific or educational credentials that rules them out altogether. So what *is* special about science must be something besides mere credentials: namely, a set of methods or practices aimed at reducing the opportunity for such biases to operate, and methods for detecting them if they do occur.

The Rosenthal results clearly indicate how an observer's expectations and attitudes can skew both the conduct and interpretation of an experiment, without any suggestion of deliberate fraud. This is the primary reason for having studies that are **double-blind** when any possibility exists for the experimenters (including assistants) to consciously or unconsciously nudge the outcome in a particular direction, whether by a biased selection of control and test group; by letting the group members know which group they are in, including by actions as minor and unintentional as body language; by interpreting data in light of expectations; or by any similar process. A double-blind study is one in which neither the subjects nor the experimenters know which subjects are in the test group and which are in the control group. This is usually accomplished by having the division of the subjects into control and test groups performed by someone at arm's length from the experiment itself: a collaborator not involved in the administration of treatment or data-gathering, or a graduate student or assistant hired specifically for that purpose.

Each of the four intercessory prayer studies discussed at the outset of this chapter was to have a fundamentally double-blind method, although the details were different in each study. In fact, they were all inherently more complicated than the two-way relation presupposed by the double-blind label, since each involved people praying for other people as part of the apparatus, and the people doing the praying had to know at least *something* about whom they were praying for. As long as the intercessors in turn had no contact with the patients, the researchers, or with anyone else who knew enough about the assignments and the treatments to use the intercessors' limited information (a name, clinical details, a photograph, etc.) to skew the recording or interpretation of patient data, the information in the hands of the intercessors should not have confounded the studies. Provided the blinding elsewhere in the study was kept airtight, no measurable differences should have arisen from the patients' *believing* they were being prayed for (in the Harris study patients were not even aware of taking part in a study), nor by the conscious or unconscious decisions of the researchers. Setting aside some substantial differences in method, the intended structure of all four studies was blind in all ways that could have constituted information leakage. But in reality at least three of the four studies showed signs of serious flaws on this score. (Again, however, I will not comment on the IVF pregnancy study until the end of the chapter.)

The Byrd study of prayer on heart patients had at least two documented failures of the double-blinding.[10] First, the published version of the data that indicated overall results for patients in the study (categorized as Good, Intermediate, or Bad overall outcomes) was constructed by Byrd himself, in light of feedback he received from reviewers on an earlier draft of the article. But this entails that Byrd had already unblinded the data for publication at that earlier point and then performed further analysis of it. That is, he had already presented his conclusions once, which means that he had put the medical data for each patient together with the information about whether they were in treatment or control groups. Hence this raises a red flag, the worry being how effectively he could reblind the study—strip out the group membership information from the medical data—in order to make his further work on the data analysis properly safe from the effects of his knowledge of the outcomes.

Moreover, although Byrd merely thanked an assistant named Janet Greene in the Acknowledgements section of his original article, in another article summarizing the study for a Christian nursing journal he explained that Janet Greene in fact did *both* the treatment-control group assignments *and* the medical record-keeping for all patients in the study. This represents a particularly serious confound, since the potential for conscious or unconscious information leakage is enormous when a single person possesses all this information and has the ability to influence how the data are recorded.

A similar worry holds for the Sicher article.[11] The data in the study were unblinded by the study's biostatistician, but in order to collect information that was later thought to be relevant the data were reblinded by Sicher himself. Yet he already had access to a great deal of information about the individual patients, both having interviewed some of them repeatedly and being privy to the treatment and control lists. Even if we can't make any judgment as to what specific mechanism might be implicated, or whether such information might be used consciously or unconsciously, this sort of breach in the blinding immediately confounds the results of a study or experiment. The revelation of circumstances that allow such information to contaminate the results—in other words, a revelation that forces everyone, including the researcher himself, to trust his belief that he didn't allow that inside knowledge to colour his decisions and judgments—is a red flag, meaning that we should at least regard the results as questionable if we don't reject them altogether.

Simplicity and Transparency

The structural and functional features of experimental design that we have been considering share at least one trait: there is a clear reason for each of them, given the constraints of the situation, in terms of the need to maximize the data gathered while minimizing confounds. There are many other common styles and practices of experimentation, and they too are used appropriately when they share that trait. Making sense of a scientific report requires thinking about whether the methods employed are fitting to the circumstances.

A scientific report that relies on data gathered in a single-blind study when a double-blind would be more appropriate is automatically under a cloud—not simply because of the confounds this introduces, but because in the absence of some very good explanation it indicates a lack of sound methodological judgment that might permeate the research in many ways. Similarly, a scientific report that makes use of data from an observational study when a controlled experiment could have been performed is not only less compelling, in the general way that observational studies are less reliable than controlled experiments, but also raises red flags about the conduct of the work. In general, a good experiment employs the simplest familiar methods necessary to deliver non-confounded data.

Of course, every new field or subfield of intellectual inquiry may be characterized by novel, hence unfamiliar, methods. But roughly and readily, it is a red flag when a field of study or a practice has been in existence for a substantial time and yet has not settled on any generally recognized methods for testing or confirming hypotheses. Such a situation at least raises the worry that there really is nothing there to measure or to theorize about.

PEER REVIEW

Scientific claims, reports, and conclusions should be willingly placed before the community of informed experts for their critique and analysis. Avoiding the open critique of the scientific community, attempting to shepherd a work through the normal processes of critical review or shelter it from analysis, and failing to respond to or acknowledge the criticisms that are presented are all red flags.

The Peer-Review Process

Scientific research, and indeed intellectual research more broadly, has come to be presented and communicated through a set of specialized conventions known collectively as the **peer-review process**. The aspect of the peer-review process that gets the most attention is publication in specialized academic journals. Indeed, journal publication is often depicted as the *end* of peer review. But this is highly oversimplified. Peer review begins with the refereeing process for journals, but it continues long after an article appears in print.

Scientific journals serve as the primary means of sharing research results with a wider community of specialists. But in theory this goal could be achieved just as effectively, and certainly more cheaply, if researchers instead distributed their results through a mass e-mail list. What, then, is special about the journal system? More than merely communicating research results, journal publication *vouches* for these results. Anyone could send out an e-mail making whatever fraudulent or crackpot claims they chose, but journals publish articles only if they pass the scrutiny of experts in the relevant field. This is a crucial stage in the process by which scientific results become recognized as genuine contributions to knowledge. These scrutinizing experts are known as reviewers or referees; their role is quite complicated.

Referees are not normally in the business of deciding whether the contents of some submitted paper are true or false. Of course, if a paper depends on a demonstrable falsehood it will not be accepted for publication, but the more usual problems that referees monitor involve method and novelty rather than content specifically. Does the report of the study or experiment make it clear that obvious confounds were investigated and ruled out? Were the right statistical or analytical tools used? Does the research merely duplicate (without realizing it) a study or experiment already published?

These and similar questions are used to determine whether, roughly speaking, a submitted article is worth talking about in the journal to which it has been submitted (it doesn't hurt to think of *worth talking about* as the basic status that journal publication effectively confers on a piece of research.) This judgment has at least two parts, then: whether the article is worth publishing, period; and whether it's worth publishing in that particular journal. It is not uncommon for referees to recommend against publishing a paper but to recommend that it be submitted instead to some other journal having a mandate more suited to the topic or methods of the paper.

The question of whether the conclusions or even the factual claims made in the article are *true* is very important but is often just left to the discipline more broadly to explore—by attempting to replicate the study, for example, or by testing it in various indirect ways. For this reason peer-reviewed publication is properly regarded as occupying a role near the beginning of the peer-review process, and not as being the end of the process. For researchers personally and professionally, it may be the fact of publication itself that matters most, or most immediately, since the number of journal publications that one produces is a key measure of performance at virtually every university. But to the discipline more broadly, what matters is how the article is received: whether it is accepted and incorporated into the stock of received knowledge or dismissed as a flawed or irreproducible piece of work. In this deepest sense, the peer-review process never really ends. As long as the observations and conclusions of an article are in print, they are open to review, analysis, and testing.

Scientific journals are special publications in several important respects. First, while they are often owned by publishing companies, they are in theory (and sometimes even in practice) not primarily aimed at making a profit. Publishers do make money from journals if enough subscriptions are sold, the key market being university libraries. But the editorial board of a journal typically has as its main mandate to uphold quality standards for the articles published, within the journal's area of focus. The aim of increasing the journal's readership, when it exists, may be as much a matter of enhancing prestige as improving the financial well-being of the publication.

Area of focus is another distinguishing feature of scientific journals. Some journals, including a few of the most famous and influential ones, have a very broad scope of interest, publishing articles in many different sciences. Most are quite narrow, however, aiming to present research mainly of interest only to the people working in a particular sub-discipline or employing a particular methodology. For better or worse, this just reflects the general phenomenon of fragmentation within the sciences. Whatever the extent to which theorizing unifies a broad range of data, in practice scientists often professionally focus on tightly circumscribed fields of study. It is common for people to talk along the lines of "Scientists now think that . . ." or "According to scientists . . .", as if there was a common core of interest and understanding among all or most scientists. But the professional development and research of many scientists is quite insular, a perhaps inevitable consequence of the sheer volume of data generated by other scientists in that particular subfield. There is little reason to expect a scientist who publishes in the *Scandinavian Journal of Metallurgy* to share many interests, or even much background knowledge, with one who publishes in the journal *Population Ecology*.

To a first approximation, then, scientific claims are at least worth taking seriously if they have been published in a respected academic journal as the result of a blind peer-review process. We might even say that they have a basic credibility in this case, though this credibility is of course defeasible for any given paper. Publication doesn't guarantee correctness, nor does it even guarantee general acceptance within a discipline, but it indicates two important things. First, it indicates a willingness to submit one's claims to critical scrutiny by those with the expertise to judge its quality and significance. And second, it is evidence that some competent referees have already recognized the work as demonstrating at least basic methodological competence and good judgment. The referees might miss some serious errors, of course, and the authors' data and conclusions might not stand up to further analysis even if the referees' judgment was reasonable based on the information provided. For that matter, a biased journal editor might occasionally shepherd a paper into publication by shunting it off to sympathetic or uncritical referees, or even by skipping the refereeing process altogether. This is rare, but not unheard of. A mild version of this may have been at work in at least one of the studies we have been examining, since just as the Byrd article included a note thanking God for helping the patients, the *Southern Medical Journal* included a commentary that seemed directly to endorse Byrd's conclusion that prayer is medically efficacious—a conclusion that by any standard would have to be seen as revolutionary, startling, a potential breakthrough requiring substantial confirmation. So there is at least some indication that a normally critical attitude was not adopted by the journal in its treatment of Byrd's article.[12] Despite its weaknesses, though, the journal system is at least a very useful gateway into the give and take of scientific discourse.

This is not to say that scientific claims must be false if they have not been published in a respected academic journal, but such a failure is a red flag. Scientists who take their claims directly to the mainstream media, for example, immediately face questions as to why the work was not first independently validated through the normal process. When peer-reviewed publication is the standard basic measure of sound methods and sound judgment, the deliberate avoidance of that system invites the concern that the work is unsound. Similar remarks can apply to scientific claims made first in popular books, or even academic books, rather than in journals. In many academic disciplines books are a perfectly acceptable, even a preferred, way of presenting research results. In most sciences, though, the reviewing process for books is much less demanding than for journals. Book refereeing is only occasionally a double-blind process, for one thing, and a measure of evaluation for the publishers tends to be whether the book will sell well, besides (and possibly instead of) whether it meets appropriate standards of rigour.

If research is not publishable in reputable journals, that is a default reason to regard it as less credible than if it had been. But the fact that research *is* published in reputable journals is very far from the end of the story. Over time, experiments and studies that are known to be mistaken in their conclusions or their alleged data accumulate in the literature; if they are debunked, the debunkings are added to the literature rather than the original publications being expunged (except in the most serious cases of academic fraud). So of course it remains strictly true that the flawed study is published in a reputable journal, and someone may well appeal to it without mentioning (perhaps without even knowing about) the fact that it subsequently came to be seen as flawed. Based on the very prayer studies we've been discussing, in fact, one Internet-based M.D. even draws the conclusion that doctors who *don't* employ prayer therapy should be held legally culpable!

> There appears to be no question that prayer works. We have many studies now that document that. The science is very solid in excellent peer-reviewed publications. The science is so solid, that it is criminally negligent for physicians not to recommend it.[13]

Word of the studies themselves can spread independently of word about their flaws. Notice how the claim that "the science is very solid" is bolstered by the allusion to studies appearing "in excellent peer-reviewed publications." But if this is the reasoning, it would get the significance of scientific publication very wrong even if the studies it cites had *not* been largely debunked. Again, sometimes scientific studies or theories lead very short lives, going directly from publication to demolition as the wider field notices problems that the referees did not, or as further inquiry reveals the result to be irreproducible. But a short list of peer-reviewed publications that agree on some conclusion carries little weight in any case, for reasons that ought to be familiar since Chapter 6 at least: what's also needed is wider information about how many studies *failed* to get concurring results. With many articles in print on a topic, each aiming for a .95 significance level, the odds are not really outrageous that someone can find two or three methodologically sound studies that get a significant result in support of a falsehood. The mere fact that one can cite two or three perfectly conducted published studies supporting some position does not in itself mean that there is good evidence for that position. Information is missing from any claim that lists a small number of studies in its support—namely, how many studies of that sort have been performed, what specific discussions of those studies exist in the literature, and how the specialists in the field generally regard those studies.

This sets the standards for careful debate or belief-formation rather higher than one might have first expected, at least when it comes to much-studied scientific questions. It is important to bear in mind that even if publications have subsequently been revealed as flawed, flukes, or even fraudulent, they can still be cited by the cynical or the ill-informed. Basing your opinion on the authority of a cited publication is risky, unless you are prepared to do some reading on how that article is regarded by the wider discipline and how it has stood up to criticism through the peer-review process.

CHAPTER 9 *Critical Reasoning about Science: Cases and Lessons*

REPRESENTATION OF DATA AND CONCLUSIONS

There are two main virtues of reliable science with respect to its presentation and use of data. Good science reports data conscientiously, and it quantifies data with both mathematical and explanatory competence and neutrality. But these aspects are expressed in a wide variety of practices. Here in particular the serious problems with the prayer studies emerge and in some cases interact with the failures of blinding noted earlier.

One indicator of good science is that researchers decide upon and can justify their means of quantifying and statistically measuring data before collecting it, wherever possible. Doing this in the reverse order is a red flag, suggesting that a metric was chosen, or the data statistically massaged, with the purpose of deriving a specific conclusion. As we saw in some detail in Chapter 4, this is the fallacy of Multiple Endpoints: trawling through the data after the fact and looking for statistically significant correlations, rather than specifying correlations of interest in advance and testing to see whether they are observed. It's one thing to theorize that two people each had a great-grandparent from the same town and then discover that they did; it's another thing to wonder whether two people have something, *anything*, in common, and then discover that they each had a great-grandparent from the same town. To depict the latter situation as if it was the former all along is to claim a significance for the data that it does not really possess in that circumstance.

So it is important to note that the Byrd study employed 26 separate indicators of illness, yet the treatment group performed statistically significantly better than the control group on only 6. A revised probability of getting the significance levels in question on 6 of 26 indicators can in turn be calculated, and Byrd did base his conclusion on such a revised score. But this step was insufficient to rescue his conclusion from the Multiple Endpoints fallacy, since, as critics observed, the indicators that came up as significant were all too tightly interrelated as causes and effects.[14] The six significant indicators in Byrd's data were pneumonia, cardiopulmonary arrest, congestive heart failure, taking antibiotics, taking diuretics, and receiving respiratory ventilation. But any one of these is likely to be accompanied by one or more of the others—indeed, most are likely to *cause* one or more of the others. Choosing the indicators in this way therefore artificially multiplied the number of statistically significant poor health categories on which the treatment group did better than the control group. If it isn't a significant correlation that two people both own shoes, we can't make it more significant by pointing out that they *also* both own things that have soles, and *also* occasionally purchases laces, and *also* both have feet.

Still more worrisome is the fact that the indicators of health that were used to measure how well patients had performed were chosen *after* Janet Greene had collected the data, and *after* Byrd had unblinded and reblinded the data.[15] This is not simply another concern; rather, it promotes the red flag of the blinding failures to the status of a very serious confound. This is just the reason that a failure of blinding deserves close attention in the first place, requiring us to confirm that the information thus accessed could not in fact have influenced the conduct of the study. In this case we discover obvious ways in which it could have. Put simply, you're not allowed to peek at the data before deciding what to measure. If you do, your results are suspect no matter what you're investigating.

What about the matching red flag for dubious blinding that we noted in the Sicher study of prayer on AIDS patients? It receives a matching promotion to serious confound. The reason that Sicher had to reblind the study was to gather data for a set of health indicators after the data had *failed* to generate non-confounded significant results for a range of factors, including not only death, the outcome it was intended to measure, but also a specific measure of HIV symptoms, a measure of quality of life, and even the key HIV diagnostic measure of "CD4+ count."[16] In short, they seem to have kept looking until they found measures on which the treatment group was better and then reported this as their statistically significant result. The use of multiple endpoints seriously undermines the conclusions drawn on the basis of alleged correlation.

While the Harris study did not show any sign of blinding irregularities, it shared the use of multiple endpoints with the Byrd and Sicher studies. Unlike Byrd, whose results he was attempting to replicate, Harris used not 26 but 34 distinct health measures to compare the treatment and control groups, plus length of hospital stay, plus a third system of weighted scoring for a set of different health indicators—a system developed specifically at the hospital where the study was conducted. It was this third system of overall weighted scoring that generated an 11 percent superior score for the treatment group after the other measures—including length of hospital stay, which was listed as a pre-study test objective—individually failed to produce any significant difference. By multiplying its opportunities to hit on one or another source of significance, the study clearly committed the Multiple Endpoints fallacy; as one researcher observed in reply, the plurality of outcomes made the probability nearly 1 in 3 of randomly getting significance on at least one measure.[17]

Both the Byrd and Harris studies suffered additionally from the use of data measures that were not validated by the wider discipline. Harris's weighted scores, through which he derived his claimed statistical significance, represent a particularly dubious use of a numerical scale, of the sort we considered in Chapter 5. These scores were derived by noting the number of events for each patient, giving each event a score of 1 to 6 depending on its medical severity, and then adding up the total points for each patient. Death alone was worth 6, cardiac arrest alone worth 5, and a range of other interventions or problems worth 1 to 4 points each. Lower scores were taken to mean healthier patients (or perhaps a superior course of treatment in some other sense; the article is not clear on this definitional point!).

The problem with this sort of ranking, as we saw in Chapter 5, is that it presupposes that each Category 5 event can be meaningfully said to be five times worse than each Category 1 event. Yet the Harris article makes no mention of any rationale underlying this very strong assumption of a linear relation between the categories. What could it even mean to say that the need for a diuretic drug (Category 2) is half as difficult to prevent through prayer as the need for an intra-aortic balloon pump (Category 4)? Obscure data manipulations like this mean that the study's weighting of the data itself is an enormous red flag. Indeed, according to the weightings used by Harris, a patient who came into the cardiac care unit, suffered cardiac

In Chapter 4 we saw an example of a biased definition at work. The InnerChange Freedom Initiative, a private religiously oriented prison rehabilitation program, was studied to determine its effectiveness in reducing recidivism (re-offending) among criminals.

Based on information from the study's "executive summary," the study was represented as showing that InnerChange was effective in dramatically lowering rates of re-arrest and re-imprisonment. The second and third of the summary's ten points attributed a 17 percent re-arrest rate to IFI program graduates versus a 35 percent re-arrest rate to a control group during the two years after inmates were released from prison, with 8 percent of IFI graduates being re-imprisoned compared to 20 percent of the control.[18] Pretty impressive results! The program organizer was invited to a photo-op at the White House; the results were cited in favour of more publicly funded evangelical programs; and the mainstream press widely reported the program as a proven success.

Yet a closer look reveals the apparent success to be effectively a failure, because the fourth point of the summary notes that factoring in the inmates who began but did not complete the IFI program produces the re-arrest figures of 36 percent for IFI participants—again, versus 35 percent for the control. Since the definition of a program graduate included things like holding down a job and remaining drug-free for at least six months after release from prison, the success of the program for its *graduates* became nearly a matter of definition. But presumably what we were interested in was the success of the program at rehabilitating prisoners—that is, not whether convicts who do well after their release do better than convicts who do badly, but whether IFI helps convicts do well after their release, statistically speaking.

Hence the primary conclusions in such a study should be drawn from the **intention to treat group:** the ones to whom a treatment is initially applied. Whether some of those people get bored or turned off by the treatment along the way is, after all, relevant to whether the treatment is effective overall. If one is allowed to pare away the failures and only (or disproportionately) count the successes, of course one's treatment will almost certainly look like a success. But when we look overall at those who enrolled in the IFI program and those who did not, we see essentially no difference. By presenting these misleading comparisons as significant—worse, by presenting them first, as if they were the main lessons of the study—the authors confused the issue and contributed to a misinformed public discussion about prison reform programs.

arrest, and died right there would score 11 points. A patient who suffered cardiac arrest, was revived and given a permanent pacemaker, and then recovered from a bout of pneumonia after a course of antibiotics would have 12 points. In other words, dead people can quite easily be healthier than living patients, according to this scale! That seems like a good reason to doubt that a valid, responsible system is being used to represent and evaluate the data.

Another aspect of scientific "best practice" on the handling of data involves presenting more data than the most economical presentation of its conclusion might strictly require. Good science errs on the side of generosity in providing data and explanations to colleagues and evaluators. Working in this spirit, a researcher would perhaps leave outlying data-points out of the calculations, but would nevertheless provide those results and clearly explain the rationale behind their exclusion from the calculations. Ideally this sort of approach will result in conclusions that flow clearly and intelligibly from the data. And should there be weaknesses in the research, the scientific community more broadly will be better positioned to diagnose and resolve them, or to reject the conclusions if no resolution can be found, when the data are fully available and clearly represented.

It is a very serious problem when we discover methods used or data generated by the authors that are obviously relevant to interpreting the study yet that have been de-emphasized or hidden, especially when these would tend to weaken the force of the conclusion. Depending on the circumstances, this sort of discovery can easily vitiate the alleged results and bring the researchers' reliability still further into question. For example, the Sicher study didn't just commit a Multiple Endpoints fallacy; it was moreover worded in a way that clouded the issue. The paper noted that "an important intervening medical factor changed the endpoint in the study design," meaning that the study went from looking at death rates to looking at other things. This wording suggests that it was *during the design phase* of the study that this change was made. What actually happened was that new AIDS therapies cut the mortality rate to zero *while the study was in progress*, so the authors went looking at various outcomes after the data had been gathered, until they found significance in one set of them. A full description of this procedure would almost certainly have sunk the paper's chances of being published. So the wording of this passage appears crafted to disguise a serious problem—thus making it reasonable for us to hold everything in the paper up to greater scrutiny and to see it as less credible in general.

On the matter of hidden methods or data, here too we find red flags in each of the three studies currently under discussion. Not only did both the Byrd study and the Sicher study have double-blinding issues that any evaluator would *obviously* want to know about, but they also either left this information very implicit or left it out of the published version altogether—to the extent that something verging on detective work was required to reveal it.[19] The Harris study did not have this particular problem, but it did present its conclusions in a very strange way, choosing an interpretation of its own data that would predictably lead many casual readers (and a study claiming to validate prayer *is* going to have non-specialist readers) down a garden path.

After all, Harris intended his study as an attempt to replicate Byrd's result. Yet as his article notes, Harris's data did not show a statistically significant effect on *any* of the six indicators for which Byrd's study did. In fact, using Byrd's method of weighing the data, Harris's data didn't show statistical significance on *anything at all*. For every positive result claimed by Byrd, Harris drew a blank—neither Byrd's method nor his observed findings could be validated.[20] Yet the Harris article summarizes these results as "consistent with those of Byrd" as well as "findings [that] support Byrd's conclusions despite the fact that we could not document an effect of prayer using his scoring method."[21] Of course there may be suitably permissive interpretations of "consistent" and "Byrd's conclusions" to make these claims strictly true. But this wording seems an extravagant attempt to depict the two studies as essentially consonant evidence for a single phenomenon, rather than essentially unrelated evidence (of whatever independent credibility) for quite distinct phenomena. It is predictable that a reader skimming the article for comprehension would read Harris's wording as the claim that his study *more or less* confirmed Byrd's result, when the most natural understanding of the data is precisely the opposite.

Obfuscation, spin, and the minimizing or hiding of potential sources of bias are reasons to hold a scientific report in question, though a good deal depends on how these problems interact with others that may also be present—as is the nature of a syndrome, after all. While it may be relatively rare in its purest form, the attitude of erring on the side of generosity in providing information (described by physicist Richard Feynman as a kind of *bending over backward* approach) has been formalized and made conventional in many respects. For instance, researchers are now conventionally expected to include information about private or corporate sources of funding for their research. This makes it more than just one more fact that a researcher might decide to include or to omit, if she is doing research on the effects of cigarette smoke and has received funding from the tobacco industry. Part of being a responsible audience for scientific claims is being sensitive to and informed about the nature, extent, and significance of the range of confounding or biasing factors that can arise in science—and in particular, the significance of attempts on the part of a researcher to disguise those factors when they exist.

THEORETICAL UNITY

Good science tends to fit together fruitfully with other good science. A theory is implausible on its face when accepting it would require that we reject not only whatever other theory deals with the same specific phenomena, but a range of other highly confirmed theories as well. Hence data and theories from across our intellectual spectrum are always potentially relevant to one another's credibility; a serious failure to dovetail with what is more broadly known counts as a red flag for a theory.

On the plus side, when the predictions and explanations offered by a theory in one field or discipline turn out to correspond with those made by a theory in another field or discipline, at least one of the two theories (maybe both) becomes more highly confirmed as a result. The term "**consilience**" is sometimes used to indicate a similar phenomenon: the virtue of success for a theory or method in one domain when it was originally formulated to explain something else. For example, the discovery of the molecular structure of DNA, the famous "double-helix" model published by James Watson and Francis Crick in 1953, was intended in the first instance to explain data fairly specific to the question of biochemical structure: that the substance was a nucleic acid had been known since the nineteenth century, while much other information about DNA had been accumulating through techniques such as X-ray diffraction and some experiments involving different strains of disease-causing bacteria. It was this sort of data that Watson and Crick had to explain through their model. But once the model was proposed and tested, and seen as highly evidenced on its own grounds, its application to other domains added further warrant both to it and to the theories with which it interacted. There was no guarantee, for instance, that the model that satisfied the immediate explanatory demands of biochemistry upon DNA would also turn out to afford mechanisms for the occurrence, conservation, and spread of mutations, as predicted by evolutionary theory of common ancestry. Once the structure and operation of the DNA molecule were known, the hypothesized sorts of mutation from evolutionary theory could be evaluated, and new kinds of mutation could be observed to occur. That's not what the double-helix model was proposed for, but the fact that it broadened and deepened an independently warranted theory made both theories still more rationally justified.

Ideally our theories aren't fragmented stories about isolated bits of reality; the world itself fits together, and our explanations of the world may therefore fit together in a range of different ways. Conversely, when a claim or theory is in serious disharmony with a range of highly confirmed theories or more broadly in tension with what is known about how the world works, we are justified in taking a particularly close look at the theory or research to see whether everything was above-board. In particular, such a decision does not amount to the fallacy of moving goalposts, confirmation bias, or scientific pig-headedness, even though we may not automatically subject research *consistent* with highly confirmed theories to the same painstaking scrutiny. All we are doing is taking account of the evidence of our wider scientific knowledge, making it reasonable to expect some methodological problem that explains the alleged result in the research. Even should the research pass inspection, we are still justified in taking seriously the prospect of mere chance as an explanation.

As at least one researcher noted this about the Harris study: apart from all its other serious problems, the most it could claim was a 1 in 25 chance of getting that result purely by luck.[22] Considering the inherently low probability of prayer effects, given a highly confirmed picture of how the world works, this would make the chance hypothesis an entirely natural conclusion to take away from a single study. Imagine, for example, a poker game in which I need an ace on the last card to win. I have one ace, two others have already been dealt away, and there is one more among the (say) 25 cards left in the deck. Now I pray, "Odin, oh Odin, great god of the Norse, give me that ace or may fleas bite your horse!" And when the card is flipped, behold! It's the last ace. Is there any temptation whatever to explain this event by reference to my prayer? Divorced of the cultural familiarity of faith healing and mainstream religions, the appeal to the efficacy of prayer rather than to mere chance in a 1/25 probability situation is simply unconvincing.

Of course, if we keep doing a prayer experiment, and each repetition of it is methodologically sound so far as we can tell, and we keep getting a positive result, then our rational justification in treating the phenomenon as genuine must increase—irrespective of how it fits with our broader theories. But depending on how poor that fit is, our confidence in the reality of the effect may increase quite slowly, and our scrutiny for methodological impropriety—for shenanigans, in short—may justifiably be very sharp indeed. Certainly we have already seen that the prayer studies in question have flaws that would undermine the acceptance of *any* study that displayed them. Given that their particular conclusions are moreover so deeply at odds with what is known about how things interact in *all* the sciences, their methodological flaws take on a still greater significance.

PREDICTIVITY

A property closely related to falsifiability, predictivity is the virtue possessed by a scientific law, theory or hypothesis when it enables us to say specifically and accurately what will occur under the circumstances to which it is relevant. For example, Einstein's General Theory of Relativity predicts that light rays (from stars) passing near the sun will be deflected farther than Newtonian physics predicts, and repeated observations confirm this with great accuracy. Evolutionary theory and its associated accounts of phylogeny predict that the entire class of mammals will be absent from the fossil record of the Cambrian era and, more precisely, that mammalian fossils will not be found in the same layers of rock as, say, trilobite fossils; again, this is just what paleontologists observe (so far). Predictivity not only enables us to test theories and hypotheses, it lets us do something else that is crucial to the prestige and significance of modern science: *intervene*. The germ theory of disease doesn't simply let us *say* what will happen when a source of bacteria contacts an open wound; it lets us *make a difference*, or alter what would otherwise occur, by preventing germs from entering a wound, for example. A theoretical proposal that affords us no predictive power that we didn't already possess is an indicator of science done poorly.

This is a major problem for the prayer studies we have examined, since even by their own lights they offer no common predictions—at least, not at any useful level of specificity. The Byrd study concluded that prayers from intercessors self-identifying as "born-again" Christians reduced the occurrence of pneumonia and reduced the need for assisted breathing, but did not reduce the length of hospital stay. The Harris study concluded that Christian prayer from across the spectrum of sects (but nearly 90 percent women) improved a general weighted health measure, but did not reduce the need for assisted breathing and did not reduce the length of hospital stay. The Sicher study utilizing a wide range of prayers, shamanic healing rites, and psychic intercession showed no effect for pneumonia, but *did* reduce the length of hospital stay (though this claim was confounded by variations in medical insurance among the patients).[23] What predictions are afforded as a result? Not only are the results radically at odds with what is known about how the world works, but they seem too much at odds with one another to produce any sort of predictions or methods for intervening. In both the Byrd and Harris studies, intercessors were instructed to pray for the *rapid* or *speedy recovery* of patients; that is, to pray both for their recovery, and that the recovery be fast. Yet in both cases there was no measurable effect on either mortality rates or the speed with which survivors recovered. How are we to plan our intervention in light of these alleged phenomena? Should we intervene by asking people to pray for what we *don't* want to happen?

The only reasonable prediction available is that future prayer studies will at most show scattered hits of significance when large numbers of health indicators are measured, consistent with chance, multiple endpoints, and informationally porous experimental structures. But that's a prediction *about* the research program, not a prediction *made by* the research program.

SCIENTISM AND THE LIMITS OF SCIENCE

The many explanatory successes of various sciences over the past century and more justify a great confidence in the knowledge-building institutions and methods of science. Is it possible nevertheless to be too confident in the explanatory capacities of science? And does that confidence mean that we should also dismiss intellectual practices that are not, by some clear reckoning, scientific? Sometimes an excess of enthusiasm for the methods of science is called *scientism*.

I say "sometimes," because the term "scientism" can also be used simply to denote the methods or attitudes characteristic of science. It's a good word for that, because it means that someone who applies scientism (in this sense) is a scientist— just as someone who applies socialism is a socialist, someone who applies capitalism is a capitalist, and so forth. By contrast, the use of "scientism" to mean something bad like the misapplication of scientific methods is very confusing. What do we call someone guilty of scientism in this sense? A scientist? Plainly not. A scientismist? Yuck.

Anyhow, we have the word now and the best we can do is make good sense of it. But even within the pejorative sense, scientism is not very clearly defined. According to one definition, scientism is the belief that the methods of science are appropriate to every domain of inquiry and every aspect of the human experience, including such phenomena as art, love, morality, and others that might not immediately leap to mind when we think *science*. People often think that the excitement of really great music, or that delicious squushy feeling of being infatuated, or the utter wrongness of truly heinous crimes could never be expressed by some dry set of empirical laws and data. The suggestion that art or love or morality are open to scientific explanation therefore strikes such people as scientism.

This is not a very useful or interesting definition of scientism, though. In particular it doesn't seem to support the negative connotations associated with the term. While it might seem unusual to think of science as the primary means of addressing questions of art or love or ethics, the idea that science could turn out to be *relevant* to, and hence *appropriate* to, such questions is quite straightforward. The history of intellectual inquiry is largely the history of discovering surprising connections, so it just seems like good sense to leave open the prospect that empirical study, scientific methods, or insights from established domains of scientific inquiry will turn out to be relevant to even the least scientific-seeming topic. At a minimum, then, it is very difficult to think of what state of information could justify the conclusion that no science, current or yet to come, could be relevant to some domain of inquiry. As a matter of fact, scientific insights do influence how we think of issues in, for example, morality: questions regarding a person's responsibility for her actions very often require answers informed by scientific work in neurology and psychology.

So is *anything* scientism? It depends in part on what one will count as science. The more one's conception of science includes things like conceptual analysis, methodological discussion, an openness to criticism, and interdisciplinary thinking, the less inclined one will be to regard the idea that only *experimental science* generates knowledge as an over-application of science, properly speaking. That attitude will instead appear to be just a garden variety silly mistake, provincialism from someone with too narrow an understanding of science itself. As with words like "pseudoscience" or "supernaturalism," "scientism" is very often used only as a rhetorical bludgeon, a convenient alternative to explaining the specific problem with some claim or approach. Just as we've tried to replace the search for a definition of pseudo-science with an analysis of specific research problems that can arise singly or in groups, and to varying degrees, so we should look for specifics rather than labels when some claim about science strikes us as over-optimistic as well.

POSTSCRIPT: THE COLUMBIA UNIVERSITY IVF PRAYER STUDY

I will close this chapter merely by summarizing some salient facts about the IVF prayer study.[24] The assessment of these facts in light of the hallmarks of reliable science we have examined is the topic of Review Question 1.

1. The IVF pregnancy study had three authors. Dr. Rogerio Lobo of Columbia University was at first listed as the lead author (that is, the primary author). He told the media in September of 2001 that he had worked closely with the other authors in *designing* the study; a press release from Columbia University reiterated this message. Yet by December of that year Lobo asserted that he had become involved in the project only months after the study itself had been completed. He later withdrew his name from the paper altogether without explaining this discrepancy. The journal issued a short note stating that Lobo's name had appeared on the article "in error."

2. The second author, Dr. Kwang Cha, left Columbia University in the aftermath of the study's publication to work in private fertility clinics, also without public comment.

3. The third author, Daniel Wirth, turned out not to have any medical qualifications whatever (though he has a law degree and a master's degree in "parapsychology").

4. In 2004 Wirth was indicted on over twenty-five counts of fraud and subsequently imprisoned; the FBI also uncovered false identities that Wirth had employed over the years.

5. Wirth was in charge of many of the practical arrangements for blinding and data gathering in the study.

6. The published study makes a point of claiming that the authors expected prayer *not* to be an effective means of increasing the likelihood of pregnancy. Yet Daniel Wirth had by that point authored or co-authored popular articles claiming the effectiveness of faith healing and paranormal phenomena in various magazines and alternative journals.

7. When the study was published, Rogerio Lobo was a member of the editorial board of the *Journal of Reproductive Medicine*, the journal in which the study appeared.

8. The treatment or intervention employed by the study was as follows: women in the treatment group were directly prayed for by four blocks of mutually acquainted intercessors in one tier, while those first-tier intercessors themselves were directly prayed for by other intercessors in a second tier. The second-tier intercessors also prayed non-specifically for God's will to be done with respect to the patients. A third tier of three people prayed non-specifically for God's will to be done with respect to the members of the first and second tiers.

9. The randomization and transmission of data were attributed to two independent statisticians, one in South Korea and one in the United States, who were never identified by name despite the subsequent controversy.

10. The *Journal of Reproductive Medicine* refused to answer inquiries about the paper and the process by which it was published. It also refused to publish letters to the editor that criticized the study. In 2004 the journal published Kwang Cha's reply to criticisms, without having published the criticisms themselves.

11. In 2005 the journal published one letter critical of the study.

12. In May 2004, when news of Daniel Wirth's arrest received coverage in some media outlets, the *Journal of Reproductive Medicine* removed the IVF prayer study from its website. In November of that year, it returned the study to the website.

CONCLUSION

Science is a way of using the contents of our best intellectual toolkit as the situation requires, in order to detect, categorize, and explain phenomena of all sorts. These tasks are relentlessly subject to biases and errors of all sorts and at all levels, which the methods and traditions of science are intended to filter out, and to correct when they occur. It is counterproductive and probably inaccurate to think of science (or even *good* science) as an all-or-nothing thing. The reasonable evaluation of information that is given to us as scientific depends instead upon a wide range of factors, including its consonance with a loose set of hallmarks of reliable science. Fruitful and reliable science may well fail on one or more of these hallmarks to some degree, but serious failures, or failures on multiple fronts, destroy the credibility of the purported result. Science is a broad endeavour that is distributed over time; no single result compels our trust, though the broad trends shown by well-conducted research do. By seeing how some scientific research fails to be credible, we can recognize similar failings in other cases—and recognize credible research by contrast.

REVIEW QUESTIONS

1. Compare each point in the summary of the IVF prayer study with the hallmarks of reliable science. Identify the three most important points for the purposes of understanding and reasoning critically about the study, briefly justifying your choices.

2. Write one or two paragraphs defending a view on whether the *Journal of Reproductive Medicine* should have left the IVF study off its website.

3. Find and document three examples of published newspaper or magazine articles (from any time and any place) that cite the Byrd study without citing the known problems with it. Expanding your search to Internet sites, see how many sites you can find that *favourably* cite all four problematic prayer studies analyzed in this chapter.

NOTES

1. K. Y. Cha, D. Wirth, and R. Lobo, "Does Prayer Influence the Success of In Vitro Fertilization-Embryo Transfer: Report of a Masked, Randomized Trial," *Journal of Reproductive Medicine* 46 (2001): 781–87. Dr. Lobo was initially described as the lead author of this article. He has since withdrawn his name from it.

2. R. Byrd, "Positive Therapeutic Effects of Intercessory Prayer in a Coronary Care Unit Population," *Southern Medical Journal* 81, no. 7 (1988): 826–29.

3. W. Harris, M. Gowda, J. Kolb, C. Strychacz, J. Vacek, P. Jones, A. Forker, J. O'Keefe, and B. McCallister, "A Randomized, Controlled Trial of the Effects of Remote, Intercessory Prayer on Outcomes in Patients Admitted to the Coronary Care Unit," *Archives of Internal Medicine* 159 (1999): 2273–78.

4. F. Sicher, E. Targ, D. Moore, II, and H. Smith, "A Randomized Double-Blind Study of the Effect of Distance Healing in a Population with Advanced AIDS," *Western Journal of Medicine* 169 (1998): 356–63.

5. K. Popper, "Science—Conjectures and Refutations" in *Conjectures and Refutations— The Growth of Scientific Knowledge*, ed. K. Popper, 33–65 (New York: Harper and Row, 1965).

6. Popper, "Science—Conjectures and Refutations."

7. H. Benson, J. Dusek, J. Sherwood, P. Lam, C. Bethea, W. Carpenter, S. Levitsky, P. Hill, D. Clem, M. Jain, D. Drumel, S. Kopecky, P. Mueller, D. Marek, S. Rollins, and P. Hibberd, "Study of the Therapeutic Effects of Intercessory Prayer (STEP) in Cardiac Bypass Patients: A Multicentre Randomized Trial of Uncertainty and Certainty of Receiving Intercessory Prayer," *American Heart Journal* 151, no. 4 (2006): 934–42.

8. T. Chalmers, "Effects of Ascorbic Acid on the Common Cold: An Evaluation of the Evidence," *American Journal of Medicine* 58, no. 4 (1975): 532–36.

9. R. Rosenthal and L. Jacobson, *Pygmalion in the Classroom* (New York: Holt, Rinehart & Winston, 1968).

10. I. Tessman and J. Tessman, "Efficacy of Prayer: A Critical Examination of Claims," *Skeptical Inquirer* 24, no. 2 (2000): 31–33.

11. P. Bronson, "A Prayer Before Dying," *Wired* 10, no. 12 (2002): 174–79, 221–23. Po Bronson wrote an investigative article that explored the Sicher 1998 study, the pilot study that preceded it, and the tragic circumstances of the death of Elisabeth Targ, Sicher's co-author, from a brain tumour.

12. G. Posner, "God in the CCU?" *Free Inquiry* 10, no. 2 (1990): 44–45.

13. J. Mercola, Comment on L. Dossey's "Prayer and Medical Science: A Commentary on the Prayer Study by Harris et al and a Response to Critics." http://www.mercola.com/article/prayer/dossey.htm. Accessed February 9, 2006.

14. Posner, "God in the CCU?"

15. Rosenthal and Jacobson, *Pygmalion in the Classroom*.

16. Bronson, "A Prayer Before Dying."

17. W. Van der Does, "A Randomized, Controlled Trial of Prayer?" *Archives of Internal Medicine* 160 (2000): 1871–72.

18. B. Johnson and D. Larson, "The InnerChange Freedom Initiative: A Preliminary Evaluation of a Faith-Based Prison Program." Report from the Center for Research on Religion and Urban Civil Society, University of Pennsylvania. Available at ccrucs.org.

19. Tessman and Tessman, "Efficacy of Prayer: A Critical Examination of Claims," and Bronson, "A Prayer Before Dying."

20. B. Bolton, "Intercessory Prayer," *Annals of Internal Medicine* 135, no. 12 (2001): 1094.

21. Harris et al., "A Randomized, Controlled Trial of the Effects of Remote, Intercessory Prayer on Outcomes in Patients Admitted to the Coronary Care Unit."

22. D. Sandweiss, "*P* Value out of Control," *Archives of Internal Medicine* 160 (2000): 1872.

23. Bronson, "A Prayer Before Dying."

24. B. Flamm, "The Columbia University 'Miracle' Study: Flawed and Fraud," *Skeptical Inquirer* 28, no. 5 (2004): 25–31; and B. Flamm, "The Bizarre Columbia University 'Miracle' Saga Continues," *Skeptical Inquirer* 29, no. 2 (2005): 52–53. Dr. Bruce Flamm was the earliest and most persistent critic of the IVF prayer study, investigating the circumstances of its publication and pressing the *Journal of Reproductive Medicine* and Columbia University for an explanation of their conduct.

CHAPTER 10

The Mainstream Media as a Source of Information

In February 2001, the city of Edmonton, Alberta, witnessed an awful and wonderful set of events. A thirteen-month-old toddler wearing only her pyjamas wandered out of her house into a −20°C night, where she succumbed to hypothermia and fell unconscious into a snow drift. Perhaps as much as several hours later, her mother awoke and noticed her daughter was missing. She found the little girl in the backyard. The toddler was frozen stiff when the paramedics arrived.

But a miracle happened. A greater power, something or someone, was on the baby's side. Before she could be placed on a sophisticated heart and lung machine intended to warm her up, her heart simply started beating again, on its own.

This was a major national news story in Canada for days, eventually making the international news as well. Each of the claims mentioned above in italics surfaced widely in the media reporting on the story, feeding its popularity. The problem is that each of these claims is either false or exaggerated. The real events had been levelled and sharpened, creating an aura of mystery.

The attending pediatrician at the hospital was especially widely quoted by the press, for his assessment that the recovery was a miracle, that a higher power was responsible, and that "sometimes it takes something beyond just the personnel and the equipment." These are themes that appeal to the love of the mysterious and the unknown in many of us, but the reality was quite different. The baby's heart did not start beating "on its own" in the hospital, as stories from Canada to China had it. It was precisely "the personnel and the equipment" that were the real story and the real heroes.

First, there were four emergency medical technicians who attended the little girl in her own house, two teams that arrived in quick succession. The baby was given cardio-pulmonary resuscitation from the moment they arrived until the moment her heart restarted in the hospital. The paramedics also injected her with medicine designed to revive her. They warmed her in the ambulance itself and inserted a breathingtube into her airway.

At the hospital, the baby was wrapped in a special warming blanket that blows hot air onto the patient. She was then transported to the room where the heart and lung machine was warming up, with a nurse actually kneeling astride her body and continuing the CPR treatment nonstop.

Then her heart started beating again.

Now, what's true is that this is an uplifting and surprising story of an innocent life saved from what looked like certain tragic death. But what seems the exact opposite of true—*false* is the word I'm looking for, really—is each of the following:

- The girl's heart started beating on its own.

- Her recovery is not explained by the actions of the personnel and the equipment they used.

- Her revival was an inexplicable miracle.

We rely on television, radio, newspapers, and magazines for a vast amount of our information about our world. I will refer to the most popular and influential of the broadcasters and publishers in each of these categories, in both Canada and the United States, by the usefully vague term *the mainstream media*. Much of the mainstream media accessible in Canada, especially broadcast media, originates in the United States, and for critical thinking purposes most observations about either nation's home-grown media are true to some degree of the other's. So it makes sense to extend the discussion to the American media as well. While I will focus on the Canadian case, the extent of American media consumption in Canada means that concerns about the content and methods of American information media are automatically critical thinking issues for readers and viewers in Canada as well.

I should also note, for those inclined to care, that I'll sometimes use the term "media" as a singular mass noun. This is strictly improper both grammatically, because "media" is a plural form, and conceptually, because it suggests that the mainstream media is some unified, undifferentiated whole, when this is no more than very approximately true. On both counts I offer the virtues of convenient expression as my excuse.

The mainstream news media is primarily what informs us about events at all levels, from the local to the national to the international, and on a vast range of special interests, from business news to sports to politics to science. This makes the question of its reliability quite pressing. We've examined in considerable detail how to reason well with the information at our disposal, but for obvious reasons this can all be rendered moot if we receive systematically mistaken or incomplete information. The strictest adherence to valid forms of argument is little use if we have no reliable premises to plug into them. GIGO, as a computer programming acronym has it: Garbage In, Garbage Out.

What makes the above example a useful cautionary tale about interpreting the mainstream media is not that it was a nationally significant story nor that it involved some intent to deceive the public. Quite the opposite. The story was short-lived, and the inaccuracies cannot reasonably be explained as deliberate deceptions. That, in fact, is the lesson. Inaccuracies in key details occur in garden-variety reports and need not result from any explicit bias or anything as grand as an implicit world-view on the part of the reporter. The factors that can introduce misleading details into a story and filter important details out are for the most part mundane institutional factors of various sorts. The fact that something is reported, or for that matter the fact that something is not reported, is insufficient information for judging its credibility, in the absence of informed critical reasoning about the story and media presenting it. This chapter notes the kinds of factors relevant to our judgments of story credibility.

So why were the exaggerated claims communicated in this example, in some cases at the expense of the actual details? A few factors may have been working together.

For one thing, the mistaken or exaggerated aspects of the story made it simpler. A good lead story has a "hook" that can be expressed in a headline, in the large-print caption for the front-page photograph, and in the story itself. It was a miracle; there's no explanation; a greater power was on her side—the framework of the story is straightforward. By contrast, a story that hinges upon the cumulative and complex efforts of many people may be harder to express briefly.

The element of mystery also lends appeal to the story. As discussed in Chapter 8, the inexplicable often gives us a thrill and makes for good casual conversation. Not only is the real story hard to express in a headline or photo caption, it's less effective at appealing to our sense of things unseen, of deep and unknown forces at work. The reporters working the story seem to have gone out of their way to emphasize this aspect of it. The day after the toddler's revival, as it became clear that she had suffered little or no brain damage, her doctor made a telling remark in a televised interview. "This," he said, "is the miracle story you guys were looking for twenty-four hours ago."[1] The doctor apparently perceived that the reporters were making a specific effort to get quotes or descriptions of the events framed in terms of the miraculous or the magical—presumably because this gloss on the story would spice it up. The more accurate version is less emotionally gripping; in our stories we prefer either mystery or solitary heroes to committees and collaboration.

Another factor is likely to have been inertia. The first stories that broke quoted the doctor and presented the events in the levelled and sharpened ways already mentioned. It is a quite common practice for follow-up stories or reports from other sources to use the initial reports at least as a guide to the basic facts—that is, as a basis for further independent investigation. So the focus of the first reports on some event can play an important role in determining the shape of subsequent coverage.

The main purpose behind these observations is to emphasize the range of factors that can explain the content and slant of stories that appear in the mainstream commercial news media. A commitment to presenting relevant truths about events on the part of the media itself is but one of the reasons that stories appear in newspapers, on television, and on radio. As with cognitive and perceptual biases, understanding how factors other than the truth or relevance of a report can explain its appearing enables us to judge whether such factors are likely to be at work in a given context. In this way we can tailor our confidence or caution about news reports in a way appropriate to the situation. This certainly does not mean a blanket rejection of all that is seen or read, though. After all, the more accurate information summarized above *also* came from various print and broadcast media reports. If the initial lesson is that news media can have a positive preference for misleading stories, a second key lesson is that more balanced information is often there to be had as well, as long as one is prepared to read the follow-up reports and sample widely from the media outlets covering any particular story.

CONTENT, SPIN, AND EVIDENCE

Some of the most important lessons for readers and viewers of news media can be applied directly from material we have already covered. For among the main questions that arise when we try to extract reliable information from a reported story are *What is being claimed?*, *How is it being presented?*, and *What evidence is available for these claims and this way of framing them?* Answering the first question depends on understanding how much information can be asserted or presupposed by just one apparently simple sentence, as discussed in Chapter 3. A single word or a brief clause in some statement from a journalist or newsreader can have important ramifications for the overall content of the report, actually changing the informational content of the statement. Choices about which words to use, the word order, and other forms of emphasis can also have powerful framing effects of the kind discussed in Chapter 7. In both respects, the task of extracting reliable information from the media requires that we take note of these assertions and insinuations, and habitually ask ourselves whether the report provides evidence for them.

Suppose, for example, that the Saskatchewan Widget Company is publicly accusing Manitoba Gadget International of industrial espionage, and this is being reported in the Business segment of a national news program. Both of the following newsreader "lead-ins" to the story would seem fairly normal:

> (1) In other news, the questions continue today for Manitoba Gadget International, as the company fends off allegations of industrial espionage from the Saskatchewan Widget Company. . . .

> (2) In other news, the Saskatchewan Widget Company today continues its attack on Manitoba Gadget International for alleged industrial espionage. . . .

Both lead-ins serve to introduce the story well enough and communicate roughly the same information. But (1), on reflection, insinuates that Manitoba Gadget International is on the defensive, making it seem that "the questions" are embarrassing or difficult. The wording of (2), though, emphasizes the aggressiveness of the Saskatchewan Widget Company, giving some intimation that the company is acting in a hostile manner.

These rhetorical effects can be quite subtle or astonishingly unsubtle. For example, the front-page headline of the *Globe and Mail* on August 8, 2001, read, "77% Oppose Neutering National Anthem." The article reported a national poll on changing the Canadian national anthem, which currently makes specific reference to male citizens ("in all thy sons") and no reference to female citizens. Deliberate or not, the use of the word "neutering"—as a transitive verb, it means to castrate—rather

ANOTHER EXAMPLE

Deliberately spicing up a story or obfuscating through innumeracy? In January 2006, a *Toronto Star* editorial commented on Conservative Party leader Stephen Harper's election platform. "Clearly," the editorial explained, "voters like the sound of Harper's promise of a big, 29 per cent cut in the goods and services tax."[2] This statement may have well puzzled someone under the impression that the GST was then only 7 percent! In fact Harper's platform proposed cutting the tax down to 5 percent. Since 5 is around 71 percent of 7, the claim is technically accurate. But it obscures more than it educates, a bit of spin seemingly performed only to make the statement more striking.

than, say, "changing," puts a strongly negative spin on the proposal, over and above just reporting on the poll. This is a framing effect, of the sort described in Chapter 8. It has a rhetorical force that can constitute a message in itself, one that a critical reader or viewer must weigh against the evidence on offer in the report itself, and one that can be relevant to how we evaluate the literal information that is presented. Any reasonable worry about spin contributes to a reasonable worry about the completeness and accuracy of a story's factual contents as well. In short: if they're going out of their way to *spin* the content, it's reasonable to worry that the information itself has been selectively culled or distorted.

On the question of factual content, our earlier observations about the surprising complexity of apparently simple claims is particularly important when we evaluate media reports. For example, the following statement (call it [S]) is not unusual for contemporary journalism. (It is not, to my knowledge, an actual quote.)

> (S) In a bid to reverse the downward trend in his popularity, the prime minister has proposed sweeping new tax-reform legislation.

Statements of this sort can occur in news articles, as opposed to explicitly editorial pieces; at a quick reading (S) looks like a simple report of some fact, with little or no guesswork or leaps of logic. Actually, it encodes or entails a surprising number of separate claims, which vary quite dramatically in the probability one might reasonably assign to them. In reading (S), you are really being told several things. I place these propositions in a rough and ready order of decreasing reliability.

1. The prime minister has proposed legislation.
2. The legislation is about tax reform.
3. The legislation is new.
4. The legislation is sweeping.
5. There is a downward trend in the prime minister's popularity.
6. The Prime Minister's intent in proposing the legislation is to reverse a downward trend in his popularity.

It might seem that (1), at least, is entirely reliable, on the grounds that only truly catastrophic incompetence or an outright intent to lie could explain the reporter's presenting (S) if (1) were false. However, it is one thing to say that (1) is very likely not false, and another thing to say just what its truth amounts to. Sentence (1) may appear a fairly simple statement of fact, but it contains at least one imprecise term in "proposed." This could mean anything from "publicly mused about" to "formally presented in Parliament." Claim (2) might also come across as inherently reliable, but it implicates at least some reporter expertise in the details of legislation. It's possible to mischaracterize legislation primarily about one issue as being primarily about an issue on which it bears indirectly. Measures to protect the environment can be implemented by levying taxes on polluting technologies, for instance, and one might mistake the point of the legislation to be revenue generation rather than environment protection. So deciding whether (2) should be accepted at face value requires knowing something about the reporter's background and political knowledge.

Other claims are like (1) in being reasonable only to the extent that they are imprecise and hence easily satisfied in some sense or other: each of (3), (4), and (5) hinges on a vague judgment call about what makes for novelty, sweepingness, and a trend, respectively. If similar legislation was passed previously and is extended by the current proposal, does it count as new? Is legislation sweeping if its focus is narrow, but its foreseeable consequences are wide? How narrow, and how wide? And of course we've seen just how dubious claims about trends can be. These three claims really aren't saying much of anything, at the end of the day.

The least reasonable aspect of (S), however, is expressed in (6). The line between reporting and analysis may be fuzzy, but a critical reading of media reports requires distinguishing statements that attempt to report events from statements that are *clearly* the writer's inferences from events. One of the more common unreliable inferences to be presented as fact is just this sort of mind-reading: the writer of (S) is purporting to describe not just the prime minister's actions, but his *motives*. Unless these motives are somehow well-evidenced, however, such attributions have little or no credibility. They are also likely opportunities for value judgments to find their way into a story, since the motives a writer assigns to one of the people discussed can make the person's actions seem inherently noble or cynical, wise or unwise, honest or dishonest. The assignment of motives in (S), for example, connotes a degree of cynicism.

For each of (1) to (6), then, a careful reading will search for grounds to think the claim plausible. A casual reading of (S) may altogether miss just how many, how strong, and how freighted the claims are that it implicitly presents. Often a casual reading is all that is wanted, but it is important to understanding how to read (or listen, or view) more carefully, when the situation warrants. And, of course, with practice a somewhat more careful reading can become second nature.

Real-life examples are not hard to find, either. Political journalist Tim Harper, writing for the *Toronto Star,* reported in December 2004 on the United States military's *stop-loss* or "backdoor draft" plan for personnel involved in the occupation of Iraq. "Many believe the program, which allows the Pentagon to extend voluntary deployments in time of war or national emergency, is the single most morale-damaging program in place," Harper wrote in one passage.[3]

While claims of this sort are very common in reporting, the claim is at once unhelpfully vague and puzzlingly specific. The context here doesn't give us much

FURTHER REFLECTION

Recall from Chapter 3 that the term "many" can be a weasel word. Usually we use contextual cues to help us understand roughly how many are meant by "many" in an utterance—the number of people required to make it correct to say, "Many people have sunstroke" is very different, depending on whether I am understood to be talking about all the people in a swimming pool or all the people in the world. In the former case, eight sunstroke victims would make it true, while in the latter case eight sunstroke victims would make it false.

information to work with. Many of *who* believe that the stop-loss plan is the single most morale-damaging program? Citizens in general? Politicians? Military specialists? Without this information, there's no way even to assess how many would be *many*, still less whether the claim is actually correct when adjusted to that context. There's no suggestion in the report that a poll was conducted on the matter. Speaking in practical terms, how many people does a reporter have to hear espousing a view, before he or she can write that *many* people hold the view? Two? Fifty?

Equally important is the specificity of the view being attributed to the many people in question. How explicitly do they hold that the stop-loss policy is the *single* most damaging program, rather than, say, one demoralizing policy among several? Around the time this article was written there were also reports of serious ongoing problems in the supply of body armour and properly armoured vehicles to American soldiers stationed in Iraq. If any steps were taken to measure and compare beliefs about the morale-damage arising from this problem with beliefs about the morale-damage arising from stop-loss, the report makes no mention of them. So what warrants the journalist's specific claim here?

An instructive remark is found just one paragraph later in the same article. Harper continued, "Republican Senator John McCain . . . this week called the stop-loss program the single most damaging morale issue for the military . . . " Although the senator did say some similar things prior to Harper's article, neither the phrase "the single most damaging" nor its strict meaning traces directly to Senator McCain, as far as I can discover. But the form of words does seem unmistakably shared between Harper's two remarks in the same article. One possible explanation is that the second occurrence is the writer's interpretation of the senator's remarks, while the first occurrence transforms that interpretation into an opinion shared by "many." On what grounds is, again, not clear.

Now, we're talking about one or two sentences in a whole article. Am I just being too picky, too literal? Maybe in some contexts this sort of careful analysis would be unnecessary. The point of the example, though, is to illustrate how even quite common journalistic statements can encode claims that not only lack evidence within the report, but would be very difficult to properly warrant under any circumstances. It's precisely because a statement like this one seems so typical and innocuous that its message is easily internalized. When we read a claim like this in a publication assigned some degree of authority or reliability, in other words, it makes a difference to how we think. Examples like this one are useful for showing the sort of habitual questioning required to separate the often interwoven warranted and unwarranted claims presented in the mainstream media.

PSEUDO-NEWS

It may be tempting to categorize a great deal of mainstream news providers as pseudo-news. But we should reserve the term for cases in which mainstream media blurs the line between explicitly non-news items, such as advertising, and "genuine" news, even if the latter is often superficial or poorly reported. A phenomenon worth monitoring is the increasingly common insertion of advertising features in newspapers or newscasts that are deliberately produced to resemble the news sections themselves—perhaps having the news anchor serving as a product spokesperson or having the advertising copy printed in the same font and column design as the newspaper.

Sometimes the entire information source itself is a pseudo-news outlet, devoted to advocacy for some particular viewpoint or cause, but adopting some visible features of an objective news source. A website simply called "thenewspaper.com" turns out to be "a journal of the politics of driving" with an emphasis on claimed injustices of traffic law enforcement. One story on the website explains how a driver in Scotland was ticketed and had his licence suspended merely "for the crime of showing disrespect to a mobile speed camera van."[4] According to the website, "Police became enraged when they noticed he had given the camera a 'V-sign'," a gesture considered rude or obscene in British culture. A more careful look at the story, however, reveals that in fact the camera caught the driver making *two* V-signs at the same time—one with each hand. As it would for any driver who lacked a third hand, this manoeuvre left the driver with a total of zero hands remaining on the steering wheel, while he leaned over into the middle of the car and glared across at the traffic camera. So was the charge of dangerous driving really "for the crime of showing disrespect"? An important first step in the evaluation of any report packaging itself as a news story is confirming that it originates from a source having at least a basic claim to describe itself as a news source; a second step is to begin following up on red flags, such as the vague and editorializing phrase "the crime of showing disrespect."

THE NEWS AS A BUSINESS

Many news organizations worldwide, and virtually all of the major ones in North America, have one thing in common: they are owned by corporations. With the exception of public broadcasting institutions, news sources normally are in the business of business. Their fundamental business mandate is profit.

In this respect the motivations of the media corporations themselves, if it makes sense to think of corporations as having motives, may diverge sharply from the motivations of the personnel they employ. Whatever other commitments these organizations may have—to truth, integrity, or objectivity—the pressure to maximize profits

"The news is what fills up the space between the ads."

—Anonymous

is an inescapable constraint. Indeed, the corporations may even have a legal obliga-tion to their shareholders to pursue the greatest possible profit as their overarching goal. Naturally there are two main ways of doing this: by minimizing expenses, and by maximizing revenues. Both approaches raise critical thinking issues when it comes to treating commercial media outlets as information sources.

REDUCING COSTS AND PROTECTING REVENUES

A way to reduce expenses in media businesses, as elsewhere, is to employ as few full-time journalistic staff as possible or to pay them as little as possible. The need to have a sufficiently good "product" may set lower bounds on how few staff there are, but there are ways around that problem, from the corporation's perspective. A means of filling white space or air time, cheaper than spending time and money on internally researched stories, is to run reports that are mass-produced via "the wire"—large press consortiums—along with ready-made articles in the form of poll results and modified press releases. While this minimizes costs, it also tends to reduce the diversity of investigations and perspectives in the media as a whole. (In effect it gives rise to a large-scale problem of *pseudo-independent confirmation,* dis-cussed elsewhere in the book.) Not only do many distinct news outlets across the country end up running substantially the same report even on familiar issues, but when new or unfamiliar issues become newsworthy, these outlets may lack the per-sonnel to investigate them thoroughly. The result is a tendency toward fewer avenues of independent inquiry and a smaller range of perspectives, even though the number of media outlets may be quite large.

Similarly the protection and maximization of profits can have a powerful effect on the kinds of information made available via the mainstream media. For business reasons, these news sources must avoid acting in ways that would seriously disrupt their sources of revenue. This amounts to a strong motive not to scandalize public, private, or government groups that could pressure advertisers to withdraw spon-sorship. A related pressure is that of avoiding stories or opinion pieces that could alienate advertisers on "image" grounds.

In the most straightforward cases of advertiser influence over media content, the sponsors may demand "complimentary copy," stories that directly promote the products in question. Much more common is the sponsors' simply having a vested interest, quite reasonably from their perspective, in the topics and tone of the cov-erage matching that of the advertisements located near it—spatial proximity for newspapers, temporal proximity for broadcast media. For example, graphic images of those killed or wounded on either side of a war are almost never shown in major news outlets, in part because they might violate the standards of regulatory agen-cies, but also because few advertisers would accept the negative associations. Who wants their product to be advertised on the page facing a photograph of bombing victims? Yet the information conveyed by such unhappy images or graphic descriptions might be relevant to our opinions about the events, were we exposed to it.

In short, there are several ways in which the need to keep advertisers can influence what we learn from the media, often in systematic ways that apply across the mainstream news outlets. Critical thinking about the media requires an awareness how this might be happening at any given time, regarding any given story. Checking the mainstream media against foreign and alternative sources is one useful way of monitoring for these effects. Equally important, though, is developing the habit of checking for indirect evidence that reporting and advertising are converging in their perspective and content.

"INFOTAINMENT" AND THE SELECTION OF STORIES

In an effort to increase viewership, many news outlets and programs introduce a greater emphasis on blending—perhaps debasing—the presentation of news or other information with aspects of pure entertainment. This phenomenon is by no means new. Newscasts and newspapers have long included stories on quirky or funny events in order to broaden their appeal and perhaps to lighten the tone. But traditionally these stories were flagged as distinct from the real news, by some means or other. ("And now, on the lighter side of the news. . . . ") There is a worry that infotainment is becoming almost inescapable and is being felt not only in the presentation of the news—short and superficial reports focusing on flashy graphics and sexy newscasters—but also in the selection of the stories themselves.

For example, on November 2, 2004, the United States held a presidential election. At issue were some matters of great national and international significance, including the erstwhile administration's policies on terrorism, an enormous domestic fiscal deficit, and especially, the motives for and conduct of the invasion of Iraq in 2002. According to the LexisNexis media archive, in the ten days following the election there were 160 stories in major newspapers having either headlines or lead paragraphs that mentioned Vice-President Dick Cheney, whose administration won a second term in the election. Over the same time period, and in the same set of newspapers, there were 159 stories the headlines or lead paragraphs of which made reference to the trial of Scott Peterson, a California man accused (and found guilty) of murdering his pregnant wife.

The Peterson case was a classic example of the manufactured story: while it obviously had a horrible significance for the family and friends of both the victim and the convicted killer, it had no national significance—only a useful commercial appeal based partly on its being presentable as a sort of real-life soap opera. Indeed, it seems to be a recurring phenomenon for the major news media to converge on one particular story of this sort and elevate it to the status of headline news. (The usual storyline involves a young, pretty, white woman who goes missing or is murdered; rarely do stories about missing elderly people, non-white people, or men of any description make this sudden jump to international celebrity case.) The major news networks not only devoted more broadcast time to the Peterson case than to many issues of national or international importance, in some respects they researched the story more thoroughly as well. The timeline of events, the personal histories of the main actors, the details of extramarital affairs, discussion of jurors' dispositions, legal analyses of possible trial outcomes—all were elaborated at considerable length. Indeed, if I may be forgiven an anecdote for a particularly vivid example, I recently witnessed a conversation in which someone, a Canadian, recalled her loss of respect for a cable television legal specialist, saying, "I remember watching during the Peterson trial, when [the show's host] kept saying her theory that on December 20, when Laci had her ultrasound, maybe Scott saw the baby's image and flew into a rage. But I knew Laci didn't have an ultrasound that day. It made me so angry, how she kept saying it!" The speaker of this remark was someone who had earlier, independently, remarked that she wasn't completely certain who currently the prime minister of Canada was! Certainly in fall 2004 it was not always clear that the American election campaign received a comparable depth of analysis to that devoted to the Peterson trial on the major cable news channels. Viewers could watch a good deal of coverage of the campaign without becoming particularly informed nor having their horizons broadened about the candidates and the issues.

A related phenomenon to monitor when consulting the media for news and opinions is that of systematic oversimplification. This may be due to the interaction of several factors, including the increased time and costs required for in-depth analysis, the lack of informedness and subtlety from the presenters themselves, and, not least, the tendency for highly simplified reporting to get better ratings—or at least no worse ratings.

Oversimplification in the media takes the same forms it takes more generally: speaking in platitudes and clichés, or substituting slogans for explanations. But more systematic issues emerge in the form of reporting *templates*: conventions or master narratives for stories of various kinds, on which accepted conventions serve as the framework around which the stories are constructed. For example, Canadian political reporting is sometimes built around an interpretive template on which Conservative Party politicians are fiscally responsible but socially uncaring; the New Democrats are socially caring but fiscally irresponsible; and the Liberals are somewhere in the middle on both counts. This set of conventions makes it easy to fit speeches, quotes, policies, and platforms into tidy news stories. Whether it has much to do with reality, however, is far from clear. The existence of such assumptions ought to raise a red flag about possible confirmation biases on more or less an ongoing basis in the political reportage of the Canadian media. They make it likely and perhaps inevitable that cases of fiscally irresponsible Conservative governments, socially conscientious Conservative politicians, fiscally responsible New Democrat governments, socially regressive New Democrat politicians, and extremist Liberals of one sort or another, will be underreported in the news and ignored in analysis, simply because they have no neat place in the simplified template for stories and editorials. Critical thinking about the information gleaned from the media places a burden on the reader or viewer to recategorize the data presented there, with an eye to cogent explanation rather than speed and simplicity—the canons that may have dictated its original presentation.

OTHER BIASING EFFECTS OF COMMERCIAL ORIENTATION

The commercial appeal of a "feel-good factor" can contribute to systematic biases in the reporting of certain events or phenomena. Public lotteries are a pretty clear example. Local media frequently report on local winners of the lottery; if the prize is large enough, the story may be reported nationally. These reports effectively function as advertisements for the lottery. By contrast, it is rare indeed for the mainstream media to report on people spending their food money on the lottery and losing it. But most people must lose, in order to provide the large payout for the winner, plus the percentage typically donated to charities and the profit for the company administering the lottery. Many people watching local news to learn the lottery numbers presumably don't want to see a depressing story every week about economically vulnerable people wasting their money on public gambling in the desperate hope of striking it rich. So although there are many more losers than big winners in the lottery, the big winners are reported while the losers are not. This illustrates how the media's representation of an event or phenomenon, formulated with the aim of securing a viewership or readership rather than accurately depicting relevant outcomes, can systematically misrepresent situations. Nobody needs to specifically intend the misrepresentation in order for it to occur.

Similar remarks may apply during times of war, when one compares the coverage of soldiers returning home alive and well with the coverage of those returning wounded or dead. Again, the better sales potential of some sorts of "feel good" stories can skew entire trends of information delivery, as can the commercial appeal of doom and gloom in other social contexts. Often the commercial appeal consists more in conforming to the viewer's preconceptions than in any particular level of optimism or pessimism. People may find it reassuring to see news that confirms their strongly held opinions; this is a form of confirmation bias discussed in Chapter 7. Since there can be major differences of opinion within a population, there can be distinct market niches for media outlets that emphasize different stories or different aspects of the same stories. Unfortunately, this gives rise to a kind of paradox: the existence of a more diverse range of media outlets with different perspectives may result in people individually getting a *less* diverse range of media perspectives. It might just result in more people having access to one or two outlets that cater specifically to their preconceptions. A greater range of information sources might lead to less informed people!

FORMS OF MEDIA CONTROL

Another pressure operating on both commercial news media and public broadcasters is the need to conform to regulatory or governmental bodies of various sorts. In the case of public broadcasters this is a fairly obvious worry; a truly independent public news source must be at "arm's length" from the government agencies that oversee it. But even private broadcasters have to apply for the right to use airwaves, which are regarded as essentially public property.

ANOTHER EXAMPLE

Journalist and news anchor Knowlton Nash remarked: "[American president Lyndon B. Johnson] couldn't stand criticism or even a pause in adulation, and this attitude extended to the media. He wanted reporters not just to be sympathetic to him but to be syco-phantic. Being a sycophant had rewards of sorts. . . . [A] friend of mine and a brilliant journalist who wrote for the Manchester *Guardian*, succumbed and wrote outrageously flattering stories about LBJ. . . . I found it embarrassing. . . . But I suppose he found it a worthwhile tradeoff for the reward he got of hours alone with Johnson for exclusive interviews."[5]

A political movement to censor or control the broadcasting and entertain-ment industries is rarely altogether absent, though there are more extreme cases from time to time, and varying from one context to another. In Canada, for example, it is unusual for news cameras to be permitted in criminal court pro-ceedings, though this is common in the United States. Canadian judges, moreover, are much more likely than American judges to order a publication ban on all or part of a trial, partly to protect the rights of the accused, partly to protect the rights of the accuser, and partly to preserve the integrity of the trial process itself (especially in jury trials, since Canadian juries are rarely sequestered in isolation from media coverage). Obviously, such constraints on publication limit the rele-vant information one can learn through the mainstream media. In these cases, however, we are at least able to get a key piece of information: that there is indeed a publication ban. To the extent that we seek information about a matter the details of which have been legally banned (at least for a time), we might find the situation frustrating, and possibly even unjust. But at least we know what we don't know. Less explicit ways of suppressing information can be more insidious, since the fact that information is being suppressed may not be clear. Falling under this description are indirect governmental pressures that can be brought to bear on the news media.

These indirect pressures can include many different kinds of information-control strategies, such as denying access to press conferences or informal press meetings to reporters or commentators who have criticized the government. To get its positive message conveyed, for that matter, a government may simply resort to hiring journalists. In 2004, for example, the American government quietly paid syn-dicated radio host Armstrong Williams nearly a quarter of a million dollars to report favourably on its education policies. Another source of both direct and indirect control of news media is a form of restriction on wartime journalism: the requirement that reporters be "embedded," or formally assigned to military units. This not only enables direct censorship of militarily sensitive—or embarrassing— details, but can erode the reporter's sense of independence and objectivity. Militarily "embedded" reporters can come to identify with the unit they join. In a sense this is only natural: embedded reporters are dependent on the soldiers for food, trans-portation, information, and perhaps most importantly for protection. Many of the

FIGURE 10.1

The Importance of Media Scrutiny

Who's watching and what is being watched? The media's awareness of events and stories keeps us all informed. It is equally important for us to be aware of the media as people and organizations, to pay attention to who and what may influence the media's work, and to discern the biases that may be present.

Evan F. Sisley-Pool/Getty Images

socialization factors that contribute to common opinion and esprit de corps among soldiers themselves can quickly condition a reporter's way of thinking too, whatever efforts are made to the contrary. Embedding can therefore affect the reporter's ability or willingness to report in an independent spirit. In wars in the Persian Gulf, embedded American reporters sometimes came to describe the actions of the units to which they were assigned using the term "we" and sometimes seemed more soldierly than journalistic in their comments.

Finally, sometimes national governments control news media by the direct means of concealing information from them or forbidding them to publish information already discovered. This can be done within the law, by invoking legislation that allows information to be classified when its publication would harm the greater national interest. Whether these laws are used appropriately from case to case is a question of great importance; certainly they are open to abuse by governments seeking merely to hide their own wrongdoing or incompetence. And of course a government may suppress such information by the simple expedient of destroying or hiding it illegally, or at least without legal sanction.

All in all, this can place us in a difficult position when we are attempting to judge the plausibility of a sketchy or unconfirmed report of an event that a government *would* have both the ability and good reason to hide, if it had occurred. On one hand, the mere absence of evidence cannot be taken to confirm the charges in the manner of a pure conspiracy theory. On the other hand, there may be indirect evidence, perhaps including a track record for that particular government, or for governments in general given events of the reported kind, that makes the report worth taking seriously. Thinking critically about such cases requires one to learn something about the historical circumstances under which the news media have been silenced or misled by governments, in order to gain some sense of the likelihood that this could be happening in any particular situation.

SOURCES OF BIAS IN REPORTING

Claims that various news media are biased in some respect are as old as the news media itself. The claim that there is some single overarching bias in the media of a nation or a region is also not new, but has certainly become a more refined point of rhetoric over several decades. It is perhaps inevitable that someone attaching importance to a particular issue or point of view will find it easy to convict the media of giving that issue or viewpoint short shrift. With so many issues to cover, the coverage of every issue might seem insufficient to its devotees. The appearance of bias in the amount and tone of coverage can be an artifact, to some extent, of the critic's own confirmation biases. And finally, there are indeed genuine biases in the media; sometimes the reason there seems to be a bias is because there is one.

Media biases are of many different sorts. They can attach to contexts as narrow as a single journalist on a particular day, and as broad as the entire industry over decades. Their object can be highly specific issues or very general ideological leanings—or of course any middling degree or combination of these. And their occurrence can be the result of anything from an explicit and self-conscious intention to advance a viewpoint to wholly unintentional small factors that add up for accidental institutional reasons. As we've already seen, it's a mistake to suppose that media bias, if it existed, would have to consist of something conspiratorial or deceptive. For a story, a media outlet, or the media in general to be biased in some way does not require that any single person be overtly biased in that way. Part of understanding how the media can supply misleading information is understanding the many ways in which biases can arise and make themselves known. The biases of individuals within the media are only part of that bigger story, and in any case the individuals whose biases matter are often not those directly covering the news.

REPORTER'S BIAS

Reporters can have personal biases, and these can have an effect on the selection and emphasis of information for a story. The mechanisms by which this can happen should now be familiar: they might range from the deliberate skewing of a story out of some overt desire to convince people regardless of the facts—very rare, no doubt—to a spectrum of biases, with varying degrees of self-awareness on the part of the reporter. These may include anything from perceptual biases, in the case of eyewitness reporting, to interpretive or recollection failures arising from preconceptions or other top-down factors. And they may include social biases as well, in particular those that can stem from a reporter's workplace or social environment. For journalists, pundits, and editors, this environment can include both the particular newsroom in which they are based, and the wider social environment of other media workers and the newsmakers themselves.

Political journalists, reporters, and commentators, for example, sometimes work and socialize as a group   conditions under which they may sometimes think as a group as well. Michel Gratton, former press secretary to Prime Minister Brian Mulroney, recalls the journalists of the Parliamentary Press Gallery who were travelling on the campaign airplane of then-Prime Minister John Turner singing satirical songs about him "while the leader cringed in his seat at the front of the plane."

ANOTHER EXAMPLE

When was the last time you used the phrase "Attack attack attack"? It's not the kind of thing that one would expect several people to spontaneously utter in a brief period purely by coincidence. American political media critic Bob Somerby noted this example of a catchphrase taking root in the minds of media commentators, who then repeat it back and forth to one another.[7] Such catchphrases can come to seem like received wisdom by sheer repetition, but it's unclear whether they convey any insight or reveal any analysis on the part of the people uttering them.

The Beltway Boys, Fox News, April 30, 2000
Mort Kondracke: Gore is behind in all the polls, so he's doing what worked with Bill Bradley, **attack attack attack,** and, you know, and he's hoping that it'll work on George W. Bush.

Fred Barnes: . . . But look, Gore was **attack attack attacking,** and he's—in the beginning, and now he's been going down as a result of that **attack attack attacking.**

Hardball, MSNBC, May 5, 2000:
Chris Matthews: ...[Y]ou see Al Gore picking away at [George W. Bush] with these left jabs of his. . . .It's the same thing he did to Bill Bradley—**attack, attack, attack.**

Russert, CNBC, May 6, 2000:
Joe Klein: The concern I have about the Gore campaign is that he has learned one lesson and he's kind of becoming a one-trick pony.

Tim Russert: **Attack. Attack. Attack.**

Klein: **Attack. Attack.**

Russert: Governor Bush put forward a Social Security plan calling for a partial privatizing, and he **attacks,** saying that is risky. . . .Why—why—why does Gore just, almost knee-jerk, **attack, attack, attack?**

Inside Politics, CNN, May 17, 2000:
Charles Cook: . . . **Al Gore is very good at the attack,** just look at what he did to Bill Bradley on health care. . . .

Bernard Shaw: What comes to mind, Stu?

Stuart Rothenberg: . . . **Once again, here, attack, attack.**

CHAPTER 10   *The Mainstream Media as a Source of Information*

Later these journalists and others would compose and sing similar songs about Mulroney, too, on his campaign bus.[6] Like any group of people working the same job and in frequent communication, journalists can adopt common attitudes of approval or disapproval toward people and issues in ways familiar to all of us—that is, in ways that can be self-reinforcing and sometimes not especially warranted. This is neither unethical nor surprising. But it does mean that readers and viewers should be open to the possibility that a convergence of opinion from reporters and commentators is partly explained by a shared social context. Reporters and pundits are rarely independent observers, unaffected by the attitudes of their colleagues. There is always the potential for "groupthink."

EDITOR'S BIAS

Much more significant than reporter bias is editorial bias. Whatever the reporter's personal views, the editor is in a position to assign stories for coverage, to edit the reports that are submitted, and to arrange the stories in order of importance in a broadcast or publication. Of course editors of newspapers also write the main opinion column in each issue of the publication—called, unsurprisingly, the *editorial* column.

Editorial bias can be reflected not only in the content of editorial columns and the choice of stories to be written or printed, but also in how the reporters themselves present information. In any job it's a rare employee who has no idea of what appeals to the boss. Conforming to those perceived expectations can be a way of getting ahead—not necessarily in some crass mercenary sense, but just as a matter of subtly shading one's reportage in light of explicit or implicit cues from the editorial staff. Sometimes a reporter may be aware of conforming, sometimes not. Patricia Pearson, former columnist for the *National Post,* writes: "When my editor, of whom I am fond, revealed a deep suspicion of environmentalism, I self-censored in favour of conviviality."[8] There is no suggestion of compulsion here, just a polite deference to the stated opinion of the boss. Similarly, journalist Tim Falconer recalls an environmental protest taking place in Calgary in June 2000. Local media had predicted violence from the protesters; it turned out to be an entirely peaceful affair. Unfortunately, some newspaper editors only wanted a story about environmentalists if they could be depicted as rioters:

> I chatted with an *Edmonton Sun* reporter [who] was worried about what
> his editors were going to say. "I can only get so much colour," he fretted.
> "What do they want, pepper spray?"
> "Yep."[9]

OWNERSHIP BIAS

Just as editorial biases can make themselves felt in the stories that reporters are assigned to cover, in the hiring of reporters themselves, and in the way that news workers go about their jobs, so can the biases of media owners or managers be felt throughout the institution.

For example, the *Toronto Star* bases its editorial policies on the "Atkinson principles," adopted by its parent corporation Torstar and named after the paper's long-time editor. These six principles include such commitments as "social justice" and "the rights of working people." While the editors profess to adapt the principles to contemporary situations as appropriate, this clearly counts as some sort of management constraint on the focus and attitudes of the newspaper.

Perhaps more overtly, the CanWest media corporation instituted a top-down editorial policy for its newspapers across Canada, including the *National Post*, Montreal's *Gazette, Ottawa Citizen*, Regina's *Leader-Post, Calgary Herald, Edmonton Journal, Vancouver Sun, The Province* (Vancouver), and Victoria's *Times Colonist*. Starting in 2001, first one editorial column per week, and then three per week, were to have been written for these newspapers at the corporation's head office and printed throughout the chain, though the practice quickly tailed off since the policy was introduced amid much controversy.

The concentration of media in the hands of a few huge corporations is well established in Canada: CanWest Global also owns the national Global Television network and several local television stations; Thomson (co-publisher of this book) owns or has owned several newspapers, including the *Globe and Mail*; Torstar owns not just the *Toronto Star* but a range of small- and medium-market newspapers. For the most part the editors of individual newspapers have been relatively free to write their own editorials, reflecting their own views of issues. Yet because owners hire and fire editors and can exert direct pressures on their newspapers or broadcasters, they can take steps to present news and analysis that reflect their own views—personal or corporate. (After the editor of the *Ottawa Citizen* publicly spoke out against the possible consequences of the CanWest editorial policy, he was fired from his position.)

ANOTHER EXAMPLE

The Irving family of industrialists, based in New Brunswick, owns hundreds of companies, including virtually every New Brunswick newspaper. Sociology professor Erin Steuter writes:

"When the national media reported on the case of . . . federal Industry minister Allan Rock, who made highly favourable policy decisions affecting the Irving empire after he went on a fishing trip hosted by the Irvings, the national newspapers' headlines read: 'Rock faces new conflict-of-interest questions' (*Globe and Mail*, Oct 14. 2003) 'Rock disregarded ethics ruling to advance Irvings' cause' (*National Post*, Oct. 20) 'New questions arise over Rock, Irvings' (*Toronto Star*, Oct. 14). Yet a review of headlines in the New Brunswick papers finds: 'Rock defends Irving trip' (Fredericton *Daily Gleaner*, Oct. 11) 'Audit of Irving deal shows no evidence of conflict' (Saint John *Telegraph-Journal*, Oct. 18) 'No Conflict in Fishing Trip' (Moncton *Times & Transcript*, Oct. 11). Similarly, when it became apparent that local MP Claudette Bradshaw had also benefited from Irving trips, the Irving papers covered the story with the headline: 'Bradshaw free flight scandal overblown' (Moncton *Times & Transcript*, Oct. 23)."[10]

Here, again, the imperatives for running a successful business may give rise to viewpoints that are specific to a corporate perspective, or the owners and managers may simply have idiosyncratic personal views. That corporations or persons are entitled to their views is not in question. But critical reasoning about information presented in the mainstream media surely requires the greatest possible awareness of such attitudes, since they may colour media coverage in so many different ways. For example, the founder of Canada's largest media conglomerate commented in an interview on his corporation's financial contributions to political parties: "We contribute to Liberals, [Progressive] Conservatives and the [Canadian] Alliance. We don't contribute to the Bloc [Québécois] because it stands for separation, and we don't contribute to the national [New Democratic Party] because it has policies that are odious to us."[11] Of course, the executive of any corporation might completely disagree with the policies of any political party. But when the corporation in question is one largely responsible for *informing* the public about the political parties, the existence of such strong attitudes is something that ought to be known and kept in mind by a critical consumer of mainstream media perspectives.

Nor is the issue solely one of private ownership of media. Public broadcasters can be influenced by various top-down means as well, including the appointment of partisan administrators that may favour one party, the reduction of funding as punishment for unfavourable reporting, or direct attempts at political interference. Awareness of such factors is particularly important in Canada, which has a large and influential public news broadcaster in the Canadian Broadcasting Corporation. Effective public broadcasting means having an "arm's length" relationship between the government of the day and the programming decision-makers, in order to prevent the government from exercising an undue influence over what information is disseminated. But this gap can be narrowed by the kinds of tactics listed above, a fact of which listeners and viewers should be aware.

Funding for the CBC was dramatically cut under Prime Minister Brian Mulroney, for example, who felt its coverage of his government to be unfairly critical. When the content of a state-funded broadcaster's news and programming is outside the government's direct control, turning off the money taps can be a way of exerting indirect control. Under Mulroney's government the then-president of the CBC had his salary frozen for seven years—over which time the salaries of his deputy and vice-presidents surpassed his own. Years earlier, Prime Minister Pierre Trudeau had also complained about the CBC, specifically its French news division, which he believed was campaigning for separatism in Quebec. Trudeau threatened at one point to place the entire French network under new management. In a concise demonstration of the concept of an arm's-length relation, CBC president George Davidson replied, "Mr. Trudeau is a taxpayer and he's got the same right to express his opinion about the CBC as any other taxpayer. And we'll pay the same amount of attention to his comments as to any comment we get."[12]

FALSE NEUTRALITY

It may seem strange to list neutrality as a source of bias. After all, it's a platitude that there are at least two sides to every story. How could presenting both sides amount to a bias? In fact, a policy of always treating the two sides as equally *serious* can create misleading impressions. It can happen that one of the two sides to a story is plainly false or dishonest, and when this is the case, treating both sides equally seriously can be a grave mistake resulting not from partisanship toward either side, but from a misapplied ethos of neutrality. The idea of the news media as neutral is an important and good one. It applies especially to cases of partisanship: news media ought not be boosters or cheerleaders for or against one political party, religion, ethnicity, or class over another. But the news media *should* be biased in favour of reasonableness, good judgment, and the truth.

Suppose a reporter for a news program or special report interviewed two people: one a scientist explaining that Earth revolves around the Sun, and the other a layperson claiming that the Sun goes around Earth. Merely placing the two on an equal footing—juxtaposing them on the screen—may give viewers the impression that each side has a roughly equivalent claim to respectability. A great deal depends on how the interview is conducted, too. If the questions are pitched at a level that does not permit the rational differences between the two positions to come through, or if the interviewer closes the segment with a typically open-ended remark like "One thing is certain, the dispute is not over yet," then the overall effect will be a quite strong suggestion of equal plausibility, of a debate too close to call. Obviously, though, one of these positions is reasonable and one is not. Sometimes a determination to show balance between the sides of an issue amounts to a simple misrepresentation of facts.

PRESS RELEASES

What gets reported or discussed, even in major broadcasts and newspapers, can simply be a matter of the key phrases or themes that sound worth repeating at that time. Punchy or pithy snippets may be widely repeated just for the sheer ease of it, not because reporters and pundits are evil, stupid, or particularly lazy, but because they are much like everyone else: that is, occasionally inclined to do things just well enough to finish up and go home for dinner.

The writers of press releases count on it, in fact. The idea behind writing a successful press release, as any public relations professional knows, is not to somehow convince reporters of the fundamental truth and justice of your group's claims. A press release that is too earnest or otherwise overstated is a bad one; in general you're taking your chances if you expect a reporter to read your press release, weigh its claims, make his or her own assessment of the situation, and then write up a story from scratch on the basis of that judgment. That's a lot of work to expect of someone with an anxious editor and lots of white space to fill. Instead, a good press release tries to already look like a newspaper article or to sound like a broadcast report. This often means deliberately underselling one's position somewhat, writing something that pushes one's views more subtly. On one hand, this makes the press release a more modest endorsement of whatever it's advocating, but on the other hand it makes the actual words of the press release much more likely to get published, in whole or in part. The point, in short, is to make it as tempting as possible for the reporter to cannibalize the press release in constructing the story—perhaps quoting it for your side of the story or perhaps just borrowing some content for the body of the piece. This can border on (what would in other contexts be called) plagiarism, but of course the press release writer is not going to complain! Indeed, if there is any reason to think that this is not plagiarism as usually conceived, it is that this use of press releases is precisely what they are intended for. Plagiarism in a journalistic context normally means passing off *another journalist's* words as one's own; it rarely applies even to modest rewrites of press releases.

Whatever the specific explanations from case to case, the incorporation of press release material directly into articles is not rare. Writing in the *National Post* on February 6, 2004, columnist Elizabeth Nickson argued that challenges to evolutionary theory should be taught in high school. Nickson observed that "in 2001, 100 scientists, from institutions such as MIT, Yale, and Rice, published a statement questioning the creative power of natural selection." If this observation had a familiar ring to readers who follow this controversy, the explanation may be that the Discovery Institute, a conservative American lobby organization, had issued a press release one year earlier, on February 10, 2003, which read in part: "In 2001, more than 100 scientists including scholars at such institutions as Yale, Princeton, MIT and Rice, published a statement questioning the creative power of natural selection."

In fact the phrasing had been used repeatedly in various published articles issuing from the Discovery Institute. Less than two weeks after Nickson's article appeared, for that matter, Discovery Institute affiliate Dr. Stephen Meyer used substantially the same sentence in a column for the *Atlanta Journal-Constitution*—although, given his audience, he prudently added the University of Georgia to the list of MIT, Yale, and Rice.

There is reason to think that press release and wire story rewriting find their way into many stories. They have the potential to introduce, by turns, subtle or unsubtle biases within the particular story, and pseudo-independent confirmation (discussed in Chapter 8) when more than one media source is consulted.

JOURNALISTIC COMPETENCE

Question: *What do you call the person graduating with the lowest marks in a medical class?* Answer: *Doctor.*

This old joke hints at an uncomfortable truth: that the people we most want to be uniformly outstanding at their work can be of uneven abilities. Even among generally competent practitioners of some profession there can be a wide range of quality, and then there are those who are only marginally competent, or outright disasters.

This point is quite general. It applies to software engineers, to plumbers, to police officers, and (unbelievable as this may seem) to university professors. Certainly it applies to journalists, reporters, political commentators, and others whose job it is to create and present news reports. When considering how to evaluate any particular piece of information offered by a media source, it is important to allow not only for the fact that a very good reporter or editor can have a bad day, but that some reporters and editors may have a lot of them.

It may be tempting to think that anyone consistently bad at the job of reporting or editing is sure to be fired or retrained. This is a bit too optimistic. First, there is nothing to suggest that any corporation, media-based or otherwise, is entirely successful at identifying and correcting incompetence. And second, we have already seen that there are ways of being good at the *job*—for example, being good at filling white space; having a pleasant voice; having good looks—that do not automatically imply competence at presenting truths or informed insights. Our attitudes toward news sources ought to strike a balance between, on one hand, uncritically assuming that the people responsible for delivering the news know what they're talking about and have a concern for the truth as their highest goal, and, on the other hand, completely rejecting as unreliable anything that is reported.

The middle ground is simply to recognize the human frailties of media workers. Practically, we need information from the media. Realistically, we have to take seriously its potential to be misleading. These two facts jointly speak in favour of a habit of context-sensitive caution. How extreme the caution ought to be varies according to the specific information available about that particular reporter, that media source, and the topic in question. A reporter may not be well-qualified to see or explain the details of the story he or she has been assigned to cover. Again, this is not to say that there's a general problem of bumbling incompetence; presumably that occurs among journalists at no higher a rate than among the rest of us. Rather it's a point about *degrees* of competence. Neither the dedicated acquisition of critical thinking skills, nor an understanding of scientific methods, nor statistical numeracy, nor reasoning about states of information is much emphasized in most journalism training programs. Some are not taught at all, depending on the program. The upshot is not that reporters and analysts aren't smart, hard-working, or well-intentioned; the upshot is that there's no guarantee that reporters or commentators are much better-versed in the details of an issue, or significantly less susceptible to reasoning errors about the issue, than the people to whom they are reporting the issue.

As thoughtful inquirers after information, we must be alive to the prospect that any particular story might presuppose background knowledge that the assigned reporter lacks. The chances that the average bright person could say something insightful or informative about any specialized topic on two days' notice are slim. Reporters may receive training in how to assemble that information from people who are themselves experts, but that assembling process itself is one that can require background knowledge of the topic. In short, non-specialists reporting specialized stories—and what story is not specialized?—to other non-specialists is a process liable to result in an ongoing level of error, ranging from errors of emphasis to errors of fact. Useful news reporting on a proposed change in tax policies, to return to our earlier example, would explain the relevant details of the legislation and its predictable consequences for wider issues. In fact, this sort of story may be reduced to uninformative slogans and clichés or simply passed over altogether in favour of stories less difficult for both the media personnel and the public. Again, the lesson is that it is unwise to consider ourselves well-informed unless we have consulted multiple sources, including less mainstream but more reliably expert sources on any particular issue.

SPECIALIZED REPORTING

SCIENCE IN THE MEDIA

The mainstream media, even in its dedicated science reporting, is not particularly good at communicating either the methods or the results of scientific research. For reasons considered in detail in Chapter 9, science can produce results worthy of great confidence. But it is nevertheless a collection of methods and attitudes involving uncertainty, defeasibility, and competing explanations. It is easy for popular reporting of science to misrepresent both of these aspects: to treat what's known with confidence as if it were known with perfect certainty and, when confronted with evidence of uncertainty and disputes among scientists, to conclude that the field is in disarray or that any guess is as good as any other.

Newspapers, news programs, and magazines, for instance, often have sections presenting snippets of what scientists proved that week or that month. Boiled down to a sentence or two, an experimental result that may have been qualified or preliminary in its original form becomes a simple statement of fact. Over time these reports may even contradict one another, with the main result being a public confused not only about the output of scientific research, but with a view of scientists as themselves issuing such nuance-free declarations of certainty. At the same time, the popular media has been fertile ground for breeding the "just a theory" error—the idea that when scientists call something a *theory,* or state explicitly that a thesis is *probably* true, they are effectively confessing to having a mere conjecture or wild guess.

Often the problem is just a specific example of the competence worry we have already discussed. A firm grasp of both scientific concepts and the state of play in some scientific discipline may require background knowledge that few reporters possess. Sheer confusion, or at least reportage that is difficult to understand, may result when news stories are written without this background knowledge. One Canadian newspaper reports that "[s]ome scientists say that homeopathy works because of the placebo effect. Others, especially those in the field of quantum physics, say the opposite."[13] Even if we interpret this merely as saying that some scientists deny that homeopathy only induces a placebo effect (setting aside the writer's apparent suggestion that the placebo effect works because of homeopathy!), there is an oddity in the brief, unexplained allusion to quantum physicists that raises a large red flag. Why should quantum physicists in general, of all people, even hold a professional opinion on homeopathy? Why should the opinions they may individually hold of homeopathy be taken as authoritative? And who, exactly, are the physicists in question? While the article is appealing to scientific authority for a (partial) vindication of homeopathy, the way it's written suggests too little familiarity with the workings of science for a careful reader to draw any conclusions about homeopathy (pro or con, that is).

Popular science reporting moreover tends to misrepresent the focus of scientific research. For understandable reasons, the reports that attract the most public attention are those relating to the personal interests of viewers, listeners, and readers. As a result, the media disproportionately reports the results of health and medical science, and science with immediate technological applications, while rarely touching on research of a less anthropocentric sort—say, the mating habits of tortoises. Even within the domain of health and medicine, moreover, mainstream reporting does not accurately reflect the state of the sciences. For example, a study published in the *British Medical Journal* reported that scientific articles on women's health (at least, those published in *BMJ* and *The Lancet*) tend to be over-reported in major British newspapers. Twelve percent of the scientific articles in the two journals were on women's health, but these were over-represented among the studies for which press releases were written, making up 18 percent of these. When it came to the question of which press releases were then reported in the popular press, the over-representation occurred again, as a full 31 percent of newspaper reports about scientific articles from the two journals were written about the women's health studies.

Why might this sort of unrepresentative reporting matter? Consider a reader of these newspapers, when encountering the claim that research into women's health is underfunded. A natural response, given merely an impression garnered from the newspaper reporting, is that this claim is unwarranted: it will seem that roughly a third of health research is devoted to women's health, when a closer estimate, according to this study, would be roughly one-tenth. Reading the newspapers in question for an understanding of medical science is likely to give one an inflated estimate of the amount of research into women's health. Something as simple as emphasizing the stories that interest viewers can result in mistaken impressions having important political and scientific overtones.

It is also increasingly common for scientists running studies with potential commercial appeal or public interest to issue press releases on their preliminary results—especially if the preliminary results are promising or interesting. This can be part of a marketing strategy if the research is privately funded, as in the pharmaceutical industry, for example, or it can simply be "grantsmanship" by the scientists in question: an attempt to secure further research funding by making a splash in the media.

Another motivation for announcing preliminary results before they have been peer-reviewed is suggested when the scientists either work for or are funded by a corporation, so that share prices or further funding or both are contingent on a public perception of success. Whatever the motivations, the key critical thinking point is that preliminary results are *preliminary*. If they were reliable, we wouldn't bother with further study. One of the details to note in a report about some scientific result, therefore, is any suggestion that the result has not yet been critically examined via the peer-review process. Claims based on preliminary studies should

FURTHER REFLECTION

The same *British Medical Journal* study described here also gave reason to think that less reliable forms of research are more widely reported. "[R]andomized trials, which represent the gold standard for evaluation of medical interventions, were underreported in newspapers despite their being more likely to be included in press releases. Observational studies, which are more prone to bias than randomized trials, were more likely to be included both in press releases and in newspaper reports."[14]

be treated with appropriate caution. It is also worth bearing in mind that if the full study or experiment fizzles or otherwise betrays its early promise, this will almost certainly fail to be a media-worthy event.

BUSINESS NEWS

Most governments at all levels in North America have at least some "access to information" regulations making it possible to discover facts that the government might wish to hide. In theory, such laws guarantee that any citizen can examine information on file about the workings of government, including information about budgets, internal communications, and paper trails more generally. In practice, a government will occasionally take every legal measure to drag out the application process for accessing the information, hoping either to discourage the applicant into leaving embarrassing information unexplored, or to at least delay the process for one reason or another. When the news media do choose to research a story about government, the successful use of these laws can be crucial.

Large businesses and corporations can also be powerfully motivated to keep their internal workings private, but there is no comparable general citizens' right to gain access to this information. Even company shareholders may have only limited rights to company information, while professional auditing companies, who are normally hired by a corporation to conduct an investigation of its finances and practices, have a vested interest in getting hired again and are not granted general access to information in any case. In short, it can be very difficult for media to unearth sensitive business news.

Even when such evidence is available, moreover, the prospects for bias in reporting it are relatively serious. Both business columnists and business reporters can be in a conflict of interest regarding the news and opinions they present, since they may well own stocks in the companies on which they are reporting, or they may have plans to buy it. Part of the worry, especially when we consider stock markets, is that stock prices are determined not simply by the inherent efficiency or track record of the company in question, but by the elusive quality of *investor confidence*. Both positive and negative reports on a company are therefore apt to be self-fulfilling prophecies: a good report may cause investors to purchase the company's stocks, driving up their price, while a bad report can undermine confidence and lead to a drop in the company's share values. That such reports can be self-fulfilling not only skews one's sense of the accuracy of the reporting after the fact, but can place the power and incentive to influence stock prices in the hands of the reporters and commentators.

DOCUMENTARIES AND SPECIAL REPORTS AS ENTERTAINMENT

Many cable or satellite television channels carry regular series that purport to *study* or *investigate* ghosts, hauntings, psychics, and "paranormal" claims more generally. Even the major American broadcast networks—that is, the non-cable broadcasters—air special reports on these or related themes. What confidence should we have in the claims and methods of such programs?

It is important to bear in mind just how few and how weak the constraints are that govern accuracy in most programming. Neither Canada nor the United States has any "Commission for Truth" ensuring that purportedly informative or educational shows are largely correct in their assertions. The monitoring that does occur is devoted for the most part to maintaining standards of decency rather than truth. It is easy to assume that any program having the look of a news report or documentary must be held to some standard of factual accuracy. In fact, such standards are mostly a matter of self-regulation by the industry; in practice, the ratings tend to be the biggest concern. It is in general a critical thinking error to reason, "They couldn't say it unless they had good reason to think it's true." They could indeed, and often do. More importantly, the bounds of truth can be more permissive than one would think. It is very common for shows of the kind mentioned here to begin with the promise that all the events depicted in the show are "based on" or "inspired by" true events. This might sound like a promise to stick to the truth as closely as possible, but in fact it amounts to a powerful disclaimer, since the "based on" and "inspired by" relations are very weak indeed. A story depicting elves, leprechauns, and time travel could be *based on*, or *inspired by*, the minutes of an office meeting. Sometimes a voice-over saying that the story is true can itself be understood as part of the entertainment package.

THE UNTOLD STORY: THE MEDIA'S BLIND SPOT

The genuinely critical and reflective content of the mass media may have diminished in recent times. But the mainstream media in North America has never been particularly good at delivering such content in at least one key area: analysis of itself. As the social, political, and economic roles of the media have expanded, it is an increasingly glaring blind spot in its orientation that it so rarely turns a critical eye on its own operations. Critical thinking about the media must therefore regard the information it delivers as emerging from a set of institutions that are not subject to any serious self-scrutiny for methods or accuracy.

The full range of explanations for media behaviour that we've seen in this chapter come into play here. It's simply human nature not to be volubly critical of one's own actions or statements, and this reluctance is only accentuated when there is a sense either of solidarity or of living in glass house among media workers. Pundits may criticize politicians, for example, but will rarely set themselves the task of criticizing even the most obviously mistaken or foolish work of other pundits—perhaps partly out of fear of having their own work placed under a microscope and partly from professional courtesy. There are also powerful commercial reasons for any newspaper or broadcaster to uphold its own image as error-free, besides the mere desire to avoid embarrassment. We saw in Chapters 2 and 8 that admissions of ignorance or error are often seen as forms of weakness or as "backing down." For better or worse—worse, more likely—many viewers are inclined to take a more positive view of brazening out an error than of apologizing and vowing to do better. The idea that an apology only advertises one's mistakes is hardly confined to the media, after all.

Whatever the explanation, the fact that the mainstream news media is so ineffective at self-criticism means that monitoring the media for accuracy, along with the task of ensuring that poor methodology, double standards, and outright mistakes aren't just promptly erased from public memory, falls to still less regulated and still less uniformly reliable parties like Internet bloggers, think-tanks, and self-described media watchdogs. Some of these are relatively even-handed and competent, but many are themselves only instruments for the advancement of a specific viewpoint. And even these informal approaches to media criticism and analysis require laws permitting the "fair use" of intellectually copyrighted material: the ability to freely quote and reproduce small sections of copyrighted material for the purpose of critically discussing it. Without such access to fair use, the mere threat of an intellectual property lawsuit can have a powerful silencing effect on critics who might otherwise speak out against media malfeasance by quoting it, reproducing a video clip, reprinting or posting an image, and so forth. This is not a new problem when it comes to advertisements, for example, which occupy so much of the mainstream media. Many advertisements would have made outstanding examples of shoddy argumentation for this book. Yet they could not be used, since the companies in question would not give permission for the images and text to be reproduced, not even with the corporate identifying information removed. So those examples were dropped, for fear of a lawsuit. There is some danger that a similar silencing phenomenon will arise for non-advertising material as well, leaving the media still less subject to effective criticism and damaging its role as a communicative medium with at least a perceived mandate for reliability.

CONCLUSION

A great deal of our information about the world is gleaned from the mainstream media. The news media is far from completely reliable, though. Some stories are over-reported, some under-reported, some are framed in biasing terms, and some are just plain wrong. The way these problems occur, moreover, is not entirely random. For reasons that range from the specific biases of reporters, editors, and owners, to institutional, interpersonal, and educational factors, media outlets can be unreliable in roughly predictable ways. Awareness of these tendencies and of the situation can help one be appropriately cautious about the media; special efforts to sample a wide range of media outlets can help minimize the quirks of any small set of them.

REVIEW QUESTIONS

1. What news sources do you consult most frequently? How would you characterize their viewpoints?
2. What steps do you take to remain aware of alternative stories and perspectives? What further steps could you take?
3. Choose two different newspapers, radio news broadcasts, or television news broadcasts. For one week read, listen, or watch them both as thoroughly as

you can. Make a note of any systematic differences of perspective you detect between them, as well as any questionable reports or opinions you encounter. On the basis of your observations, do you consider either to be overall superior to the other as a source of information? Add any other remarks you wish, regarding what you learned from the comparison.

NOTES

1. CTV News, February 25, 2001; transcript on LexisNexis Academic. http://web. lexis-nexis.com/universe. (May 2005).

2. *Toronto Star* editorial. January 11, 2006. "Can Voters Afford Harper Promises?" http://www.thestar.com/NASApp/cs/ContentServer?pagename=thestar/Layout/ Article_Type1&c=Article&cid=1136933411373&call_pageid=968256290204&col= 968350116795. Accessed January 12, 2006.

3. T. Harper, "U.S. Soldiers' Grilling Fields," *Toronto Star*, December 12, 2004.

4. "UK Speed Camera Tickets Non-Speeding Protester," report, January 11, 2006. http://www.thenewspaper.com/news/08/891.asp. Accessed January 12, 2006.

5. K. Nash, *History on the Run* (Toronto: McClelland & Stewart, 1984), p. 195.

6. M. Gratton, *So What Are The Boys Saying?* (Toronto: McGraw-Hill Ryerson, 1987), pp. 48–49.

7. B. Somerby, The Daily Howler, "Four Years Later!" http://www.dailyhowler.com/ dh120204.html. Accessed January 2005.

8. P. Pearson, "See No Evil, No More," *The Globe and Mail*, April 19, 2003, p. A19.

9. T. Falconer, *Watchdogs and Gadflies* (Toronto: Penguin Books, 2004), p. 120.

10. E. Steuter, "The Irving Media Monopoly in New Brunswick," Conference presentation posted at www.yourmedia.ca/modules/irving/overview/overview.shtml, 2003.

11. M. Radler, "Mogul with a Message," *Jerusalem Post* (Online Edition), August 7, 2003.

12. K. Nash, *The Microphone Wars* (Toronto: McClelland & Stewart, 1994), pp. 391–2, 468.

13. G. Niosi, *Harbour City Star*, August 11, 2004, p. A20.

14. C. Bartlett, J. Sterne, and M. Egger, "What Is Newsworthy? Longitudinal Study of the Reporting of Medical Research in Two British Newspapers," *British Medical Journal* 325 (2002): 81–84.

CHAPTER 1

Readings and Discussions

This chapter contains five readings, each of which has a preface giving its context and a discussion of some of the critical thinking issues it raises. The readings range substantially in length and technical complexity and cover topics ranging from education to the media, from police work to medicine. In many respects they tie into themes that have been raised throughout this book. They challenge you to think of further critical thinking issues as well.

To varying degrees these readings raise critical reasoning both in their topics and in their execution. That is, on one hand they talk about critical thinking to some extent, and on the other hand we can analyze the readings themselves for persuasiveness or red flags. The guidance questions before each reading are intended to inspire that sort of analysis as you read the selections, and the discussions that follow the readings are meant to illustrate an approach to reading critically and answering such questions.

This approach can impose clarity where it is needed and expose lack of clarity where it is hidden, but I have certainly not made an exhaustive catalogue of the critical reasoning issues with any of these readings. In keeping with a theme of this book, we can see that fallacies, biases, accuracy problems, and other critical thinking concerns tend to travel in groups. I will normally select only a few such concerns for discussion. The idea is to get you started by presenting examples of how to carefully read and evaluate different sorts of readings: opinion columns, news stories, and special reports in the mainstream media; a technical scientific journal article; and an article in the specialized magazine of an interest group.

READING 1

EVIDENTIAL REASONING ABOUT CANADIAN UNIVERSITIES

Barbara Kay is a Canadian writer dealing with political, social, and cultural issues. She has been a regular contributor to the *National Post* for years, and her work is often reprinted and widely read in other venues as well. In the following article from 2005, Kay argues (among other things) that the humanities and social sciences departments in Canadian universities are hotbeds of intellectual dogmatism and intolerance.

This reading raises critical thinking issues mainly from Chapters 2, 3, 6, 8, and 10. As you read:

1. Make a list of any words whose definitions are not entirely clear to you.
2. Note any evidential red flags for Kay's claims.
3. Note any other critical thinking issues raised by the reading.

Compare your observations with the brief critical analysis that follows the reading.

Academic Freedom Is Under Attack
Barbara Kay

National Post, 12 January 2005, A14. Reprinted by permission of the author.

Canadian students in the arts and social science departments of our universities are being recruited to the hyperorthodoxies of multiculturalism, feminism, Marxism, postmodernism and bio-politics. Proponents of these ideologies prefer social engineering and the subversion of Western values to the advancement of learning and respect for Western achievements. Furthermore, today's welfare campus fosters a culture of comfort/grievance for women, aboriginals, other visibly distinct races and all sexual orientations: for everyone, that is, except Americans, Israel-sympathizers and heterosexual men of European descent.

Last month I posed a series of questions about ideological harassment in academia. I asked students if it is still possible to get a classic, broadening education in public universities today. The vast majority of the 100-odd respondents to my unscientific poll say no. More than 90% agree that campus political correctness generates a frosty anti-intellectual climate hostile to academic freedom.

Out of 500,000 university students in Canada, 100 responses is a picayune representation. Yet every anecdote reflects an opinion or behaviour exposed to a classroom of between 20 and 300 students. Multiply that figure by every class the same instructor offers per semester, and then factor in a lifetime of teaching. Consider how many students are actually affected when an individual student reports that:

- Comparative Politics teachers wouldn't admit *The Economist* (in one case) or Fraser Institute reports (in another) as source material because of their "right wing, biased writers";

- An International Relations professor pronounced political realism as a method of inquiry "dead" and inadmissible in argumentation;

- Political Science students taught by a feminist were not permitted to use statistics to bolster an argument because "mathematics is a male construct for a male-dominated world";

- A professor in a course on terrorism said: "No educated person can support Israel . . . educated people don't have those kinds of views."

- A feminist teacher in a school of nursing insisted that her male students participate in a "Montreal Massacre" commemoration. When one refused (on the grounds that he is no more responsible for Marc Lepine's sins than his teacher is for Karla Homolka's), he was made to submit to corrective counselling.

My poll tells me that students are no longer offered "the best which has been thought and said in the world," the traditional mantra of humanities professors. Left-wing ideologies have turned all but the hard sciences into hustings for the social empowerment of collectivities rather than groves of academic freedom, where individual students are owed—with scholars hired on merit to teach—a liberal education.

I didn't hear only from students. Ideological harassment is a two-way street. Several academics wrote with harrowing tales of university careers derailed or ended by well-coached (and anonymous) student grievance collectors, and some even by their colleagues and/or university administrators. Graham L. Smith, a geography professor at the University of Western Ontario, won an award for excellence in undergrad teaching, yet, "I have had my course grades changed arbitrarily, been accused of being a fascist and been told I am brain-washing students, all because I present a dynamic perspective that challenges the hegemony of the present paradigm."

The "present paradigm" is bound to blunt the ambitions of any young academic striving to meet a traditional ideal of ideological neutrality. Last semester a McGill student took "Canadian-American Relations since 1939." Her instructor, a PhD candidate, was "the most gifted teacher I've encountered at McGill. . . . I haven't the faintest idea where he stands politically. . . and that's exactly how it should be. . . . He received outstanding evaluations." She goes on to say that he was replaced this semester by a "more qualified" teacher who said all Canadian-American relations since 1939 would be viewed "through a gay/lesbian/transsexual lens" and that they would devote part of the course to "lesbians who are claiming refugee status in Canada after Bush's re-election." How long will it be before the "gifted" teacher gives up, and abandons—or is pushed—from academic life?

Parents of students wrote to remind me that indoctrination begins well ahead of university, citing instances of secondary school aggression their children are ill-equipped to resist. In one case, a mother of a Grade 12 student sent me a copy of a simplistic questionnaire her son's class was made to fill out to assess their respective stances on social issues: "[B]ased on the answers to 10 or 12 questions [they] were categorized as to their political sympathies. [My son] was humiliated when the teacher publicly labelled him a Nazi for having a conservative viewpoint."

In a recent *Post* column, Susan Martinuk quoted Abraham Lincoln: "The philosophy of the schoolroom in one generation will be the philosophy of governance in the next." Not a comforting thought in the age of political correctness, but my job isn't to comfort. I will be returning to this subject in future columns.

DISCUSSION

There is a general interpretive problem with this article, as well as three loosely distinguishable evidential problems. The basic interpretive problem stems from the fact that many key terms in the reading are either undefined or are used in unclear ways. What, for example, is a "hyperorthodoxy"? An orthodoxy is a belief or doctrine identified as correct within a community; a connotation is that membership in the community requires acceptance of the belief. So a hyper-orthodoxy (I'll hyphenate the term) must mean a belief to which the community demands an especially universal unquestioned allegiance. The first sentence of the article, therefore, is the complex assertion that Canadian university faculty teaching in arts and social sciences have a universal unquestioned commitment to positions called "multiculturalism, feminism, Marxism, postmodernism and bio-politics," and that they actively recruit students to these perspectives.

It is well beyond our scope to comprehensively determine whether the distinct claims implicit in that complex claim are true. But we can at least get a sense of the truth-*conditions;* that is, what would have to be the case in order for the claims to be true. Again, the fundamental question is how each of these key terms is being used. Each may be open to a range of stronger and weaker interpretations, and some are simply ambiguous. To focus on one example, I confess to having never encountered the word "bio-politics" before reading this article. Nor had the authors of any of my dictionaries, for that matter. Fortunately the Internet had heard of it; one web encyclopedia listed six distinct meanings for the term.[1] Of the six definitions I found, three made some reference to reproductive technology or genetic engineering. But these three also defined the term neutrally, referring to a generic activity or a spectrum of views in the same way that the word "politics" itself does. This leaves it unclear how one could be *recruited* to the hyper-orthodoxy of bio-politics any more than one could be recruited to the hyper-orthodoxy of politics.

Another definition of "bio-politics" alluded to a concept introduced by the late French author Michel Foucault. This definition was barely familiar to me before I read up on it. (It remained almost as unfamiliar to me *after* I read up on it. I wish you better luck.) A fifth definition involved the study of politics as it applies to living things—again, a neutral or generic definition. And yet another sense of "bio-politics" defined it as political action or lobbying in the interests of all life forms, an idea similar to one I have encountered before, under the label "deep ecology." While there is a lot of guesswork involved here, my inclination would be to take this last definition as the one intended by Kay. This would make the relevant sub-claim into the following: *Canadian students in the Humanities and Social Science departments of our universities are being recruited to a universal unquestioned commitment to political advocacy on behalf of all life forms.* That at least gives us a rough and ready truth-condition for one of the sub-claims, depending on what the political advocacy is supposed to comprise. For instance, does it mean that one should advocate *equally* for all life forms, treating individual bacteria as equal in moral or political value to individual humans? This too would have to be settled before we could usefully move on to the question of whether the claim is even *true*.

Indeed, most of the key terms that seem central to the author's claims are of dubious clarity, in the absence of some indication of how they are intended. Such terms include these:

recruited

social engineering

Western values

Western achievements

ideological harassment

classic, broadening education

political correctness

academic freedom

The truth-conditions and hence the plausibility of many individual claims in the article depend on how these terms are to be understood. At the same time, they should be interpretable in a fashion that makes the claims hang together as well.

These two requirements may make it difficult for an overall plausible interpretation of the article to be constructible. For example, the more extreme a notion is meant by "feminism," the less plausible the individual claim that Canadian university students are being recruited to a feminist hyper-orthodoxy. Yet the more moderate the interpretation of "feminism," the less likely the further claim that feminism (so defined) is inconsistent with (some definition of) Western values. Similar remarks apply to most or all of the generalizations in the piece.

Hence the interpretive problem also amounts to the first sort of evidential problem with the article, and particularly with the claims made near its start: if the claims are understood as strongly as they seem to be meant, then particularly extensive and detailed evidence would be required to support them.

The second sort of evidential problem is statistical. The sampling method described in the article is a clear case of a selection bias, with respondents self-selected for having a complaint by the very nature of the questioning process. The sample size of 100, moreover, is trivial ("picayune," as Kay aptly observes) in comparison to the population of university or college students in Canada whose educational experience it is taken to illuminate. Indeed, depending on the time period from which the anecdotes are drawn, this minuscule sample may be still more trivial than the author observes, since the relevant cohort comprises all the people who were in university over the period from the earliest anecdote to the latest. But we are not given the dates of these alleged events.

That leads us to the final kind of evidential problem, which is broadly a problem with fact-checking and with testimonial evidence. Neither we as readers of the article nor Kay as the author (barring the existence of an army of research assistants) has access to information confirming the accuracy of these reports. For example, the professors alleged to have said and done these things were not consulted to see whether they or others who may have been present remembered the events in the same way. As with anecdotal evidence more generally, a basic default concern with each incident reported is whether it happened at all. But the worry persists even if we assume that some genuine event underlies each report. What makes most of the incidents described in the article seem so outrageous, after all, are the very specific motivations and precise words attributed to the instructors (or colleagues) in question. So it is important that the events not only happened, but also that they happened *essentially as described*. Any tendency for Kay's respondents to have done things like gradually shifting—unintentionally—from "My prof's attitude was basically that P" to "My prof said that P" would render the resulting anecdote a construction rather than a report of what was (even approximately) said. The lessons about levelling and sharpening from Chapter 8 come to the fore here, along with more general problems known to attend on unconstrained or unconfirmed testimonial evidence. Not only do we lack sufficient grounds to accept these anecdotal reports at face value, but we also have no way of investigating the reports for ourselves. This makes it reasonable to exercise great caution in assigning credibility to these individual reports (or reports of reports).

Overall the reading provides virtually no rationale for its central claims, which are so general and strongly worded that we couldn't really expect to find better evidence for them elsewhere. The biggest reservation about this judgment is just the lack of clarity of some of those claims. Of course, a lack of clarity and specificity may just be a cost of presenting complex and provocative views in a venue as limited in space (and with such tight deadlines) as a newspaper. And it might be a cost worth paying if one's aim is more to stimulate public discussion than to give reasons for believing one's assertions.

At least two lessons emerge: it's time-consuming and difficult to present a case that is clearly worded and tightly argued on one hand, while yet being controversial or provocative on the other; and opinions that are neither clearly presented nor tightly argued are apt to end up a mass of red flags.

READING 2

NUMERACY AND THE MEDIA

Peter Calamai is the national science correspondent for the *Toronto Star* and an active advocate of greater literacy and numeracy in Canadian society. In this 2006 article, he puts his own profession under the microscope and argues that a combination of poor training, mathematical incompetence, and the temptation of convenience results in the publication of many statistical and mathematical errors in the news media.

This reading raises themes common to Chapters 4 and 10: numeracy, and the orientation and competence of the news media.

As you read:

1. Make a note of any (non-trivial) assumptions the author makes but does not support with evidence. Explain which, if any, you find contentious.
2. Explain what you think is meant by "convenient numbers," and summarize the author's explanation(s) for how these numbers find their way into reports.
3. Identify one passage in which the author is not quite living up to the standards he is defending. Explain your choice.

Compare your observations with the brief critical analysis that follows the reading.

The Tyranny of the Convenient Number: More Powerful Than Words?

Peter Calamai

Toronto Star, Sept. 24, 2006, D1. Reprinted by permission–Torstar Syndication Services.

Being intimidated by numbers is troubling enough in a society that views so many issues through a quantitative lens. Even worse, however, is the harm to critical thinking from the numeracy shortcomings that afflict so many Canadians.

Especially journalists.

It's best to admit this failing right up front—journalists are often poor at handling numbers. The reasons are many but the outcome is depressingly predictable. All sorts of nonsense gets into print or on the air, because many reporters and editors check their critical thinking facilities at the door when numbers arrive on the scene.

The failings of journalists are on display every day but lots of Canadians share the problem, as shown by recent international surveys of literacy and numeracy skills. The Adult Literacy and Life Skills Survey, released last year, concluded that half of Canadian adults age 16 to 65 lack the minimum numeracy skills necessary to cope with the everyday demands of an advanced society.

This leaves us vulnerable to "commercial chicanery, financial foolery, medical quackery and numerical terrorism from pressure groups," in the words of A.K. Dewdney, a math professor at the University of Western Ontario and author of a

1993 book on public innumeracy (*200% of Nothing: An Eye-Opening Tour through the Twists and Turns of Math Abuse and Innumeracy*).

Consider how the Harris government in Ontario in the mid-1990s was able temporarily to bamboozle most of the media and the public with claims of a crime wave among the province's youth by using carefully massaged statistics as justification for setting up special boot camps.

The absolute number of crimes committed by those age 12 to 17 had, indeed, been rising. But the number of young people in the province was rising even faster, which meant that the youth crime rate—the number of crimes committed per 1,000 young people—had actually been dropping since 1991.

Solicitor General Bob Runciman sidestepped this inconvenient fact by using Canada-wide statistics and restricting his example to an earlier period from 1986 to 1991, when the rate of youth violent crime had actually soared.

Spotting this deception didn't demand the ability to solve quadratic equations, calculate square roots, or even figure out percentages. It simply required people to use their noggins in a critical fashion. After all, looking at the rate or incidence of some phenomenon is familiar territory. Health officials do it all the time to find out if particular diseases are increasing or decreasing in the general population, or in sub-groups such as the elderly.

Not asking the critical question—such as, is the rate of youth crime increasing, not just the absolute numbers?—is what distinguishes the big concerns from the little ones in the media's uneasy relationship with numbers.

The little concerns constitute the "numeracy mischief" we journalists do to ourselves. They're the slips people usually notice: repeated confusion between per cent and percentage point, meaningless decimal places, laughable conversions between Imperial and metric measurements, the shoddy and self-serving presentation of public opinion surveys, mixing up millions and billions, and so on.

The big concerns constitute the numeracy mischief inflicted upon the numbers-challenged media. They involve uncritical acceptance of numbers supplied by others, often people pushing an agenda, as Runciman did with that phantom explosion of youth crime.

Among the most blatant instances have been the media's treatment of supposed health dangers from the threat du jour (toxins in salmon, silicone breast implants, etc.), the fictional poverty line, gender pay inequities, race and crime, violence against women, drug use in schools, the education gap with other countries, and more.

The media numeracy problem isn't limited to Canada. In the U.S., the Statistical Assessment Service, based in Washington, D.C., operates as a numbers "truth squad," keeping tabs on journalists and politicians. In the U.K., Ben Goldacre's "Bad Science" column in *The Guardian* newspaper regularly exposes numbers malfeasance in the media and names individual reporters.

And it's a big problem. After studying a 150,000-circulation newspaper for three months, journalism professors at the University of North Carolina concluded that "an example of blatant misuse of numbers could be found, on average, in the newspaper every other day."

Or consider the numbers boner perpetrated this summer by *New Scientist*, a weekly magazine in Britain that prides itself on covering science and technology with style and authority. A July 1 article about the global boom in desalination plants reported that the Earth harboured 1,400 million cubic metres of water.

Two weeks later the magazine acknowledged that "we managed to get the quantity of water wrong by a factor of 1 billion. The correct figure is 1,400 cubic kilometres, not cubic metres."

That wasn't the end. After two more weeks, *New Scientist* reported that the correction itself was "missing some zeros" and should have been 1,400 million cubic kilometres.

Surveys have found that reporters are well aware of their inadequacies on the numbers front. Many chose their craft because of a fascination with words and often a corresponding aversion to even simple math, such as calculating percentage increases.

Overwhelmingly, newsrooms are populated by arts and humanities graduates who spent the four years after high-school math coddled in a numbers-free environment at university. John Brynner, a leading British social-science researcher, has shown that numeracy skills have a half-life of roughly 3.5 years when they're not used.

So many "experienced" journalists 10 years into their craft have lost whatever facility they might have had with numbers. And there's no numerical counterpart to Spell Check on computers.

What there is, however, is a constant demand for numbers in reporting. Numbers make news. How does the city's murder rate now compare to a year ago? What percentage of hospital emergency wards are redirecting ambulances? What is the added health risk from hormone-replacement therapy?

Journalists have a love-hate relationship with numbers. They believe they need them "to add verisimilitude to an otherwise bald and unconvincing narrative," as Gilbert and Sullivan said in *The Mikado*.

Matters of great public interest are reported poorly, or not reported at all, because of pervasive numbers anxiety in the media.

Yet since they aren't really comfortable around numbers, reporters tend to grab the first one handy and quickly hang it on the prose, like an ornament on a Christmas tree. This behaviour leads to the Tyranny of the Convenient Number.

Consider the *Star* story in August last year about a 48-year-old man killed by lightning at a remote campsite in a Killarney wilderness park. The first question any editor would ask is how many people are killed by lightning every year in Canada. So the story quoted a figure of "about 16 people a year" from a website operated by an amateur "storm chaser."

But that number is patently nonsense. It's obvious to anyone who thinks for a few seconds that the number of lightning strikes must vary greatly from year to year depending on thunderstorm frequency and intensity. Equally obvious is that human exposure to dangerous lightning would also be highly variable.

Sure enough, the official number of deaths annually from lightning in Canada, as verified by Statistics Canada, fluctuated widely over the past dozen years from just one in 2002 to a maximum of 11 in 1994. The median was five, a mere third of the website's figure.

Such Convenient Numbers abound in our society, often supplied by groups with a vested interest in making some social problem seem large and pressing. Claims about the numbers of Canadians who supposedly suffer from a severe allergy to peanuts rested for years on a meagre research base. And the alarming 940,000 figure often quoted for the number of birds that collide with lit office towers and other artificial structures annually in Toronto is speciously precise for what is basically an extrapolation from whatever proportion can't fly away after colliding and manage to be picked up.

All too often the numbers that find their way into print or onto air simply don't make sense. Stephen Lewis was once quoted as saying in a speech that AIDS was killing 300 million people a year. You would think someone would have noticed, since at that rate Africa would long ago have been depopulated.

Yet a reporter typed that nonsensical number and an editor read it and it got into all editions of a newspaper. (The correct figure is 3 million.)

Or take the chart that appeared in a Toronto-based newspaper (not the *Star*) that compared health resources between Canada and other countries.

According to the numbers, Canada has a mere 10.3 CT scanners per 1,000 population, while Japan boasted 92.6. Which would mean one CT scanner for every 10 Japanese. (The correct figure was 92.6 per million people.)

Yes, mental alarms should have sounded in both cases. Yet as embarrassing as they are, such slips aren't the media's real numbers problem.

The true concern is that matters of great public interest are reported poorly, or not reported at all, because of pervasive numbers anxiety in the media.

Journalists who aggressively question politicians on policy matters suddenly become silent stenographers when those same public figures start throwing numbers around. Look at the confusing reportage on climate change, a subject founded on numerical modelling and the detection and attribution of statistical trends.

Because most reporters don't have the background or the inclination to tackle the numerical underpinnings of climate change, the story becomes transformed into something they do understand: a political controversy.

When the media do handle numbers well, the force of the resulting coverage has the power to change public policy. Remember the recent investigative series by the *Star* and its sister papers about airline safety? The reporters ferreted out elusive numbers, explained them well, and marshalled them as big weapons in the stories. Action followed.

Such triumphs are the exception to the generally unsatisfactory handling of numbers in the media. Hand wringing and finger pointing, however, aren't much of a solution.

Some media outlets, like the *Star,* already offer numbers workshops for reporters and editors. Many more are needed. Journalism schools are starting to at least try to tackle numbers proficiency but there's plenty of room there for improvement.

Perhaps editors could even take the daring step of hiring even half as many new reporters with science or engineering backgrounds as with arts or humanities degrees.

After all, in today's quantitative-obsessed society, shouldn't a facility with numbers be considered just as important by the media as the ability to craft a telling metaphor or the familiarity with history required to put current developments into context?

The issue goes far beyond how we journalists handle numbers. The poor numeracy of the Canadian public ought to be the real cause for concern, especially the fact that almost no one in authority seems to care, and that otherwise intelligent people offer up the idiotic excuse that they were "never any good at math."

All this matters greatly, because we construct the world around us as much with numbers today as with words. Yet people will willingly do battle over the perversion of language by a phrase like "The Coalition of the Willing," because they understand how words can be used to shape reality, but similar flim-flammery with numbers mostly escapes critical scrutiny and thought.

That actually makes numbers more powerful than words, because often they shape reality without many people being any the wiser. As Temple University math professor John Allen Paulos wrote in his book, *A Mathematician Reads the Newspaper*:

> Mathematics is not primarily a matter of plugging numbers into formulas
> and performing rote computations. It is a way of thinking and questioning
> that may be unfamiliar to many of us, but is available to almost all of us.

DISCUSSION

A first set of questions to ask about this (and any) article has to do with its factual accuracy. We need to determine, for example, whether the then-Solicitor General Bob Runciman really did use "Canada-wide statistics . . . restricting his example to an earlier period from 1986 to 1991," as Calamai states. Claims of this sort might be confirmed by looking for independent evidence gathered via the Internet or library records.

A second set of questions we should ask involves the clarity of Calamai's explanations of the numeracy problems he mentions in connection with Runciman's arguments. One alleged problem is the confusion between a rise in the absolute number of youth crimes and a rise in the youth crime *rate*. If Runciman committed this confusion, then it clearly was a serious evidential error. In other cases it's less clear what problem Calamai is reporting. Notice, for example, that while Calamai clearly takes Runciman's presentation of Canada-wide data to have been part of "bamboozling" the media, he does not explain why the use of nation-wide data should have been considered irrelevant or statistically incorrect. Perhaps the details of Runciman's press releases would make this clear, but it is not clear from the article itself.

The charge that Runciman cherry-picked data from an earlier period ("restricting his example to an earlier period from 1986 to 1991") that is known to differ from the current situation is serious if accurate, but again it's unclear that this is the best description of Runciman's reasoning. We would have to know more about the situation than Calamai explains before we could judge whether in the mid-1990s it was bamboozling on Runciman's part, and innumeracy on the media's part, to rely on data that was, by Calamai's own account, as recent as 1991.

To see why this is so, suppose that the issue instead was something like Canadians' attitudes toward their pets. In that case, survey data from five years earlier would probably be quite reliable; national trends in attitudes toward pets are unlikely to change very rapidly, other things being equal. On the other hand, if the year was 2004 and we were considering the wisdom of investing heavily in technology stocks, then using only data from 1994 to 1999 would be indefensible; the collapse of the market in 2001 makes for a significant distinction between the situation in 2004 and the situation between 1994 and 1999. So the question is whether the use in 1995 of youth crime statistics from 1986 to 1991 is more like the pet attitudes example or more like the stock market example. The article itself doesn't give us enough information to decide.

Much of the article is a straightforward defence of the idea that journalists should possess (and should exercise) at least basic skills in statistics and numeracy more generally. To that extent it is hard to fault. At a minimum, however, Calamai's description of critical thinking is worth questioning. He writes that the relevant sort of numerical reasoning does not require "the ability to solve quadratic equations, calculate square roots, or even figure out percentages." Seeing the problems with the Runciman claims "simply required people to use their noggins in a critical fashion. After all, looking at the rate or incidence of some phenomenon is familiar territory." This may well be an oversimplification, though. As was discussed in the Introduction, using your head is very often a matter of using something else: the library, an expert, a database, or a calculator. A failure to do so might indicate the lack of specifically numerical skills, but it might also just indicate a lack of general research skills or, for that matter, a lack of motivation. This indicates at least one confounding explanation for Calamai's suggestion of a lack of numeracy skills among media reporters: perhaps reporters are simply not given an incentive to write stories that explain numerical or statistical fallacies. The problem may be editorial policies and practices as well as journalistic numeracy.

Finally, Calamai cites British researcher "John Brynner" as having shown a 3.5-year half life for unused numeracy skills. Ironically, this is a tidy example of a journalist using a statistic in a meaningless fashion. Even if that number made sense in its original context, the stark assertion of a 3.5-year half-life for unused numeracy skills is opaque when thrown out on its own. Half-life is a concept originating in physics, where it means the time it takes for half a sample of some radioactive isotope to decay into another isotope. What could the corresponding phenomenon be, when it comes to numeracy skills? Are some particular skills (e.g., factoring) lost altogether while others are wholly retained, or do people just become half as good at all their skills? (Could you lose your ability to perform division on whole numbers, but retain your ability to multiply by fractions?) Or is it some combination of these?

A quantification of numeracy appropriate to the claim in question could be performed, in one sense: we could give many people a mathematics test, and then give groups of them the same test (or a very similar one) over the years. In this way we might determine how long it takes for those who haven't been using their numeracy skills to decline as a group to an average test score that's half the original average test score. Of course, it would be ferociously difficult both to define and to measure *disuse of numerical skills*. But even could we do so, the people who did half as well on the subsequent test would not very clearly have become half as numerate. It would just mean they had lost whatever one has to lose in order to do half as well on that particular test. Without knowing what that test is, and what it measures, the 3.5-year figure is just an impressive-looking number with no concrete interpretation—the very thing that Calamai is more generally (and correctly) arguing that journalists should not reproduce.

Does that statistic even make sense in its original context? There's a further lesson here about the difficulty of accurate reporting and of critical reading. When first reading Calamai's article I had never heard of British researcher John Brynner, and a search of social science publication databases turned up no relevant results. Internet search to the rescue! Yet that search also generated depressingly few hits for a supposedly "leading British social-science researcher." Working through the few available Internet links, and following on from links within them, I was eventually led to an old press release about a John Brynner at the Joint Centre for Longitudinal Research in the Institute of Education, University of London. Scrolling through the institute's web pages, I discovered the existence of a John *Bynner,* no "r," who did in fact look very much like a leading British social-science researcher. Unfortunately Calamai misspelled his name; but fortunately his own university committed the same misspelling, and kindly left it on a web page for me to find.

Armed with the correct spelling of Bynner's name, I was able to find several pieces of published work dealing with adult numeracy skills and employment. None of them seemed to contain the claim of a 3.5-year half-life for unused skills, not even in different wording. One of the papers reported a study indicating that the average score among men on a numeracy test dropped to 55 percent of the original average, after five years of unemployment, but that is not a statement about numeracy *skills;* nor is it strictly half the original score; nor is it 3.5 years; nor is the correlation with lack of use. Given that the half-life claim has the problems already noted, there is reason to think a responsible social scientist would not make it. My failure to find it with some reading (and some computerized text-searching for the string "half-life") made it reasonable for me to conclude that the claim is probably not supported by Bynner's work. Indeed I eventually contacted Professor Bynner directly and asked him whether he makes this claim explicitly or implicitly in his published work. The short answer is no. (The longer answer is, no, and he can't imagine having said it in conversation, either.)[2]

To quote Calamai himself: "[A] reporter typed that nonsensical number and an editor read it and it got into all editions of a newspaper." In this case, surely the problem is not innumeracy but sheer *convenience,* the factor that figures in the title of the article. The 3.5-year half-life is an impressive number that seems to support the general argument, so it's easy to use without very careful consideration of what it might mean, nor of how an audience could parse it. The story of my chase for the details shows once again that getting things right can be harder work than someone working to media deadlines might always be able to afford. Still, the biggest problem with the half-life claim was apparent on a first reading, with no web searching required: it was simply unclear what the number could mean. Even if you could not devote that much time and energy to chasing down the details, you would be justified in not taking that claim as evidence of any sort.

The article makes a borderline-successful case for its main conclusions—which is, remember, a separate question from whether its conclusions are plausible on independent grounds. Where the article lacks evidence for its claims, at least the claims tend to be sufficiently specific and sufficiently matters of public record that we can investigate them directly ourselves. (Compare this with the mix of vague generalizations and specific claims based on unconfirmable appeals to private personal communication, in the previous reading.) Calamai argues more through illustrative examples than through industry-wide representative data, but most of the examples seem genuine, at least.

The article is weakest when its unargued assumptions are thickest, as when "toxins in salmon, silicone breast implants, . . . the fictional poverty line, gender pay inequities, race and crime, violence against women, drug use in schools, [and] the education gap with other countries" are suddenly presented as having been handled innumerately by the media, without any evidential support. Though it also contains one or two outright confusions or errors, a core of reasonable evidence remains for the conclusion that numeracy and critical thinking are important but underemphasized virtues in the mainstream news media. The article moreover gives us cues, names, and citations (not always successfully, as we saw), helping us to investigate the matter further ourselves. It may be more useful for that, in fact, than for making a compelling argument itself.

FIGURE 11.1

Critical Thinking in Practice

The goal of this text is to develop habits of monitoring our own thinking and the thinking of people around us in order to gradually improve our skills of distinguishing reliable from unreliable reasoning on the fly. This chapter is your chance to practise those skills.

Gary Conner/Photo Edit

READING 3

SOCIAL CONSENSUS AND WEIRD BELIEFS

Print and broadcast journalist Dan Zakreski wrote for the Saskatoon *Star-Phoenix* regarding two similar stories of alleged cult-based child abuse that occurred in and around Saskatoon, Saskatchewan, in the early 1990s. Both involved accusations of horrifying abuse. In both cases, multiple adults were charged with crimes based on the testimony of children, and in both cases the testimony included outrageous claims of apparently Satanic or ritualistic torture and murder. Finally, in both cases few or none of the charges, and certainly none of their most bizarre aspects, were supported by independent evidence. The most extreme charges or details of the accusations seemed to be artifacts of both the preconceptions and the methods used by some police and other interviewers to elicit the testimony from the children.

The first case occurred in the city of Saskatoon itself. In 1991 more than a dozen adults were charged with crimes based on children's testimony that implicated them in ritualistically murdering and eating children, in rites of black magic, and in pedophilic orgies involving dozens of people. These charges were dropped before the cases came to trial—although the Crown suggested that this was done partly to spare the children the trauma of a trial and not simply because the evidence overall was incredible, self-contradictory, and corrupted by the use of shoddy methods. This case eventually became notorious across Canada after it was reported as "The Scandal of the Century" by the CBC investigative program *the fifth estate*.[3] In 2005 twelve of the accused finally won a civil judgment for malicious prosecution against a senior Saskatoon police office, a child therapist, and a Crown prosecutor, who had as a group taken the lead in collecting evidence and pressing charges against the twelve.

Just as the Saskatoon case was disintegrating from a lack of credible evidence, however, a similar investigation was beginning to run out of control in the nearby town of Martensville. Amidst a tangle of personality clashes, poor training, and lax supervision, the town's small police force consulted with the Saskatoon city police and the Crown prosecutor to lay charges of sexual abuse and forcible confinement, based on testimony that included accusations of child murder, torture, and (what would have been) crippling sexual abuse conducted at a "Devil Church." Eventually 173 charges were laid against nine people, including the owners of a daycare facility and several officers from the Martensville, Saskatoon, and Royal Canadian Mounted Police forces.

Most of the accused have now received apologies, or settlements, or both, from the government of Saskatchewan in light of how the investigations were conducted. The Martensville case too was the subject of a damning report by *the fifth estate* and was the focus of an RCMP inquiry.[4] The following selection is from an article written by Zakreski about one phase of the Martensville investigation.

This reading raises issues discussed in Chapters 2, 7, and 8.

As you read:

1. Think of some possible origins for the police chief's apparently detailed knowledge about local Satanic cults.

2. In terms of hypothesis-testing and evidence, describe the deputies' reasoning during their nighttime patrol.
3. From the deputies' description of the consequences of expressing their scepticism, what do we learn about the consensus among local officials regarding the existence and dangers of Satanic cults?

Compare your answers with the observations that follow the reading.

Nightmare in Martensville
Dan Zakreski

"Nightmare in Martensville: Part 1." Saskatoon Star-Phoenix, *March 24, 2001, E1. Reprinted with permission.*

It's Easter 1992 and Const. Mike Swan, armed with a riot shotgun, revolver and assault rifle, is dispatched to the streets of Martensville to confront and do battle with a busload full of bloodthirsty Satanists. Chief's orders, issued directly. Martensville police chief Mike Johnston had summoned Swan and Const. Mel Neufeld to an emergency meeting earlier that same day. Johnston had it on a tip from a source that Satanists from Weyburn and Estevan were driving up to hunt humans in the town of 3,500.

Martensville, a quiet little community north of Saskatoon, is on alert. "We were given explicit instructions they were coming," Swan recalls.

Unusual orders, yes, but not unprecedented. Johnston had the devil on his mind a lot that spring. Martensville police reports from the time are cluttered with his references to Eohippus Draconis, Elderbeast, the Clan, Star of Seven and scarab beetle tattoos.

In a report dated April 16, 1992, Johnston writes how "the indications were that tonight was a very important night with the Occult in the preparation of potential victims." He believed there were two independent groups of Satanists living in the area.

"The group in town is known as The Brotherhood of the Ram, with the Ram being a reference to Satan," he wrote.

"The other group operating around Mennon is also Satanic in nature, however, is a separate Sect known as The Temple of Seth and is generally the upper class types. The two groups use different types of rituals however both can and do offer human sacrifices."

Johnston believed the out-of-towners were coming to "take out" a local family. Swan swallowed his incredulity, "he's our chief and we had to do what he told us," and suited up.

"He called us in and armed us to the teeth. I had a riot shotgun and an FN assault rifle with 30-shot clips, taped back to back. He wanted us to get whatever we could," Swan said in an interview.

"He had us on the lookout, he made it out as if, like, these guys are coming and we're going to be in the fight of our lives that night."

The busload of gun-toting Satanists never did materialize on the streets of Martensville that Easter night.

Const. Mike Swan recalls becoming increasingly skeptical of his orders as he patrolled the empty town.

"And then as the night went on, if we're in such a fight, where's our backup? Where's he (Johnston)? Shouldn't the RCMP be in on this? Saskatoon city police? What are two guys going to do against 30 or 40 coming, armed, in a school bus?"

Within months, disillusioned, Swan and Neufeld concluded the investigation and hysteria over Satanic cults was "a crock of shit" and took their concerns to Martensville mayor Rob Friesen.

The mayor was unswayed.

"Once we made our stand, said this isn't happening, it never did happen, and we can prove a lot of it, disprove a lot of it, they just blocked us. We weren't allowed to see any reports, we weren't allowed to have nothing to do with it because we could blow a lot of it apart," Swan said.

Welcome to the Martensville child sexual assault investigation, circa 1992.

DISCUSSION

Despite being very short, this excerpt from Dan Zakreski's article raises some interesting critical thinking questions. Before we consider those issues, however, we should first do some critical thinking about the reading itself.

This article raises few serious red flags in its reporting. Since Zakreski directly quotes the deputy, the non-quoted descriptions of the deputy's experiences are presumably also based on a direct interview with him. The article also clearly gives the impression that Zakreski has viewed the police chief's reports that he quotes. So there is no obvious worry about second-hand or third-hand information being circulated in the article itself. Moreover the details of police chief Mike Johnston's reports can (or could, at the time of writing) be confirmed by viewing copies of them posted online by *the fifth estate*.[5] Whether former Constable Swan was accurately reporting events to Zakreski is of course a further question—and one that might have more to do with his memory than with his honesty, as we saw in Chapters 7 and 8. We should bear in mind the possibility that he is misremembering or misdescribing events in hindsight. But the details about the weapons sound plausible, and the police chief's attitudes and beliefs, independently confirmable, would provide an explanation for such an apparently extreme set of orders. That this report about the events of Easter 1992 is generally accurate seems a good working hypothesis.

We might regard it as less certain that Swan and Neufeld really were excluded from the investigation after expressing doubts about it, since here Swan is speaking about more general events, and speaking for Neufeld as well. Ideally we would have input from the other constable too, and a more specific account of the "freezing out" process by the mayor (and, presumably, others). But this element of Swan's report is supported not just by his own say-so, but by the fact that it helps explain something that calls out for an explanation: namely, that the prosecutions took place at all, given the lack of credible evidence for virtually all of the allegations. We can return to this momentarily.

The article presents a nice example of critical thinking in action. By Swan's description, he and his partner engaged in (literally, now) a textbook case of testing a hypothesis or conjecture against independent evidence. We get an image from the reading of Swan driving around Martensville and asking himself, in effect, "What would the world have to be like, in order for what the Chief told us to be correct?" Of course, the immediate answer is that Estevan and Weyburn would have to be home to bands of murderous Satanic cultists. But Swan indicates the still wider scope of the ramifications through his rhetorical questions.

Even supposing that Estevan and Weyburn *were* home to bands of murderous Satanists, why would the defence of an entire town against busloads of armed attackers be left to two constables in the Martensville town police force, if there were evidence in advance of the impending attack? There are logically possible explanations, of course: because nobody cared; or because key personnel in the Saskatoon city police force and the RCMP were also part of the murderous cultish plot.

Apparently neither of these answers struck Swan as having the credibility of a third answer: that there simply *was* no reasonable evidence of an impending attack. *This* hypothesis seemed to be supported by such facts as that no backup forces had been called, and that Chief Johnston himself was not out on patrol. In other words, the chief had not done the things a reasonable person would do, if in possession of evidence that a group of murderers was en route to a town. Swan concluded that there was no such evidence, though he put the matter in rather blunter terms. The reasoning can be put in the form of a Modus Tollens argument:

1. If the chief had good evidence for what he told us, a range of very specific things would be happening.
2. But those things aren't happening.

Therefore,

3. The chief does not have good evidence for what he told us.

One question, then, is why the police chief made these statements at all or sent the deputies out on patrol so heavily armed. A partial explanation can be found in the fact that he was receiving information from citizens he considered reliable, regarding the existence and nature of various bands of Satanic abusers in Martensville.[6] Of course this raises the further question of why he would have found such reports reliable in the first place. His file notes, quoted in Zakreski's article, are a highly revealing insight into his view of the world; the comments suggest a detailed theory about devil-worship, including such subtleties as its class distinctions and some very specific regional variations. It is implausible, though, that the particular theory underlying those file notes arose in all its confidence, complexity, and ramifications, with no relevant precursor, from whatever the chief heard over the course of a few weeks during the investigation. Presumably he already had a broad conception of how the world works that contained elements of this theory, or at least constituted fertile ground in which the thought of a massive local conspiracy of Satanists would take root as a likely explanation for something or other.

Moreover, the article mentions that the population of Martensville was around 3,500. The remarks attributed to Chief Johnston by his deputies are perhaps more explicable if one notes that Weyburn's 1991 population was roughly 9,700, while that of Estevan was roughly 10,000. For people unfamiliar with small-town life it may seem strange to think of a town of 10,000 as large, but from the perspective of a much smaller town it may have seemed more believable that Weyburn and Estevan could be home to "a busload" of human-sacrificing Satanic cultists.

Given that officers—even lower-ranking ones—within the Martensville force were prepared to say, "This isn't happening," how did the perception that it *was* happening last long enough for charges to be laid and a trial to occur? Again, the article provides a suggestion. Of course, it provides only one side of the story in reporting Swan's contention that he and Neufeld were shut out of the case once they voiced scepticism about it. But this would certainly help explain the otherwise astonishing continuation of the prosecution in spite of a virtually complete lack of confirming evidence. Convinced of the truth of the allegations and uncomfortable with challenges to them, the investigation's insiders may have maintained an atmosphere of confirmatory feedback simply by excluding any naysayers from their discussions. This implicates both confirmation biases of the sort explored in Chapter 7 and social biases as described in Chapter 8.

For a short reading, this article raises many critical thinking issues. Most of these implicate further details about the events in question, which I will not explore. But the details that have been presented enable us to see a few phenomena at work: hypothesis testing and critical reasoning in a stressful situation, the ability of very strange beliefs to gain a sudden and wide currency in a group, and the interplay of psychological and social biases in the spread and persistence of those beliefs. Among the lessons here is one about the consequences of holding strange and unwarranted beliefs. If you already think that Satanists may well be everywhere among us, kidnapping and sacrificing human beings, it becomes much more likely that you'll send deputies out armed to the teeth to fend them off or that you'll contribute to the prosecution of innocent people for cult-related crime with no compelling evidence. The point has nothing essential to do with beliefs about Satanism, though. More generally: it's hard to keep crackpottery confined to a single shelf in your mental kitchen.

READING 4

BIASES AND STATISTICS IN HOMEOPATHY AND CONVENTIONAL MEDICINE

Homeopathy is a popular form of alternative health treatment in Canada and many other countries. Dating from the middle of the eighteenth century, it is based on just a few principles. These include the "Law of Similars," according to which diseases are cured by substances that replicate their symptoms, and the principle of minimal dosage, that these substances have their curative effects when prepared at extremely low levels of concentration, dissolved in water. Jointly these amount to the view that if one concentration of a substance *causes* something like the symptoms of the disease in question, then a much lower concentration of that substance *cures* that disease.

Partly because no known mechanisms of medical intervention cohere with these principles, there is considerable scepticism in the wider medical community about the efficacy of homeopathy. Indeed, the concentrations of supposedly active ingredients in some homeopathic dilutions are so low that there may be zero molecules of the active substance (the *solute*) in a sample. In other words, the patient is just being given water.

Some homeopaths argue that in these cases the water itself has been "imprinted" or "potentiated" by exposure to the solute, in some way that persists even after dilution completely eliminates the presence of the solute. Because there is no clear idea of *how* this could happen, the question is whether there is sufficiently strong evidence to conclude that *something* chemical or mechanical must be happening with these solutions anyhow (though we don't understand what, precisely) in order to explain that evidence. Think of it this way: we might tentatively accept weak evidence for the existence of a phenomenon, if the phenomenon coheres with things that are already known about the relevant field. And strong evidence for the existence of a phenomenon, even one that does not cohere well with things already known, can nevertheless drive us to accept that some unknown explanation must exist. But when we have weak evidence for a phenomenon that moreover does not cohere well with what is known, we can reasonably treat this evidence as ambiguous or misleading, a result of chance, bias, and misinterpretation (though of course any such judgment is defeasible).

The question, then, is whether there is sufficiently robust evidence for the clinical effectiveness of homeopathic treatment to support the conclusion that something besides chance, bias, or misinterpretation must explain the reports of its success. For a variety of reasons like those just sketched, many medical scientists have been disposed to see alleged homeopathic benefits as mere placebo effects. That is more or less the null hypothesis of the following article by Aijing Shang et al. in the medical journal *The Lancet*. (The expression "et al." is an abbreviation for the Latin *et alii*, meaning "and others." It is widely used in the sciences to truncate long lists of co-authors.) This article is a special form of scientific publication: a **meta-analysis**, which is a statistical analysis of a collection of other studies. Meta-analysis is a useful approach to the problem of understanding what a broad swathe of the scientific literature, and not just an individual study, tells us about some phenomenon or problem.

While the article raises many issues about homeopathy, medical science, and science more broadly, at its heart is the meta-analysis comparing the statistical results in a set of homeopathic studies with those in a set of *allopathic,* or conventional, medical studies. According to the authors, their analysis of the data shows that a range of biasing factors alone is sufficient to explain the apparent efficacy of homeopathy, but is not sufficient to explain the apparent efficacy of conventional medicine in the selected studies. Hence there is no need to propose more than a placebo effect for homeopathy, while the same is not true of conventional medicine.

A NOTE ON ODDS RATIOS

In Chapter 6 we introduced a set of statistical concepts mainly in terms of normal distributions. The approach we used is particularly suited for measuring and representing properties that can vary by degrees in a population or sample—as height varies by degrees among people. A statistical concept we did not cover, but which is very useful in more specialized contexts, is the notion of an **odds ratio.** The article by Shang et al. makes heavy use of this concept, so it's worth explaining the basic idea first.

In ordinary talk we often use the term "odds" to mean the same thing as "chance" or "probability." "What are the odds of that?" might be taken to mean nothing more than "What is the probability of that?" Strictly speaking, though, the odds of an event are expressed as a ratio: the probability that the event occurs divided by the probability that it does not occur. If I win 60 percent of the card games I play, then the *probability* that I win a randomly chosen game is 0.6. The *odds* that I win a randomly chosen game, however, are the probability that I win divided by the probability that I don't win, which is 0.6/0.4, or 1.5. (The probability that I don't win, remember, is 1 minus the probability that I do win.) There are advantages and conveniences to this way of representing the likelihood of an event, particularly having to do with tracking the simple occurrence or non-occurrence of events or properties.

So odds are already a kind of ratio. But what is *called* an odds ratio (or *relative* odds) is something further: a ratio between odds. To see the point, suppose that we wanted to measure the effects of a proposed driver education program. The overall incidence of car accidents in our city might be 80 in 100,000, meaning that the probability of an accident on a randomly chosen car trip is 80/100,000 or .0008. Hence the odds of an accident are .0008/.9992 ≈ .0008. Now we randomly choose 200 drivers. After giving them our driver training course, we monitor them each on their next 100 trips, giving us a total of 20,000 trips from trained drivers. In those trips, suppose we find a total of 6 accidents, for an accident probability of 6/20,000, or .0003. This makes the odds of an accident among our trained drivers .0003/.9997 ≈ .0003. Now we have two sets of odds: the odds of having an accident without the new driver training, and the odds of having an accident with

DETAILS MATTER

This "difference from 1" measure for odds ratios is non-linear, since there is no highest value that an odds ratio can take, but it cannot be lower than zero. Taking the logarithm of odds ratios addresses this problem, producing an approximately normal distribution, more straightforward confidence intervals, and a spatial proportionality on graphs. For a "log odds ratio" a null effect is represented as the value 0, with kinds and sizes of effects indicated by values below and above 0. Often, though, odds ratios are transformed into log odds ratios to simplify the calculation of standard deviations and confidence intervals, and then are transformed back by taking the antilog of these values.

the new driver training. The ratio between these odds is an odds ratio. In this case it would work out to .0003/.0008 = .375. This would be a measure of the effect of driver training on the probability of having an accident.

The utility of this concept in the medical science literature is not hard to see, since it's very well suited to expressing the comparative effects of a treatment between the test group and the control group in a study. From each group we can calculate the odds of getting some effect—say, whether patients get the measles in a control group and in a vaccinated group. Using those odds we can then construct an odds ratio that expresses in a single number the size of the treatment effect. Depending on how we describe the situation (whether we define our interest as the property of having measles or that of not having measles), the kind of effect will be indicated by whether the odds ratio is below 1 or above 1, and the size of the effect will be shown by how far from 1 the odds ratio is.

An odds ratio of exactly 1 means that the treatment or test condition has had no measurable effect. If 75 out of 100 ulcer patients experience nausea without any treatment, and 30 out of 40 ulcer patients experience nausea when they eat raw ginger every day, we can see that the odds of nausea in the untreated group are $75/25 = 3$, and in the ginger-treated group are $30/10 = 3$, so the odds ratio of treatment to control (forgoing the conversion into probabilities) is $3/3 = 1$. Which is just another way of saying that, according to this data, eating raw ginger had no measurable effect on nausea among ulcer patients. Moreover, odds ratios are every bit as subject to degrees of confidence and margins of error as the statistical concepts we examined in Chapter 6. As we saw in that chapter, our confidence in the accuracy of some statistical conclusion depends in part on how precise we want the judgment to be. When we deal with odds ratios, it is a red flag if the confidence interval, calculated to achieve whatever level of significance we are aiming for, overlaps the value 1. (Again, 95 percent and 99 percent are standard confidence levels in many fields.) If the confidence interval includes 1 at the appropriate level of significance, then there is an elevated chance that the treatment has no effect at all. The article uses "CI" as an abbreviation for "confidence interval."

As you read:

1. For each factor listed as making a significant difference to the probability that a trial reports positive effects, suggest an explanation for why that factor might

amount to a bias. For example, why might "analysis not by intention to treat" (covered in Chapter 9, recall) bias the outcome of a study?

2. Note what the authors claim about earlier meta-analyses that were performed on the homeopathic literature. Explain the problems they attribute to those meta-analyses.

3. Explain any evidential red flags you notice in the article.

Compare your observations with the brief critical analysis that follows the reading.

Are the Clinical Effects of Homoeopathy Placebo Effects? Comparative Study of Placebo-Controlled Trials of Homoeopathy and Allopathy

Aijing Shang, Karin Huwiler-Müntener, Linda Nartey, Peter Jüni, Stephan Dörig, Jonathan A.C. Sterne, Daniel Pewsner, Matthias Egger

THE LANCET, V366 (9487): 726–732. @2005.

SUMMARY

Background

Homoeopathy is widely used, but specific effects of homoeopathic remedies seem implausible. Bias in the conduct and reporting of trials is a possible explanation for positive findings of trials of both homoeopathy and conventional medicine. We analysed trials of homoeopathy and conventional medicine and estimated treatment effects in trials least likely to be affected by bias.

Methods

Placebo-controlled trials of homoeopathy were identified by a comprehensive literature search, which covered 19 electronic databases, reference lists of relevant papers, and contacts with experts. Trials in conventional medicine matched to homoeopathy trials for disorder and type of outcome were randomly selected from the Cochrane Controlled Trials Register (issue 1, 2003). Data were extracted in duplicate and outcomes coded so that odds ratios below 1 indicated benefit. Trials described as double-blind, with adequate randomisation, were assumed to be of higher methodological quality. Bias effects were examined in funnel plots and meta-regression models.

Findings

110 homoeopathy trials and 110 matched conventional-medicine trials were analysed. The median study size was 65 participants (range ten to 1573). 21 homoeopathy trials (19%) and nine (8%) conventional-medicine trials were of higher quality. In both groups, smaller trials and those of lower quality showed

more beneficial treatment effects than larger and higher-quality trials. When the analysis was restricted to large trials of higher quality, the odds ratio was 0·88 (95% CI 0·65 − 1 ·19) for homoeopathy (eight trials) and 0·58 (0·39 − 0·85) for conventional medicine (six trials).

Interpretation

Biases are present in placebo-controlled trials of both homoeopathy and conventional medicine. When account was taken for these biases in the analysis, there was weak evidence for a specific effect of homoeopathic remedies, but strong evidence for specific effects of conventional interventions. This finding is compatible with the notion that the clinical effects of homoeopathy are placebo effects.

INTRODUCTION

Homoeopathy is a widely used but controversial complementary or alternative therapy.[1–3] The basic premise is that like is cured by like (*similia similibus curentur*)—diseases can be treated by substances that produce the same signs and symptoms in a healthy individual.[4,5] The preparation of remedies involves serial dilution, commonly to the extent that no molecules of the original substance remain, and vigorous shaking between dilutions (potentisation). During this process information is thought to be transferred from the diluted substance to the solvent,[6] which in the light of current knowledge seems implausible. Many people therefore assume that any effects of homoeopathy must be non-specific placebo effects.[7]

Bias in the conduct and reporting of trials is a possible explanation for positive findings of placebo-controlled trials of both homoeopathy and allopathy (conventional medicine).[8,9] Publication bias is defined as the preferential and more rapid publication of trials with statistically significant and beneficial results than of trials without significant results.[10] The low methodological quality of many trials is another important source of bias.[11] These biases are more likely to affect small than large studies; the smaller a study, the larger the treatment effect necessary for the results to be statistically significant, whereas large studies are more likely to be of high methodological quality and published even if their results are negative. We examined the effects of homoeopathy and conventional medicine observed in matched pairs of placebo-controlled trials, assessed trial quality and the probability of publication and related biases, and estimated results of large trials least affected by such biases.

METHODS
LITERATURE SEARCH AND DATA SOURCES

We updated a previous comprehensive search for placebo-controlled trials of homoeopathy, which covered publications up to August, 1995.[12] We searched 19 electronic databases, including specialised homoeopathic and complementary-medicine registries, covering the period from 1995 to January,

2003: MEDLINE, Pre-MEDLINE, EMBASE, DARE, CCTR, CDSR, CINAHL, AMED, MANTIS, Toxline, PASCAL, BIOL, Science Citation Index, CISCOM, British Homeopathic Library, the Homeopathy Abstract page, HomInform Homoeopathic library, NCCAM, and SIGLE. The search terms in MEDLINE were (homeop* OR homoeop* OR homeopathy (MeSH)) AND (placebo* OR placebos (MeSH) OR placebo effect (MeSH) OR sham). Search terms for the other databases were much the same. We also checked the reference lists of relevant papers, including reviews and meta-analyses of homoeopathic interventions, and contacted experts in the specialty. There were no language restrictions.

We searched the Cochrane Controlled Trials Register to identify placebo-controlled trials of conventional medicine. This bibliographic database of controlled trials is maintained by the Cochrane Collaboration. As part of an international effort to search systematically health-care journals worldwide and other sources of information, the collaboration has combined results of electronic searches and searches by hand to create a comprehensive database of trials.[13] We searched issue 1, 2003, of the Cochrane Controlled Trials Register, which included 353 809 bibliographic references.

STUDY SELECTION

We defined inclusion and exclusion criteria a priori and applied the same criteria to trials of homoeopathy and of conventional medicine. Inclusion criteria were: that the trial was controlled and of treatments or preventive measures with clinical outcomes; that it had a parallel-group design with placebo control; that there was random or quasi-random assignment to treatment and placebo groups; and that a written report (eg, journal publication, abstract, thesis, conference proceeding, unpublished report, book chapter, monograph) was available with sufficient data to allow the calculation of odds ratios. We excluded trials of homoeopathic "provings" in which remedies are given to healthy individuals to assess their effects, cross-over trials, and N-of-1 trials.

PROCEDURES

We used prespecified criteria to identify outcomes for inclusion in the analyses. The first choice was the main outcome measure, defined as the outcome used for sample-size calculations. If no main outcome was specified, we selected other outcomes, in the order: patients' overall assessment of improvement; physicians' overall assessment of improvement; and the clinically most relevant other outcome measure (for example, the occurrence or duration of an illness). Outcomes were selected randomly if several were judged equally relevant. For each homoeopathy trial, we identified matching trials of conventional medicine that enrolled patients with similar disorders and assessed similar outcomes. We used computer-generated random numbers to select one from several eligible trials of conventional medicine. Outcomes were selected and trials matched without knowledge of trial results.

We used a piloted data-extraction sheet, which covered descriptive information on the trial and study population, intervention, outcome measures, and trial quality.

Data were extracted independently by two observers, and discrepancies were resolved by consensus.

Homoeopathic interventions were defined as classical, clinical, or complex homoeopathy, or as isopathy. Classical homoeopathy was defined as comprehensive homoeopathic history-taking, followed by the prescription of a single individualised remedy, possibly with subsequent change of remedy in response to changing symptoms. If no comprehensive homoeopathic history was taken and all patients received a single, identical remedy, interventions were classified as clinical homoeopathy. Complex homoeopathy was defined as the prescription of a mixture of several different remedies. Interventions were classified as isopathy if the agent that was judged to be the cause of the disorder was used (for example, pollen in pollinosis). Indications for treatment were classified as acute or chronic or primary prevention or prophylaxis (interventions with the intention of preventing the occurrence of a disorder or complication). The duration of follow-up was measured in weeks from the start of the treatment to the assessment of outcomes.

Assessment of study quality focused on three key domains of internal validity:[11,14] randomisation (generation of allocation sequence and concealment of allocation), masking (of patients, therapists, and outcome assessors), and data analysis (by intention to treat or other). Random-number tables, computer-generated random numbers, minimisation, coin-tossing, card-shuffling, and lot-drawing were classified as adequate methods for the generation of the allocation sequence. Sealed, opaque, sequentially numbered assignment envelopes, central randomisation, independently prepared and coded drug packs of identical appearance, and on-site computerised randomisation systems were classified as adequate methods of allocation concealment. Analysis by intention to treat was assumed if the reported number of participants randomised and the number analysed were identical. Descriptions of other methods were coded either as inadequate or unclear, depending on the amount of detail provided. Trials described as double-blind, with adequate methods for the generation of allocation sequence and adequate concealment of allocation, were classified as of higher methodological quality.

GRAPHICAL AND STATISTICAL ANALYSIS

We expressed results on the odds ratio scale and used the method described by Hasselblad and Hedges[15] to convert differences in continuous outcomes to odds ratios. We recoded outcomes if necessary, so that odds ratios below 1·0 indicated a beneficial effect of treatment in all cases. We used descriptive analyses to compare characteristics of homoeopathy and conventional-medicine trials. We examined heterogeneity between trials with standard x^2 tests and calculated I^2 statistics, which measure the proportion of variation in treatment effect estimates due to between-study heterogeneity.[16] We investigated the association between study size and trial results in funnel plots, by plotting odds ratios on the horizontal axis (on a logarithmic scale) against their SE on the vertical axis.[17] The extent to which study-level variables were associated with log odds ratios was examined by fitting of univariable and multivariable meta-regression models.[18] The following variables were considered: SE of log odds ratio, language of publication, indexing of the publication in

MEDLINE, trial quality (masking, generation of allocation sequence, concealment of allocation, intention-to-treat analysis), duration of follow-up, and clinical topic. For homoeopathy trials, we also examined whether effects varied between types of homoeopathy and types of indications (acute, chronic, primary prevention, or prophylaxis).

We combined treatment effects from larger trials of higher quality by use of standard random-effects meta-analysis and used meta-regression analysis to predict treatment effects in trials as large as the largest trials included in the study. Trials with SE in the lowest quartile were defined as larger trials. Results are given as odds ratios, ratios of odds ratios, or asymmetry coefficients with 95% CI. Ratios of odds ratios of less than 1·0 correspond to a smaller odds ratio for trials with the characteristic and hence a larger apparent benefit of the intervention. Funnel-plot asymmetry was measured by the asymmetry coefficient: the ratio of odds ratios per unit increase in SE of log odds ratio.[19] All analyses were done in Stata version 8.2.

ROLE OF THE FUNDING SOURCE

The funding sources had no role in the study design; collection, analysis, or interpretation of data; or the writing of the report. The corresponding author had full access to all the data in the study and had final responsibility for the decision to submit the paper for publication.

RESULTS

We identified 165 potentially eligible reports of placebo-controlled trials of homoeopathy and excluded 60 reports. The commonest reasons for exclusion were insufficient information (precluding the calculation of odds ratios), ineligible study design, multiple publication, and inability to identify a matching trial of conventional medicine (Figure 1). We included 105 publications that reported on a total of 110 independent trials of homoeopathy (webappendix 1) and 110 publications of 110 matched trials of conventional medicine (webappendix 2).

The clinical topics studied in pairs of trials ranged from respiratory infections to surgery and anaesthesiology (Table 1). The outcomes studied were closely matched; overall assessments of response were analysed in 49% of homoeopathy trials and 45% of trials of conventional medicine (Table 2). More detailed information on outcomes is given in the webtable. The average study size was similar for the two groups, with a median of around 65 participants. Overall, study size ranged from ten to 1573 participants. Among homoeopathy trials 48 (44%) concerned clinical homoeopathy, 35 (32%) complex homoeopathy, 18 (16%) classical homoeopathy, and eight (7%) isopathy. For the remaining trial, the nature of the homoeopathic intervention was unclear. 101 (92%) of the conventional-medicine trials investigated drugs, eight (7%) immunotherapy, and one a vaccine. The drugs most frequently tested were non-steroidal anti-inflammatory agents (11 trials), anti-allergy drugs (11 trials), virostatic drugs (11 trials), and antibiotics (seven trials).

FIGURE 1

Identification of 110 Eligible Placebo-Controlled Trials of Homoeopathy That Could Be Matched to an Equal Number of Placebo Controlled Trials of Conventional Medicine

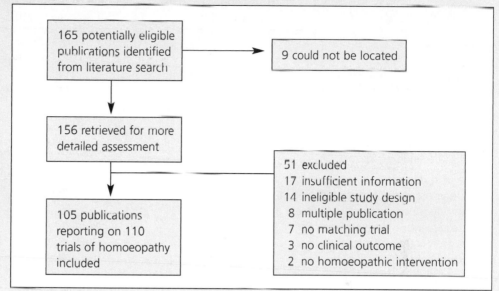

TABLE 1

Distribution of Pairs of Placebo-Controlled Trials by Clinical Topic

Clinical topic	Number of trial pairs
Respiratory-tract infections	21 (19%)
Pollinosis and asthma	16 (15%)
Gynaecology and obstetrics	14 (13%)
Surgery and anaesthetics	12 (11%)
Gastroenterology	12 (11%)
Musculoskeletal disorders	11 (10%)
Neurology	10 (9%)
Other	14 (13%)

53% of homoeopathy trials were published in English compared with 85% of trials in conventional medicine. 50 homoeopathy trials were published in German or French. The two groups of trials also differed in the proportion published in MEDLINE-indexed journals. The two groups had similar methodological quality in terms of masking, generation of allocation sequence, and analysis according to intention to treat, but a higher proportion of homoeopathy trials reported adequate concealment of patients' allocation. 21 (19%) homoeopathy trials and nine (8%) conventional-medicine trials were of higher quality (Table 2).

TABLE 2

Characteristics of Placebo-Controlled Trials of Homoeopathy and Conventional Medicine

	Homoeopathy trials (n = 110)	Conventional-medicine trials (n = 110)
Sample size		
Median (range)	65·5 (10–1573)	65 (12–1367)
Mean (SD)	117 (211)	133 (226)
Median year of publication (range)	1992 (1966–2003)	1994 (1974–2002)
Type of publication		
In English	58 (53%)	94 (85%)
Journal article	94 (85%)	110 (100%)
MEDLINE-indexed journal	45 (41%)	95 (86%)
Type of outcome		
Overall assessment of response	54 (49%)	49 (45%)
Occurrence or duration of disorder	26 (24%)	26 (24%)
Assessment of symptoms	21 (19%)	26 (24%)
Measurement of function or state	6 (5%)	6 (5%)
Assessment of clinical signs	3 (3%)	3 (3%)
Trial quality		
Described as double-blind	101 (92%)	96 (87%)
Adequate generation of allocation sequence	27 (25%)	30 (27%)
Adequate concealment of allocation	49 (45%)	21 (19%)
Analysis by intention to treat	33 (30%)	40 (36%)
Higher quality*	21 (19%)	9 (8%)

*Trials described as double-blind, with adequate generation of allocation sequence and adequate concealment of allocation.

Most odds ratios indicated a beneficial effect of the intervention (Figure 2). SE ranged from 0·12 to 1·65 for homoeopathy trials and 0·13 to 1·52 for conventional-medicine trials. Heterogeneity of trial results was less pronounced for homoeopathy (heterogeneity x^2 = 309, df 109, p < 0·0001) than for conventional medicine (heterogeneity x^2 = 481, df 109, p < 0·0001). This difference is unlikely to be due to chance (p = 0·011 by F test). The proportion of total variation in the estimates of treatment effects due to between-study heterogeneity (I^2)[16] was 65% for homoeopathy and 77% for conventional medicine.

Funnel plots were asymmetrical, with smaller trials (larger SE) in the lower part of the plot showing more beneficial treatment effects than larger trials (smaller SE, Figure 2). In meta-regression models, the association between SE and treatment effects was similar for trials of homoeopathy and conventional medicine: the respective asymmetry coefficients were 0·17 (95% CI 0·10 − 0·32) and 0·21 (0·11 − 0·40). Therefore, with each unit increase in the SE, the odds ratio decreased by a factor of 0·17 for homoeopathy and 0·21 for conventional medicine (Table 3).

FIGURE 2

Funnel Plot of 110 Homoeopathy Trials and 110 Matched Conventional-Medicine Trials

Solid lines indicate predicted treatment effects from meta-regression, with dotted lines representing the 95% CI.

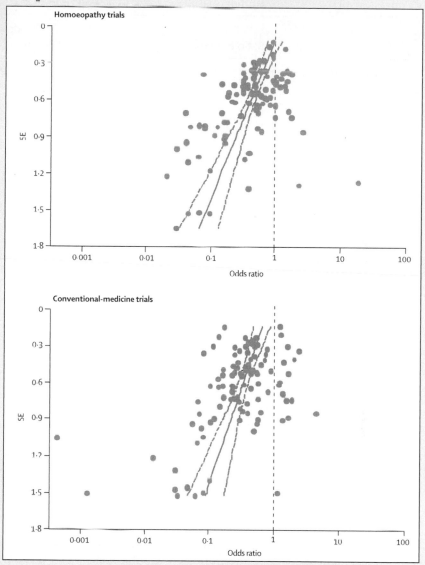

Other sources of heterogeneity between homoeopathy trials included the language of publication (more beneficial effects in trials published in languages other than English), indexing in MEDLINE (more beneficial effects in trials not indexed in MEDLINE), and indicators of trial quality (more beneficial effects in trials of lower quality). The effects of these variables were generally similar for conventional-medicine trials but did not reach statistical significance (Table 3). There was little evidence that treatment effects varied according to duration of follow-up ($p = 0.862$ for homoeopathy, $p = 0.594$ for conventional medicine) or

CHAPTER 11 *Readings and Discussions*

TABLE 3

Univariable Meta-Regression Analysis of Treatment Effects in 110 Placebo-Controlled Trials of Homoeopathy and 110 Matched Trials of Conventional Medicine

Study Characteristics	Homoeopathy		Conventional medicine	
	Ratio of odds	p	Ratio of odds ratios* (95% CI)	p
Asymmetry coefficient[†]	0·17 (0·10−0·32)	<0·0001	0·21 (0·11−0·40)	<0·0001
Publication				
Non-English vs English	0·73 (0·53−1·00)	0·05	0·67 (0·40−1·14)	0·144
Not MEDLINE-indexed vs MEDLINE-indexed	0·69 (0·50−0·94)	0·019	1·03 (0·61−1·75)	0·906
Study quality				
Not double-blind vs double-blind	0·44 (0·22−0·87)	0·017	0·63 (0·36−1·11)	0·107
Generation of allocation sequence not adequate or unclear vs adequate	0·67 (0·48−0·95)	0·024	0·98 (0·65−1·46)	0·913
Concealment of allocation sequence not adequate or unclear vs adequate	0·78 (0·57−1·07)	0·117	0·76 (0·48−1·16)	0·193
Analysis not by intention to treat or unclear **vs** by intention to treat	1·25 (0·87−1·80)	0·225	1·14 (0·78−1·66)	0·506
Not higher quality or unclear vs higher quality	0·62 (0·43−0·90)	0·011	0·61 (0·34−1·09)	0·095

*Odds ratio with characteristic divided by odds ratio without characteristic. Ratios below 1·0 correspond to a smaller odds ratio for trials with characteristic and hence a larger apparent benefit of interventions. Trials published in languages other than English show a more beneficial treatment effect than those published in English, for example.
[†]Ratio of odds ratio per unit increase in SE of log odds ratio.

clinical topic (p = 0·660 for homoeopathy, p = 0·360 for conventional medicine) or that effects differed between different types of homoeopathy (p = 0·636) or type of indication (p = 0·487). In multivariable analyses, the SE of the log odds ratio (asymmetry coefficient) was the dominant variable in both groups. Coefficients of other variables, including study quality, were attenuated and became non-significant.

When the analysis was restricted to the larger trials of higher reported methodological quality, the odds ratio from random-effects meta-analysis was 0·88 (0·65 − 1·19) based on eight trials of homoeopathy and 0·58 (0·39 − 0·85) based on six trials of conventional medicine. Similarly, for prediction of treatment effects in trials as large as the largest trials, the odds ratio was 0·96 (0·73 − 1·25) for homoeopathy and 0·67 (0·48 − 0 ·91) for conventional medicine.

DISCUSSION

We compared the effects of homoeopathy and conventional medicine that are seen in placebo-controlled trials, examined the presence of bias resulting from inadequate methods and selective publication, and estimated results in trials least affected by these biases. We assumed that the effects observed in placebo-controlled trials of homoeopathy could be explained by a combination of methodological deficiencies and biased reporting. Conversely, we postulated that the same biases could not explain the effects observed in comparable placebo-controlled trials of conventional medicine. Our results confirm these hypotheses: when analyses were restricted to large trials of higher quality there was no convincing evidence that homoeopathy was superior to placebo, whereas for conventional medicine an important effect remained. Our results thus provide support for the hypothesis that the clinical effects of homoeopathy, but not those of conventional medicine, are unspecific placebo or context effects.

In 1991, Kleijnen and colleagues[20] argued that there is no reason to believe that compared with homoeopathy "the influence of publication bias, data massage, bad methodology, and so on is much less in conventional medicine". Indeed, we found that trials of homoeopathy tended to be of higher methodological quality than conventional-medicine trials, although most trials of either type of medicine were of low or uncertain quality. In both groups, smaller trials and those of lower quality showed more beneficial treatment effects than larger trials and those of higher quality. Between-trial heterogeneity was less pronounced among homoeopathy trials. This finding might be expected if heterogeneity between homoeopathy trials is essentially due to biased reporting and conduct of trials, whereas in the conventional-medicine sample treatment effects represented an additional relevant source of heterogeneity. When we discussed results with practitioners of homoeopathy, they contended that classical homoeopathy and homoeopathic treatment of chronic disorders, in trials with longer follow-up, would yield specific effects. We addressed these points in additional analyses but found no strong evidence in support of these hypotheses.

This study directly compared the presence of biases and their influence on effect estimates in homoeopathy and conventional-medicine trials. Identical definitions were used, and data were abstracted independently by two observers. The search of homoeopathic publications was comprehensive, and we are confident that we identified a near-complete set of published placebo-controlled trials of homoeopathy. The identification of unpublished studies is notoriously difficult, and we probably missed some of these trials. Conventional-medicine trials were randomly selected from the largest existing database of clinical trials (the Cochrane Controlled Trials Register) and were carefully matched to homoeopathy trials for clinical subject and type of outcome.

Different sources of bias are difficult to disentangle. The methodological quality of randomised trials cannot be reliably assessed from published articles because reporting on important features of the methods is incomplete in many cases.[21] Indeed, deficiencies in methods of smaller trials that were either not reported or not assessed by us could also have contributed to the asymmetrical shape of the funnel plot. We have argued elsewhere that the funnel plot should be seen not only as a means of detecting publication bias, but also as a generic tool for examination of small-study effects—the tendency for the smaller studies to show larger treatment effects.[22] If reporting is inadequate, study size can be a more precise measure of trial quality than formal assessments of trial quality. We addressed this possibility by modelling the effects expected in trials as large as the largest trial included in our study; again, we found little evidence for an effect of homoeopathy but stronger evidence for conventional medicine. Another limitation of our study is the exclusive focus on the beneficial effects of homoeopathy and conventional medicine, rather than on both benefits and risks. However, the trials included in the study were small and lacked the power to reveal infrequent but important adverse effects. Furthermore, reporting on adverse effects is inadequate even in larger trials.[23] A comprehensive and valid assessment of adverse effects would probably not have been possible within the framework of this study.

A previous review, which did not include a meta-analysis, also found that many trials of homoeopathy show beneficial effects but are of low methodological quality.[20] A meta-analysis by Linde and co-workers[12] was based on an extensive literature search, which we updated for our study, but it did not include trials of conventional medicine. These researchers concluded that their results were "not compatible with the hypothesis that the clinical effects of homoeopathy are completely due to placebo". However, in a subsequent, more detailed analysis of the same data,[24] they observed that more rigorous trials yielded smaller effect sizes and that their meta-analysis[12] probably "at least overestimated the effects of homoeopathic treatments." In a separate study, the same group observed that many trials in complementary medicine have important methodological weaknesses.[25] Finally, a study of 23 trials of homoeopathy that were considered to be of high methodological quality found that the few trials that used objective endpoints were all negative.[26]

Our study has implications beyond the question of whether homoeopathic remedies have specific effects. First, an important point to keep in mind is that most systematic reviews and meta-analyses are based on relatively few trials. Simulation studies have shown that detection of bias is difficult when meta-analyses are based on a small number of trials.[22] For example, for the eight trials of homoeopathic remedies in acute infections of the upper respiratory tract that were included in our sample, the pooled effect indicated a substantial beneficial effect (odds ratio 0·36 [95% CI 0·26–0·50]) and there was neither convincing evidence of funnel-plot asymmetry nor evidence that the effect differed between the trial classified as of higher reported quality and the remaining trials. Such sensitivity analyses might suggest that there is robust evidence that the treatment under investigation works. However, the biases that are prevalent in these publications, as shown by our study, might promote the conclusion that the results cannot be trusted. We submit that similar studies should be done in other types of both complementary and conventional medicine. Such studies would "borrow strength" from a large number of trials and provide empirical information to assist reviewers and readers in the interpretation of findings from small meta-analyses that focus on a specific intervention and disorder. Second, although important progress has been made lately,[11,27] further research is needed to identify the dimensions of methodological quality that are important in different clinical contexts, different outcomes, and different types of trials. Finally, the relation between the probability of publication of a study and its methodological quality should be examined in more detail.

We emphasise that our study, and the trials we examined, exclusively addressed the narrow question of whether homoeopathic remedies have specific effects. Context effects can influence the effects of interventions, and the relationship between patient and carer might be an important pathway mediating such effects.[28, 29] Practitioners of homoeopathy can form powerful alliances with their patients, because patients and carers commonly share strong beliefs about the treatment's effectiveness, and other cultural beliefs, which might be both empowering and restorative.[30] For some people, therefore, homoeopathy could be another tool that complements conventional medicine, whereas others might see it as purposeful and antiscientific deception of patients, which has no place in modern health care. Clearly, rather than doing further placebo-controlled trials of homoeopathy,[3] future research efforts should focus on the nature of context effects and on the place of homoeopathy in health-care systems.

Our study powerfully illustrates the interplay and cumulative effect of different sources of bias. We acknowledge that to prove a negative is impossible,[31] but we have shown that the effects seen in placebo-controlled trials of homoeopathy are compatible with the placebo hypothesis. By contrast, with identical methods, we found that the benefits of conventional medicine are unlikely to be explained by unspecific effects.

CONTRIBUTORS

M Egger conceived the study and wrote the first draft of the report. All the authors contributed to the final draft. A Shang, K Huwiler-Müntener, L Nartey, S Dörig, and P Jüni did the literature searches, identified eligible studies, and extracted data. P Jüni advised on data extraction and quality assessment. D Pewsner helped with data extraction and classification of homoeopathy trials. A Shang, J A C Sterne, P Jüni, and M Egger did the statistical analyses and contributed to data interpretation.

CONFLICT OF INTEREST STATEMENT

We declare that we have no conflict of interest.

ACKNOWLEDGMENTS

We thank Fritz Grossenbacher for valuable help with literature searches. This study was funded by the Complementary Medicine Evaluation Program (Programm Evaluation der Komplementärmedizin [PEK]) of the Swiss Federal Office for Public Health. We thank Marianne Amiet and Florian Mitscherlich from the PEK coordinating office and Felix Gurtner from the Federal Office of Public Health for their support. Peter Jüni was supported by grants from the Swiss National Science Foundation (grants no. 3233-066377 and 3200-066378).

REFERENCES

1. Eisenberg DM, Davis RB, Ettner SL, et al. Trends in alternative medicine use in the United States, 1990–1997: results of a follow-up national survey. *JAMA* 1998; **280**: 1569–75.

2. Ernst E. The role of complementary and alternative medicine. *BMJ* 2000; **321**: 1133–35.

3. Vandenbroucke JP. Homoeopathy trials: going nowhere. *Lancet* 1997; **350**: 824.

4. Vickers A, Zollman C. ABC of complementary medicine: homoeopathy. *BMJ* 1999; **319**: 1115–18.

5. Jonas W, Jacobs J. Healing with homeopathy. New York: Warner Books, 1996.

6. Schulte J. Effects of potentization in aqueous solutions. *Br Homeopath J* 1999; **88**: 155–60.

7. Skrabanek P. Is homoeopathy a placebo response? *Lancet* 1986; **2**: 1107.

8. Gotzsche PC. Trials of homeopathy. *Lancet* 1993; **341**: 1533.

9. Rennie D. Fair conduct and fair reporting of clinical trials. *JAMA* 1999; **282**: 1766–68.

10. Egger M, Davey Smith G. Meta-analysis: bias in location and selection of studies. *BMJ* 1998; **316**: 61–66.

11. Schulz KF, Chalmers I, Hayes RJ, Altman D. Empirical evidence of bias: dimensions of methodological quality associated with estimates of treatment effects in controlled trials. *JAMA* 1995; **273**: 408–12.

12. Linde K, Clausius N, Ramirez G, et al. Are the clinical effects of homoeopathy placebo effects? A meta-analysis of placebo-controlled trials. *Lancet* 1997; **350**: 834–43.

13. Dickersin K, Manheimer E, Wieland S, Robinson KA, Lefebvre C, McDonald S. Development of the Cochrane Collaboration's CENTRAL Register of controlled clinical trials. *Eval Health Prof* 2002; **25**: 38–64.

14. Jüni P, Altman DG, Egger M. Assessing the quality of controlled clinical trials. *BMJ* 2001; **323**: 42–46.

15. Hasselblad V, Hedges LV. Meta-analysis of screening and diagnostic tests. *Psychol Bull* 1995; **117**: 167–78.

16. Higgins JPT, Thompson SG. Quantifying heterogeneity in a meta-analysis. *Stat Med* 2002; **21**: 1539–58.

17. Sterne JAC, Egger M. Funnel plots for detecting bias in meta-analysis: guidelines on choice of axis. *J Clin Epidemiol* 2001; **54**: 1046–55.

18. Thompson SG, Sharp SJ. Explaining heterogeneity in meta-analysis: a comparison of methods. *Stat Med* 1999; **18**: 2693–708.

19. Sterne JAC, Egger M, Davey-Smith G. Investigating and dealing with publication and other biases in meta-analysis. *BMJ* 2001; **323**: 101–05.

20. Kleijnen J, Knipschild P, ter Riet G. Clinical trials of homoeopathy. *BMJ* 1991; **302**: 316–23.

21. Schulz KF. Randomised trials, human nature, and reporting guidelines. *Lancet* 1996; **348**: 596–98.

22. Sterne JAC, Gavaghan DJ, Egger M. Publication and related bias in meta-analysis: power of statistical tests and prevalence in the literature. *J Clin Epidemiol* 2000; **53**: 1119–29.

23. Ioannidis JP, Lau J. Completeness of safety reporting in randomized trials: an evaluation of 7 medical areas. *JAMA* 2001; **285**: 437–43.

24. Linde K, Scholz M, Ramirez G, Clausius N, Melchart D, Jonas WB. Impact of study quality on outcome in placebo-controlled trials of homeopathy. *J Clin Epidemiol* 1999; **52**: 631–36.

25. Linde K, Jonas WB, Melchart D, Willich S. The methodological quality of randomized controlled trials of homeopathy, herbal medicines and acupuncture. *Int J Epidemiol* 2001; **30**: 526–31.

26. Morrison B, Lilford RJ, Ernst E. Methodological rigour and results of clinical trials of homoeopathic remedies. *Perfusion* 2000; **13**: 132–38.

27. Moher D, Pham B, Jones A, et al. Does quality of reports of randomised trials affect estimates of intervention efficacy reported in meta-analyses? *Lancet* 1998; **352**: 609–13.

28. Di Blasi Z, Harkness E, Ernst E, Georgiou A, Kleijnen J. Influence of context effects on health outcomes: a systematic review. *Lancet* 2001; **357**: 757–62.

29. Kleijnen J, de Craen AJ, van Everdingen J, Krol L. Placebo effect in double-blind clinical trials: a review of interactions with medications. *Lancet* 1994; **344**: 1347–49.

30. Kaptchuk TJ, Eisenberg DM. The persuasive appeal of alternative medicine. *Ann Intern Med* 1998; **129**: 1061–65.

31. Altman DG, Bland JM. Absence of evidence is not evidence of absence. *BMJ* 1995; **311**: 485.

DISCUSSION

The opening Summary of the Shang article gets the main points out in the open: there are published studies testing homeopathic treatments, and other published studies testing treatments from conventional (allopathic) medicine. The meta-analysis concludes that for *both* approaches the trials with smaller samples and less rigorous methods were most likely to report beneficial results of the treatment being tested. But when only larger and more rigorous studies were considered, the statistical evidence supporting beneficial effects for homeopathy became too weak to justify rejecting the null hypothesis that homeopathic effects are placebo effects. Statistical evidence for the efficacy of conventional medicine remained significant, however, when only the higher-quality studies were included. Finally, according to the authors, the effect of biasing factors on the tendency of homeopathic studies to report positive results is sufficient to account for the appearance of effectiveness of homeopathy in the trials as a group. While these same biasing factors may have just as large an effect on conventional medical studies, those biases are *not* sufficient to entirely account for the appearance of effectiveness in the allopathic studies. In other words, both kinds of medicine are influenced by biases, but after this is factored in there is still clear evidence for the efficacy of conventional medicine. Not so for homeopathy, the authors claim.

The authors' reasoning about homeopathy is somewhat complex. Shang et al. test a range of factors that have the potential to bias a study. Some of these factors relate mainly to good scientific methods, like the importance of double-blinding in medical studies, and the need to specify an "intention to treat" group in order to avoid both trimming the sample size *post hoc* (as with the InnerChange study described in Chapter 9) and Multiple Endpoints reasoning (as with the Sicher study described in Chapter 9 and in the next reading). Other potential biasing factors relate to assumptions about the wider scientific world, such as the higher representation of prestigious refereed medical journals among English-language journals. Shang et al. compare homeopathic studies with and without each factor, with respect to the effects the studies reported for homeopathy. This produces odds ratios for each factor: for example, an odds ratio representing the effect of double-blinding on whether trials reported a beneficial effect for homeopathy. They do the same thing for their selection of conventional medical studies, moreover, indicating how each factor correlated with trials reporting a beneficial effect for whatever treatments they are testing. Table 3 summarizes the results.

It's important to note that each of the odds ratios listed in Table 3 indicates the effects of the listed factor on whether the trials reported a beneficial effect. They do not indicate the effects of homeopathy itself on some medical condition (nor of the relevant conventional treatment, in the second column). So the relation of the odds ratios to the effectiveness of the treatments is somewhat inverted in Table 3. For example, the homeopathic odds ratio listed for non-indexing in MEDLINE (a bibliographic database for thousands of significant journals in medicine and health care) is .69, with a confidence interval of .50 to .94 at 95 percent confidence. For the same factor in the conventional medical trials, the odds ratio is 1.03, with confidence interval .61 to 1.75. Effectiveness, remember, is indicated by an odds ratio of less than 1, with a confidence interval that does not include 1, in this meta-analysis. So the numbers in that row of Table 3 tell us that publication in a journal that didn't make it into MEDLINE is significantly correlated with reporting a beneficial result among the homeopathic trials, but is not significantly correlated with reporting a beneficial result among the conventional trials. Looking at all the factors listed in Table 3, you can see that they are typically significant for homeopathic trials and not for allopathic trials.

In many respects the article is even-handed. It certainly does not indulge in mere cheerleading on behalf of conventional medical science, as the authors clearly point out that conventional medical studies and homeopathic studies are largely subject to the same kinds and degree of biases, and that "most trials of either type of medicine were of low or uncertain quality." This aspect of the data is an interesting one, quite apart from the issues of homeopathy's effectiveness. It reinforces a familiar theme from other meta-analyses of medical studies (one of which is discussed below) regarding sample sizes. Finding and administering human subjects for studies is enormously expensive and difficult, which creates pressure to extract statistical conclusions from small numbers of subjects where possible. Both positive and negative conclusions drawn from such samples are suspect, though, since the tendency for a sample to misrepresent the nature of the population (or the nature of the treatment) through random variation becomes likelier as the sample sizes get smaller. In short, small sample sizes are more apt to produce both false positives and false negatives.

Moreover, false positives at the level of the whole study are likely to be over-represented in the scientific literature owing to **publication bias**, which is why the authors flag this issue in their Introduction and Discussion sections. Publication bias is the tendency for studies or experiments with positive outcomes to be published at a higher rate than studies with a negative outcome (or, more accurately, at a higher rate than studies in which the null hypothesis cannot be rejected given the data and the relevant significance level required). Again, as we saw in Chapter 6, the smaller the sample size the greater the probability of getting a misleading sample just by bad luck. When a treatment or test condition genuinely has no effect or only a small effect, large trials will tend to show this. But small trials will be likelier to vary between showing misleadingly large and misleading small effects. The worry about publication bias is that, by preferentially publishing studies that show positive results, scientific journals (and particularly medical journals) will in fact end up publishing a disproportionately high number of those small-study false positives. (Similar remarks apply to methodology: by selecting for studies showing positive results, journals may unwittingly over-represent methodologically inferior research over the long term.) The bias in favour of positive results is sometimes called the **File Drawer Effect,** as unexciting results that fail to reject the null hypothesis have a greater tendency to end up sitting in the researcher's file drawer rather than getting published.

The graphs in Figure 2 are **funnel plots** intended to convey the apparent publication bias in a visual way. A funnel plot in a meta-analysis is a graph that displays (among other things) a relation between the sample sizes of trials and the degree and kind of effect the trials indicate. The vertical axis on each graph shows the **standard error** of each trial in the meta-analysis. Setting aside its technical definition(s), which you can easily track down if you wish, the standard error reflects both the sample size of a trial and the standard deviation of the trial's method of sampling the population. The larger the standard error (SE, in the article), the smaller the trial and hence the more susceptible the trial is to misrepresenting the population purely by chance. Notice that zero SE is at the top of the vertical axis in a funnel plot; lower "points" represent smaller trials with greater SE.

The horizontal axis shows the odds ratios of the trials (or the log odds ratios, sometimes). While the vertical position of a point indicates the size of the trial, in other words, its horizontal position indicates the effectiveness of the treatment according to that trial. In the absence of bias, we should therefore expect the points representing the studies to fall roughly into an upside-down triangle, or funnel shape. The larger studies near the top should tend to converge on a consensus of treatment effect, while the smaller studies near the bottom of the graph should over-estimate and underestimate the treatment effect symmetrically. When the funnel plot is asymmetrical—when the points angle off in one direction near the bottom of the graph—this suggests that some bias in the study or in the publication process has filtered out the inaccurate trials drawing one conclusion while accepting inaccurate trials that draw the opposite conclusion. This is only a tentative explanation of an

False negatives stemming from small samples can also be problematic in the scientific literature, especially when these are presented as evidence of a non-effect and not as insufficient evidence of an effect. This issue emerged in Chapter 2 as well, in the discussion of whether absence of evidence is evidence of absence. It is complicated here by the use of sharp cut-offs for standards of statistical significance.

There is a pre-existing worry about oversimplified negative conclusions in scientific publications, of the sort that describe a near miss for statistical significance as having shown *no effect*, or words to a similar effect. One meta-analysis of seventy-one published "negative" medical trials concluded that in nearly half the trials the data were nevertheless consistent with a 50 percent improvement from the treatment, at the same confidence level adopted for the trials![7] Because the trials aimed to detect a larger effect than this, the results were classed as negative, but *simply* calling them negative or describing them as showing "no effect" is quite misleading. In fact, such results should be described only as having failed to satisfy whatever standard was stipulated in advance as significant, possibly with the level of confidence and effect they *do* support also made clear.

asymmetrical funnel plot, but it's simple to use and handy for at least showing the need for further investigation. In Figure 2 the distribution of points tends to angle leftward as it moves down in both graphs, suggesting that both homeopathic and allopathic trials of smaller size were more apt to be published if they showed beneficial effects of a treatment than if they did not. These are visual arguments for the authors' cautious conclusion that publication bias affects medical science in general.

The Shang et al. meta-analysis is not without its critical thinking red flags, though. For the casual reader one red flag is the problem of undefined terms, since the article is written for experts. (Still, it is interesting to note the number of presumably familiar expert terms that receive brief definitions anyhow.) I have tried to explain some of the key concepts already, but a medical science dictionary, which can be found online from various plausible sources, would no doubt be useful on this front as well.

The more serious issues here are evidential and interpretive. One evidential red flag is the fact that the authors do not tell us which trials they have selected to study. Even the relatively small set of trials considered to be higher in quality are not named, though this would only have been fourteen in total. So direct confirmation of the selection procedures is difficult or impossible, given the information provided.

A related evidential red flag is the relatively small number of trials that generates the overall odds ratios for treatment effectiveness in homeopathic and allopathic studies, as reported under *Findings* in the Summary section. Probably the single most important conclusion of the meta-analysis is that when we consider those trials least likely to be biased, when we factor in known biases, homeopathic (but not allopathic) studies produce results consistent with placebo effects. But this conclusion and the odds ratios on which it is mainly based stem from the comparison of *eight* higher quality homeopathic trials and *six* higher quality conventional medical trials. "These are not large numbers, though the studies seem to have been chosen in a methodologically sound fashion." So it is important that we don't over-interpret these statistics. The authors themselves do not claim to have disproved homeopathy, but the issue of *The Lancet* in which the article was published also contained an editorial entitled "The end of homeopathy."[8]

Is the judgment expressed in that title justified? Not on the basis of the information in the Shang et al. study alone. But here it becomes particularly important to consider the wider evidential context. The facts about homeopathy that I covered in the preface to this reading may reasonably lead medical scientists to assign homeopathic treatment a low **prior probability** of efficacy. In other words, general background evidence can lower the credibility of homeopathy before we even get around to specifically considering this meta-analysis and can perfectly reasonably colour our interpretation of the new evidence. So our information might weigh more decisively against homeopathy, all things considered, than the authors' quite neutral phrase "compatible with the placebo hypothesis" would suggest in its own. After all, the homeopathic hypothesis is that people can be cured of many illnesses by consuming what is, by the lights of known chemistry and physics, mere water. If that's implausible on its face, then a failure to detect such curative powers in the highest quality trials, and the greater appearance of such curative powers in lower quality trials may reasonably support a stronger negative conclusion than that we just don't know either way. Absence of evidence for an effect within a given study or set of studies may not demonstrate an absence of the effect; but it does mean that *independent* or *background* evidence of absence—including the lack of any plausible explanation for the alleged effects—wins the day as a result.

READING 5

ANOTHER PERSPECTIVE ON A "REMOTE HEALING" STUDY

In Chapter 9 we examined several badly flawed studies that were nevertheless published in scientific journals. One of these was the Sicher et al. study, which purported to test the effects of "distant healing" on AIDS patients. As we saw, the biggest methodological problem with the article was the Multiple Endpoints fallacy half-hidden within it. Originally designed and conducted with the aim of measuring the effects of prayer (among other things) on mortality among AIDS patients, the study generated no relevant data after new drug treatments sharply reduced the number of people dying of AIDS. The measures on which a statistically significant result appeared in the treatment (prayed-for) group were sought out after the fact, as the researchers passed over other measures on which no difference was observed, or even measures on which the control group performed *better* than the treatment group. This is classic Multiple Endpoints reasoning: trawling through the data looking for comparisons of the desired sort that rise to the level of statistical significance.

Sicher's primary colleague in that study was Elisabeth Targ, a medical doctor and the daughter of Russell Targ, himself a well-known defender of the view that psychic phenomena are scientifically confirmable. In the article reprinted here, Elisabeth Targ summarizes that study and some related work for the readers of the *Noetic Sciences Review*, a publication that has since been renamed *Shift*. It is not a scientific journal, but the main publication of the Institute of Noetic Sciences (IONS), an organization that describes its mission as the study of the "potentials and powers of consciousness."

One of the main lessons that emerged from the case studies in Chapter 9 was that the peer review process so characteristic of academic inquiry depends on norms of openness and transparency. The process is defeated or debased when crucial information is withheld or downplayed—especially information that clearly counts against the conclusions drawn by the researcher. In Chapter 10, moreover, we saw that factual constraints, professional norms, or editorial expertise do not strongly govern the presentation of science (or alleged science) in the popular media, obliging us to be particularly cautious towards information we encounter in that context. This reading highlights both lessons, and provides a further lesson about the contrast between the two.

As you read:

1. Note and briefly explain any red flags you may find in the background information Targ provides regarding the phenomena of distant healing.
2. Given what you know about the Sicher et al. study from Chapter 9, make a note of any key information that is missing from the summary given here.
3. Comment on the experimental design Targ describes.

Compare your observations with the brief critical analysis that follows the reading.

Distant Healing

Elisabeth Targ, M.D.

First appeared in IONS' Noetic Science Review *(No. 49, August–November, 1999, pp. 24–29), the former quarterly publication of the Institute of Noetic Sciences, now titled* Shift: At the Frontiers of Consiousness, *and is reprinted with permission of IONS (www.noetic.org), all rights reserved. Copyright 2006.*

Can one person's thoughts influence the experience or the health of another—far away? While there are many complex and meaningful aspects to the practice of prayer or hands-on healing, a sixty-four million-dollar question remains: Is there an effect at a distance?

In December 1998, forty scientists from universities and research laboratories around the United States gathered at the Swedenborg Chapel at Harvard University for a three-day conference jointly sponsored by the Institute of Noetic Sciences and the Harvard University School of Medicine. Their focus: to examine and evaluate data on a remarkable phenomenon baffling to modern medical science. The attendance list was confidential, and the proceedings closed. Preliminary data presented at this conference suggested that we are on the verge of an explosion of evidence to support the efficacy of distant healing.

The term "distant healing" and the more precise but cumbersome "distant mental influence on biologic systems" (now adopted by the National Institutes of Health)—is an attempt to find a way to objectively describe the outcome of what others call psychic healing, energy healing, or prayer.

While distant healing has historically received little attention from mainstream medical institutions and laboratories, a substantial body of published data supports the possibility of a significant effect. Over the last forty years, more than 150 formal, controlled studies of distant healing have been published—more than two-thirds of them showing significant effects (a less than one-in-twenty likelihood of the effect having occurred by chance; in scientific terminology, $p < .05$).*

The most exciting and the most controversial studies in the area of distant healing have involved human beings as subjects. These studies are challenging to design because of uncontrollable factors such as hope, expectation, and the role of the relationship between the healer and the patient.

A seminal paper presented at the 1998 conference was "A Study of Distant Healing as an Adjunctive Intervention for People with Advanced AIDS," initiated by IONS member Fred Sicher. This project, recently published in the *Western Journal of Medicine*, represents five years work by a research team at California Pacific Medical Center (CPMC). While many studies of distant healing have focused on more benign conditions—such as headache, high blood pressure, or recovery from minor surgery—after interviewing numerous healers, Sicher had observed that many healers feel they do their best work when the need is greatest.

The healers suggested that if we want to see a significant effect on someone's health, there has to be a significant motivation—the patient should be *in extremis*. Continuing his survey, Sicher also found that, unlike in many healing studies, distant healing is not usually performed as a one-time effort. Most of his interviewees stated that they tend to work with patients over a period of time, often many weeks. In an effort to bring the scientific approach in line with this "community standard," Sicher then proposed that a study of distant healing should involve people with an incurable disease such as AIDS, that the treatment should occur over at least two months, and that many healers be involved.

THE CPMC RESEARCH TRIALS OF DISTANT HEALING FOR AIDS

In 1994 Sicher joined our team at the California Pacific Medical Center to design a methodologically airtight collaborative research project. The CPMC trial of distant healing for people with AIDS was a "proof of principle" trial. It made no effort to investigate any mechanisms. The sole purpose of the study was to determine whether or not there is an effect of healing intentions over distance. Because of the controversial nature of this area of investigation, the research protocol was discussed and reviewed by numerous scientists, by AIDS specialists, and by self-identified healers before the first patient was enrolled.

Two studies were eventually completed, a pilot of twenty patients, followed by a confirmatory study of another forty patients. The pilot, considered exploratory, produced the surprising finding of 40 percent mortality in the control group, but no deaths in the treatment group. This striking result occurred despite the fact that patients and researchers did not know who was in the treatment group, and that the two groups were balanced for CD4 count. Both of these studies are reported in the December 1998 issue of the *Western Journal of Medicine*.

THE PATIENTS

In each study, patients were recruited from around the San Francisco Bay Area, using flyers, physician contacts, and newspaper advertisements. In the first study only men were included; the second study included women. Because of the variable course of HIV at different stages it was important to choose a group of patients at a similar stage of illness. The study inclusion criteria required all patients to have T-cell counts less than 200 and a history of at least one AIDS-defining illness (such as pneumocystis pneumonia, Kaposi's sarcoma, or cytomegalovirus).

The patients were randomly divided into two groups using a formula that equalized both groups on factors relevant to disease course (CD4 count, age, number of previous AIDS-defining diseases). Patients in the study had an average age of forty-three years, and had been HIV-positive for an average of eight years. Baseline illness severity was calculated by summing severity scores for previous and current AIDS-defining illnesses. No significant differences were found on any of twenty-seven baseline variables. The study was triple blind: None of the patients, physicians, or researchers knew which patients were in the treatment group and which were in the control group.

THE HEALERS

Healers for the study were recruited by word of mouth and from schools and professional organizations all over the country. Because the study itself was a test of the efficacy of distant healing, there was no objective test that could be used to determine which healer might be "the best." Healers were therefore selected using the same type of criteria that might be used in selecting any healthcare practitioner. Researchers collected names based on healer reputation among colleagues and patients. Healers were required to have had at least five years of experience as professional healers, to have performed at least ten healing attempts at a distance, and to have worked with at least two people with AIDS. The healers selected significantly surpassed these criteria, averaging more than seventeen years of experience performing healing-at-a-distance on an average of 106 people. In addition, just as one would select only a physician who believed one could get better from an illness, for the study, we selected only healers who believed the study would succeed.

The healers had an average age of forty-seven and represented a wide variety of educational backgrounds, including several medical doctors, nurses, and psychologists who also maintain a regular professional practice using nonlocal healing. Other healers included a Baptist minister, a cu-gong master, a Native American shaman, and a Philippine woman with no formal education who performed healing in the Christian tradition. Half of the healers in the study described their healing techniques as "energetic," 25 percent described their work as meditative or contemplative, 15 percent came from devotional or religious traditions, and 10 percent described their work as "shamanic." Many had received training or were now instructors at well-known schools of energetic or spiritual healing. A majority of healers reported working with chakra imagery for healings; other frequently reported modalities included prayer, visualization, and work with crystals.

THE HEALING INTERVENTION

The healing intervention consisted of each patient in the treatment group receiving healing efforts from one healer at a time, one hour per day, six days per week, for ten weeks. The healers worked on a rotating schedule so that each week, each patient was treated by a new healer. Thus, by the end of the study, each patient had received "healing effort" from a total of ten different healers. Each week, a head and shoulders photograph of one of the treatment patients was sent via overnight mail to a healer who was then instructed to "hold the intention for the health and well-being of the patient" for one hour a day during the time the patient was assigned to them. The healers were given the first name of the patient, the patient's CD4 count, and two or three sentences describing active elements of their illness. Healing techniques were quite varied.

THE STUDY OUTCOME

Patients in the study were followed for six months. Three categories of outcome were assessed: progression of illness, medical utilization, and quality of life. Eleven specific outcome measures were used. Medical data were collected by blind chart review, and quality of life/psychosocial data were collected using standardized paper and pencil tests. At the end of six months, patients in the treatment group had acquired significantly fewer new AIDS-defining diseases than people in the control group, their overall illness severity scores were significantly lower, they had had significantly fewer hospitalizations, and those hospitalizations were significantly shorter. In addition, treatment patients showed significant improvement on psychological status, including decreased depression, decreased anxiety, decreased anger, and increased vigor, compared to controls. There were no significant differences between groups on CD4 counts, which went up slightly for both groups. The treatment group also showed more recoveries from AIDS-defining diseases (six versus two), but this result did not reach statistical significance.

Extensive statistical analyses were performed by the research team and were reviewed by several biostatisticians from outside institutions to determine whether some factor other than the distant healing intervention might have accounted for the differences between groups. Analysis did not reveal evidence that any baseline factor (such as medications, ethnicity, gender, age, religious orientation) could have accounted for any of the medical outcomes. By chance, the patients who were randomized to the treatment group were individuals who had initially higher scores on measures of psychological distress; this observation opens the possibility that their improvement on psychological outcomes may represent a regression to the mean. Interestingly, changes in psychological outcomes, for example becoming more depressed, did not correlate with medical outcomes, such as becoming more ill.

Historically, the usual scientific explanation for medical improvement in the context of distant healing or prayer is that the patients' hopes or expectations in the context of the treatment are what lead to any benefit. In the above studies, the main effect of hope or expectation is eliminated because the study was double blind. Neither group knew whether or not they were receiving the treatment, thus neither group should be differentially influenced by being in the study. This assertion relies on the assumption that the two groups had equal levels of expectation about the possibility of being treated.

The question arises: Did the group that received the treatment simply contain more patients who "guessed" or believed they were being treated? If that were the case, it would be possible that their increased level of expectation might have influenced the outcome. This question was addressed in two ways. First, the two groups were compared to see whether one group showed significantly greater likelihood of believing that they were in the treatment group. The answer to this question was— no. Despite the fact that only one group was receiving the treatment, nearly half of the patients in the control group had (mistakenly) guessed they were in treatment. More important, despite the fact that they were doing significantly better than the control group, nearly half the patients in the treatment group guessed that they were not being treated.

The second approach to this issue was to ask whether those patients in either group who thought that they were being treated showed significantly better outcomes on any measure. It turned out that in the early stages of the study, patients who thought they were being treated were those whose T-cell counts had been rising (a fact that would have been known to them and may account for their guess). In the later part of the study, patients who were showing more recoveries from AIDS-defining illnesses were more likely to guess they were being treated. Significantly, believing one was being treated did not correlate with severity of illness, with development of new illness, with psychological outcomes, or with medical utilization. Thus it appears expectation does not account for the differential benefits seen in patients in the treatment group.

CONCLUSION

No single study can be decisive in demonstrating an effect. The two studies presented here represent only the latest work in a nearly forty-year process of developing, refining, and repeating studies to evaluate the effects of healing attempts at a distance. The two current studies, like the majority of other published studies, confirm such an effect. This work raises many more questions that will be the focus of future studies. What healing techniques or attitudes are the most helpful? Are certain individuals more likely to be able to develop healing abilities? Is distant healing more effective for some conditions than others? What is the role of the patient in the healing process? Is healing additive? Is it beneficial to have groups of people sending prayers or making healing efforts? Are there certain biological pathways that are specifically affected by healing efforts? And last, of course, how does it work?

The work described here is one piece in a puzzle that is bringing together medicine, philosophy, physics, and spiritual science to create a new picture of a highly connected and interactive universe. We look forward to seeing the results of the many other studies which are ongoing, and to exploring ways of introducing these interventions into mainstream medical settings.

* D.J. Benor, *Healing Research,* Vol. 1. Deddington, England: Helix Editions, 1992.

DISCUSSION

One problem noted in Chapter 9 concerned the fit between the Byrd prayer study and the subsequent Harris prayer study. The two featured very different, even contradictory, outcomes and very different "treatments"—in terms of both the prayers and pray-ers—yet the Harris study was presented as *confirming* the Byrd study. It is entirely unclear how these two sets of results could be mutually supportive when not only is there no particular kind of outcome that some shared treatment produces, but there is also no particular shared treatment that produces the outcomes.

In this reading we discover the same sort of conceptual problem with the treatment Targ describes. The distant healers include "a Baptist minister, a cu-gong master, a Native American shaman, and a Philippine woman with no formal education who performed healing in the Christian tradition." The healers' self-described methods are energetic, meditative, contemplative, devotional, religious, or shamanic, and the "modalities" they employ include chakra imagery, prayer, visualization, and crystal power. Now, it's true that if a statistically significant effect appeared in a large and well-conducted study of this sort, and were replicable in further such studies, that in itself would be sufficient to compel the conclusion that *something* was happening. But for a single small study to be deliberately constructed in this hodge-podge manner, with such a heterogeneous mixture inappropriately presented as one kind of treatment, is a large red flag. It simply does not reflect a serious intent to test for something in particular. So it confirms a reasonable suspicion when we discover that the Sicher and Targ study produced a statistically significant result only by *not* testing for anything in particular.

A related point overlaps with something we observed about the homeopathy example in Reading 4, moreover. Our broader theories of the world, which have robust evidential support, don't really provide for or cohere with any mechanism for such an effect of prayer. And as in the homeopathy case, a low prior probability for the phenomenon, coupled with systematic flaws in the purported sources of evidence for the phenomenon, makes it reasonable to conclude that there *is* no phenomenon (besides a placebo effect). The mere claim that large numbers of studies nevertheless confirm distant healing is properly rejected under these circumstances.

A distinct worry is found not in what the reading says, but in what it fails to say. Targ writes that the pilot study "produced the surprising finding of 40 percent mortality in the control group, but no deaths in the treatment group." Yet this is less surprising when one considers a major problem with the pilot study: it was confounded by the ages of the patients, which were not balanced between the treatment and the control groups. All four of the patients who died during the study were in the control group, but they were also the four oldest patients in the study. As we saw in Chapter 9, studies based on small samples often have to be sorted into treatment and control groups on some basis other than mere randomization, since mere randomness is apt to lead to confounds when small numbers of subjects are involved. Instead we need to use pair-matching, or some other means of intervening, to help ensure an even distribution of potentially relevant properties among the subjects.

As one of the collaborators in the Sicher study, that is, one of the authors of the *Western Journal of Medicine* article to which she refers, Targ clearly knew that the pilot study was confounded by age. The *Western Journal of Medicine* article even says of the pilot study: "Four of the 10 control group subjects died, with no deaths occurring in the treatment group, but the result was confounded by age (those who died were older)." In *that* article, the authors Sicher, Targ, Moore, and Smith explicitly cite this problem as their reason for deciding in the follow-up study "to control for factors shown to be associated with poorer prognosis in AIDS, specifically age, T cell count, and illness history." The bottom line is that the pilot study really only showed something that was already known: that greater age was associated with a poorer prognosis for AIDS patients.

Yet in the reading reproduced here, originally published a full year after the *Western Journal of Medicine* article, Targ still calls the pilot study a "striking result." Even having gone out of her way to say something about its methodology, and in particular about the matching of treatment and control groups in the pilot study, she makes no mention of the single most salient and scientifically important fact about the matching: namely, that it was compromised by an imbalance in older patients. Instead she goes out of her way to note how *well* the control and treatment groups were matched, writing only that "patients and researchers did not know who was in the treatment group, and that the two groups were balanced for CD4 count." There is no mention of the confounding factor. Nobody reading just this article could know that the pilot study was undermined by a major methodological flaw to which its authors, including Targ herself, had already admitted elsewhere.

For that matter, imagine reading this article on its own, knowing that its author was a co-author of the scientifically published paper on which it is based, and amenable to the thought that distant healing could be scientifically confirmed. Would this article convey the strong impression that it had been substantially confirmed? Given what you do know about the studies in question, is that impression well-founded?

I did not read (and could not find in any nearby library) the book that Targ cites for her claim that over one hundred "formal, controlled" and published studies have shown statistically significant effects for distant healing. At a minimum this is a clear case of appeal to an authority whose accuracy is unsupported. Yet we can actually draw a stronger conclusion than that. At this point, in light of Chapter 9's investigations, we are thoroughly justified in taking Targ's claim of a large body of successful studies supporting the medical efficacy of prayer to be based on exaggeration or on poorly conducted or poorly reported investigations. We have broadly inductive reasons to think this, based on the serious failings we have seen, in what are typically presented as the *best* examples of distant healing studies.

Altogether these observations point to a larger lesson. As critical thinkers we are obliged to carefully consider the scientifically dubious claims of distant healing, psychic phenomena more generally, astrology, crystal energy, aura-reading, palmistry, and the like. We do this preferably by examining original sources, using not just our heads but our libraries, the Internet, a calculator, and a careful accounting of the information we gather. This can be hard work. But the payoff comes in the form of a justified confidence when we encounter some reference to the studies that allegedly confirm these effects. We've read the studies (unlike the person appealing to them, typically!) and considered them in light of an understanding of good reasoning and good scientific practice. Moreover, when some new study surfaces that purports to scientifically confirm a phenomenon the previous confirmations of which have been revealed as consistently poor in quality, we are justified in regarding the new claim as having very low credibility. We've seen that story before, after all. Knowledge acquisition has no end, and beliefs must remain defeasible; but for all that, after walking long enough in a cow pasture we gain the ability to identify a slippery patch without stepping in it first.

NOTES

1. Wikipedia contributors, "Biopolitics." Wikipedia, The Free Encyclopedia. Date of last revision: 20 September 2006 21:54 UTC.
   http://en.wikipedia.org/w/index.php?title=Biopolitics&oldid=76869238.

2. While this may seem the most decisive sort of evidence, it is also evidence that you, the reader, cannot (or ought not) directly confirm in this case. Direct confirmation of specific claims, including directly approaching the source of some alleged information, is a good idea when you are following up your own red flags, but please don't

bother Professor Bynner about this particular example in your fact-checking exuberance. He was helpful in response to my inquiry and shouldn't suffer for it by being deluged with messages!

3. *the fifth estate,* "The Scandal of the Century." http://www.cbc.ca/fifth/scandal/index.html.

4. *the fifth estate,* "Hell to Pay." http://www.cbc.ca/fifth/martin/scandal.html.

5. *the fifth estate,* "The Scandal of the Century."

6. *the fifth estate,* "Hell to Pay."

7. J. A. Freiman, T. C. Chalmers, H. Smith, Jr., and R. R. Kuebler, "The Importance of Beta, the Type II Error and Sample Size in the Design and Interpretation of the Randomized Control Trial. Survey of 71 'Negative' Trials," *New England Journal of Medicine* 299(13) (1978): 690–94.

8. Editorial, "The End of Homeopathy," *The Lancet* 366 (2005): 690.

INDEX

A page reference that includes the letter F refers to a Figure or Table.

Percentage figures
  non-literal conventional
    meaning, 129–30
Percentile
  vs. percentage, 134–36
Perceptual bias(es), 188–95
  Cutaneous Rabbit, 192
  face detection, 189–90
  Hollow Face Illusion, F190–91
  low-level, 189–92
  McGurk Effect, 191
  neurological mechanisms
    for, 189
  self-monitoring, 191
  and Top-Down effects, 192–95
Perceptual and neurological
    mechanisms, 189
Performative purpose of
    language, 62
Persuasive Definition, 116, 213
Peterson, Laci, 299–300
Phlogiston, 262, 262
Photographs, see Images
Pictures, communication with,
    83–87. See also Visual
    arguments
Placebo effect, 268–71, 353
Poisoning the Well, 112–13
Polls, selection bias, 152–53
Polysemy, 69
Popper, Karl, 261–62
Popular Opinion, Appeal to,
    103–104
Population, 148–49
Possible worlds, 28–29
Post Hoc Ergo Propter Hoc, 105
Pragmatic fallacies, 109–19. See
    also Procedural fallacies
Praise and blame, moral
    arguments, 81–82
Prayer studies, 252–53, 267–68,
    270, 286–87, 363
  double-blind, 272–73
  predictivity, 284
  remote healing study, 358–59
Prediction, 205–206
Premise(s)
  defined, 4, 8
  essential, of argument, 6
  implicit, 63
  must be mutually accepted, 7
  true, for sound argument, 4–5

Press releases, 309–10
Presupposition, 63–64
  false, 115
Priestley, Joseph, 261
Prison reform program, 117
Prison rehabilitation program, 280
Probabilistic concepts, 162–65
  and critical reasoning, 163
  heuristics, 163
  and Monty Hall problem,
    163–65
  mutually exclusive events,
    169–71
  and probabilistic reasoning, 163
  vs. statistics, 163
Probability, basics of, 165–78
  axioms, 166
  and background
    information, 177
  categorical, 175–77
  comparing, 179–80
  of complex events, 169–74
  conditional, 173, 174–78
  dependent events, 173
  of an event, 165
  fallacies and pitfalls, 178–82
  Gambler's fallacy, 178–79
  independent events, 172–73
  information and Base-Rate
    Error, 177
  maximally specific re events, 177
  of a necessary event, 166
  outcomes and, 167
  possible outcomes, 166–67
  prior, 357
  relative long-run frequency
    of events, 166
  relevant outcomes, 167
  regression effects, 181
  Regression Fallacy, 180–81
  Simpson's Paradox, 179, F180
  state of information
    re events, 177
  of three disjoint compatible
    events, 171–72
  of two conjoint events, 172
  of two disjoint events, 169
Procedural fallacies, 109–19
  Argument by Dictionary, 118
  confusions, 113–19
  distractors, 109–13
Professing Feminism, 72

Professional judgments, and
    hindsight bias, 209
Proof, 58–59
  burden of, 63
  direct, 9
Proposition, defined, 8
Prosentences, negation as, 30
Prosody, 64, 66
Proximate causes vs. remote
    causes, 53
Pseudo-explanation, 12
Pseudo-independent confirmation,
    248–49, 298
Pseudo-news, 297
Pseudo-science, 255, 263
Publication bias, 355

Qualifiers, 66
  existential, 95
Quantification,
    confused/incoherent, 141
Quantifier expression, 16
Quantifiers, 67
  universal, 95
Quantifier Scope Fallacy, 95
Quantitative reasoning, 124–26
  and numerical reasoning, 124
  and persuasive reasoning, 125
Quantum logic, 10
Question-begging arguments, 12
Questionnaires
  and numerical reasoning,
    140–41
  and student feedback, 140–41
Questions
  loaded, 118–19
  rhetorical, 62–63
Quotations, 71–74
  direct, 70
  indirect, 70
  misattributions, 72
  misquote, 71
  stitched together, 73
Quote-mining, 72–73

Racial bias(es), 222–23
  Implicit Association Test, 222
Ranking(s), 134–36
  Globe and Mail report card,
    140–41
  Maclean's of universities,
    136–39